SCANDALIZE MY NAME

Volume 13

Critical Studies on
Black Life and Culture

Advisory Editor
Professor Charles T. Davis, Chairman
Afro-American Studies, Yale University

Assistant Advisory Editor
Professor Henry-Louis Gates
Afro-American Studies, Yale University

SCANDALIZE MY NAME
Black Imagery in American Popular Music

Sam Dennison

GARLAND PUBLISHING, INC. / NEW YORK AND LONDON
1982

Acknowledgments of permission to quote copyrighted song lyrics
appear on pages xv–xxiii.

Library of Congress Cataloging in Publication Data

Dennison, Sam.
  Scandalize my name.
  (Critical studies on Black life and culture; v. 13)
  1. Afro-Americans—Songs and music. 2. Music, Popu-
lar (Songs, etc.)—United States—History and criticism.
3. Racism in literature. I. Title.
ML3556.D448   784.6′8305896073   80-9027
ISBN 0-8240-9309-7   AACR2

Printed on acid-free, 250-year-life paper
Manufactured in the United States of America

To
Patricia, Lee Ann, and Leslie

Contents

Illustrations

Preface

Few people today realize that practically all of the American songs about the black are to some extent demeaning to the black image. Even fewer realize how, why, or to what extent this is so. The purpose of this study is to investigate racism as it appears in our popular songs on the black subject. It is *not* a study of black music; it is a study of the black as he appears *in* music throughout the musical history of America.

To one dealing for any length of time with the polemics of the so-called Negro problem in America's past, the lack of dispassionate discourse becomes readily apparent and the tendency to be drawn into a "for" or "against" position becomes virtually irresistible. The point of view from which the materials of this study are presented is frankly liberal; whether this viewpoint invalidates the analysis and judgment of the material is for others to determine. The actual methods employed in this study are explained in Appendix II as a convenience for the scholar. It should be remembered, however, that the songs speak for themselves; no great perspicacity is needed to discern the racism in them. To repeat, the problem is to determine how, why, and how much racism exists within this body of song.

The black theme in American popular music reflected generally accepted stereotypes associated with blacks, in almost total disregard of the validity of such images. Only rarely did the black image in song exhibit desirable qualities until the decades following World War II, when the strong movement toward guaranteed civil equality made the entire subject an embarrassment to performers and audiences alike. Significantly, the production of songs on the black subject decreased during the same period.

A central theme of songs about the black concerns the myth of the happy, indolent slave, bound to his master by strong ties of devotion—something of an Uncle Tom. This myth, in turn, is derived from the so-called Cavalier myth, or that of the Southern white as the symbol of chivalry and daring, with honor foremost among personal values. The picture of the plantation as the central social unit comprised of devoted slaves, gallant masters, and their crinolined women became the embodiment of the South in song for more than a century. The image of the black evoked by the Cavalier myth was not limited to the happy plantation slave, however. The black was portrayed in song as thieving, lying, lazy, hopelessly addicted to gambling and gluttony, and so on. His woman, the Negress, was seen as a shrew and a wanton: a female possessed of few desirable traits who yet remained somehow an irresistible sex object to males.

During the first decades of the new nation, a greatly expanded output of songs on black subjects coincided with the revitalization of slavery in the South and the appearance of the Cavalier myth in literature. Popular music aligned itself—whether by design or accident is impossible to state with certainty—alongside those forces whose interests lay in the subjugation of blacks. Pro-slavery arguments came from politicians, clergymen, and intellectuals as the "peculiar institution" came under attack from liberals. Most arguments in support of slavery took a position presumptive of the inherent inferiority of the black, a position heartily endorsed in popular song of the same period. Inasmuch as the songs gave rise to a wholly new American form of entertainment, the minstrel show, there can be little doubt as to the effectiveness of the songs as propaganda supportive of the stereotypical black. Even some of the anti-slavery arguments echoed the myth which, translated into the various stereotypes, had stripped the black of his very humanity.

Nothing seemed capable of shaking the myth of the inherently inferior black. The four years of sheer agony suffered in the Civil War taught the nation very little by way of understanding either slavery or the black. Within a few years after the close of hostilities, the nation was singing songs of intensified nostalgia for the mythological South, along with an even wider-ranging misrepresentation of the black.

The vast numbers of songs on the black subject, and their endurance as a genre, bespeak a considerable influence in the formation of racial attitudes in the collective American mind. Through song, the Negro came to be seen as Americans were expected to see him. The songs were an integral part of the cultural learning process which directed its population to see blacks as inferior to whites—a lesson that even blacks themselves were required to assimilate before being allowed to participate in white society on any level. There were of course no evil conspirators directing our thoughts through song; whatever plot existed had to be part of our national subconscious. We *wanted* and *needed* to see the black as we did in order to assuage the collective guilt and fear surrounding the hideous creation, slavery. Once slavery was destroyed, the black continued to be treated as an inferior in song because of the threat he posed to the purity of the white race—or so the argument ran. At any rate, the fact remains that no realistic view of the black was successful in American song until relatively recent times.

This study is devoted, then, to social, political, psychological, economic, and musical ramifications bearing on the black theme in American popular song throughout its history. Within this context the songs can be seen as a means by which popular attitudes can be revealed and traced to their roots, thus providing insights into forces which guided our attitudes to their present state. It is hoped that the study of past prejudices will in some small measure explain and alleviate those of the present.

Acknowledgments

This study, begun in 1966, has benefitted from the assistance and cooperation of many people and institutions. My wife, Patricia, contributed not only vast amounts of understanding but also assisted in editing the earlier sections of the study. My daughter, Lee Ann, spent an entire summer typing portions of the text, the bibliography, and the indexes.

My secretary, Leslie Wilkins, provided the impetus for the book and aided in gathering songs for the larger sample. The bibliography was prepared by Mary Longenecker Frorer.

Elizabeth Hartman, former Head of the Music Department of the Free Library of Philadelphia, and her successor, Frederick James Kent, made accessible the resources of the magnificent collection of sheet music, songsters, and song collections, offering advice and assistance on the progess of the study. Manuel "Manny" Kean, Curator of the Kean Archives, materially aided in the research by providing material and information available nowhere else. Black music scholar Arthur LaBrew offered a guiding hand and research material from the outset. Richard Jackson, of the Music Division of the Library and Museum of the Performing Arts, New York Public Library, and Peter Fay at the Library of Congress freely gave of their time in locating obscure songs. The late Harry Dichter, aptly characterized as the *pater familias* of sheet music collecting, presented me with a number of rare and valuable songs for my research, while many other collectors materially aided the study by suggesting and locating needed songs.

Special thanks are due to sociologist Dr. John Shope, who gave generously of his time and advice, critically reading the manuscript and providing valuable insights into sociological implications of popular music. My secretary, Marsha Richardson, worked long and diligently typing the multitude of letters connected with preparing the book for publication.

The following publishers are acknowledged for permission to quote lyrics of copyrighted songs:

Shapiro, Bernstein & Co. Inc. "AWAY DOWN SOUTH IN HEAVEN" (Bud Green & Harry Warren) Copyright 1927 Renewed by Shapiro, Bernstein & Co. Inc., New York, N.Y. 10022 "USED BY PERMIS-SION" "BRING BACK THOSE MINSTREL DAYS" (Ballard MacDonald & Martin Broones) Copyright 1926 Renewed by Shapiro, Bernstein & Co. Inc., New York, N.Y. 10022 "USED BY PERMIS-SION" "CHICKEN SONG" (William Jerome & Jean Schwartz) Copyright 1909 Renewed by Shapiro, Bernstein & Co. Inc., New York, N.Y. 10022 "USED BY PERMISSION" "I MAKES MINE MYSELF" (Francis DeWitt & Robert Hood Bowers) Copyright 1921 Renewed by Shapiro, Bernstein & Co. Inc., New York, N.Y. 10022 "USED BY PERMISSION" "I WISH I WAS IN DIXIE" (William Tracey & Dan Dougherty) Copyright 1927 Renewed by Shapiro, Bernstein & Co. Inc., New York, N.Y. 10022 "USED BY PERMISSION" "THE MOON SHINES ON THE MOONSHINE" (Francis DeWitt & Robert Hood Bowers) Copyright 1920 Renewed by Shapiro, Bernstein & Co. Inc., New York, N.Y. 10022 "USED BY PERMISSION" "SEVEN OR ELEVEN" (Lew Brown and Walter Donaldson) Copyright 1922 and 1923 Renewed by Shapiro, Bernstein & Co. Inc., New York, N.Y. 10022 "USED BY PERMISSION" "SHINE" (Cecil Mack, Lew Brown and Ford Dabney) Copyright 1924 Renewed by Shapiro, Bernstein & Co. Inc., New York, N.Y. 10022 "USED BY PERMISSION" "SKOKIAAN" (August Msarurgwa, English lyrics by Tom Glazer) Copyright 1952 Renewed and Copyright 1954 by Shapiro, Bernstein & Co. Inc., New York, N.Y. 10022 "USED BY PERMISSION" "WAY DOWN YONDER IN NEW ORLEANS" (Creamer and Layton) Copyright 1922 Renewed by Shapiro, Bernstein & Co. Inc., New York, N.Y. 10022 "USED BY PER-MISSION"

G. Schirmer, Inc. "WID DE MOON, MOON, MOON" (William Moore and Will Marion Cooke) Copyright 1907 G. Schirmer, Inc., New York, N.Y. "USED BY PERMISSION" "MAH LINDY LOU" (Lily Strickland) Copyright 1920 G. Schirmer, Inc., New York, N.Y. "USED BY PER-MISSION" "RUN ON HOME" (Lily Strickland) Copyright 1920 G. Schirmer Inc., New York, N.Y. "USED BY PERMISSION" "VOO-DOO" (Marie Lussi and David Guion) Copyright 1929 G. Schirmer, Inc., New York, N.Y. "USED BY PERMISSION"

Fred Fisher Music Company, Inc. "CANNIBAL LOVE" (Will J. Harris and Harry I. Robinson) Copyright 1909 by Will Rossiter, Chicago, Fred Fisher Music Co. Inc., New York, N.Y. "USED BY PERMISSION" "WHEN THE WAR BREAKS OUT IN MEXICO I'M GOING TO

SCANDALIZE MY NAME

I met my sister the other day,
She gave me her right hand,
But jus' as soon as ever my back was turned,
Scandalize my name.

You call that a sister? No! No!
You call that a sister? No! No!
You call that religion? No! No!
Scandalize my name.

I met my brother the other day,
He gave me his right hand,
But jus' as soon as ever my back was turned,
Scandalize my name.

You call that a brother? No! No!
You call that a brother? No! No!
You call that religion? No! No!
Scandalize my name.

I met my neighbor the other day,
He gave me his right hand,
But jus' as soon as ever my back was turned,
Scandalize my name.

You call that a neighbor? No! No!
You call that a neighbor? No! No!
You call that religion? No! No!
Scandalize my name.

                    (Negro spiritual said to have
                       originated in Alabama)

Vous avez crié pour un rêve—
Je vous ferai crier pour la réalité!

[You make a stir about a dream—
I will make you roar about reality!]

                    (*La Belle Helene*, III, ii)

Chapter One

The Beginnings

When Thomas D'Urfey (1653–1723) published his *Wit and Mirth; or, Pills to Purge Melancholy* (London, 1684), one of the songs included concerned a subject which was destined to become a major stereotype in the popular song of subsequent generations—that of the young black prostitute. Entitled "A Song," D'Urfey's little satire cut both ways, showing that the black female was considered as an easily obtainable sex partner while at the same time showing the "Good Captain Thunder" as tactless and cheap. Although the black is depicted as having rather dubious morals, D'Urfey demonstrates a sense of justice along with his sense of humor as he has his "Dear Pinckaninny" spurn the "half a Guinny" proffered by Captain Thunder, she declaring:

> Other Town Misses,
> May gape at Ten Pieces,
> But who me possesses,
>   Full Twenty shall Pay;
> To all poor Rogues in Buff,
> Thus, thus I strut and huff,
> So Captain kick and cuff,
>   March on your way.

The musical settings for D'Urfey's collection were made by some of England's best composers of the period, including Henry Purcell, Thomas Farmer, and John Blow. There is no evidence that these composers attempted to infuse Negroid elements into any songs with a black subject, however. The Negro was not unknown in seventeenth-century England, of course, but he was remote—mainly an object of concern to those with interests in the distant colonies of the New World.

3

The association of blackness with popular entertainment was known both in England and on the Continent from at least the beginning of the seventeenth century, when blackened face and hands were utilized for comic effect in such amusements as Jan van Arp's *Singhende Klucht, Van Droncke Goosen*, a Dutch farce jig published in 1639, and the Elizabethan jig *The Blackman*.[1] In the fourteenth-century Dutch farce *Buskenblaser*, an old husband pays a quack to make him young and handsome for his wife, and has his face and hands blackened instead; a similar incident is portrayed in the English farce *John Swabber*.[2] It would be pure conjecture to connect these stage jigs to the black subject on the American stage; yet the evidence does suggest that they, along with folk drama, minor dramatic forms, and other literary forms reflecting popular tastes represent the real roots of the American minstrel show.

Twenty years before the publication of *Singhende Klucht, Van Droncke Goosen*, the black was brought to the North American continent as a laborer—twenty Africans brought to the port of Jamestown, Virginia, in a Dutch ship and exchanged for "Victualle." The colony was only some dozen years old and laborers were sorely needed for the plantations established along the James River. The early black in Virginia was not at first considered a slave but was accorded status similar to indentured servants. Gradually, however, the demand for cheap labor converted the length of servitude from a fixed term to life.

It is not certain when the first black slaves were brought to New England, but a reasonable amount of evidence places the date somewhere between 1624 and 1628.[3] From the outset there were subtle differences in attitude toward the black among the New England colonies as contrasted to the southern and middle colonies. Yet special concessions, geography, and prospects of huge profits soon made New England foremost in the slave traffic.[4]

The Founding Fathers felt compelled to rationalize slavery on both spiritual and moral grounds, which they accomplished by declaring that slavery was established by the law of God in Israel and that they, as the Elect of God, were granted the enslavement of Indians and blacks as a sacred privilege. It was their sacred duty, they reasoned, to bring the godless savage into the Christian fold, no matter how many Christian ideals were violated in the process.[5] The Virginia colonists paid lip service to this rationale, but the exigencies of the labor situation outweighed moral and religious considerations. The establishment of slavery rested heavily on economic and legal grounds. But race was the dominant factor; had the laborer been white, it is inconceivable that the history of slavery in America would have taken the course it did. These combined factors produced an attitude of righteous paternalism toward the black, relegating him forever to the bottom rung of society's ladder.

Musically, the first century of the colonies produced virtually nothing of interest to this study. Although music was very much a part of early colonial life, it was based entirely on the tastes of England. Sacred and secular music depended on the Mother Country for both style and content until well into the eighteenth century, when a distinctly American hymnody developed in New England.[6] This English dominance explains in part the dearth of songs on black subjects and the tone of the few that did appear; the black was everywhere in American colonial life whereas he was a rarity on the streets of London.

The black began to figure as a sympathetic subject in the literature of the period, however, as authors awakened to the horror of slavery. English men of letters formed the vanguard of the movement to end the evils of slavery—poets, dramatists, and writers who attacked the institution of slavery on moral grounds, and who almost succeeded in their effort to shame their countrymen were it not for unforeseen technological developments which wrecked their arguments.

Shakespeare's *Othello* and Thomas Southerne's *Oroonoko* were conspicuous examples of the portrayal of blacks in drama. The mass of commentary on Shakespeare's work renders further discussion unnecessary. The Southerne work—less familiar and decidedly inferior dramatically—deserves our attention in that the subject is black slavery as seen through a white man's eyes.

Oroonoko is the story of an African prince taken captive by treacherous whites. The prince, whose name gives the play its title, leads a slave rebellion which is crushed perfidiously by his white captors. His lady chooses death over dishonor in rejecting the passionate advances of a white man, equalling her prince in courage and virtue. It is a complicated plot, with many long dialogues; yet it has a primitive power which is capable of making its impact felt even today.

Needless to say, *Oroonoko* was not an overwhelming success with early American plantation owners, although the addition of the comic song "The Gay Negro Boy," sung in blackface to the accompaniment of a banjo, made it somewhat more congenial to American audiences.[7]

On the British stage, however, *Oroonoko* found favor for almost a century after its appearance in 1695. One of the reasons behind this difference of British and American opinion lay in Southerne's treatment of his tragic figure within the context of aristocracy—Oroonoko was no ordinary slave, he was a prince outraged by unscrupulous men. An affront against him was symbolically an affront against all nobility. Unimpressed, the colonists saw *Oroonoko* only as an attack on their cherished institution of slavery.

Southerne's conception of the black shows an unfamiliarity with the subject. Oroonoko is given the manner of speech of Whitehall rather than his African kingdom as, for example, in his exhortation to the whites as he leads them in an attack against the Indians who have plundered the plantations:

> A lover cannot fall more glorious,
> Than in the cause of Love. He that deserves
> His Mistress's favour wonnot stay behind:
> I'le lead you on, be bold, and follow me.[8]

The other slaves are also grotesquely misconceived, singing two songs after a day's forced labor which, except for the obviously serious intent of the author, would lend the play an appearance of travesty:

> A SONG by Sir Harry Sheers;
> set by Mr. Courtevill
>
> A Lass there lives upon the green,
>   Cou'd I her picture draw;
> A brighter nymph was never seen,
> That looks, and reigns; a little queen,
>   And keeps the swains in awe.
>
> Her eyes are Cupid's darts and wings,
>   Her eye-brows are his bow;
> Her silken hair the silver strings,
> Which sure and swift destruction brings,
>   To all the vale below.
>
> If Pastorella's dawning light
>   Can warm, and warm us so;

Her noon will shine so piercing bright,
Each glancing beam will kill outright,
    And every swain subdue.

A SONG by Mr. Cheek; set by Mr. Courtevill

Bright Cynthia's pow'r divinely great,
    What heart is not obeying?
A thousand Cupids on her wait,
    And in her eyes are playing.

She seems the queen of love to reign,
    For she alone dispences
Such sweets, as best can entertain
    The guest of all the senses.

Her face a charming prospect brings;
    Her breath gives balmy blisses;
I hear an angel when she sings,
    And taste of heav'n in kisses.

Four senses thus she feasts with joy,
    From nature's richest treasure;
Let me the other sense employ,
    And I shall die with pleasure.[9]

The black and slavery began to appear in American music and literature around the middle of the eighteenth century. Freedom and slavery were conceptualized for the most part, while the black himself emerged primarily as a comic figure. It must be noted that the references to freedom and slavery applied only to whites, in the growing awareness that strictures imposed by England made the colonists little better than slaves to a system that was more interested in profit than the welfare of its subjects. Americans found ways in which to express their feelings about freedom without appearing disloyal, however.

James Lyon expressed his loyalty to the Crown in his *Ode, Set to Music*, performed in 1759 upon his graduation from Princeton.[10] The *Ode*, intended as a glorification of Amherst's victory over the French in Canada the previous year, made only passing reference to slavery:

Cheerful, fearless and at ease,
On the downing lap of Peace,
In the gentle Muses Seat,

> Unmov'd at War's tremendous Roar
> That Consternation spreads from Shore to Shore
> O'er solid Continents, and Falling Waves,
> From haughty Monarchs down to Slaves
> Low cringing at their feet. . . .

The music to which this ode was set has not survived; but the text was published in the *New American Magazine* (Woodbridge, New Jersey, 1759), under the title *Louisburg Taken*. Without realizing it perhaps, Lyon revealed a current attitude toward slavery. The "classical" education of American universities in the 1750's ignored classical attitudes toward slavery—attitudes which certainly did not require all slaves to cringe at the master's feet.[11]

More to the point of this study, *The Disappointment; or The Force of Credulity* (1767), by Andrew Barton (possibly a pseudonym for Thomas Forrest), is generally credited as being the first ballad opera published by an American in America.[12]

The Disappointment is noteworthy on other counts as well: it is the first native work to present a black character and, perhaps because of this, it is also the first American ballad opera to suffer the consequences of censorship.[13] The story concerns four "humourists"— Hum, Parchment, Quadrant, and Rattletrap—who hoodwink a number of "dupes" into searching for a nonexistent buried treasure. The black character, Raccoon, is presented in a most unorthodox way even by today's standards: he is not only obviously a free black, but rich and debauched, keeping a white mistress with whom he plans to share his part of the treasure. His part is in dialect and is intended for comedy; yet he suffers no overt discrimination at the hands of any of the other characters during the treasure hunt. He also introduces, in the fourth song of the play, what may be the earliest version of "Yankee Doodle" in American literature, thereby overthrowing certain fondly held notions concerning its origin in the American Revolution.[14] The version included in the play relates to the action, however:

Air IV

YANKEE DOODLE

O! how joyful shall I be
  When I get de money,

> I will bring it all to dee;
> O! my diddling honey!

The part of Raccoon stands in marked contrast to the black characters portrayed by later playwrights. While the part is comic and dialect is used, the character of Raccoon is accorded equal status with the other characters, who speak in comic Irish and Scottish dialects. The treatment of Raccoon as a human being may well have been one of the unspecified reasons why *The Disappointment* was withdrawn as being "unfit for the stage."[15]

Close on the heels of *The Disappointment* came Charles Dibdin's *The Padlock*, performed in London in 1768 (or 1769, according to some authorities).[16] Probably the best-known, and certainly one of the most prolific, songwriters in England before the turn of the century, Dibdin achieved further fame through his characterization of the black in his opera and played the part himself in England.

The libretto of *The Padlock*, by Charles Bickerstaff, is an adaptation of Cervantes' *El Celoso Extremeño*, the story of an old miser who locks his wife in his house in order to prevent temptation. The miser's servant, Luys, becomes in the Dibdin opera a comic black character called Mungo. Dibdin's characterization of Mungo as a servile lout, shiftless and cowardly, devoid of most virtues, was the standard by which most playwrights and songwriters depicted black males during the following century and a half. Success in the part of Mungo brought Dibdin personal glory; it also established on two continents a stereotypical stage-black, an image which satisfied the white need to see the black as an essentially inferior being.

The Padlock came to the colonies in 1769, after a run of fifty-three nights in Drury Lane in 1768.[17] It was performed at the John Street Theatre in New York in May, 1769, and ran throughout the rest of that summer, with Lewis Hallam in the role of Mungo. It was said that Hallam was "unrivalled" in the part until his death, surpassing even Dibdin, the original.[18] Hallam, it was further suggested, owed much of his excellence as Mungo to his study of black character and dialect in the colonies and in Jamaica. It is extremely ironic that this evaluation—based on white standards of observation of the black, concerning a white actor on a white stage performing a white opera for a white audience—should have been given credence, since those involved could claim only a superficial knowledge of the black under conditions as they existed at that time. Claims of authenticity in the presentation of the stage-black became one of those unsupported myths surrounding the origin of later representations, eventually deluding many authorities into the belief that the black himself approved of such material.

Dibdin capitalized on the popularity of the black theme in his songs, although the bulk of his work was dedicated to the glorification of England, with particular emphasis on the British tar and the Royal Navy. A partial list of his songs on black subjects includes: "Kickaraboo," from *Christmas Gambols* (performed in 1795); "The Negro and His Banjer," from *The Wags; or, The Camp of Pleasure* (performed in 1790); "Negro Philosophy," from *The General Election* (performed in 1796); "Poor Orra Tink of Yanko Dear," from *The Islanders* (1780); "One Mountain Neger" and "The Sun Go Down," from *The Round Robin* (1811).

"Poor Orra Tink of Yanko Dear" is a maudlin lament for a departed lover, with only the pseudo-dialect attributed to the black distinguishing it from other English sentimental songs of the period. Dibdin's "Negro Philosophy" gives a dramatic view of the condition of slavery, describing the whippings which make the slave "jerk like pea 'pon drumhead." The unending "worky, worky" forces him to work "a Sunday," and, when "soon something good begin to grow, take away a Monday." The song further describes how the white slave owners cuckold the black husband, his only recourse being to "lie down flat while Overseer he jerk [i.e., whip] ye." Incredibly, this description of the conditions of slavery was found to be comical, not only by audiences of the day, but even today, as Nathan finds it "amusing rather than pitiful."[19]

This point should be made absolutely clear: the humor, such as it is, that may be found in songs of this type is entirely from a white perspective, representing the deriding of an oppressed minority by a white majority either unwilling or unable to realistically see the black.

Charles Dibdin was, in all likelihood, unconscious of the part his songs played in the slander of the black. In common with most composers of popular songs throughout the ages, he wrote according to the fashion of the moment, using Irish, Scottish, or black dialect as the occasion demanded.[20] But there is a difference which distinguishes his use of those dialects; the Scottish and Irish songs were essentially favorable to the cultures represented, whereas Dibdin's unfamiliarity with the black resulted in an ambivalent and superficial attitude in the songs.

As the eighteenth century drew to a close, references to the black in popular song became both more numerous and more specific. The ambiguity with which the subject was treated was a reflection of popular uncertainty concerning the status of the blacks. Many songs attempted to strike a sympathetic note for the black, while others continued to exploit the comic possibilities of the subject.

"The Poor Black Boy," by Stephen Storace, combines a clumsy pseudo-black dialect with excessive emotionalism to create a panegyric to the imagery of the contented slave who could not bear separation from his "massa." This canard was destined to become one of the basic themes of songs on black subjects. Through constant repetition it gained the status of accepted doctrine.

THE POOR BLACK BOY

You care of money ah care no more
No tink if you be rich or poor
No tink if you be rich or poor
My mind employ me stay wid you
No sorry no and where away my Massa go
Go poor black boy go poor black boy
And where away my Massa go—go black boy.

You good to me dat keepy here
No Massa dat you never fear
No Massa dat you never fear
Long time destroy me know death kill
But leave one part he never kill
The loving heart of poor black boy
Of poor black boy he never kill
The loving heart of poor black boy.[21]

The popularity of "The Poor Black Boy" is indicated by at least five American printings between 1794 and 1796.[22] It formed part of the musical score of Storace's *The Prize*, which was called "a musical farce"—aptly enough, to judge by this example.

"The Desponding Negro" was a far more realistic account of what might have been the fate of an African Negro caught in the vicious snare of slavery during the 1790's. The British Museum Catalogue

attributes the song to William Reeve, there being three known
American editions dating from 1793 to 1798.[23]

THE DESPONDING NEGRO

On Africk's wide Plains, where the Lion now roaring,
With freedom stalks forth the vast Desart exploring,
I was dragg'd from my Hut, and enchain'd as a Slave,
In a dark floating Dungeon upon the salt wave,
    Spare a Half-penny, Spare a Half-penny,
    Spare a Half-penny to a poor Negro.

Toss'd on the wild Main, I all wildly despairing,
Burst my Chains rush'd on Deck with mine Eyeballs wide
    glaring,
When the Lightning's dread blast struck the Inlets of Day,
And its glorious bright beams shut for ever away,
    Spare a Half-penny, &c.

The despoiler of Man then his prospect thus losing,
Of gain by my sale, not a blind bargain choosing,
As my value, compar'd with my keeping, was light,
Had me dash'd overboard, in the dead of the Night.
    Spare a Half-penny, &c.

And but for a Bark to Brittannia's Coast bound then,
All my cares in the deep by that plunge had been drown'd then,
But by Moonlight decry'd, I was snatched from the wave,
And reluctantly robb'd of a watery grave.
    Spare a Half-penny, &c.

How disastrous my fate freedom's ground tho' I tread now,
Torn from Home, Wife, and Children, and wand'ring for bread
    now,
While Seas roll between us which ne'er can be cross'd,
And Hope's distant glimm'rings in darkness are lost.
    Spare a Half-penny, &c.

But of Minds foul and fair when the Judges and the Ponderer,
Shall restore light and rest to the Blind and the Wanderer,
The European's deep dye may outrival the Sloe
And the Soul of an Ethiop' prove as white as the Snow.
    Spare a Half-penny, &c.[24]

Here, in song, is a clear and detailed protest against the outrages
committed against the African black in the name of commerce. The

last verse pinpoints the nagging fear of many white Christians that there might actually be an avenging God who would prove color-blind in the evaluation of men's souls. The conviction that all men are alike *under* the skin recurs many times in the songs on black subjects, but William Blake, in his haunting poem "The Little Black Boy," expresses it more forcefully:

> My mother bore me in the southern wild,
> And I am black, but O, my soul is white.[25]

William Cowper, an active abolitionist from around 1788, puts a wry twist to the same idea with his epigram:

> To purify their wine, some people bleed
> A lamb into the barrel, and succeed;
> No nostrum, planters say, is half so good
> To make fine sugar as a negro's blood.
>
> Now lambs and negroes are harmless things
> And thence perhaps this wondrous virtue springs,
> 'Tis in the blood of innocence alone—
> Good cause why planters never try their own.[26]

One of the earliest songs to become internationally popular was the poignant "I Sold a Guiltless Negro Boy," by John Moulds, an English songwriter active in the 1790's. The song is also known by a shorter title, "The Negro Boy." It was sung by the noted Mr. Tyler, perhaps as early as 1796, in Samuel Arnold's opera *Inkle and Yarico*, and in concerts presented in New York during 1798 and 1799.[27]

It is said that "I Sold a Guiltless Negro Boy" was inspired by an incident which allegedly took place in the early 1790's; the story concerns an African prince who, when asked what he had paid for his fine watch, replied, "I gave a fine boy for it."[28] Although both words and music of the song are stylistically contemporary European and sentimental to the marrow, it has an emotional impact that is still capable of being felt. It is the exposition in song of that greed which is within mankind—greed so strong that it can lead one human being to actually sell his fellow human beings.

Nathan discounts "I Sold a Guiltless Negro Boy" on the grounds of its excessive sentimentality and his characterization of the words as

unintelligible.[29] Evidently Nathan examined some different version of
the song, inasmuch as he quotes variants of the title, words, and
composer.[30]

In point of fact, the English sentimental ballad style dominated the
songs of this period, making Nathan's judgment seem a bit harsh in
this instance. Perhaps it might be well to remember that congruity of
elements has never been the deciding factor in establishing the
popularity of these or any other popular songs.

A case in point is "An African Love Song," the words to which
were written by "A Lady," with music composed by James Fisin, an
Englishman known for his songs, glees, sonatas, etc.[31] "An African
Love Song" is cast as the importunate warning of a black lover to his
lady to eschew the flattery of whites bent on enslaving her. There is
no attempt at realism in the musical setting, nor is the pseudo-black
dialect evident in the words. Shunning the use of artificial Negrisms
reflects a certain sincerity of purpose in this particular instance while
at the same time assuring the virtual extinction of the song. American
audiences were unaccustomed to crediting the black with humanity,
preferring to see their "coloreds" as dialect-spouting clowns.

AN AFRICAN LOVE SONG

Dear Colyzs will you leave me,
    Can you leave your Lover true,
Can you have the heart to grieve me,
    Why dislike my sable hue,
Nature ever just and kind,
    To that sable hue has joined,
Candour and a constant mind,
    Free from guilt to Love and you.

White men flatt'ry too engaging,
    Tempts you to a distant shore,
O'er the waves the storm is raging,
    Round their ship the waters roar.
Now the swelling surges foam,
    Do not dearest, do not roam,
Hie thee to thy peaceful home,
    There delight unfolds her store.

Fans of palm around thee playing,
    Sweet and coolness shall combine,
Swells thy jetty neck arraying,

In contrasted lustre shine.
Twining plants shall guard thy bower,
    From the noon beams' fervid power,
Pleasures varied ev'ry hour,
    Dear Colyzs shall be thine.

Samuel Arnold's "Poor Negro Woman," from his "entertainment" *Obi; or, Three Fingered Jack*, is another example of the songs dealing with the humanity of the black. The pseudo-black dialect is employed in this song obviously in the interest of realism, but the effect of the device is distracting to the serious intent of the text.

POOR NEGRO WOMAN

My Cruel Love to danger go,
No think of pain he give to me,
Too soon me fear like grief to know,
As broke the heart of Ulalee,
    Poor Negro Woman Ulalee,
    Poor Negro Woman Ulalee.

Poor Soul to see her hang her head,
All day beneath the Cypress Tree,
And still she sing "my Love be dead,"
The Husband of Poor Ulalee:
    Poor Negro Woman Ulalee,etc.

"My Love be kill'd" how sweet he smiled,
His smile again me never see,
Unless me see it in the Child,
That he hath left Poor Ulalee:
    Poor Negro Woman Ulalee, etc.

My Baby to my breast I fold,
But little warmth poor Boy have he,
His Father's death make all so cold,
About the heart of Ulalee:
    Poor Negro Woman Ulalee, etc.[32]

The idea that the black was endowed with human qualities according to Western concepts was given additional impetus in the last decade of the eighteenth century with the publication, in 1798, of the abstract of *Travels in the Interior Districts of Africa . . . in the Years 1795, 1796, and 1797*, by Mungo Park.[33] Park related an incident which he experienced as he sought shelter in a native village, where he sat for many hours, "weary and dejected," until he was provided with food and a place to rest. As he was waiting, the women of the village went about their work, as described by Park:

They lightend their labour by Songs, one of which was composed extempore, for I was myself the subject of it. It was sung by one of the young women, the rest joining in a sort of chorus: The air was sweet and plaintive, and the words, literally translated, were these, "The winds roared, and the rains fell; The poor white man, faint and weary, came and sat under our tree. He has no mother to bring him milk; No wife to grind his corn. (Chorus) Let us pity the white man; No mother has he, &c. &c.

The thought of the black, in his own territory, aiding the white man who represented the most dreadful danger known to blacks, held many intriguing possibilities for Western imaginations. Anti-slavery forces saw in the incident proof of the humanity of the black; white pro-slavery interests found in it irrefutable evidence that blacks were by their very nature the servant of whites. The story was irresistible to songwriters of the period, and many versions were published within the next few years.

The first of these, according to Nathan,[34] was by F.H. Barthelemon, a French composer living in England at the time. A literary paraphrase of the text by Georgiana Cavendish, Duchess of Devonshire, was used by most of the composers in their settings. Among those composers were some of the leading figures in music, including G.G. Ferrari, Joseph Dale, F. Mallet, and America's own leading composer, Benjamin Carr. A paraphrase of the story by S.S. Coleman was set by John Moorehead.

One version, "The Poor White Man," was "versified by 'A Lady' " (not the Duchess of Devonshire) and set by "A Lady of Fashion," who in all likelihood will unfortunately remain unidentified. This version follows the Park text with reasonable faithfulness, making a concise poem of striking quality. The music is well within the common practice of the day—sentimental and thoroughly European.

The setting of the Park incident by Benjamin Carr is of interest not only as an American work, but for its obvious musical and moralistic ties with British anti-slavery sentiments. The text for the Carr version is that of the Duchess of Devonshire, and the Carr setting, while more suited to the text than most, is devoid of Negroid elements.

The loud wind roar'd, the rain fell fast,
The white man yeilded [sic] to the blast,
He sat him down beneath our tree,
For weary sad and faint was he,
And ah! no wife or mother's care,
For him the milk or corn prepare,
The white man shall our pity share,
Alas! no wife or mother's care,
For him the milk or corn prepare,
For him the milk or corn prepare.

The storm is o'er, the tempest past,
And mercy's voice has hush'd the blast,
The wind is heard in whispers low,
The white man far away must go,
But ever in his heart will bear,
Remembrance of the Negros' care.

Go white man, go and with thee bear,
The Negros' wish, the Negros' pray'r,
Remembrance of the Negros' care.[35]

Of course, there is no accurate measure of the effect of the Park incident on whites at the turn of the century; but the number of times it was set to music is a fair indication that it was considerable. It added fuel to the abolitionist movement, but there was no perceptible change in white attitudes toward blacks, who had become fixed in the minds of most whites as naturally inferior beings.

Another European import sympathetic to the black was "The Negro's Song," by Thomas Thaarup, set to music by C. Stokes[36] sometime before 1815.[37] The song speaks directly to the moral issue of slavery in a nominally Christian society. Most slaveholders, of course, considered themselves devoted Christians, actively carrying out God's will in the practice of slavery. The European moralists thus exposed in song one side of the slavery question—why should blackness be a justification for enslavement—which was to dominate the first half of the nineteenth century. The pro-slavery element was put on the defensive, finding slavery increasingly difficult to abandon on both moral and economic grounds.

To return to "The Negro's Song," the distinction can be made, even at this early date, between the slavery issue and the question of the status of the black. For all the thundering prose and sentimental songs, it was a rare abolitionist who could bring himself to admit the black as his social equal. To picture the black as present in a social gathering, as does "The Negro's Song," was something of a rarity in itself.

THE NEGRO'S SONG

I will fly the social room,
   I will weep in lonely sadness;
The poor negro's cherish'd gloom
   Must not mar the hour of gladness.
Let my fate your sighs command,
Fetter'd in a distant land.

Say, what is the negro's crime,
   Ye who in our blood engrave it?
Can the colour of our clime
   Plead for sin with him who gave it?
Gloomy is the negro's breast,
Robb'd of her he loves the best.

God of Christians, God of men!
   Thou canst melt the heart of scorn;
May none e'er the bridegroom chain,
   From his new-espoused torn!
Let our fate thy pity move,
Robb'd of country and of love!

While there was more hope than evidence that slavery was dying as expected at the end of the eighteenth century, the issue continued to be a point of controversy and embarrassment in a society built upon the premise of individual freedom. The songs discussed thus far are indicative of two points of view: the black as an inferior, ideally suited to be a comic figure; and the black as an object of sympathy. Neither of these was a finely drawn, fully established type, however. Not until the 1820's, when slavery became an economic factor vital to the interests of the South—in the opinion of Southerners, at any rate— would the songs become fixed in style and content.

    The rather unclear picture of the black as seen through the songs of this period is consistent with the unsettled economic, political, and social conditions which prevailed in the infant nation. As ties with the Mother Country were severed, it became evident that refined European musical imports were hardly suited to the tastes of the boisterous new nation; many of these imports, both sacred and secular, were "Americanized" to remove all references to the "King and Motherland" so recently discarded.

American tastes in entertainment, in contradistinction to the English or European, inclined toward the spectacular and the sensational, creating a demand for music which exceeded the abilities of local composers to provide. Thus, the reliance on imported music continued until around the second decade of the nineteenth century, when a typically American style generated its own body of material. This characteristically American style developed around the subject of the black, culminating in the truly American form, the minstrel show.

During the early days of the republic, however, the British influence on American popular song continued, but not entirely as a one-way affair—particularly if the subject happened to be the American black. Charles Mathews, the English actor designated by Francis Hodge as the "pater-familias of Yankee theatre,"[38] made two visits to the United States during this formative period, demonstrating not only an impressive array of impersonations of European types, but collecting an equally impressive number of observations of distinctively American types which he brought to the stage in his *Trip to America* and *Jonathan in England*. Mathews performed alone on stage, ridiculing in skits, songs, and monologues the Scottish, Welsh, Irish, or any of the many European types which he developed according to his observations. However clever these conceptions may have been, Mathews was in grave error when he allowed his preconceptions to interfere with his observations of the American black (see Appendix I).

Mathews included a song in his *Trip to America* which he claimed to be "a South Carolina Negro Air," going so far as to assert that the song was "from the original Negro Melody, of which this is the only correct copy extant." The song, "Possum Up a Gum Tree," is, of course, familiar today, but the commonly sung version differs widely from Mathew's version. Perhaps he actually did hear the song and, believing it to be authentic, presented it to his audiences, but no other source verifies his extravagant assertions of the folk origin of the song. In fact, Mathews made three transcriptions of the tune himself, none of which are identical.[39]

The Mathews "Possum Up a Gum Tree" examined for this study reveals a preoccupation with trivia which is exploited as the ingenuous observation of a disinterested party—commerical artlessness, as it were. In an amateur zoological excursion into fantasy, the song purports to explain certain peculiar habits of the oppossum and the raccoon, in an explicatory foreword:

The burden of this little ballad is founded on a Circumstance in Zoology reported by Naturalists, The Oppossum climbs a Tree, the hollow of which is occupied by the Raccoon, He seizes the tail of the Oppossum as he ascends, who loudly exclaims against this unjust invasion of his property, but is notwithstanding too slothful to quit the vicinity of his Oppressor.

This inane observation is continued through the first verse of the song, after which the actual purpose of casting the black in a ridiculous light becomes evident:

> Possum up a Gum-tree
>   Up he go, up he go
> Racoon in the hollow
>   Down below, down below
> Him pull him by hims long tail
>   Pully hawl, pully hawl
> Then how him whoop and hallow
>   Scream and bawl, scream and bawl.
>
> Possum up a Gum-tree
>   Racoon in the hollow
> Him pull him by hims long tail
>   Then how him whoop and hallow.
>
> Massa send we Negro Boy
>   Board a ship, board a ship
> There we work and cry "Ye hoy"
>   Cowskin whip, cowskin whip
> Negro he work all day
>   Night get groggy, night get groggy
> But if Negro he go play
>   Massa floggy, Massa floggy.
>
> Possum &c.
>
> Caesar steal him Massa's boots
>   Last whitsunday, last whitsunday
> 'Cause him marry Polly Cootes
>   Look fine and gay, fine and gay
> Caesar all day walk in pain
>   Boot so tight, boot so tight

He no get them off again
   All de night, all de night.
Possum &c.

Miss Polly say "You nasty brute
   "Get out of bed, get out of bed
"If you come near me wid de boot
   "I break your head, I break your head."
Caesar he no more entreats him
   He quite dummy, he quite dummy
Massa see his boots and beat him
   All to mummy, all to mummy.
Possum &c.

Thus Mathews turns a song dealing with animal lore into a comic song with a black subject. Compared with the versions collected by folklorists, the Mathews version appears to be the sole example which mentions the "work all day, play all night" idea, as well as the assumption that slaves were natural thieves and ludicrous husbands.[40] Indeed, such comparisons would seem to indicate that the extraordinarily great difference between the Mathews version and those collected by later scholars shows Mathews to have been either a strikingly inept collector of folksongs or the victim of those who wished to impress him with their own misconceived notions of black music.[41]

While Mathews made the harsh effects of slavery a sick joke, at least two British imports which appeared during this period tried to deliver a more realistic appraisal of slavery as seen through British eyes. "The Negro Slave," and "The Negro's Lamentation" deliver essentially the same message: slavery is a rotten business.

"The Negro Slave," a "favourite, pathetic ballad," was written by C.I. Pitt and set to music by V. DeCleve around the turn of the century. The case against slavery is presented in the third person, without a trace of pseudo-black dialect, implying a white point of view. Loaded with sentiment, "The Negro Slave" expresses the same feeling as does "The Negro's Song," in *Danish and Norwegian Melodies* (see p. 18).

THE NEGRO SLAVE

Ye Children of pleasure, come hither and see
   A sight that shall check your irreverent glee;

Ye Children of woe, hear a tale which a while
   A sense of your own various griefs shall beguile;
Thy tear at that tale divine, sympathy! shed;
   Rejoice, sweet compassion! at viewing this grave;
Here wretchedness hides unmolested its head;
   For under this turf lies a poor Negro slave!

Depriv'd of whatever endears us to life;
   His country, his freedom, his Children, and Wife;
Grown mad with Reflection, his spirit he freed—
   With pity, ye rigid, contemplate the deed.
His Corpse, unregarded, disgrac'd the highway,
   'Til, blushing, humanity's credit to save,
With tenderness, charity hasten'd to pay
   Mortality's due to the poor Negro Slave!

Ye kind passers by, who this spot turn to view,
   The tribute bequeath to his memory due—
May Peace watch his Pillow whose Breast can bestow
   A generous Sigh o'er the Annals of woe!
The Sigh that you heave, and the tear that you shed,
   Remembrance on Heaven's blest Records shall 'grave;
But vengeance shall heavily fall on each head
   That spurn'd and oppres'd him, a poor Negro Slave!

"The Negro's Lamentation," composed by W. Howard at the close of the eighteenth century, is akin to the earlier "The Desponding Negro." The enunciation of the evils of slavery is made in the first person without resorting to the pseudo-black dialect. This device had its limitations, however. The shock of hearing the black—even an imaginary type on stage—declaiming in perfectly acceptable English must have been great to audiences already accustomed to hearing the catachrestical dialect-spouting pseudo-black onstage.

THE NEGRO'S LAMENTATION

Behold me torn From Afric's Shore,
The Place which gave me Birth,
A Foreign nation to explore,
Where interest dazzles worth.

Behold me bound with heavy Chains,
And forc'd from all I love,
My Wife, my Child—the Dear remains,
They know not where I rove.

Let all prevailing nature speak,
And wear Compassion's Face,
Let pity smile upon your Cheek,
Thus shade your own Disgrace.

Alas! I see no merit reign,
Triumphant on your Brow,
Then farewell all, but ah, the shame
Proud Briton, rests with you.

To counterbalance the excessive sentimentality of the songs attacking slavery, there stood Michael Kelly's "Mister Mug," the first really funny comic song on the subject. Sung by Liston in George Coleman's *The Africans*, the classic switch in comedy is employed to depict Mug, a white man, becoming the slave of "A woolly old Humbug." This of course was heresy to the doctrine of white superiority, regardless of how amusing it might have been for the moment; the song rescues itself, therefore, in having Mug take advantage of his unique skin color (along with generous helpings of good luck) to become "His black Mandingo Majesty's white Minister of State."

MISTER MUG

By Trade I am a Turner,
  And Mug it is my name,
To buy a lot of Ivory
  To Africa I came,
I met a trading Blackamoor,
  A woolly old Humbug,
He coax'd me up his land
  And made a Slave of Mister Mug.

Crying won't you, won't you,
  Won't you come, Mister Mug,
Won't you, won't you, won't you,
  Won't you come, Mister Mug.

My skin is lily white,
  And my colour here is new,
So the first man whom they sold me to,
  He thump'd me black and blue.
The Priest who bought me from him,
  In a tender hearted tone,

> Said come from that great blackguard's house,
>   And enter in my own.
>
> Good lack! but to behold
>   The vicissitudes of fate!
> I'm his black Mandingo Majesty's
>   White Minister of State:
> For hours, in my lobby,
>   My petitioners shall stay,
> And wish me at the Devil
>   When I hold my Levee day.

"Yankee Doodle; or, The Negroes Farewell to America" is quite another story. This song, bearing absolutely no resemblance to the well-known American patriotic song with the same title, reflects a sentiment of many leaders of the day, both black and white, that the best solution to the entire black question lay in deportation. In this instance, the desire to leave the land of slavery is expressed through the lips of a pseudo-black who sees England as his promised land. It is not certain whether the song was meant for the English stage or as an affirmation of anti-slavery feelings; it might even have been considered propaganda in the British effort to gain defectors to their cause among the black population in the colonies during the Revolution and, more possibly, during the War of 1812.

The role played by black Americans in the American Revolution and subsequent wars is—or should be—common knowledge. They fought at Bunker Hill and were recruited by all the states except Georgia and South Carolina. This recruitment came, however, only after the British had offered freedom to those slaves who would defect to their side. Some blacks did gain freedom as a result of their service in the Revolutionary forces; but for the most part, their services were quickly forgotten.[42]

While some blacks favored deportation, and a significant number did defect to the British, most black leaders saw deportation as merely another white ploy which avoided the fundamental issue of justice for blacks in America. Those opposed to deportation took the position that America was, after all, the home of blacks as much as whites, and that it was better to try to improve conditions here than to avoid the problem by moving to new and totally unfamiliar lands.

Within this context it can be seen that "Yankee Doodle; or, The Negroes Farewell to America" strikes closer to the heart of the black question in America at this time than any of the comic or sentimental songs heretofore considered. Both words and music for this song were by "T.L."[43] Nathan characterizes the black portrayed by this "Yankee Doodle" as realistic,[44] although there is no indication of just how he arrived at this peculiar evaluation. It might be considered realistic if viewed as British propaganda, but it is difficult to imagine a Southern slave addressing his master and mistress in the defiant manner of the text—unless perhaps it were done from the safety of the British shore.

YANKEE DOODLE;
or, THE NEGROES FAREWELL TO AMERICA

Now farewell my Massa, my Missey adieu
  More blows or more stripes will me e'er take from you,
Or will me come hither or thither me go,
  No help make you rich by de sweat of my brow.

Yankee doodle, Yankee doodle dandy I vow
Yankee doodle, Yankee doodle bow wow wow.

Farewell all de Yams & farewell de salt Fish,
  De Bran & Spruce Beer at you all me cry Pish,
Me feed upon Pudding, Roast Beef & Strong Beer,
  In Englan', old Englan' when me get dere.

Farewell de Musketo, farewell de black fly,
  And Rattle Snake too who may sting me to dye,
Den Negro go 'Ome to his friends in Guinee
  Before dat old Englan' he 'ave a seen'e.

Farewell de cold Winter, de Frost & de Snow,
  Which cover high Hills and de Valley so low,
And dangling & canting, swearing & drinking,
  Taring and Feath'ring for ser'ously thinking.

Den Hey! for old Englan' where Liberty reigns,
  Where Negroes no beaten or loaded with chains,
And if Negro return O! may he be bang'd
  Chain'd, tortured & drowned—Or let him be hang'd.

The songs discussed up to this point reflect considerable variation in attitudes toward the black. The imports from Europe—British, Dutch, Danish, and Norwegian—show the two tendencies of seeing the black as an object of pity or as a comic figure. The lack of a vital element hinders their effectiveness, however: the lack of ambiance deprives them of a sense of reality. Certain of the stereotypes that were to become firmly fixed in white minds have their roots in this period. The sexuality of the black female is seen in D'Urfey's "Song"; the association of blackness with comic situations is found in the Dutch and English farce jig; *Oroonoko* introduced the tragic black slave and the image of the black entertaining himself and others at the close of a hard day's work—an image which was to become the later "contented, happy and carefree slave." His undying loyalty to "massa" was presumed in "The Poor Black Boy," later to be developed into the distinctive "Uncle Tom" type. While the Park incident focused on the humanity of the black, songs such as Mathews's "Possum Up a Gum Tree" presented the black as a thief and an inept husband. In short, the influence of these songs from overseas provided a basis upon which indigenous types were developed. Songs of pity laid the foundation for later propagandism of the abolitionist movement while the comic songs developed into the vigorous and utterly degrading minstrel types.

Chapter Two

Antecedents of
the Minstrel Show

The American Revolution gained for the colonies independence from England, but it was through the War of 1812 that a strong national unity was achieved. The patriotism engendered by these wars erupted in a great wave—an influence which diverted American literature and music from the dominance of England and infused native efforts with a distinctively American savor. "Freedom" and "liberty"—along with other catchwords—became commonplace through constant repetition in countless songs and poems. It was a period which produced some of our most cherished patriotic songs, including "The Star Spangled Banner" and "Hail Columbia."

When Yankee tunesmiths wrote of freedom, however, they had in mind a whites-only freedom. They did not attempt to explain the glaring inequity—nay, hypocrisy—of phrases proclaiming "death to the tyrants," or "give me liberty or give me death," with the bitter actuality of thousands of black slaves daily suffering hardships far worse than whites had ever suffered under the British yoke.

The doctrine of the natural rights of man as manifested in the Declaration of Independence was given a whites-only interpretation when Jefferson's reference to slavery was taken out. Freedom as an ideal thus lost its meaning in America, becoming part of the jingoistic phraseology employed mainly as a means of inspiring chauvinistic responses. Official sanction of slavery and the silence of most Americans acted to suppress the enthusiasms of those who felt the theory of freedom endangered by the presence of the anachronism of slavery in America.

The emancipation of the slaves was not easily dismissed as an untimely or unworkable idea, however. The spirit of liberalism gained some headway with the abolition of the slave trade in 1808, and the freedom—at least nominally—of the blacks in the North. The South, on the other hand, saw economic disaster and social chaos resulting from a free Negro population, and so proceeded along totally different lines to kill any thought of emancipation, becoming grimly and rigidly united in the cause of slavery.

The Southerner was hard-pressed to justify his stance in the face of the international movement toward the abolition of slavery. He relied heavily on the arguments that the black was inferior—incapable of fending for himself—and thus required the paternal white hand to guide him; the slave, it was further held, was *happy* on the plantation and actually lived a better life than many "white slaves" in the North and in England.

One can imagine the delight felt by Southern slaveowners as Yankee songwriters abandoned the sentimental songs of sympathy for the image of the comic black figure. Gratuitously, the Northern songsmiths provided pro-slavery elements with a body of musical propaganda which helped their cause greatly. Southerners were not even imposed upon in the dissemination of the songs; the Northerners did it for them.

The patriotism which figured so heavily in the establishment of the American song style was perverted to humorous ends in the early treatment of the black subject by songsmiths. A battle or event became a comic situation were the protagonist pictured black, as in "The Guinea Boy," a song representing the black as a volunteer in the service of the British, fighting in the Chesapeake Bay with the "redoubtable Admiral Cockburn."[1] The comic possibliities of the black in a military role were clearly perceived by Micah Hawkins (1777–1825) in his "Backside Albany" (also known as "The Seige of Plattsburgh") and "Massa Georgee Washington and General La Fayette," songs which set the pattern for a long-lived stereotypical black figure.

"Backside Albany" was quite popular after its appearance in 1815 and was printed several times in songsters until as late as 1850. The sheet music version was published in 1837.[2] In contrast with similar songs with white protagonists, the adoption of the pseudo-black narrative style with the absurd dialect pointed to the black himself, rather than to the story, as being the object of humor.

BACKSIDE ALBANY[3]

Back side Albany stan' Lake Champlain,
  One little pond half full a water

    Pla-te-bug dare too, close pon de main,
      Town small—he grow bigger de hereafter
    On Lake Champlain Uncle Sam set he boat,
      An Massa M'Donough he sail 'em;
    While Gen'ral M'Comb make Pla-te-bug he home
      Wid de army who courage never fail 'em.

    On 'lebenteenth ob September,
      In eighteen hundred an fourteen,
    Gubbener Probose an he British soger
      Come to Pla-te-bug a tea party courtin;
    An he boat come too, arter Uncle Sam boat,
      Massa M'Donough he look out de winder,
    Den Gen'ral M'Comb (ah! he always at home)
      Catch fire too, just like tinder.

    Bang, bang, bang! den de cannon gin to roar,
      In Pla-te-bug, and all 'bout dat quarter;
    Gubbenor Probose, try he hand upon de shore,
      While he boat take he luck 'pon de water—
        But Massa M'Donough,
        Knock he boat in he head.
    Break he heart, broke be shin, tove he caffin in
      And Gen'ral M'Comb,
      Start old Probose home—
    Tot me soul den, I mus die a laffin.

    Probose scare so, he lef all behind,
      Powder, ball, cannon, tea pot an kittle—
    Some say he cotch a cold—truble in he mine
      Cause he eat to much raw an cold vittle—
      Uncle Sam bery sorry,
      To be sure for he pain;
    Wish he nuss himself well an hearty—
      For Gen'ral M'Comb,
      An Massa M'Donough home,
    When he notion for nudder tea party.

Hawkins's "Massa Georgee Washington and General La Fayette" is a far more ambitious effort than "Backside Albany." It was written supposedly as an honor to Lafayette on the occasion of his visit to the United States in 1824, but history does not record how this famous Frenchman, well-known as an exponent of liberal causes, received this dubious tribute. The song itself is a crudely constructed account of the entire American Revolution in a pseudo-black dialect that reflects nothing so much as the author's total ignorance of blacks. The music is weak and, to use Nathan's generous evaluation, "fairly nondescript" stylistically.[4]

There are important points of interest to be found in Hawkins's tour de force, however. The cover illustration (Figure 1) is one of the earliest representations graphically of a white performer in blackface on sheet music. This feature was destined to become in some cases fully as important in demeaning the black as the message contained in the song text. The very size and scope of the song indicate some degree of success for the genre, although the "unrivalled applause" claimed by the title page may be taken as early press-agentry. "Massa Georgee Washington and General La Fayette" accomplished still another important function for whites: it disposed of the need to take the black contribution toward gaining our independence seriously. Hawkins, with only two songs, showed future song writers the method of treating the black as a military figure.

Henceforth, the black military figure was rarely, if ever, presented except as a posturing comic character. From the vantage point of today, however, it seems incredible—something of a joke in itself—that this vacuous, homespun piece would have been offered in homage to Lafayette, who was reared in the genteel traditions of French aristocracy.

The ambivalence in attitude toward the black in popular song began to disappear in the second decade of the nineteenth century, to be replaced by pointed reference to him as an object of humor. Songs reflected the hardening attitudes of whites, contributing to the virtual extinction of reality concerning the institution of slavery. Common stereotypes were established which obliterated the true black image. These stereotypes became so entrenched in the white mind that no amount of logic could muster the strength required to supplant them. The white audience did not wish to be reminded, least of all in popular entertainment, of the horror of its creation.

Thus one of the cornerstones of the pro-slavery argument, the image of the black as a contented ward of the slave owner, became fixed as a basic theme in popular song. The black, free or slave, was seen as happy to remain "in his place," a view which was reinforced, alas, by those unfortunate blacks who were forced into servile roles, acting out real-life parts designed to satisfy white egos. Whites interpreted this as irrefutable proof that all "good darkies" were

Figure 1

overjoyed to have the opportunity to work themselves to death for "ol massa"; and the tunesmiths churned out literally thousands of songs in support of this preposterous notion.

Storace's "The Poor Black Boy" had postulated the black as the faithful servant, but the style was that of the English sentimental ballad. The same idea, treated humorously, may be found in a song which appeared in the United States around 1814 in a songster entitled *The Nightingale*.[5] The song, "Negro and Buckra Man," is of unknown origin, sung to the tune of "Hamlet Travestie."[6] The "Buckra Man," of course, is an early expression of the blacks in reference to the white man. The various white owners of the slave depicted in this song were blessed with a genial servant of the rarest type: the black with insight into his master's personality.

NEGRO AND BUCKRA MAN

Great way off at sea, when at home I benee,
Buckra man steal me, from the coast of Guinea;
Christian massee pray, call me heaten dogee,
Den I run away, very much he floggee.

    Ri tol lol lol la.

White man bring me here, and good christian makee,
Lady fair—oh dear, for a sarvee takee.
Stand behind her chair, faro play for guinea,
Always she play fair, and yet she always winee.

    Ri tol lol lol la.

Lady run away, den de lawyer takee,
Latin word he say and great rogue he makee;
Poor man den I saw, go to law so funnee,
He have all de law, massa all de monee.

    Ri tol lol lol la.

Actor man so gay, for a sarvee hire me,
Tragedy he play, play-house never tiree;
Massa often die, den good wine he quaffe,
All de people cry, I and massa laughee.

    Ri tol lol lol la.

After dat I go, vid de doctor livee,
Hold him hand out so—and de fee dey givee;
Dey be fool enough, massa make great fussee,
Give de patient stuff, and make de poor man worsee.

Ri tol lol lol la.
Neger girl I see, love her sweet as honey,
Soon she marry me, she and I get money;
Happy she and I, live among our betters,
Heaven go when die—if Buckra Man will let us.
Ri tol lol lol la.

There are several features in the "Negro and Buckra Man" beyond the calm acceptance of slavery which show embryonic, yet important, ideas that were to become part of the successful formula of later songs on the black subject. The paradoxical attitudes toward the black taken by Christian whites is reflected by the casual remark that the "Christian massee pray, call me heaten dogee," yet the attempt of the protagonist to flee the un-Christian situation results in a beating. White superiority of the various masters is acknowledged in the song as each is observed as having the upper hand in every situation. This desire to be on the winning side is not entirely a fabrication, of course. In real-life situations, it was to the slaves' benefit to have a successful master; the only difficulty lay in the fact that few masters met this ideal. The total dependence of the slave is shown by the assertion that even entrance into heaven is dependent on the whim of the white man. The reference to marriage is purely fictional, inasmuch as marriages between blacks were not recognized by whites.

White superiority was further bolstered by picturing the white as proudly suffering the world's blows while the carefree slave basked under his protective wing. This idea, which assaults both common sense and any sense of decency, was put forward in "Bonja Song," which was published between 1815 and 1816. The composer of the music is unknown, but the words have been attributed to R.C. Dallas.[7] The song achieved considerable popularity, appearing in several editions over the next thirty years. Its title associated it with the beginnings of the banjo in America and, predictably, lent a sense of authority to the false statement that it was "A Favorite Negro Air." The style, in point of fact, is derivative of eighteenth-century buffa, without a trace of black elements.

BONJA SONG

What are the joys of white men here,
    What are his pleasures say?

> Me want no joys no ills me fear,
>> But on my bonja play.
> Me sing all day me sleep all night
>> Me hab no care my heart is light,
> Me tink not what tomorrow bring
>> Me happy so me sing.
>
> But white mans joys are not like mine,
>> Dho he look smart and gay,
> He great, he proud, he haughty, fine,
>> While I my Bonja play.
> He sleep all day he wake all night,
>> He full of care, he heart no light,
> He great deal want, he little get,
>> He sorry so he fret.
>
> Me envy not dhe white men den,
>> Me poor, but me is gay,
> Me glad at heart, me happy when
>> Me on my Bonja play,
> Me sing all day me sleep all night,
>> Me hab no care, my heart is light,
> Me tink not what tomorrow bring,
>> Me happy so me sing.

The myth of the happy plantation slave, singing and dancing as an expression of innocent joy, was reinforced by numerous accounts of white visitors to the South. Visitors were usually shown what slaveholders wished them to see, or their own preconceptions prevented their seeing anything other than a well-organized system working to the benefit of the black as well as to his master. The callous, brutalizing effects on slave and master alike were ignored or, when recognized, passed off as so much abolitionist propaganda. The testimony of the slave himself could not alter this preconception, as evidenced by Frederick Douglass's observation:

I have often been utterly astonished, since I came to the north, to find persons who could speak of the singing, among slaves, as evidence of their contentment and happiness. It is impossible to conceive of a greater mistake. The songs of the slave represent the sorrows of his heart; and he is relieved by them, only as an aching heart is relieved by its tears.[8]

But reality was not the point at issue here; what was required was reassurance that slavery was a positive good for blacks, and the songs provided this reassurance in abundance.

The beneficent effect of slavery was further enhanced by picturing the slave as expected to produce less than his free white counterpart, the workingman. The stereotype of the lazy black became a popular necessity, one which was admirably suited to treatment in song. Thus emerged the image of the slave in his idyllic existence repaying his master's generosity with a marked reluctance to work. Credulous whites accepted the image, convinced that the black, rather than the system, was responsible for the relatively inefficient method of production. Accounts of the actual working conditions of slaves, such as that provided by Solomon Northrup,[9] should have constituted sufficient evidence that this image of the black was false, but whites were not interested in truth.

"Do I Do I Don't Do Nothing" is typical of the early songs depicting the slave's indolence. Arranged by "An Amateur" and published in 1825, it purports to be of black origin, as stated on the title page. The short repetend in the melody gives a surface appearance of Negroid influence, but analysis shows the song to be of white parentage.

The humor of the doggerel text is meaningless today. Indeed, it should have been meaningless in its own day, in view of the known conditions of life under slavery, in which there was hardly any motivation to work beyond the threat of the lash.

DO I DO I DON'T DO NOTHING

Do I do I don't do nothing
  Master say I don't do nothing
Work all night work all day
  Master say you don't do nothing.

Do I do I don't do nothing
  Mistress say I don't do nothing
Work all day work all night
  Morning come I don't do nothing.

Do I do I don't do nothing
  Lasy dog I don't do nothing
Work all night work all day
  Lasy dog I don't do nothing.[10]

In a system which denied the laborer any of the fruits of his labor, the imagination is strained to believe that the slave was actually expected to adopt white values concerning the virtue of work.

Song writers stepped up the pace of production of songs demeaning to the black during the latter days of the 1820's and throughout the 1830's. Songs were in some cases directed toward one preconceived black trait, while others served as a sort of catchall for whatever supposed black characteristics struck the composer as humorous. Within fifteen years, it is safe to say, no stereotype, no preconception, no opportunity had been overlooked in the process of belittling blacks in America.

Sometime between 1828 and 1830, George Washington Dixon introduced to American audiences a song which firmly fixed the stereotype of the comic, jealous, black lover. "Coal Black Rose," said to be the "first burnt-cork song of comic love,"[11] has as its central plot the discovery of a rival by Rose's suitor, in whom love turns to hate as the interloper is driven from the house. Damon informs us that the melody of "Coal Black Rose" is "appropriated from an old ballad"[12] without further identification. There were dozens of editions of the song in sheet music and songsters which appeared during the following thirty years, evidence which confirms it as one of America's first popular hits. Various editions inform us that the song was performed by W. Kelley and "Daddy" Rice, in addition to Dixon.[13]

The message contained in "Coal Black Rose" was certainly not new, but the blackface presentation added a new dimension to the old theme. More importantly, it tended to confirm a widely held preconception that blacks were incapable of a love relationship comparable to that of whites. In fact, romantic love and marriage according to white customs presented a somewhat sticky problem to slaveowners. Should the parties involved belong to different masters, or should one happen to be free, complicated questions of ownership and status of offspring could arise. Even when both man and wife belonged to the same master the problem remained complex, since selling members of the family to the highest bidders was always a messy business, although slaveowners managed to do it often enough. It was far more efficient to discourage slaves from marriage in the white sense, letting them breed indiscriminately and without entanglements of social sanction. Slaveowners hotly denied this as an accepted policy, but in practice it had existed since the early days of slavery.[14]

Figure 2

Given these circumstances, the capacity of blacks to understand or adopt heterosexual love as a white value was minimized through ridicule. White institutions and concepts dealing with love and marriage were serious matters which were to be kept racially pure at all costs; black imitations were not, under any circumstance, to be credited with importance. Racial purity and sex thus became intertwined to produce the most formidable of all the preconceptions surrounding the relationship between black and white in America. It was inevitable that Coal Black Rose was created in an entirely different mold from Colyzs, of "An African Love Song."

In addition to establishing the absurd notion that blacks were incapable of adopting white cultural values regarding heterosexual love, "Coal Black Rose" established the stereotypical fickle, sensuous Negress. She became the symbol of forbidden fruit to the white male. Like a magnet, she both attracted through her sex and repelled through her color. The considerable mulatto population of the United States is evidence that these were not mere fantasies confined to expression in popular song. "Coal Black Rose" was the prototype which determined the direction composers would take in their songs about the young black female—songs which encompassed all the sexual fantasies and weird racial preconceptions denigrating her relationship with the male, white or black.

COAL BLACK ROSE

Lubly Rosa, Sambo cum,
Don't you hear de Banjo—tum, tum, tum;
Lubly Rosa, Sambo cum,
Don't you hear de Banjo—tum, tum, tum;
　　Oh Rose, de coal black Rose,
I wish I may be cortch'd if I don't lub Rose,
　　Oh Rose, de coal black Rose.

Dat you, Sambo? yes I cum,
Don't you hear de Banjo—tum, tum, tum;
Dat you, Sambo? yes I cum,
Don't you hear de Banjo—tum, tum, tum;
　　Oh Rose, de coal black Rose,
I wish I may be burnt if I don't lub Rose,
　　Oh Rose, de coal black Rose.

Tay a little, Sambo, I cum soon
As I make a fire in de back room;

Tay a little, Sambo, I cum soon
As I make a fire in de back room;
    Oh Rose, de coal black Rose,
I wish I may be burnt if I don't lub Rose,
    Oh Rose, de coal black Rose.

Make haste, Rose, lubly dear,
I froze tiff as poker tandin here;
Make haste, Rose, lubly dear,
I almose froze a waitin here;
    Oh, Rose, I almose froze,
I wish I may be burnt if I don't lub Rose,
    Oh, Rose, I almose froze.

Cum in, Sambo, don't tand dare shakin,
De fire is a burnin, and de hoe cake a bakin;
Cum in, Sambo, and top dat shakin,
De peas in de pot and de hoe cake a bakin;
    Oh, Rose, bress dat Rose!
I wish I may be burnt if I don't lub Rose,
    Oh, Rose, bress dat Rose.

Sit down, Sambo, an warm your shin,
Lord bress you, honey, for what make you grin;
Sit down, Sambo, an toast your shin,
Lord bress you, honey, for what make you grin;
    Oh, Rose, bress dat Rose!
I wish I may be burnt if I don't lub Rose,
    Oh, Rose, bress dat Rose.

I laff to tink if you was mine, lubly Rose,
I'd gib you a plenty, the Lord above knows,
Ob possum fat and hominey, and somtime rice,
Cow heel an sugar cane an ebery ting nice;
    Oh, Rose, bress dat Rose!
I wish I may be shute if I don't lub Rose,
    Oh, Rose, bress dat Rose.

What in de corner dar, Rose, dat I py?
I know dat nigger Cuffee by de white ob he eye;
Dat not Cuffee, 'tis a tick ob wood, sure,
A tick ob wood wid tocking on, you tel me dat, pshaw!
    Oh, Rose, take care Rose!
I wish I may be burnt if I don't hate Rose,
    Oh, Rose, you black snake Rose!

Let go my arm, Rose, let me at him rush,
I swella his two lips like a blacka balla brush;

> Let go my arm, Rose, and let me top his win,
> Let go my arm, Rose, while I kick him on de shin;
>   Oh, Rose, take care Rose!
> I wish I may be burnt if I don't hate Rose,
>   Oh, Rose, you blacka snake Rose!
>
> I ketch hold of Cuffee, I take him by de wool;
> I ketch hold of Cuffee, he try away to pull,
> But I up wid a foot and kick him on de shin,
> Which put him breafless on de floor and make de nigger grin.
>   Oh, Rose, take care Rose!
> I wish I may be burnt if I don't hate Rose,
>   Oh, Rose, you blacka snake Rose!
>
> He jumb up for sartin, he cut dirt an run—
> Now Sambo follow arter wid his tum, tum, tum;
> He jump up for sartin, he cut dirt an run—
> Now Sambo follow arter wid his tum, tum, tum;
>   Oh, Rose, curse dat Rose!
> I wish Massa Hays would ketch dat Rose,
>   Oh, Rose, you blacka snake Rose!

The efficacy of popular song in establishing lasting stereotypes was demonstrated once again in the early 1830's as "Sambo's Address to His Bred'ren," or "Ching a Ring Chaw," as it was sometimes called, utilized religious satire to ridicule both black Christianity and the hope of some blacks that a solution to their problems lay in emigration. Black religion had been burlesqued a decade earlier by Charles Mathews (see Appendix I) in a mock sermon he claimed to have heard delivered by a black preacher, the catachrestical homily which formed the pattern for future white treatment of the subject in both story and song.

Conversion of blacks to Christianity was one of the original precepts by which whites justified slavery in the colonies. Slavery was explained as God's charge to the white man; the condition of the slave was merely the execution of the divine will.[15] But there were practical dangers involved in black acceptance of Christianity. For one thing, there was the implication that all souls were equal in the sight of God, a fine theory which nonetheless was fraught with danger to the system of slavery. There was the finger of guilt pointed straight at the slaveowners and everyone else connected with slavery; an onus of sin weighed on the conscience despite assurances by preachers who twisted Biblical teachings into sermons in support of the system. Inconsistencies were glossed over by assuring the slave that his soul would be freed upon death, and all souls would enjoy equality in heaven. This argument also helped rebut the claims of those blacks who anticipated freedom as a reward for conversion.

On a less philosophical level, conversion presented the slaveholders with immediate problems as well. In order to worship meaningfully, the slave had to be allowed freedom to attend church. He either went to a white church, which was in white eyes a defilement of the institution, or he attended an all-black church, which gave excellent opportunities for plotting rebellion. Then there was the question of teaching the slaves to read—a prerequisite for studying the Bible—but a proposition which slaveholders flatly rejected.

These problems were resolved in various ways in different localities. Generally, slaves were allowed to attend their own church with at least one white to oversee the service. In order to prevent the preacher from gaining any real power over his flock, and as reassurance to worried whites, another potent weapon was employed to defuse the dangers inherent in black religion: ridicule.

"Sambo's Address to His Bred'ren" is a mock sermon in which the flock is urged to emigrate to "Hettee" (Haiti) as a means of improving their lot. The successful rebellion of the slaves on the island of Saint Dominique in the 1790's seemed to offer hope of resettlement of blacks from the United States. As a matter of history, few blacks were willing to take their chances in an entirely foreign environment, eschewing the promise of this black paradise now known as the Republic of Haiti. "Sambo's Address to His Bred'ren" is significant mainly through its ridicule of the preacher as an authority figure rather than through its message favoring a black exodus from America. The preacher became a fixture in the popular mind, although the fullest realizaton of the genre was not reached until the period following the Civil War.

SAMBO'S ADDRESS TO HIS BRED'REN[16]

Broder let us leave,
   Buckra lan for Hettee,
Dar you be receve,
   Gran as Lafayettee;
Mak a mity show,

Figure 3

Wen we lan fom steemship,
I be like Munro,
  You like louis Fillip.

Chinger ringer ring ching ching
Ho ah ding ah ding kum darkee,
Chinger ringer ring ching chaw
Ho ah ding kum darkee.

O dat equal sod,
  Hoo no want to go-e,
Dar we feel no rod,
  Dar we hab no fo-e:
Dar we lib so fine,
  Wid our coch an hors-e,
An ebry time we dine,
  Hab one, two, tree, fore, cors-e.

No more carry hod,
  No more iceter o-pe,
No more dig de sod,
  No more krub de sho-pe;
But hab wiskers gran,
  An prominade de Street-e,
Wid butys ob de lan,
  Were we in full dres meet-e.

No more carry bag,
  An wid nail an tick-e,
Nasty dirty rag,
  Out ob gutter pick-e:
No more barro weel,
  All about de street-e,
No more blige to steel,
  Den by massa beet-e.

No more witeman stare,
  Wen we stan in mob-e,
An frite our lubly fair,
  Wich make dem sy an sob-e;
Dar our wives be gran,
  An in dimons shin-e,
Wile ebry kuler'd man,
  Hab much he drink ob wine-e.

Dar smoke de bess segar,
  Fech from de havanah,

Wile our dorters fair,
  Play on de Pianah;
No more kry hot korn,
  Or pepper pot all hot-e,
But worck de lubly lorn,
  An res in shady grot-e.

No more our son, kry, sweep,
  No more he be de lack-e,
No more our dorters weep,
  Kays dey kall dem black-e:
No more dey sarvant be,
  No more wash an kook-e,
But ebry day we see,
  Dem read de novel book-e.

No more wid black an brush,
  Make boot an shoe to shin-e,
But hab all good tings flush,
  An all ob dem subblim-e;
No more dance for eel,
  An all dem sort ob fish-e,
Nor more eat korn meal,
  But hab de bess ob dish-e.

Dar we hab partys big,
  Dar dance an play de fiddle,
Dar walse an hab de jig,
  Kast off an down de middle;
Den in de gran saloon,
  We take de blushing damsull,
Were eyes shine like de moon,
  An ebry mouf dey cram full.

Dar dance at night de jig,
  Wat witeman kall kotilon,
In hall so mighty big,
  He hole a haf a milon;
Den take our partners out,
  Den forword too and back-e,
Den kros an turn about,
  An den go home in hack-e.

Dar too we sure to make,
  Our dorters de fine la-dee,
An wen dey husban take,

> Dey bove de comon gra-dee;
> An den perhaps our Son,
>   He rise in glories splender,
> An be like Washinton,
>   He countries great defender.

The popularity of such blackface presentations of witless black imagery in the years between 1820 and 1840 led to a proliferation of native American songwriters and a greatly accelerated production of their works. The stylistic interdependence of songs of this type was no accident; most of the songwriters were known, at least professionally, to each other, as evidenced by the frequent borrowings and mentioning of one song in another. The majority of the composers were also performers. While each jealously guarded what he considered to be his "material," there was no stigma attached to appropriating the material of another performer for one's own use.

The rough-and-tumble character of the juvenile nation was perhaps nowhere more accurately reflected than in the popular songs produced during this period. Cocksure and fiercely independent, Americans reacted favorably to songs which asserted American superiority over real or imagined foes. One of the most formidable of the imaginary enemies of white America was seen in the black slave, who had to be rendered impotent in order to remain servile. The black authority figure, as represented by the preacher in "Sambo's Address," was easily discounted through ridicule; the younger, more virile male was accorded vastly more attention in popular song in order to render him harmless. It was within this context that the superhit "Jim Crow" was conceived by Thomas Dartmouth Rice.

A considerable amount of legend has grown up around Rice's "Jim Crow," the song which practically singlehandedly paved the way for the advent of blackface (American, as some prefer to name it) minstrelsy. Wildly acclaimed on two continents and assuring immortality for its creator, "Jim Crow" became a part of the American language, lending its name to the system of segregation which became the shame of the nation.

According to legend, Rice, a bit part actor in the drama *The Rifle*, was said to have noticed the antics of an old, deformed black groom who performed a curious song and dance as he went about his work. Intrigued, Rice copied the old man's song and dance, interpolating it

Figure 4

between acts of the play and causing an instant sensation which rocketed Rice to fame and fortune both here and abroad.

So far so good. But as is the case with most legends, a vast confusion surrounds the details of this account. There is a rather wide discrepancy concerning the date ascribed to the incident, for example. Some scholars declare flatly that the incident took place in 1828, others give 1830 as the date, while many merely speculate that the momentous occasion occurred sometime between 1828 and 1831.

Equally uncertain is the city in which the event allegedly happened. Louisville and Baltimore have their champions, as do Pittsburgh and Cincinnati, while Nashville and Memphis both lay claim to the dubious distinction. Even New York was nominated for the honor as late as 1970.[17] Some writers prefer to evade the issue by declaring that "Jim Crow" saw the light of day "in a midwestern town," or "somewhere along the Ohio River."

The poor creature who was the object of Rice's merciless caricature offers some degree of unanimity to researchers. He is usually described as an old deformed black stable attendant. Some versions of the story picture him as a slave; others merely describe him as an old nondescript black dressed in rags. Important as this old black was to the development of popular music in America—and despite his undeniable contribution to Rice's career—no one seems to know what happened to him after he provided his inspirational song and dance.

The tune is almost unanimously ascribed to the black groom. It is hardly ever called the creation of Rice; the inference is plain that here is a documented, authentic black melody which was copied by a white performer. But even a superficial examination of the melody casts doubt on the black origin of the song. Nathan traces the parentage of "Jim Crow" to known Irish and English examples,[18] demonstrating the weakness of the black origin theory and revealing a relationship that should have been obvious to anyone equipped to make a musical evaluation of the piece.

More discrepancies arise in the description of the dance that accompanied the song. Nathan attempts a recreation of its performance[19] which at least is more informative than vague references to the "strange shuffling motion" and the "queer jump at the end of each stanza" which constitute the general description provided by scholars of the subject.

Confronted by such an astonishing lack of solid fact concerning this song, it is surprising that many students of popular music history attach so much importance to what can only be characterized as trivia surrounding the appearance of "Jim Crow." The expenditure of so much effort to prove the black origin of the song tends to obfuscate the significant role played by the type in demeaning the American black. A footnote to the song published by Brown University states:

"Jim Crow" was the first black-face song to characterize a negro sympathetically; it introduced the negro style of dancing to the stage; it ensured the future of negro song by its success; and it was probably the first American song to make a great hit abroad.[20]

On all counts except the last, this is the sheerest nonsense. The characterization of the black in "Jim Crow" is anything but sympathetic; it is a cruel joke based not only upon the physical deformities of a defenseless old man, but upon his color as well. The allegation that black dancing was introduced to the stage by this means is equally absurd; the old man's dancing is acknowledged by all authorities as that of a cripple—hardly representative of the dancing of his race. As to ensuring the future of the black song by its success, it must be emphasized that none of the evidence shows that "Jim Crow" is in actuality a black song—the most it could possibly have ensured was Rice's own success; and that it did in abundance. It was undoubtedly a great hit. "Jim Crow" was followed by a host of editions, variants, imitations, and parodies which opened the gates wide for the flood of puerility leading to the establishment of the minstrel show and the utter destruction of the black image in any favorable sense.

The paucity of factual evidence supporting the legendary beginnings of "Jim Crow" leads the researcher to the inescapable conclusion that the whole story might well be an invention begun by Rice and embellished by those who came later. Thus it appears reasonable to disregard the hypothetical story of its creation entirely. Should this result in stripping away the romance, so much the better, for there can be little glory accruing to a song which figures as heavily in the distortion of the black image as does "Jim Crow."

Of the dozens of editions of "Jim Crow" which exist, six have been chosen for comparison in this study. The large number selected for study reflects not only the great popularity of the piece, but offers a wider view of the song. The editions have been taken from examples of leading publishers in the United States as well as one English version.

A comparison of these editions reveals the interaction between publishers and their common practice of pirating materials from one another during this period.

The edition of "Jim Crow" described in Dichter and Shapiro's *Early American Sheet Music* (New York, 1941) is presumed to be the first edition, printed around 1829, although the cover makes reference to "the original Jim Crow," suggesting that there might have been imitations of the act before the music was published.

This edition of "Jim Crow" was published by E. Riley, of New York. The forty-four verses of the piece are indicated to be performed "Alla Nigaro," a musically meaningless directive which matches the cover illustration in facetiousness.

The Atwill edition, also of New York, is probably a pirated edition of the Riley publication. Entitled "Jimmy Crow," the melody is identical with the E. Riley edition except for a slight alteration of the anacrusis; there is some attempt to camouflage that plagiarism by alteration of the accompaniment. The cover illustration is obviously an imitation. The principal difference between the two editions lies in the words; the Atwill version has only twenty-two verses, most of which are new. Since Atwill published at the address shown on this edition between 1834 and 1847, it is hardly possible that his "Jimmy Crow" preceded the E. Riley publication.

The third example, published by J. Edgar of Philadelphia, is dated 1832. There is no illustrated cover, but the title page indicates that it is a "comic song sung by Mr. Rice at the Chesnut [sic] Street Theatre." The accompaniment for this edition is a compendium of faulty writing, but the main interest again lies in the words, which show considerable variation from the original.

"Jimme Crow," the fourth example, shows a relationship to Atwill's "Jimmy Crow." No information is available concerning its date, but it is possible that it preceded the Atwill version. Similarities between these editions suggest that both were produced within a short time of each other.

The "Jim Crow" published by George Willig, Jr., of Baltimore is related to the E. Riley edition and might possibly have preceded it, although the latter is generally accepted as the first edition. The Willig example was sold at John Ashton's Music Store, which was located at the address given between 1824 and 1833. The accompaniment is identical for both editions. An interesting feature of the Willig edition is the inclusion, at the bottom of the second page, of an alternate melody. This alternate melody suggests that the original, somewhat involute melody presented some difficulty to performers or that the endless verses of the song required surcease from repetition of the same theme.

The last example, the "Jim Crow's Songs," published in broadside form in London (not dated), is by far the most fantastic of all. Its more than eighty-five (!) verses, "as sung by Mr. Lloyd at the Theatres Royal and Adelphi," cover most of the known verses plus many references to English life: a distorted version of *Hamlet*, the description of a visit to Parliament, and so on interminably. Sung in its entirety, this version would qualify Lloyd for the record for staying power, if nothing else.

Utilizing both the descriptive and narrative approaches in the words, "Jim Crow" symbolizes white attitudes toward the black in the late 1820's. "Jim Crow" describes himself in terms which point up, always pejoratively, his insolence and blustering. The fierce independence portrayed in these verses has been related to the frontier spirit, deemed charming when applied to whites,[21] but which shows, at the same time, an abysmal ignorance of the actual status of blacks at the time in which "Jim Crow" was written.

The narrative verses of "Jim Crow" relate to local and current happenings, political satire, and comic reference to leading personalities. In the main, they show the degree to which whites had removed themselves from the actual condition of black life in existence during the period.

There is a third category of verses in "Jim Crow" which can only be characterized as nonsense. These reveal the curious incoherence that many writers approached when composing songs of this type; it is almost as though words and music had become inadequate to express the depth of contempt felt by the whites toward the blacks and only putting sheer gibberish into the protagonist's mouth could solve the problem. Nonsense verses were particularly effective in reinforcing the white conviction that blacks were inherently ignorant.

While it is impractical to cite all the verses of "Jim Crow," it is equally important to examine them in sufficient depth to show their demeaning effect. The citation of only one or two verses provided by most researchers gives just a fleeting glimpse of the song without revealing much of the truly degrading aspect of the entire work.

The first verse serves not only to introduce the main characters but also sets the tone for everything that follows. The irreverent, impudent attitude and the artlessness of the protagonist Jim Crow are immediately apparent:

> Come listen all you galls and boys
> I'se jist from Tuckyhoe,
> I'm goin to sing a little song,
> My name's Jim Crow.
>
> Weel about and turn about
> And do jis so,
> Eb'ry time I weel about
> And jump Jim Crow.

The braggadocio begins at once:

> Oh I'm a roarer on de fiddle,
> And down in old Virginny,
> They say I play de skyentific
> Like Massa Pagannini.
>
> I went down to de riber,
> I didn't mean to stay,
> But dere I see so many galls,
> I couldn't get away.

In addition to the early reference to male prowess, the freedom of movement ascribed to Jim Crow in this and subsequent verses constitutes a rather witless affront, considering the dim view taken by masters toward unrestricted movement by their slaves. But Jim Crow manages to get around without apparent difficulty:

> I git 'pon a flat boat,
> I cotch de Uncle Sam,
> Den I went to see de place
> Wher dey kill'd Packenham.[22]

The next verse relates how Jim Crow spent a night in jail because he "felt so full of fight," but his release hardly occasioned contriteness:

> When I got out I hit a man,
> His name I now forget,
> But dere was nothing left
> 'Sept a little grease spot.
>
> I wip my weight in wildcats
> I eat an alligator,
> And tear up more ground
> Dan kifer [cover] fifty load of tater.

Preoccupation with his own prowess gradually reduces Jim Crow as near to speechlessness as he is likely to get:

> I sit upon a hornet's nest,
> I dance upon my head,
> I tie a wiper [viper] round my neck
> And den I goes to bed.
>
> Dere's possum up de gumtree,[23]
> An raccoon in de hollow,
> Wake snakes for June bugs
> Stole my half a dollar.
>
> A ring tail'd monkey,
> An a rib nose babboon,
> Went out de odder day
> To spend de arternoon.
>
> Oh de way dey bake de hoecake
> In old Verginny neber tire,
> Dey put de doe upon de foot,
> An hole it to de fire.

In a futile gesture aimed at proving respectability, James Crow informs us that:

> O by trade I am a carpenter,
> But be it understood,
> De way I get my liben is,
> By sawing de tick oh wood.

Turning again to his physical strength—as though the listener were not fully convinced by this time:

> I'm a full blooded niggar,
> Ob de real ole stock,
> And wid my head and shoulder
> I can split a horse block.

The reference to the strength of the head and shoulder is no compliment, however. It was (and perhaps still is) widely held that primitive, uneducated peoples were so thickheaded that blows to this region of the body were not likely to injure. Superior strength, on the other hand, was never a point denied the blacks:

> I struck a Jarsey niggar,
> In de street de oder day,
> An I hope I neber stir,
> If he didn't turn gray.

The following verse brings a hint of the true purpose of the song, however:

> I'm berry much afraid of late,
> Dis jumpin will be no good;
> For while de Crow are dancing,
> De whites will saw de wood.
>
> But if dey get honest,
> By sawing wood like slaves,
> Dere's an end to de business
> Ob our friend Massa Hays.[24]

The aggressiveness of the black is revived in the following three verses, this time reflecting a white attitude which is less than commendable, the shifting of blame for mistreatment suffered by blacks to other blacks:

> I met a Philadelphia niggar,
> Dress'd up quite nice and clean,
> But de way he 'bused de Yorkers
> I thought was berry mean.
>
> So I knocked down dis Sambo,
> And shut up his light,

> For I'm jist about as sassy
> As if I was half white.
>
> But he soon jumped up again,
> An 'gan for me to feel,
> Says I go away you niggar,
> Or I'll skin you like an eel.

The inference in the second verse above is that whiteness represents power. The following verses expand on this theme, perpetrating an even greater affront by maintaining that being black during this period was an enviable quality:

> I'm so glad dat I'm a niggar,
> An don't you wish you was too
> For den you'd gain popularity,
> By jumping Jim Crow.
>
> Now my brudder niggars,
> I do not think it right,
> Dat you should laugh at dem
> Who happen to be white.
>
> Kase it dar misfortune,
> An dey'd spend ebery dollar,
> If dey only could be
> Gentlemen ob colour.

The preoccupation over skin color continues, with Jim Crow voicing pity (!) that whites cannot enjoy his status as a black. In order to understand the full irony of this incredible point of view, it must be remembered that this was written during the period in which slavery had become a fixed institution. For their part, blacks gave the lie to the notion that slavery was a beneficent system through their numerous uprisings, the most notable of which was Nat Turner's rebellion, which took place within a short time of the inception of "Jim Crow." Reverse psychology, practiced on a crude level in this example, attempted to minimize the danger of black reprisals by asking whites to believe the preposterous idea that being black constituted some sort of advantage.

> It almost break my heart,
> To see dem envy me,

> An from my soul I wish dem,
> Full as black as we.

Had this unlikely phenomenon actually occurred, the fate of Jim Crow would have been interesting to observe. Nothing daunted, he continues to expound on the theory of skin color as a measure of good and evil:

> What stuff it is in dem,
> To make de Debbil black
> I'll prove dat he is white,
> In de twinkling of a crack.

> For you see loved brodders,
> As true as he hab a tail,
> It is his berry wickedness,
> What makes him turn pale.

The following eight verses are concerned primarily with observations made while visiting various cities. These offer little enlightenment on the white attitudes beyond the usual distortions designed to demonstrate the stupidity of the homespun philosophy of the black. Womanizing, drinking, and a slur against the "Broadway dandy," whose likeness is found in "a glass case of monkies," are among the points covered by the verses. The rather gloomy and prophetic observations which follow are of great interest, however:

> De great Nullification,
> And fuss in de South,
> Is now before Congress,
> To be tried by word ob mouth.

> Dey hab had no blows yet,
> And I hope dey nebber will,
> For its berry cruel in bredren,
> One anoders blood to spill.

> Wid Jackson at de head,
> Dey soon de ting may settle,
> For ole Hickory is a man,
> Dat's tarnal full ob mettle.

The next verses begin to demonstrate for the first time a degree of insight—almost enough to justify the song on moral grounds were it not for their inconsistency with the remainder of the song. They occur, as a matter of fact, only in the E. Riley edition, having been deleted from subsequent editions as an obvious deviation from the tenor of the times. Even in the abstract, advocacy of freedom for blacks was not to be sanctioned.

> Should dey get to fighting,
> Perhaps de blacks will rise,
> For deir wish for freedom,
> Is shining in deir eyes.
>
> An if de blacks should get free,
> I guess dey'll fee [?] some bigger,
> An I shall consider it,
> A bold stroke for de nigger.
>
> I'm for freedom,
> An for Union altogether,
> Aldough I'm a black man,
> De white is call'd my broder.

Here, after thirty-six verses, is the crux of the song. The entire Christian world was turning away from slavery by the time "Jim Crow" was composed; yet in the United States, numerous factors contributed to renewed vigor for the institution, already two hundred years old. Mechanical aids to production of Southern crops, the opening of the new territory in the Southwest, and rapidly changing attitudes toward traditional institutions of social and political power gave a curious but effective new twist to the justification of slavery.[25] The offensive verses of "Jim Crow" which pointed the finger of guilt at whites had to be expunged, and they were.

The protagonist, evidently aware of the breach of good taste occasioned by the reference to freedom for blacks, retreats to safer ground, reopening the subject of women, but not before taking a parting shot at current events:

> I'm for Union to a gal,
> An dis is a stubborn fact,
> But if I marry an don't like it,
> I'll nullify de act.

Three verses follow, continuing the rather neutral ruminations on marriage. In the final verse, however, Jim Crow reverts to the belligerent stance of the opening verses, as he issues a warning to whites:

> An I caution all white dandies,
> Not to come in my way,
> For if dey insult me,
> Dey'll in de gutter lay.

Thus the E. Riley edition of "Jim Crow" ends on the same note of bluster with which it began. The representation of the black can hardly be regarded as accidental when taken in the context of the times in which it was composed. The role given the black in this song flies in the face of all reason, far exceeding the requirements of humor. It must be seen as a significant point in the development of white attitudes toward the black, both by what it says and by its very popularity. The influence of "Jim Crow" upon the musical development of the genre was tremendous; but had the public been attuned to receiving the true black, the song would almost certainly have died aborning. As it happened, however, the public saw Jim Crow as not only howlingly funny, but as an essentially accurate picture of the black. Other songwriters, alas, were all too quick to grasp the significance of this development.

The other editions of "Jim Crow" included all the salient features of the original, adding their own distortions of the black image as fancy dictated. In the J. Edgar edition, for example, Jim Crow fantasizes:

> Wen Jim Crow is President
> Of dis United State,
> He'll drink mint jewlips
> An swing pon a gate.

This absurdity is carried even further in the Atwill edition:

> O den I go to Washington,
> Wid bank memorial;
> But find dey tork [talk] sich nonsense,
> I spen my time wid Sal.

I make de speech rite udder side,
Too Burjus ob Rode ile;[26]
I gib him sich a mighty cut,
Dat make de hole house smile.

I teld dem dare be Ole Nick,
Wat wants de bank renew;
He gib me so much mony,
O lor, dey want it too.

I den go to de Presiden,
He ax me wat I do;
I put de veto on de boot,
An nullefy de shoe.

He laff most hearty tink how smart,
I spick so mighty big;
He tole me for to go to de house,
An call dem all a pig.

Political satire in song was hardly a new device in early America; what made the device screamingly hilarious in this instance was that the sentiments were mouthed by a pseudo-black protagonist—the presumption of power by a figure who, figuratively, was castrated in social and political matters. The reality of the situation was light years away from the version presented in song, yet the public preferred this false image and accepted it without question. Thus the tone was set for subsequent treatment of the black in song and the stage prepared for the next act—the so-called blackface minstrel show.

Other songs followed "Jim Crow" in profusion, most of them imitating the style, or at least derivative of it. The steady progression of these songs shows a steadily increasing command of the material; most of the composers learned the hazards inherent in indiscriminate mixing of the narrative with the descriptive elements, for example. By the time the minstrel show was born, the style had become established to a point where composers could draw from their own material without the necessity of looking elsewhere for inspiration or method.

Few of the songs which followed "Jim Crow" achieved the lasting fame that was accorded "Zip Coon," which appeared in 1834. Better known today as "Turkey in the Straw,"[27] "Zip Coon" was sung by George W. Dixon and Bob Farrell, both of whom claimed authorship of the song. Another blackface performer of the period, George

Nichols, claimed credit for the piece, although Farrell is usually conceded the dubious honor.

Several attempts have been made to trace the lineage of "Zip Coon," Wittke comparing it to "a rough jig dance" called "Natchez Under the Hill," said to have originated among the boatmen, river pirates, gamblers, and courtesans who congregated at a rendevous in Natchez.[28] Nathan links it to the Irish hornpipe, citing two examples, "The Glascow Hornpipe" and "The Post Office."[29] Damon considers "Zip Coon" an adaptation of a "long lost" Negro original,[30] a theory accepted by Chase, who cites it as an example of a "folk song being modified, made popular, and working its way back into the domain of folk music."[31] Chase does mention the possibility of Irish origin, the theory which contains the weight of the evidence. At any rate, a moment's reflection on the comparative styles of Irish and Negro music would make Ireland the common-sense choice of parentage for "Zip Coon."

The popularity of "Zip Coon" derived in no small measure from its melody, far more natural than that of "Jim Crow." The song was soon on everybody's lips: it is said that Stephen Foster sang it as a youth, P.T. Barnum sang it in blackface, and it was standard in the repertoires of minstrel troupes throughout the country. Its natural buoyancy helped cement the style into something uniquely American—but it was not black.

Four early printed editions of "Zip Coon" have been selected for comparison with variants attributed to folk origin. The printed versions all appeared around 1834, and show no textual differences except for spelling (i.e., "Zip Koon" for "Zip Coon"; "Crocket" for "Crockett," etc.). All of these examples have identical melodies and accompaniments. The lack of variation in either text or melody suggests that the song originated as a written composition rather than as folk music, which, if nothing else, would almost always reflect regional differences.

The text of "Zip Coon" is similar to "Jim Crow" in the utilization of the descriptive, narrative, and nonsense approaches. It is a broad attack on the entire concept of the black in American society of the period. The black's intelligence, maleness, and personal predilections are all held up to ridicule. In the second verse, "Old Zip Coon" asserts emphatically the claim that he is a "very larned scholar" with the fact that he can perform "Cooney in de hollar" cited as proof.

Figure 5

> I went down to Sandy hook, toder arternoon;
> I went down to Sandy hook, toder arternoon;
> I went down to Sandy hook, toder arternoon;
> And de fust man I met dere was old Zip Coon.
>
> Old Zip Coon is a very larned scholar,
> Old Zip Coon is a very larned scholar,
> Old Zip Coon is a very larned scholar,
> He plays on the Banjo Cooney in de hollar.

From this point to the final verse, "Zip Coon" follows a meandering trail, observing current political events, natural phenomena, and his own personal experience in love and marriage. The unadulterated inanity of these verses could not be construed by any stretch of logic as a sympathetic picture of the black.

> Did you ever see de wild goose sail upon de ocean,
> O de wild goose motion is a very pretty notion,
> For when de wild goose winks he beckon to de swallor,
> An den de wild goose hollor, google, google, gollor.
>
> Old Suke Blueskin fell in love wid me,
> She vite me to her house for to take a cup of tea,
> What do you think old Suke had for de supper!
> Dare was chicken foot, sparrow grass and apple sauce butter.
>
> O my ole mistress is very mad at me,
> Because I wouldn't go wid her and live in Tennessee;
> Massa built a barn dere and put (in) all de fodder,
> Dere was dis ting and dat ting and one ting an oder.
>
> As I was a goine down a new cut road,
> I met a little Tarrapin a looking at a Toad;
> An jist at every time de toad begin to jump,
> De Tarrapin he hide himself behind a burnt stump.
>
> Dat tarnal critter Crocket, he never say his prayers,
> He kill all de wild cats, de Coons and de bears,
> An den he go to Washington to help to make de laws,
> An dere he find de Congress men sucking of deir paws.
>
> If I was de President of dese United States,
> I'd suck lasses candy and swing upon de gates,
> An dose I didn't like I'd block em off de dockett,
> An de way I'd block em off would be a sin to Crocket.
>
> I tell you what's a goine to happen now very soon,
> De United States bank will be blown to de moon,

Den all de oder bank notes will be mighty plenty,
An one silver dollar will be worth ten or twenty.

O glory be to Jackson, for he blow up de Banks,
An glory be to Jackson, for he many funny pranks,
An glory be to Jackson, for de battle of Orleans,
For dere he gib de enemy de hot butter beans.

It is difficult to imagine lyrics such as these being responsible for
the lasting popularity of "Zip Coon," and indeed, the melody must be
credited with being the major reason the song is remembered. Even
today, there is hardly a country fiddler who doesn't know the melody,
yet it is extremely unlikely that many could quote more than a few of
the verses. The melody was one of the three minstrel tunes set by
Henry Franklin Belknap Gilbert (1868–1928) in his orchestral work
"Americanesque," and has been transcribed innumerable times by
composers and arrangers. "Zip Coon" has become one of the melodic
types designated as peculiarly American, a designation which should
not, however, create the illusion that it is a melody of Negro origin.

The issue of black origin has been further clouded by rather
careless research in the present century, during which time songs such
as "Long Time Ago" (or "Shinbone Alley") were attributed to black
sources on evidence that can hardly be characterized as conclusive.
"Long Time Ago," reprinted as Number 18 of the Brown University
Harris Collection of old American songs, asserts in the annotation
that the song was rooted "deep in the Negro past," and that it had
already been altered in various ways by the time "Daddy" Rice sang it
in 1833. The original is not quoted, nor is its source given, yet the
annotations explicitly state that the song was "widely known,"
without revealing by whom it was known, in what form it was known,
or how this interesting information came to be known. The reprint
version is dated 1836, a discrepancy of some three years in relation to
the Rice version. The accompaniment was by William Clifton who
preserved, we are told in these notes, the "nine-measure rhythm of the
original." Aside from the rather undiscriminating use of musical
terminology, the student of this piece is once again asked to place his
faith in an oddly elusive original.

While the account of the origin of "Long Time Ago" admittedly
might be accurate, present-day knowledge of African music makes it
highly doubtful that much, if any, black influence exists in the printed
version of 1836. The so-called "call and response" pattern cannot be

cited effectually inasmuch as the device is common to many other types of music closer to Western experience. The melody is of distinctly European folk flavor, and the arrangement by Clifton erases any tinge of Africa which might have "tainted" the alleged original. And finally, unless the present generation is using a system of mathematics completely foreign to scholars of the past, the phrasing is in ten-, rather than nine-measure periods, as stated in the Damon annotations.

Textually, "Long Time Ago" loses still more ground in its contention for black genesis. The freedom enjoyed by the protagonist was that of a white man, as evidenced by his possession of a gun, not to mention his obvious relish at the sight of a fellow black's being shot by "Massa," who offers no reason for his action whatsoever. Far from being horrified at his master's homicidal tendencies, the protagonist pays his respects to him in the last verse, saying: "I hope dat Massa in de sky-e." This sort of lunatic logic is too closely related to established white attitudes in songs of the period to be taken seriously as the product of the black. The words of "Long Time Ago" show one thing quite clearly, however: the gradual development of a coherent narrative style. Descriptive and nonsense verses do not appear in this version of the song, leaving the story to unfold itself. In the technical sense, "Long Time Ago" was an important milestone in the development of white songs on black subjects.

LONG TIME AGO

O I was born down ole Varginee, Long time ago.
O I was born down ole Varginee, Long time ago.

O Massa die an make me free, Long time ago.
O Massa die an lef me free, Long time ago.

O I ax Massa ware he gwoin, Long time ago.
He hab a gun an dog to show im, Long time ago.

He say he gwoin to kill a Niggar, Long time ago.
He aim he gun, he pull de triggar, Long time ago.

He shoot de Niggar trough de libber, Long time ago.
Vich make de Niggar kick an quiver, Long time ago.

I ax him why he do dat darfore, Long time ago.
He neber say no why nor warfore, Long time ago.

I look I see, he only stun im, Long time ago.
De Niggar he cut dirt an run im, Long time ago.

O I den runs down Shinbone alley, Long time ago.
I saw dat Niggar in de valley, Long time ago.

I ax im if he dat dar Niggar, Long time ago.
Dat Massa shot wid gun an triggar, Long time ago.

He cum at me like Allegater, Long time ago.
I stop he mouf wid hot potater, Long time ago.

He say he offen kiss my Sally, Long time ago.
I tell im dat be one dam lyee, Long time ago.

O den I ketch im by de coller, Long time ago.
I guess I make de Niggar holler, Long time ago.

I take de gun, I pull de triggar, Long time ago.
An dat de en ob dat dar Niggar, Long time ago.

Dis appen long fore Massa die, Long time ago.
I hope dat Massa in de sky-e, Long time ago.

One cover illustration for "Long Time Ago" is an anachronism, showing the subject of the song carrying a rifle at the ready with a rather determined look on his face. Thoughtful whites might have taken this as a veiled threat, were it not for the label, emphatically pointed up with scrollwork, of "comic songs & chorus" which decorated the cover. Possession of firearms by blacks was, of course, unthinkable in real life; therefore it had to be taken as a humorous illustration (Figure 6).

Whatever the origin of "Long Time Ago," there can be little doubt concerning its influence. Not only did it serve as a prototype for early minstrel songs, it was made over into a religious song and lifted almost intact to become the pseudo-art song, "Near the Lake Where Drooped the Willow," with new words by George Pope Morris and a new accompaniment by Charles Edward Horn. The natural inclination of the melody favors sentimental treatment such as that afforded by Pope; thus, "Long Time Ago" can be considered as a precursor of the sentimental song of the ante-bellum South. This type of treatment promoted a totally fictional image of easy living on the plantations for "massa" and slave alike. It was a picture of pleasure and love within a system almost entirely devoid of such qualities. For want of a better name, the songs in this category have been designated as either the "carry me back" or the "magnolia theme" types. The former refers to the type in which the protagonist expresses the desire to return to this fictional South, whereas the "magnolia theme" categorizes those songs descriptive of it.

Figure 6

An early example of the "magnolia theme" is encountered in "Old Tar(e) River," a song which appeared close on the heels of "Long Time Ago." The first line contains a phrase destined to become an essential feature of such songs: "Oh, way down in . . . ." Songs following in this style soon adopted the "work all day and play all night" refrain, suggesting an idyllic existence which was mainly valid only in the minds of apologists for slavery. The freedom enjoyed by the protagonist of the "carry me back" and the "magnolia theme" songs represents a desire to avoid thinking of the blacks as chattel without the obligation of actually granting them freedom. The fictional black in song could do almost anything he wished; a "fact" readily accepted by whites unwilling to face reality. Thus, the songs bolstered the contention of slaveholders that slavery was necessary for the well-being of blacks.

OLD TAR RIVER[32]
(WID A LITTLE LOCAL SALT IN DE WATA)

Oh, way down in ole Tare riber,
    Hu hu lu a hu ahoo,
On de banks of Alama,
    Lum tum tum tum Toddy um de da,
Dar's war I see my ole Anna,
    Oh hu hu,
Gwaine away to ole Lusianna,
    Lum tum tum tum,
She grin dis nigga two good bye,
    Oh hu hu,
Lord, how she sweated in de eye,
    Lum tum tum,
I gib her hand a good bye shaken,
    Fur lu ah ahoo,
Twas hot enough to bake a cake on,
    Lum tum tum,
I ride upon de rollin riber,
    Hu hu ahoo,
Wid a sail made ob a waggon kiver,
    Lump tum tum,
I go down to de dismal swamp,
    Hu hu ahoo!
War alligator's ghosts do romp,
    Lump tum tum.

> I dance wid dem all in de mash, ah!
>   Hu hu ahoo!
>
> It make de trees turn all goose flesh, ah,
>   Lum tum tum,
> I sing a song to massa raw bone,
>   Hu ha ahoo!
> And play de banjo on his jaw bone,
>   Lum tum tum.
> I'm gwaine to de wild goose nation,
>   Hu hu ahoo,
> For to complete my educashin,
>   Lum tum tum,
> To England on a raff I'll scull, ah,
>   Hu hu hu,
> Den I'll print notes about John Bull, ah,
>   Tum tum tum,
> I'll larn em how to eat dar pickens,
>   Hu hu hu,
> And dey call me de Yankee Dickens,[33]
>   Lum tum tum.
> Den I'll turn a weather guager,
>   Hu hu hu,
> By rule ob star shine like old Hague, sa,
>   Hu hu ah hoo,
> Clar thro' de stone fence ob de futah,
>   Lum tum tum, toddy un de da.

It was but a short step from this somewhat primitive notion of the slave rising to the defense of the South to the sentimental "carry me back" and the "magnolia theme." At this point, however, songwriters were still preoccupied with establishing the character of the plantation "darky" in song. Songs such as "Jim Crow" and "Gombo Chaff" are associated, in the view of Nathan,[34] with frontier heroes Mike Fink, David Crockett and "a host of similar hardfisted fellows." The naive assumption that "Jim Crow" and "Gombo Chaff" types were black varieties of white heroes of popular imagination is, of course, ridiculous. The inescapable reality of slavery made any comparison impossible. While white folk heroes were products of the frontier experience and real enough to survive in American frontier lore, the black portrayed in these songs is pure fiction—a product of the wholehearted attempt to avoid the horrid reality of slavery. No actual black hero such as Denmark Vesey or Nat Turner was ever mentioned in these songs. The intent of songs such as "Jim Crow" and "Gombo Chaff" was to hold up the character of the black to ridicule—not to extol it.

"Gombo Chaff" (or "Gumbo Chaff") appeared in Baltimore in 1834. The illustrated cover shows a stylized black boatman grinning widely as he poles his craft with one hand while holding aloft in his other hand a jug, presumably filled with whatever made him so happy.[35] Its length and similarity to examples cited makes the complete version extraneous. The caption title reads: "The humorous Adventures of Gombo Chaff, as sung by Mr. T. Rice." The words follow a rambling narrative which, despite the appearance of artlessness, is a rather well organized exhibition of current white attitudes toward blacks. Beyond the characterization of the black as a ludicrous figure, "Gombo Chaff" demonstrates that songwriters were becoming increasingly skillful in the handling of the genre. In less than a decade the obliteration of the true black image had progessed from the indiscriminate mixture of unrelated verses, as in "Jim Crow," to a more coherent progression of events. This accretion of expertise added nothing to the luster of the black image; indeed, the success of these early, probing, and experimental attacks on the Negro character insured that composers would continue to exploit the theme.

"Gombo Chaff" begins with the protagonist's explaining:

> On de Ohio bluff in de state of Indiana,
> Dere's where I live, chock up to de Habanna;
> Ev'ry morning early Massa give me licker,
> I take my net and paddle and I put out de quicker;
> I jump into my skiff and I down the river driff,
> And I cotch as many Catfish as ever you could liff.

He is not as concerned with proving his prowess as is "Jim Crow," however, since he spends only two verses in telling of his bout with an alligator and the ease with which he handles bales of cotton in New Orleans. The attitude shown by "Gombo Chaff" to his "Massa" verges on impudence, as he describes his death:

> Now old Massa die on de 'leventeenth of April,
> We chuck'd him in de troff where we cotch de sugar maple;

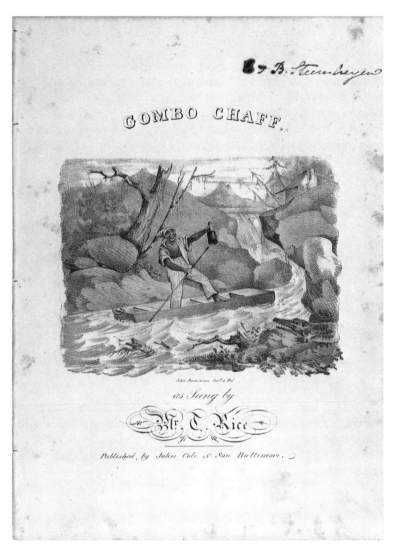

Figure 7

> We dig a big hole dere, down on de big level,
> And I really do believe dat he gone to de Debil;
> For when he live I know he light upon me so,
> Now he gone to tote de firewood and water down below.

This temporary extravagance is overlooked as the following verse relates what happened to "Massa's" widow after she married "Big Bill de weaver," who turns out to be a gay deceiver. "Gombo Chaff" decides to look for greener pastures and heads for New Orleans, after which he travels to Louisville as a stowaway on a riverboat. At this point the song expands on the subject of Gombo Chaff's capacity for learning, an exercise on the theme of the inherent stupidity of the black:

> O when I got dare, I larn'd to speak de Francey,
> Kiss ki ding—tare your shirt, a la mode de dancey;
> Bone jaw Madam sell, stevadores and riggers,
> Apple jack and sassafras and little Indian Niggers;
> O de natives dey laff, and dey swore I was corn'd,
> For dey never heard sich french since de hour dey was born.
>
> Dare Bill beats de drum and old Joe's de fifer,
> I is dat child dat can read and write and cypher;
> Twice one is five, den carry six to seven,
> Eighteen and twenty nine and thirteen's eleven;
> So 'tween you an me, it's very plain to see,
> Dat I larn'd to play de Banjo by de double rule of three.

Having demonstrated his complete stupidity to the satisfaction of whites, Gombo Chaff reveals in the final verse that he has fulfilled the requirements for acceptance in a white world. He is no longer a threat, he has found "his place," and wants merely to live peacefully on his farm:

> Now I 'rive on our farm on de Ohio bluff,
> And I tink of fun and frolic Old Gombo's had enough;
> All de white folks at home, and dey very much amuse,
> When I sing um dis song, and tell um all de news;
> So we'd music all night, and they set up sich a laff,
> When I introduced de Niggers to Mrs. Gombo Chaff.

This picture of a stupid, worn-out, and pitiful wreck is the one Nathan has compared with white folk heroes such as Mike Fink and David Crockett!

It was no accident that the majority of the pre-minstrel show songs worked toward the destruction of the male black's image; he represented the major threat to the smooth operation of a system of oppression which, despite all arguments to the contrary, was offensive to the sensibilities of Western man. Make the black less than a man and perhaps the system would work; this ideology, expressed through every means possible, including the entertainment business, partially explains why the black, rather than any other minority in the United States at the time, was singled out for public character assassination. No black characteristic—actual or imagined—was omitted in the frantic scramble to heap destruction on the black image.

Blacks in uniform, so successfully exploited in "Backside Albany" and "Massa Georgee Washington and General Lafayette," appeared again in 1835 as "Jim Brown," a military band leader. The authorship of "Jim Brown" is not stated in the 1835 song, but a later edition (*ca.* 1836) states that it was "selected, written and arranged" by William Clifton.[36] The text of "Jim Brown" is related to the pretensions of "Jim Crow" type songs, with an added fillip of military garb to serve as the means to draw attention to the preposterous figure puffed up by his own self-importance.

It is possible that "Jim Brown" was patterned after the real-life model of Francis Johnson, a black bandmaster of considerable renown during this time. Not only was Johnson one of the first black musicians to gain international fame, but his Washington Guards, Company Three Band, was considered superior to *any* of the musical groups in Philadelphia at that time. He played before European royalty, yet at home in America his band endured the same racial discrimination extended to other blacks.[37] Johnson, or one of his several black bandmaster rivals, could have provided the model for the musical insult, "Jim Brown":

JIM BROWN

I am science nigger, my name is Jim Brown,
De one dat plays de music up and down de town;
Tho' to de common niggers I would not deign my hand,

Figure 8

Be kase I'm de leader ob de fam'd brass band.
I plays upon de music, I make de hansom sound,
I am de musician dat dey call Jim Brown.

I larnt to beat de cymbals, and I larnt to beat de drum,
And all de fancy tunes, dis nigger he could cum;
I went to de Tremont, to see what was dare—
Wid dis old nigger, dey nothing to compare—
Dey make talk about de opra, de gassa Rakkaria,
Dey neber cum tell wid ole Wirginny neber tire.

De way I larnt to play de carry ob de sword,
I practis on de Banjo sugar in de gourd;
De niggers all dance when Jim begin to play,
Dey dance from de mornin, to de closin ob de day,
I plays upon de fiddle and I plays de claronet,
I plays upon de cymbals till I make de nigger swet.

I was born on Long Island close to Oyster Bay,
I worked upon de farms for three cents a day;
De genius ob dis nigger was sure to be disciver,
I jump't upon de pine raft and floats down de river,
I land at Coarlers hook, de music in my hand,
Quick I get de leader ob de famed Brass Band.

I caution all de New York niggers not to stop my way,
For if he play de fool wid me dey in de gutter lay;
For when I was at New Orleans and only three feet high,
I run before ole General Jack, and make de red coats fly.
Den I play upon de corn stalk de true Yankee fiddle,
Lick'd lasses from de punkin blow and sugar from maple.

I went on to Washington, de capitol ob de nation,
I ax massa Jackson, will you gib me situation?
Says he, Jim Brown, I give you one but what can you do?
I can nullify de boot, and put de veto on de shoe.
Says he, Jim Brown, what can you do for me?
I can go in the garden and plant a hickory tree.

Since music in de city it is all de rage,
Now I take a benefit and sing upon de stage;
Since I've appear'd and got de coppers from you,
I won't care for constable nor fear de Bug a Boo.
Since I got encouraged by de people ob dis town,
Take de eberlasting blessing ob de nigger Jim Brown.

Old Jim Brown, he sing, sing some,
But de people was not satisfy till young Jim come;

> Now I've sung you all I could and told you all de cause,
> And if you think de song is good I want your applause.
> And now I've sung you all I could, pray don't cry encore,
> Bekase you kill yourself a laffing if I sing any more.

History does not record the exact number of people who died "laffing" at "Jim Brown," but the figure of the black in a pseudo-military guise proved to be a lasting image. Actual black contributions to the military history of the United States were obscured and minimized by the pervasive image of the black in a ludicrous military posture. This stereotype reached its fullest development in the period from the Civil War through the 1890's, however. The period in which "Jim Brown" was conceived concentrated on the destruction of the male image in civilian garb for the most part, following the lead of established favorites with songs such as "Long Tail Blue," considered by some authorities as the first song of the black dandy.[38]

George Washington Dixon claimed authorship of "Long Tail Blue," although the cover of the Willig edition cited in this study shows William Pennington in the role. In addition to Pennington and Dixon, the song was made popular by other performers, such as the little known Barney Burns. It was one of the songs sung by Stephen Foster as a boy.[39]

"Long Tail Blue" not only attacked the black for his desire to be well-dressed; it attempted to show that he aspired to that unattainable and strictly taboo position of equality with whites. This reference to white aspirations was something of a blunder on the part of the author and was amended in subsequent editions of the song. The stereotype of the tawdry black remained, however, and "Long Tail Blue" became not only a standard item in the minstrel repertoire, but a prototype for songs on the subject for the next hundred years.

LONG TAIL BLUE

> I've come to town to see you all,
> I ask you how d'ye do?
> I'll sing a song not very long,
> About my long tail blue.
>
>> Oh! for the long tail blue,
>> Oh! for the long tail blue.
>> I'll sing a song not very long
>> About my long tail blue.

Figure 9

> Some Niggers they have but one coat,
> But you see I've got two;
> I wears a jacket all the week,
> And Sunday my long tail blue.
>
> Jim Crow is courting a white gall,
> And yaller folks call her Sue;
> I guess she back'd a nigger out,
> And swung my long tail blue.
>
> As I was gwoin up Market Street,
> I holler'd arter Sue,
> The watchman came and took me up,
> And spilte my long tail blue.
>
> I took it to a Tailor's shop,
> To see what he could do;
> He took a needle and some thread,
> And mended my long tail blue.
>
> If you want to win the Ladie's hearts,
> I'll tell you what to do;
> Go to a tip-top Tailor's shop,
> And buy a long tail blue.

This version, while technically superior to later versions in its conciseness, was purged of its third and fourth verses and their calumny of white womanhood, either omitting them altogether or changing them to remove the insult, as in the version printed in the *Negro Forget-me-not-Songster* (Philadelphia, *ca.* 1840):

> Jim Crow was courting a brown gal,
> And de white folks called her Sue,
> But I guess she let de nigga drop,
> When she saw my long tail blue.

As the decade prior to the establishment of the minstrel show came to a close, composers of songs on black subjects became more expert at their craft as well as more prolific. The texts began to repeat ideas from one song to another, as in the numerous references to political events and reminiscences of the war years. Stereotypes took shape and hardened into figures that would survive for more than a century. Certain food predilections, such as an assumed fondness for raccoon, were associated with the black and endlessly repeated from song to song.

The male image as delineated by "Jim Crow" and "Zip Coon" was strengthened by a host of songs in direct imitation of the style and content. In 1840, for example, no less than three songs with alliterative titles similar to "Jim Crow" appeared: "Jim Along Josey," "Jumbo Jum," and "Jonny Boker."

Both "Jim Along Josey" and "Jumbo Jum" were arranged by "An Eminent Professor" and sung by John N. Smith, who billed himself as "the celebrated delineator of Etheopean character." According to some authorities, "Jim Along Josey" was written by Edward Harper, who sang it in *The Free Nigger of New York,* around 1838.[40] The far less successful "Jumbo Jum" claimed on the cover that it was "an original Nigger ballad," an assertion which need not be taken seriously if one examines the content of the song.

The text of "Jim Along Josey" reveals the emergence of a standard pattern modelled after "Jim Crow" and similar songs; an introductory verse followed by verses attempting to draw humor from supposed black characteristics:

> I'se from Lucianna as you all know,
> Dar whare Jim along Josey's all de go,
> Dem niggars all rise when de bell does ring,
> And dis is de song dat dey do sing.
> > Hey get along, get along Josey,
> > Hey get along, Jim along Joe!

The hint is made in the next verse that the black aspires to whiteness, or to be taken as white:

> Oh! when I gets dat new coat which I expects to hab soon,
> Likewise a new pair tight-kneed trousaloon,
> Den I walks up and down Broadway wid my Susanna,
> And de white folks will take me to be Santa Anna.

The following two verses are nonsensical, but the fifth verse draws a distinction between the Northern and the Southern black:

> De New York niggers tink dey're fine,
> Because dey drink de genuine,
> De southern niggers dey lib on mush,
> And when dey laugh dey say Oh Hush.

A personal observation follows:

> I'm de nigger that don't mind my troubles,
> Because dey are noting more dan bubbles,
> De ambition dat dis nigger feels,
> Is showing de science of his heels.

This, in essence, is the entire song. The black wants nothing from life except to entertain. Whites need not consider him a threat to any of their institutions. By now, the expression of this thought could be— and of course, was—thrown into the song texts casually, as though it were accepted fact that slavery would exist unhindered by criticism forever.

The final verse of this edition of "Jim Along Josey" is a tribute to George Washington, a rather pointless anachronism which adds nothing to the song. Many variations of "Jim Along Josey" appeared in later years, and its use in extravaganzas and afterpieces assured it a permanent place in the minstrel repertoire. Adaptation of the song as a game obscured the fact that it was not of folk origin.

"Jumbo Jum" has been largely overlooked by authorities in the popular music field. Perhaps this can be explained by the crudity of the text and music, which represent something of a retrogression within the style. However, the interesting feature of "Jumbo Jum" is its direct approach to the stereotypical black: he is belligerent and independent—worst of all, he is sexually potent. The work-all-day-play-all-night theme, as well as the usual political salute to Jackson, are concessions to the formula; but the male figure is simply too strong to fit the stereotype. Indeed, "Jumbo Jum" might well be considered an example of the faults of formula writing, with its awkward melody and a character which does not fit the mold. "Jumbo Jum" was briefly successful (it was reprinted a few times in the songsters) but died soon after the realization that it had strayed far from the formula. The song's main interest to this study is to emphasize the standardization which had begun to dictate the style and content of songs in the genre; it was a rigidifying mold which nonetheless allowed some, but not too much, experimentation.

JUMBO JUM

My name is Jumbo Jum and I cum from Tennessee,
I can fight, jump and wrestle by the double rule of three,

Ev'ry morning very early this nigger can be seen,
Fireing up like the devil to raise a little steam.
    Oh! look at exquisite shin!
    Nigger you can't begin,
    Here is the Jay bird wing!
    And the back action spring!

Oh! Nashville is a nice place as any in the nation,
And all, all the niggers work dare upon the plantation,
When the day's work is done, they take hold of a fiddle,
They ballance to their partner and chassy down the middle.
    Oh! then you ought to see the niggers,
    Sporting dare elegant figures,
    I took 'em right on the wing,
    When I cum the back action spring.

Not a great way from Nashville, as snug as a mouse,
Dare lives a great man in a very nice house,
Every body ought to cherish him, you know who I mean,
It's massa General Jackson of the battle of Orlean.
    I tell you 'twas mighty big fun,
    When he pointed his blunderbuss gun,
    He made 'em all cum to a stand,
    When he rowed up old Packenham.

I recollect well what old master used to say,
Jumbo, if I lick don't you never run away;
But one night he hit me wid a big corn stalk,
And the first place I found myself was in New York.
    The niggers looked at me wid surprise,
    Oh! Moses how dey opened dare eyes,
    I nebber see darky so civil,
    Though they all was as ugly as the devil.

There was a nigger wench and I thought I'd die,
For when she looked at me she give such a sigh,
I made an impression on the wenches feeling,
That I set the coloured lady in a big fit a reeling.
    She dropt right down on the floor,
    In a state of agony you know,
    I kissed her gently on the chin,
    Says she pray do dat agin.

When the coloured lady arose, upon close inspection,
I thought I made a very fair selection,
She was a dandy wench and she carried full sail,
Round her neck she wore a thing like a foxes tail.

> Oh! she looked so very fine,
> She was the real superfine;
> Of all the wenches that I meet,
> I never see one wid such feet.

"Jonny Boker" (or "Johnny Booker") was one of the many songs associated with Joel (Joe) Walker Sween(e)y. Sweeney was one of the earliest performers on the banjo, an instrument said to have been invented by him.[41] His songs usually indicate "as sung by . . ." without actually naming Sweeney as the composer, yet there is little reason to doubt that he was responsible for the majority of them. "Jonny Boker" is, by all counts, the least offensive song in his repertoire and certainly less insulting than the two preceding songs cited. Essentially, the song is the story of a black wagoner whose vehicle breaks while on a trip to "Lynchburg town," and the many attempts he makes to find help in repairing his rig.

> As I went up to Lynchburg town,
> I broke my yoke on de coaling ground,
> I drove from dare to bowling spring,
> And tried for to mend my yoke and spring.
>   O Jonny Boker,
>   Help dat nigger, do,
>   Jonny Boker, do.

The rather good-natured attitude of this text would lead one to assume that Sweeney, at least, was not part of the movement which was assiduously attacking the black character—but no. In his "Whar Did You Cum From? or, Knock a Nigger Down," Sweeney contributes a stereotypical image of the black as a thief and a liar:

> Some folks say dat a niggar wont steal!
> But I cotch one in my corn field,
> So I ask him 'bout dat corn and he call me a liar,
> So I up wid my foot and I kick him in de fire.

The refrain shows that the white response to this supposed trait of the black was predictable:

> O whar did you cum from,
> Knock a niggar down.

> O whar did you cum from,
> Knock a niggar down.

Sweeney's "Jonny Boker" and his "Whar Did You Cum From" call attention to the phenomenon of duplicate titles, a circumambient development growing out of the intense effort to exploit the increasingly popular black theme. The duplication of titles has been a continuing source of difficulty for researchers in subsequent years, in many cases leading scholars to draw conclusions about one song from another, entirely different song. There were, for example, several "Jonny Boker" songs, none of which are alike.[42] Damon cites as a variant text of "Whar Did You Cum From" a text from "Whar Did You Cum From or, Oh, Mr. Coon," a song of the same period which bears no resemblance to the content or metrical arrangement of the Sweeney song beyond the fact that both are about the black.[43] In passing, it is interesting to note that this oversight brings to light a verse in the "Oh, Mr. Coon" version concerning miscegenation, or "amalgamation," as it was termed at that time:

> De white bird an de black bird settin' in de grass,
> Preachin' 'malgamation to de bobolinks dat pass;
> To carry out de doctrine dey seem little loth,
> When along cum de pigeon hawk and leby on 'em both.

The freed slave was no more immune to the vicious imagery than his less fortunate brothers in bondage. "De Free Nigger," presumably written by Richard W. Pelham in 1841, falls well within the established formula; it contains much of the plantation slave concept as developed in song to this point, with freedom an incidental matter of slight importance. "De Free Nigger" is essentially a vehicle for extolling "de Carolina crew," a fictional group with rather unusual proclivities, as explained in the first verse:

> Come all you Virginia gals and listen to my noise;
> Neber do you wed wid de Carolina boys,
> For if dat you do your portion it will be–
> Corn cake and harmony and Jango lango tea.

Recognition of any dignity in the status of the freed black is thwarted in the chorus:

> O Mamsele Mariache, bone cum saw;
> Mamselle Mariache, bone cum saw.

The ladies associated with "de Carolina crew" could look forward to little pleasure:

> They will take you and place you on Jango lango hill,
> Dar de ill [they'll] make you work and tary to your will.
> You work all day your fingers to be [the] quick
> Den you trample over de ground like a crooked maple stick.

But the men, however, are not without their pretensions:

> Some have de mockazins and some haves none;
> But he dat habs a pair of boots he tinks himself a man,
> Wid his big brass buttons and his long tail blue,
> Dem what we call de dandies of de Carolina crew.

As something of a concession to the title of the song, slavery and freedom are finally touched upon in the sixth verse:

> When I was a slave some elebin years ago,
> My master gib me spade, shubil and a hoe;
> But I tell him rite smack it neber would do
> For I was bound to shine among de Carolina [crew].

The seventh and final verse revert to the bluster that has by this time become typical of songs about the black male:

> Now the Carolina crew da [they] are a bery large crowd,
> They walks in de hubaras and dresses up so loud,
> And when da are on a spree, mind I tell you,
> You had better meet de debil dan dat Carolina crew.

Legal and social restrictions on the free black were severe and manifold. Upon gaining freedom, some states required the ex-slave emigrate at once to another state; some states required him to remain not only in the state, but in the locality, presumably for security reasons in both instances. He was denied most of the rights of citizenship and, of course, could never dream of social equality with the white population. Naturally, none of these limitations on the freedom of blacks were considered suitable material for songs. The free black, indeed, was an even greater threat to slavery than was the slave himself, the significance of which was not lost on songwriters who afforded the ex-slave harsher treatment, in the main, than they did those remaining in bondage. This black threat to the stability and purity of white society is one of the basic reasons why blacks were feared and had to be defused as a potential danger. The steady erosion of the imagery associated with blackness reached a peak in the period following the Civil War, when the newly freed slaves evoked a degree of terror in white minds that has not subsided fully to this day.

Songs on black subjects during this period recognized this fear and spared no pains to reassure whites that the black was, after all, an object of humor. In song the black could posture, bluster, swagger, put himself forward as a philosopher, preacher, lover—or even threaten to invade white society—it meant nothing because it was all a joke.

The sentimental "carry-me-back" was the white conception of the South which also contributed to the comforting thought that slaves were content and would cause no trouble unless they were freed.

The white performer in blackface who put these images before audiences of the day managed to convince them that blacks concurred in the imagery of the slave contented to "stay in his place" because slavery was beneficial and, anyway, he was a naturally inferior being.

The notion that the songs, dances, and mimetics of the pre-minstrel show material originated with the slaves lends authority to the pro-slavery arguments and mocks the present-day scholar who vainly gropes through Southern plantation history to find minstrelsy's roots.

If it were possible to choose one example which best exemplifies the pre-minstrel period, "Sich a Gitting Up Stairs" might well be nominated. Almost every stereotype known to songwriters of the 1830's is presented in this song: the happy, singing darky; the preacher; political and social commentary on black problems; the jealous lover; and the belligerent but cowardly black male.

"Sich a Gitting Up Stairs" has been attributed to Joe Black-burne,[44] although none of the versions located for this study confirms this point. The date of the piece is equally uncertain, but it was being sung as early as 1837, when T.D. Rice used it with "devastating" effect in his Negro farce, *Bone Squash Diavolo.*[45]

Authorities differ on the question of the musical lineage of "Sich a Gitting Up Stairs," Howard calling it "one of the least derivative and

Figure 10

perhaps the most original" of the early minstrel tunes,[46] while Nathan shows its derivation from the Morris dance tune, "Getting Upstairs."[47] Regardless of the differences concerning the parentage of "Sich a Gitting Up Stairs," Howard's assertion that it contains "true folk vigor" must be taken as a reference to European, rather than African folk tradition.

SICH A GITTING UP STAIRS

On a Suskehanna raft I come down de bay,
And I danc'd and I frolick'd and fiddled all de way.

Sich a gitting up stairs I never did see,
Sich a gitting up stairs I never did see.

Trike he [sic] toe an heel, cut de pigeon wing,
Scratch gravel, slap de foot, dat's just de ting.

Sich a gitting up stairs (etc.).

I went to de play, and I see'd Jim Crow,
Oh! nigger Isam den he swell, for Jim was no go.

I look him in de face until I make him grin,
And den I trow a backa quid an' hit him on de chin.

Oh! I is dat boy dat know to preach a sarmont
Bout Temperance and seven up an all dat kind of varmint.

Nigger hold a meeting about de Clonization [Colonization]
An dare I spoke a speech about Amalgamation!

To Washington I go dare I cut a swell,
Cleaning gemmen's boots and ringin auction bell.

I call on yaller Sal dat trade in sassenges [sausages]
An dare I meet big Joe, which make my dander ris.

Says I "You see dat door? Just mosey, nigger Joe,
For I'm a Suskyhanner boy what knows a ting or two!"

An den I show my science—prenez gardez vouz,
Bung he eye, break he shin, split de nose in two.

Sal holler out, den she jump between us,
But guess he no forget de day when Isam show his genus.

Den Big Joe went out, he gwoin to take de law,
But he no fool de Possum—I cut stick for Baltimore.

To sum up the evolution of songs on black subjects from Independence to the establishment of the minstrel show, it becomes

apparent that the South—the reality of slavery and plantation life—
had no bearing on the imaginations of the composers, singers, actors,
managers, and audiences who were in daily contact with the genre. All
of this activity was centered in the North. True, the subject was
Southern, but it was distorted beyond recognition as mythology
replaced reality in songs. Audiences were primed for almost anything
except realism with regard to slavery, which imposed a heavy burden
of guilt in return for free labor. The new nation, anxiously anticipating
the exploitation of an entire continent, had no desire to address itself
to weighty moral questions while labor was so desperately needed;
songs which allowed temporary relief or gave the illusion that no
problem existed were welcomed.

It is interesting to note that the American theatre of this period was
seriously groping to find the American mind—to discover the formula
for popular success. Imported as well as indigenous types were
thrown at audiences in profusion. At first, the characterization of the
black was merely one of many such types presented on the American
stage. Favorable reception of these "delineations" led to refinements
and exploitation of the subject which ultimately resulted in the virtual
exclusion of other types from the boards. Presentation of "Negro
extravaganzas" and farces was in many cases all that saved theatres
from bankruptcy following the panic of 1837.

But the black seen on stage represented an escape from the black
seen in everyday life. Through the songs, dances, extravaganzas, and
farces, the issue of slavery was set aside momentarily while the
pressure of reality continued to build.

Northern white producers of the theatical "Negro" took advantage of the situation, shamelessly proclaiming that what audiences
were hearing were authentic black melodies and dialogue. Meanwhile, they busily searched their own folk traditions for fresh ideas to
meet the insatiable demand for new material. The experience thus
gained through some thirty years of practice with the "Negro" genre,
a lengthy financial crisis which left managers desperate for attractions and which drew actors together for support, and the overriding
public need for respite from a tremendous and horrid moral problem
made the establishment of the so-called Negro minstrel show little
short of inevitable.

Chapter Three

The Minstrel Show

The momentum generated by the extraordinary success of the pseudo-black songs in the 1820's and 1830's nudged the entertainment business inexorably toward the establishment of a medium which would capitalize fully on the black theme. Although there were serious efforts aimed at establishing a legitimate American theatre, audiences clamored for more spectacular attractions, and managers searched diligently for novelties such as equestrian acts, India rubber men, or such amusements as "R. W. Pelham and his son in Negro Peculiarities, Dances and Extravaganzas."[1]

Songs on the black subject were presented in a multitude of ways on stage. They were interpolated between acts of larger stage works, incorporated into sketches, and were on occasion presented from the backs of moving horses. Songs were thrown together to form a rudimentary "Ethiopean Opera." Dialogue was added between verses of songs, and individual song hits, such as "Jim Crow," were expanded into complete acts, becoming *Jim Crow In London*, an extravaganza created by T.D. Rice as a means of exploiting his original idea to its fullest.

Actors' talents were being honed to perfection in the delineation of the pseudo-black on the pre-minstrel show stage. Those associated with the minstrel show in its formative period were well known to the audiences long before the genre was established. Pelham, Rice, Dixon, Farrell, Sweeney, and a host of others possessed skills essential to the maintenance of the form once it was started.

A crucial factor in the establishment of the minstrel show was the economic decline following the panic of 1837. Unemployment touched the variety stage as well as other sectors of the economy, reaching a climax in the 1842–1843 season, which Odell characterized as "the nadir."[2] Performers banded together in order to seek work or to while away the hours between engagements. While it is fairly clear that legitimate actors resented being forced by hard times into playing parts in the pseudo-black productions, there were always enough who were ready and willing to bow to expedience.

The time was ripe for institutionalizing the black theme on the American stage. This, by common consent among scholars, occurred on February 6, 1843, at the Bowery Amphitheatre in New York, when Frank Brower, Billy Whitlock, Dick Pelham, and Dan Emmett marched onstage and made their first confirmed appearance as the Virginia Minstrels. American blackface minstrelsy had been born.

Other claimants arose to challenge the Virginia Minstrels' primacy as originators of the genre. E.P. Christy went so far as to have his claim endorsed by the Supreme Court of New York.[3] But it is not the purpose of the present study to attempt a settlement of questions of priority in this instance; it is sufficient to accept the opinions of authorities on the subject, while turning our attention to the far more important question of the role this "devouring ogre," as Odell characterized the minstrel show, plays in the slander of the black.

Popular acceptance of the minstrel show was swift and complete. Critics who attacked the form for its "vulgarity" often came away from performances converted and loud in their praises. This change of face is easier to understand if it is remembered that attacks on the minstrel show were based on its lack of gentility and its sharp break with attempts to establish traditions of a legitimate American theatre; the slander of the black inherent in the form was not a consideration. At any rate, criticism began to appear as nothing more than precious pettifoggery as the minstrel show happily conquered not only the United States, but Europe as well.

How was the central figure—the black—affected by the new form? Within the songs themselves there was little change; it was through institutionalizing the pseudo-black that a new perspective was established. Individual songs had seen the black singly, whereas the minstrel show created a type: America's own lovable plantation darky. The medium enlarged the figure without enhancing it. Stereotypes were amplified and transformed into rigid images that proved durable through all subsequent changes within the American theatre.

The institutionalized black image was admirably suited to the times. Anti-slavery voices were becoming more strident in their demands for an immediate end to slavery, and the issue was beginning to assume the aspect of a national shame. Something was needed to assuage the uncomfortable feeling that condoning slavery was a violation of every precept upon which the nation was founded, and that a day of reckoning would inevitably come. The minstrel show provided a welcome relief from these anxieties by offering a view of the black as an inferior comic figure undeserving of serious worry or guilt feelings. Small wonder that American audiences took the minstrel show to its bosom and made it a whopping success!

The notion that the fictional black as represented on the minstrel stage was based on the actual plantation slave is one of the enduring myths surrounding the form. Even today, writers occasionally resurrect stories of how white men absorbed the music and dance of the plantation slaves, molding them into uniquely American forms.[4] Facts contradict these theories insofar as the American minstrel genre is concerned; those responsible for the production of such shows were, almost to a man, Northern whites with scant knowledge of black music or customs. Leading theatres in which the shows were produced were in the North, as were the larger music publishing firms. The paucity of plantation slaves on the streets of New York, where minstrelsy began, renders the theory of Southern origin of the genre absurd.

The roots of the music of minstrelsy have already been traced to English, Irish, and Scottish sources. Negrisms in this body of song are virtually non-existent. The Southern origin myth, like that surrounding the origin of "Jim Crow," might well be discounted as early press-agentry, a bit of "show-biz" designed to promote public acceptance of the fledgling form.

In the face of so little supportive evidence, the continued uncritical acceptance of the Southern origin theory does little credit to American scholarship devoted to the study of indigenous popular expression. But there is still another, even greater reason for questioning the theory: the utter inconceivability of blacks using this form of expression to demean themselves so conclusively. Known examples exist within the body of black secular music which are insulting in nature, but the language involved and the manner employed are worlds apart from the style of the minstrel songs. Black musical insults spring from within rather than from without the group. There is a vast difference between the satire of the black's own song:

> Look at that darky there, Mr. Banjo,
> Doesn't he put on airs!

> Hat cocked on one side, Mr. Banjo,
> Walking-stick in hand, Mr. Banjo,
> Boots that go 'crank, crank,' Mr. Banjo—
> Look at that darky there, Mr. Banjo,
> Doesn't he put on airs![5]

and the doggerel of the minstrel tunes, as in the "Jim Along Josey" cited previously (p. 77), the second verse of which is a far more malign commentary on the dress of the black:

> Oh! when I gets dat new coat which I expects to hab soon,
>   Likewise a new pair tight-kneed trousaloon,
> Den I walks up and down Broadway wid my Susanna,
>   And de white folks will take me to be Santa Anna.

The use of the third person in the former example indicates personal distaste for the subject's character, whereas the common use of the first person in the minstrel songs has the effect of representing characteristics of the entire race through the mouth of a spurious black protagonist. Here, as in the bulk of the minstrel show genre, it might be said that black influence exists in the same proportion that Japanese influence is present in Gilbert and Sullivan's *The Mikado.* Yet scholars persist in the assumption that black music got itself before the general public "through the minstrel troupes of the 1840's and 50's."[6] As long as scholars remain incapable of distinguishing black music from white music, little understanding of either is to be expected. The minstrel show, it must be emphasized, was white music and dance conceived and performed by whites for white audiences; its relationship to the black was based on a stereotyped myth.

This myth—the plantation fantasy which is basic to the minstrel theme—has roots extending into the early history of the South. Reverend Alexander Whitaker described an earthly paradise in his *Good News From Virginia* (1613),[7] and later writers echoed the view of the South as an Eden populated by a contented servant class at one end of the social scale, and a genteel, landed aristocracy at the other. The assumption grew that this aristocracy was descended from the emigrant Cavaliers who fled the England of the Commonwealth period. Unfortunately for the self-image of Southerners, this aristocracy was in fact descended from middle-class stock.[8]

But the Cavalier spirit—a romantic concept of personal honor and civic pride—captured the Southern imagination during the latter part of the eighteenth century, and from that time forward, this spirit became codified into a set pattern of behavior known as "the Southern way of life."[9] The white South saw itself living in the only way possible for civilized man. Stiffening resistance to change or outside interference in Southern affairs coincided with a deterioration of relations with the North and a hardened, paternalistic attitude toward the black, who was frozen into a perpetually servile role in Southern society.

The importance which Southerners attached to the Cavalier myth should not be minimized, although some of its ramifications might seem curious to outsiders. Every member of Southern society, regardless of sex, age, rank, or race was rigidly bound by the unwritten code, as exemplified by the incident recorded in the *Magazine of Wit, and American Harmonist* (Philadelphia, 1821):

Sir William Gooch, the governor of Williamsburg, walking along the street in conversation with a friend, returned the salute of a Negro who was passing by. "Do you deign," said his friend, "to take notice of a slave?" "Yes," replied the governor, "for I cannot allow even a slave to excel me in good manners."

In this rigidly stratified society, the black was expected to occupy his "place" without objection—indeed, he was expected to *enjoy* the bounties of a system which allowed him to work and live without worry, always happy and content in this materialistic white world. Slaveholders provided the necessities of life for the slave, and their hurt was great when the slave did not show proper appreciation for their goodness. The image of the contented and devoted slave was essential to the self-esteem of the South.

The "happy plantation slave" theme as represented in song had several distinguishing characteristics. He viewed work as did the white master: it might be tolerable or even pleasurable; it might be onerous and never-ending; but above all, it was necessary. In song, no slave questioned *why* he was singled out for work, while "massa" reaped the benefits.

This mythical slave was not only happy to labor all day, he eagerly joined his companions after work for an evening of frolic and fun. "Work all day; play all night" is a recurrent theme in the minstrel song which became an important and enduring ingredient in the image of the black.

Most slaves in song were seen as totally committed in their loyalty to the South. The sentimental attachment to "massa" and the South contributed the principal motif for the cloying "carry-me-back" and the "magnolia" themes which formed such a large portion of the minstrel literature. It placed the slave in the incredible position of desiring bondage over freedom. Of all the ingredients invented by whites for their stereotypical black, none is more preposterous than this presumption that he preferred servitude over freedom.

The "carry-me-back" was often linked with a love theme, one which frequently added elements of separation through death, being sold down the river, or some such circumstance. The connection between the image of the black female lover and nostalgia for the South produced a striking phenomenon: the South gradually assumed the aspect of the female in song. Female characteristics came to dominate the image of the South to such a degree that even today, many see "Dixie" as a compendium of qualities which are essentially maternal: security, gentleness, warmth, love, loyalty, and so on.

Southerners, of course, convinced themselves that they held a virtual monopoly on such civilized qualities. The expression, "Southern hospitality," exemplifies a host of assumed attitudes entirely consistent with the Cavalier myth. The charming picture of tranquil gentility and happy contentment was transformed into a scene of rage and turmoil once the threat of black equality was introduced, however.

Composers of minstrel songs were captivated by the mythical South as potential material. While perhaps ignorant of the full horror of slavery, they realized that the myth constituted the main behavior pattern of the South, and they supported it by churning out thousands of songs on the subject. A measure of their support is seen in the many vicious attacks they made on leading abolitionists while, at the same time, constantly reiterating the "happy plantation slave" theme.

It was not long before the happy, singing darky was commonplace on stage. Atlases, maps, and newspapers were searched for material. There was hardly a Southern locality which escaped fame in song as the very spot to which the slave wished to return as his years ended. Minstrelsy gave America its own Eden and, at the same time, allowed it to evade the crushing shame of reality.

Beginning with the "happy plantation slave" theme, the progress of the type through its various modifications—the "carry-me-back" and the "carry-me-back" with a love association—can be traced.

"Sweet Mississippi," characterized as "a popular Ethiopian song,"[10] approaches the "happy plantation slave" from the vantage point of a passenger on a riverboat listening to the song of the boatman as he steers onward, "unconscious of fear":

> Gaily in de cornfield, happy all de day,
> Afric's sons and daughters pass dere time away,
> Dere old massa gibs us some old Virginny rye,
> Golly, how it makes de darkies wink dar eye.

> When evening comes, de darkies home returning,
> O, happy am de niggas all dat night,
> Pompey, Dan, an all de gals a-dancing,
> While Seizer sits and laughs wid all his might.

The presumed propensity for singing and dancing among the slave population was the major premise of the minstrel show. Many of the "happy plantation darkies" were thus cast as performers eager to demonstrate to white audiences the pleasures of servitude, as in "Sing, Sing, Darkies Sing":[11]

> Sing, sing, darkies sing,
> Don't you hear the banjo ring,
> Sing, sing, darkies sing,
> Sing for the white folks, sing.

E.P. Christy's "Happy Are We Darkies So Gay," written in 1847, puts the protagonist on the stage rather than in the field, a practice which demonstrates the utilitarian function of the type within the minstrel show. This practice ignored completely the reality of slavery and concentrated on the exigencies of the stage production through the necessity for exciting opening songs, end pieces, and so forth. This, in turn, reveals the extent to which the songs avoided entanglement with the moral issue of slavery. Audiences faced with the national problem of slavery during the day could find welcome relief at night by hearing a blackface "Negro" in the theatre offer reassurance that:

Happy are we darkies so gay!
Come, let us sing and dance while we play,
We darkey minstrels' favorite lay,
With a ha, ha, ha, ha, and laugh while we play.

> Music delicious!
> O, den how sweet!
> Your kind applauses
> We hope to greet.

The situation was the same on the plantation itself; only the locale differed from the vantage point of the stage pseudo-Negro. "Gayly De Niggas Dance," reprinted in *The Negro Forget-Me-Not Songster*,[12] makes slavery appear to be little more than a frolic:

Gayly de niggas dance,
On de sand, on de sand,
Come all dat have a chance,
And join de darkey band.

Sound, sound de violin,
Show tum in de old banjo,
Let de triangle ring,
Wid de bones and de old tambo.

When de sound does rise at de broke ob day,
All in de morn, all in de morn,
To de fields dey all work away,
To hoe de yaller corn.

De niggas have a happy life,
Always gay, always gay,
Troubled with no care or strife,
But merrily work all day.

When de work's all done and de day is ober,
Dey all trots in, dey all trots in,
De niggers think themselves in clover,
Wid dere hoe-cake and de gin.

Dey hands de banjo from de wall,
And touch de string, and touch de string,
Dey join in de chorus, one and all,
And so merrily dey sing.

In song, the slave's devotion to "massa" did not always hinder the ability to see his faults, as in "Come Day, Go Day, or Massa Is A Stingy Man":[13]

> Oh, massa is a stingy man,
> And all his neighbors knows it,
> He keeps good whiskey in his house,
> And neber says, here goes it.
>
>> Sing come day, go day,
>> God send Sunday,
>> We'll drink whiskey all de week,
>> And buttermilk o' Sunday.

The mistress comes in for her share of criticism as the protagonist continues his unusually frank observation of plantation life:

> Oh, missus says we eat too much,
> An wear out too much trowses,
> She'll make us feed on atmosphere,
> And dress in nature's blowses.
>
> Oh, massa loves to hug de gals,
> And missus doesn't knows it.
> But as I like de angels too,
> I believe I won't exclose it.
>
> Oh, missus says we shouldn't eat,
> Kase we don't work a Sunday,
> But natur keeps digestion's mill,
> Agoin' as well as Monday.
>
> Massa sich a stingy man,
> I no more ketch him possum,
> I roast and eat him in de wood,
> And den I swear I loss him.

Such candid views of slave life were the exception rather than the rule. The "happy plantation darkey" was not expected to observe—merely to serve. In the sole example known in the repertoire of this period in which that most dreaded of events happened—the death of "massa" at the hands of one of his slaves—retribution came from the other slaves, who took it upon themselves to hang the culprit. This uncharactertistic piece of fantasy reinforced the myth of the happy slave, while satisfying justice against the crime of murder. But physical violence against a white person by the slave was unthinkable, so it is hardly surprising that a song on the subject was unlikely to become a lasting favorite. Audiences were not accustomed to hearing grisly details such as those recounted in "Old Master's Death":[14]

> One night, as I thought all de darkies were sleeping,
> And the wind it did moan, and my flesh it was creeping,
>> Well, what den?
> A darkey did steal from the bed which he slept on,
> And so silently crept to my old master's room.
>> Well, what den?
> Too soon I heard of my master's death,
> For I'll love him, I'll love him, while I've breath.
>
> In de morn, when de breakfast was ready to eat,
> I wondered why massy was not at his seat;
>> Well, what den?
> I went to his room—what you think there I saw?
> His corpse was all mangled and covered with gore!
>> Well, what den?
>
> We buried him in de church-yard so lowly,
> And proceeded up his grove den so lowly;
>> Solemn work!
> Our eyes filled with tears as we put the last clod on,
> To think our massy was away from us torn!
>> Our massy dear!
>
> We den took dat dark, and we bound him together;
> To see him swing up you'd a thought him a feather;
>> That was right!
> He swung to a sapling that was very tall:
> So we left him hanging, an example to all.
>> Let him hang!

The normal view of "massa" was less dramatic. He was usually seen as just and generous, and many songs mention his intention to free his slaves upon his death—a provision not always fulfilled as expected in real life.

The slave, for his part, was to be faithful and obedient. Criticism of "massa" or the conditions of bondage were to be treated as comedy or not at all. He most decidedly was not to use violence as a means of obtaining redress against the system. Fighting for his liberty did not make him a hero; it made him a serious threat to the institution of slavery—a very grave matter indeed.

The slave-master relationship was therefore standardized as the most efficacious arrangement for all concerned, somewhat in the frivolous manner described in "We Live on De Bank Ob De Ohio":[15]

> Old massa to us darkies am good,
>   Tra la la, tra la la la,
> For he gibs us our clothes and he gibs us our food,
> And we merrily work for him, for him, for him,
> And we live on de bank of de Ohio.

The "happy plantation slave" was, for all his sentimental attachment to "massa," inclined to revert to childlike behavior during his owner's absence. The fact that constant supervision was necessary to make the slave produce was seen, not as a weakness of the system, but as proof of the slave's charming but nonetheless inherent irresponsibility. In a popular hit sung by Sweeney and Whitlock, "Genny Git Your Hoe Cake Done,"[16] this theme appears in the first verse:

> Old Massa and Misses is gone away,
> Da left home one morning gest about day;
> And den you hear dat nigger say,
> Hand me down de banjo and let de nigger play.

And of course, the "happy plantation slave" was not sufficiently civilized to understand such abstract concepts as property rights; things belonging to master belonged to slave as well, as seen in "Come Back Steben."[17] The slave was not only a thief, as seen in "Whar Did You Cum From," but he showed a casual attitude toward the care of the tools which "massa" provided for his work:

COME BACK, STEBEN

> Good news, Steben—good news!
> Good news, Steben—good news!
> What is dem!
> Why, massa bought a new wagon—
> Pompey was de driver—
> An' he run agin a gate-post,
> An' smash 'em all to nofen!

Oh Lord, ladies! don't you mind Steben!
Steben am so deceiben' dat his daddy won't belieb him!

Come back, Steben—come back!
Come back, Steben—come back!
I'm a com—
Oh, come back Steben! for you am de berry man what stole
massa's blue coat!
Now fotch back de money!

Get out ob dat, you bones—get out ob dat!
Get out ob dat, you bones—get out ob dat!
Oh, get out ob dat, you bones—you am de berry man what stole
massa's sheep-head,
For to make dem dar bones out ob!

Inconsistencies in the picture of the "happy plantation slave"
were not especially bothersome to songwriters, although unpopular
images, such as the rebellious slave, were quickly dropped. Treatment
of the theme of the "happy plantation slave" evolved into two
separate types: the carefree, happy stereotype as the basis for lively
comic songs; and the contented, loyal servant as the subject of
countless sentimental ballads. The former type never lost popularity
while the latter grew into the most compelling of maudlin fantasies in
which nostalgia, love, and sheer emotion swayed many toward the
belief that here—in the flesh—was the real American black.

The "happy plantation slave" became perceptibly older in songs
of both types. Virility, when displayed by the subject of the song, was
no particular virtue. The potential threat of the belligerent young male
qualified him for special treatment in song, as will be seen later.

The comic treatment of the "happy slave" myth is exemplified by
"The Fine Old Colored Gentleman," a loose parody of "The Fine
Old English Gentleman."[18] Many versions of the song were made,
and several eminent writers claimed authorship. The 1843 edition
used in the present study cites D.D. Emmett as the author of the text
while giving no credit to the composer. Henry Russell utilized the
words in slightly altered form in another version but composed a new
melody. Songster versions rarely follow the Emmett text closely, and
comparison of these with the Emmett version reveals interesting
parallels in thought between various authors. Emmett's "The Fine
Old Colored Gentleman"[19] illustrates the point adequately, however:

In Tenn'see as I've heard say, dare once did use to dwell,
A fine old colored Gemman and dis nigger knowed him well,
Dey used to call him Sambo or somethin near the same,
De reason why da call dat was, becase it was his name;
For Sambo was a Gemman, one of de oldest kind.

His temper was very mild when he was let alone,
But when you get him dander up, he spunk to de back bone,
He whale de sugar off ye by de double rule of three
And whip his wate in wildcats when he got on a spree.

When dis nigger took a snooze,
    it was in a nigger crowd,
He used to keep them all awake,
    because he snored so loud,
He drawed himself up in a knot,
    His knees did touch his chin,
De bedbugs had to clar de track,
    when he stretched down his shin.

He had a good old banjo,
    so well he kept it strung,
He used to sing the good old song,
    of "go it while you're young,"
He sung so long and sung so loud,
    he scared the pigs and goats,
Because he took a pint of yeast
    to raise the highest notes.

When dis nigga stood upright
    and wasn't slantindicular,
He measured about 'leven feet,
    he wasn't ver partic'clar,
For he could jump and run a race,
    and do a little hoppin',
And when he got a goin' fast,
    the devil couldn't stop 'im.

Old Father Time kept rolling by,
    and age grew on apace,
The wool all dropt off from his head,
    and wrinkled was his face,
He was de oldest nigger
    what lived on dat plantation,
He didn't fear de debil den,
    nor all of his relation.

> Old age come on, his teeth dropt out,
>   it made no odds to him,
> He eat as many taters
>   and he drank as many gin.
> He swallowed two small railroads
>   wid a spoonful of ice cream,
> And a locomotive bulgine,
>   While dey blowin' off de steam.
>
> One bery windy morning,
>   dis good old nigger died,
> De niggers came from odder states,
>   and loud for joy dey cried;
> He layin' down upon a bench,
>   as strait as any post,
> De 'coons did roar, de possums howled
>   when he guv up de ghost.
>
> De niggers held an inquest,
>   when dey heard of his death,
> De verdict of de jury was,
>   he died for want of breath;
> Dey went to work and skinned him,
>   and then they had it dried,
> And de head of dis here banjo,
>   is off dat old nigger's hide.

The gruesome finale described in the last verse of the Emmett version offended some publishers, who amended it or left it out entirely in reprinted versions. The song was too popular to ignore, however; it appeared twice in *The Negro Foget-Me-Not Songster*,[20] once with the title altered to read: "De Genteel Fine Ole Nigga." The indelicate verse was changed to:

> De niggers hold an inques'
>   when dey heard ob his deff,
> De verdict ob de jury was—
>   He died for want ob breff;
> Dey laid 'im in an old pine chest,
>   So fast dey den did lock it,
> Dey found dese verses I be jist sung
>   in his old trowsers pocket.

The other version printed in the songster, as well as Henry Russell's, omitted the last verse altogether. Russell, however, was something of an opportunist and not above taking his inspiration from others, although his own imagination was fertile enough. It is possible that his version as performed was not the version he printed as original work. For all his aspirations to make music "the vehicle of grand thoughts and noble sentiments,"[21] Russell's record as a minstrel songsmith was mediocre.

Sentimental treatment of the "happy plantation slave" is in a direct line of descent from its ancestors, the English ballads of the earlier period, such as "The Desponding Negro," and "The Poor Black Boy." The eventual dominance of the sentimental treatment was perhaps a concession to the time, which placed emotion on a higher plane than discernment in most of its musical efforts.

The pinnacle of mawkishness was reached with the lachrymose effusions of Stephen Foster, whose "Old Folks At Home," "Old Black Joe," "Massa's In De Cold, Cold Ground," and numerous others convinced millions that here, at last, the "real" black was presented in song by someone sympathetic to his character. The dissembling effect of Foster's songs was—and is—tremendous. His songs are still sung today, and there are those who cling to the notion that the Foster conception of the black is fact rather than fable.

One of the first "carry-me-backs," or the treatment of the stage-black as a sentimental, happy slave, "De Floating Scow of Ole Virginia"[22] ranks as an example of that type of song whose influence exceeds its fame. Charles White is acknowledged as the composer, although some editions include James Sanford, who introduced it on stage.[23]. Historians seem to relish calling this song "Carry Me Back to Old Virginny" and drawing comparisons between this and the famous Bland song of that title. Actually, the subtitle of "De Floating Scow of Ole Virginia" is "Oh Carry Me Back to Ole Virginia Shore," admittedly a small point, but the songs are musically different as well. The sentiment is, of course, the same in both instances.

The pattern for subsequent "carry-me-backs" is fairly well defined in "De Floating Scow of Ole Virginia." The protagonist looks back on happier days as a slave and longs to return to the South to die. The female connection in this song is slight in comparison to the emphasis placed on that figure in songs of the type which followed.

Characteristic terms referring to presumed black interests in life—
"banjo," "possum," "coon"—became tearful reminders rather than
comic attributes specifically designed to elicit laughter. The melody,
while hardly as mournful as those of later "carry-me-backs," is
sufficiently grave to match the doleful theme.

DE FLOATING SCOW OF OLE VIRGINIA

De floating scow ob ole Virginia,
Dat I worked from day to day,
A raking 'mong de oyster beds,
To me it was but play.
But now I'm old and feeble too,
I cannot work any more,
Oh! carry me back to ole Virginia,
To ole Virginia shore.

O, if I was but young again,
I would lead a differet [sic] life,
And I'd save money, and buy a farm,
And take Dinah for my wife;
But now old age, he holds me tight
And my limbs are growing sore,
Den carry me back to ole Virginia,
To ole Virginia shore.

Oh, when I'm dead and gone to rest.
Lay de ole banjo by my side,
Let de Possum an de coon to de funeral go,
For dey was my only pride;
Den in soft repose I take my sleep,
And I'll dream for eber more,
Dat carrying back to ole Virginia,
To ole Virginia shore.

The formula for the sentimental "happy plantation slave"
consisted—with the exception of those emphasizing themes of love,
which will be studied separately—of three main elements: recollections of a happy childhood; separation from home and family; expression of fervent longing to return to the ambience of childhood as life
draws to a close. Allowable variations were few. The locale of the
happy childhood, for instance, was invariably Southern. "Down in"
became synonymous with Southern localities, especially the picture

of a social situation in which the black was carefree and supremely happy under the comforting and fatherly care of "ole massa."

The second element—separation—was essentially an attempt to avoid the reality of slavery. Constant repetition of the notion that either the slave or free black could move about at will in the United States endowed this fallacy with an aura of fact, while in actuality their movements during this period were severely limited by most state laws. Songwriters were aware of this, but the longing for a fictional childhood home would have made little sense had the protagonist remained there in bondage throughout his life. The suggestion of utter freedom of movement implies even more strongly that songwriters were unwilling to admit in their songs that the land of the free was indeed the home of millions of slaves.

The last element contained the consummate irony: the slave, having gained freedom, wished to abandon this most precious possession and return to the scene of his childhood because of nothing more profound than homesickness. Although such cases did occasionally happen, the overwhelming evidence of ex-slaves themselves, fighting and dying in droves to achieve liberty and to keep it once it was obtained, makes this about-face in song blatantly illogical. But logic was not, alas, a vital ingredient, nor a major virtue, of the "carry-me-back."

These elements of the "carry-me-back" withstood the test of time and, with minor variation, have been utilized in more modern song products in which the origin of the type is less clear or forgotten altogether.

Minstrel melodists managed to vary details of the "carry-me-back" without changing its essential structure, as with "Our Hut On The Old Plantation,"[24] which contains both a mother *and* father, a bow toward biological necessity which nonetheless ran counter to the myth. The father image evoked the specter of an authority set between the slave and "massa," who was supposedly the only power that the slave was bound to respect. This may account for the fact that "Our Hut On The Old Plantation" was only moderately successful. Songwriters were quick to recognize the anomaly of allowing slaves to have fathers, and soon the "happy plantation slaves" were once again being born in song through some mysterious unisexual process which left them fatherless—but which satisfied the stereotype.

In other respects, "Our Hut On The Old Plantation" obediently
follows the formula. Frank B. Somers wrote the words and music of
the song, and it was something of a minor hit to judge by the number of
reprintings that appeared in the 1850's. The version cited is taken
from a broadside published by A.W. Auner of Philadelphia. It is
copyrighted by J. Couenhoven, also of Philadelphia.

OUR HUT ON THE OLD PLANTATION

Far away down is the good old farm,
  Where we darkies used to dwell,
Oh! how we've often longed to see
  The place we loved so well.
There first we saw the morning sun,
  As it lighted up the sky,
Oh! take us back to the sweet old spot,
  For there we all wish to die.

    The darkies sing as on we roam,
    And tell throughout creation,
    The happy time we had at home,
    Our hut on de old plantation.

Father and Mother old now and gray,
  Still do hoe and shell de corn,
While we, their children, work far away,
  From the spot where we were born,
From poor old Massa 'twas hard to part,
  He always was so good and kind;
And we could search the world all over,
  His like we ne'er should find.

Oh, 'tis many years that we've been free,
  But here no longer we can stay,
Our hearts they pine for our own little hut,
  Down in the South, far away,
When will the happy time come round,
  When we darkies may go home,
And from that blessed good old farm,
  We never more need roam.

Regardless of the mention of "father," a temporary aberration in
the formula, the picture of the early life of the song's protagonist
remained relatively static. The point was emphasized in both the

comic and the sentimental "carry-me-back" types. Thus the comic "My Heart's In Mississippi"[25] contains a chorus and first verse which are hardly distinguishable from its sentimental counterpart:

> My heart's in Mississippi,
> 'Tis de place whar I was born;
> 'Tis dar I planted sugar cane,
> 'Tis dar I hoed de corn.
> Dey have taken me to Texas,
> A thousand miles below;
> Yet my heart's in Mississippi, boys,
> Wherever I go.
>
> Yet my heart's in Mississippi,
> 'Tis de place whar I was born;
> 'Tis dar I planted sugar cane,
> 'Tis dar I hoed de corn.

It is only in the second and subsequent verses that the comic character of the song emerges:

> New York may boast of beauties,
> Dat lemonade de street;
> But dey never hab a sixpence,
> To axe you to a treat.
> De Mississippi yaller gales,
> Dey always treat dar beau;
> Den my heart's in Mississippi,
> Wherever I go.

The picture of blissful contentment as seen in the first part of the "carry-me-back" turns to utter bleakness as the slave discovers that freedom is no more than the waters of Marah—a bitter disillusionment which strips him of his security and throws him at the mercy of a materialistic world. This point is made explicit in "Old River Farm; or, The Darkey's Regret," written by "R.S.M." and set to music by Stewart Macaulay:[26]

OLD RIVER FARM

The long day is done and I sit all alone,
As the night's darkening shadows creep chilly and drear,

From my o'erflowing heart will the bitter tears start,
As I list for the voices of my old friends to cheer;
There's no spot like home where I mournfully roam,
And the freedom once craved is a name at the best,
And I long for the day when they'll put me away,
And this sad heavy heart will be sleeping at rest,
My kindred are laid 'neath the old woodland shade,
And I sigh for the spot where in childhood I played,
For I'm sent to be free o'er a strange land and sea,
Where no smiles of the past light the long day for me.

I miss every charm of the old river farm,
I miss the old fields with their gold waving grain,
The small patch of soil made so dear by my toil,
All the old things I loved I shall ne'er see again;
Yet my thoughts must still cling round the cool mossy spring,
Where the grape vine I planted so leafly entwined,
And this land of the free holds no bright hopes for me,
Half so sweet as the mem'ries I've left behind.
My kindred (etc.).

It is interesting to compare the sentiments expressed in this song with the pro-slavery arguments which were flowing from the pens of Southern intellectuals and statesmen during the 1850's, when it was written. George Fitzhugh, for example, issued a scathing indictment of Northern capitalism in his defence of slavery in a pamphlet, *Slavery Justified, by a Southerner* (Fredericksburg, 1850), in which he insists that "liberty and equality are not only destructive to the morals, but to the happiness of society."[27] Slavery, on the other hand, not only assures the well-being of the slave, but ennobles the master in a South where "all is peace, quiet, plenty and contentment."[28]

But nowhere in the upside-down logic of the pro-slavery rhetoricians was there a more poetic—or insane—picture of the "happy plantation slave" painted than in Henry Hughes' *A Treatise on Sociology, Theoretical and Practical* (Philadelphia, 1854), as he rhapsodized over the future of what he chose to call "warranteeism with the ethnical qualification," rather than the more accurate but inflammatory term, "slavery":

Then, in the plump flush of full-feeding health, the happy warrantees shall banquet in plantation-refectories; worship in plantation-chapels; learn in plantation-schools; or, in plantation saloons, at the close of evening . . . chant old songs, tell tales; or, to the metred rattle of chattering castanets, or flutes, or rumbling tamborines, dance down the moon and evening star; and after slumbers in plantation-dormitories, over whose gates Health and Rest sit smiling at the feet of Wealth and Labor, rise at the music-crowing of the morning-conchs, to begin again welcome days of jocund toil. . . .[29]

Northern criticism of Southern slavery infuriated the pro-slavery forces; but the censure which came from abroad, particularly from England, caused anguished rebuttals in profusion to appear. Most replies to English critics adopted the position that foreign condemnation of American slavery was a cheap shot: the distortion of a situation which was purely an internal affair. The impulse to compare the lot of the Southern slave to that of the "wage-slaves" of English and Northern capitalists was irresistible.[30] Songwriters joined the defenders of slavery by inserting verses in songs aimed at discrediting anti-slavery arguments, as in "Pompey's Trip to New York," an oblique attack on Abolitionists who carried their campaigns to England:

> Lor' bless the Southern ladies, and my old Southern home,
> But don't come back, Aunt Sarah, in England make a fuss,
> Go talk against your country, put money in your purse,
> And when we happy darkies you pity in your prayer,
> Oh! don't forget the WHITE SLAVE that's starvin' over there![31]

And in a verse of "Pop Goes the Weasel":[32]

> John Bull tells, in de ole cow's hum,
> How Uncle Sam used *Uncle Tom*,
> While he makes some white folks *slaves* at home,
> By "Pop goes de Weasel!"

The establishment of a viable image of the "happy plantation slave" required more than irrelevant assaults against capitalism, however. The picture of the old man, alone and dreaming dreams, was also incomplete. Songs which approached the myth as pure comedy were in themselves successful in portraying the carefree slave; but the songwriters were not long in discovering a formula by which the "happy plantation slave" not only sprang to life in the popular mind, but implanted himself there as one of America's most enduring images: they presented him with a woman. Godlike, minstrel song-smiths perfected Black Adam's Eden by providing him with a helpmeet, thus completing the illusion of supreme bliss. This "carry-me-back" with added love interest assumed a predominant position in minstrel literature, and soon developed into the lachrymose, syrupy effusion which still tinctures the image many hold of the South.

There are more examples of the "carry-me-back" with the added love theme than could possibly be included in a single chapter. The formula was essentially unchanged: the "carry-me-back" was left intact, and the love theme characterized by sentiment heightened by some form of pathos—usually the death or separation of the female partner. The formula tended to obscure the father figure in its earlier stages of development; ultimately the father figure was dropped altogether. The identification of the female with the mythical, idyllic plantation existence led to the eventual identification of the entire South as an essentially feminine entity.

The father figure is still present in the early example, "The Old Corn Mill,"[33] although dominance of the female is seen to be emerging through reference to the mother figure as well as the lover "Katy." "Carry-me-back" elements are left unchanged.

THE OLD CORN MILL

De home of my childhood, dat dearly beloved spot,
Whar de yaller corn am growing round my fader's cot,
Dar many happy days I spent, I yet remember well,
Wid my kind old mudder down by de old Corn Mill.

> Den hurry me home to de old Corn Mill,
> To my fader's old cot on de top ob de hill,
> For I am getting weary and not afraid to die,
> Oh lay me side my mudder, in de ground whar Katy lie.

Full well I remember, how with boyish delight,
We met roun de pine-knot at de night,
I lub to see de ole corn mill, and watch de wheel go round,
I lub my good old mudder in de cold cold ground.

Oh for dat old corn mill to memory dear,
I would eat de bright corn cake with merry good cheer,

But de old corn mill am passing away,
And de crazy old wheel am gone to decay.

And Katy I loved, her grave am so cold,
De old folks am dead an de young ones am sold,
Dem happy days am ober, free from sorrow and ill,
When we all lived at home by de old corn mill.

Charles White's "The Old Pine Tree,"[34] written in 1849, approached the ideal more closely than the above example in its exclusion of the father figure and its concentration on the details of the formula. The main departure in this instance is the happy ending, wherein the couple is reunited after a lengthy separation.

THE OLD PINE TREE

Oh! darkies now I'm gown to sing, de truth to you I'll tell,
Ob happy days dat I hab seen wid my dear Nancy Bell,
Oh! I wish dat I was back again way down in Tennisee,
Wid my dear Nancy by my side beneath the old pine tree.

    Tis many a night since first we met,
    Neath dat old pine tree,
    An dar we told our tales ob lub,
    How happy we shall be.

My lub has left me long ago, whar she is no one can tell,
An I am nearly crazy now, for my dear Nancy Bell,
But I dreamt last night when all was still, dat she'd come
        back to me,
An I would yet see happy days beneath de old pine tree.

I quite forgot I was so old, it seems to me a dream,
Dat three score years hab past and gone since I was seventeen;
But everything is right at last, an Nancy is true to me,
An when we die oh let us rest beneath de old pine tree.

The happy ending had only a short vogue in the "carry-me-back" with the love theme. A clue to the logic which caused the happy ending to decline is shown in "Pretty Dilly Burn,"[35] a song which describes how the lovers, who belonged to different masters, were brought together after the protagonist's master purchased her and "gave her as my bride." The final verse ends with the lines:

And now we're happy in our cot, and massa's pleased to see,
How two fond hearts that truly love, tho' black, can happy be.

Blacks, since they were assumed to be less than human, were not
ordinarily considered capable of love according to white values, and
marriage for them was something of a charade. A marriage between
slaves had little moral or legal status under the system which regarded
them as chattel. Mating of slaves for breeding purposes might have
been practiced as a form of "marriage" but it most decidedly was not
wedlock in the white sense. Thus, the idea that blacks might sanctify
their union in the manner of whites found favor in song mainly as a
comic situation. Some writers treated the female of the song in the
manner of "Jane Monroe":[36]

> A darkey trader came one day,
>   And bought my gal from me,
> And left me here alone to mourn
>   Beneaf de cypress tree;
> It filled my heart wid grief an' pain
>   To think dey'd treat me so,
> But I live in hopes to meet again
>   My charming Jane Monroe.

Songsmiths found numerous ways in which to interdict a slave
marriage in song. In "Rosa Lee,"[37] the mate "Cotched a shocking
cold"; "Sweet Rose Of Caroline"[38] was bitten by a rattlesnake and
died; but "Mary Blane,"[39] a popular favorite, suffered a variety of misfortunes, depending upon which of the several versions is consulted.

Four sheet music editions of "Mary Blane" form the basis of the
present analysis and discussion, including an interesting "New Mary
Blane," with words by W. Guernsey and music arranged by George
Barker. The versions attributed to F.C. German, set to music by J.H.
Howard, are the most common, however, and here serve as the point
of departure for study. These versions are textually and musically
identical, and they were extensively reprinted in songsters, broadsides, and collections over the years; differences exist primarily in the
form of alterations of type and illustrations of the covers.

Adherence to the formula for such songs is relatively strict in all
the examples; yet the various writers often betrayed their own feelings
through alteration of details within the mold, as can be seen.

MARY BLANE

I once did know a pretty Gal
And took her for my wife,
She came from Louisiana,
I lik'd her as my life,
We happy lib'd togethder [sic]
She nebber caus'd me pain,
But one dark and dreary night
I lost poor Mary Blane.

> Oh, Farewell, Farewell,
> Poor Mary Blane,
> One faithful heart will think of you,
> Farewell, Farewell,
> Poor Mary Blane,
> If we ne'er meet again.

While in de woods I go at night,
A hunting for some game,
A nigger came to my old hut
And stole my Mary Blane.
Long times gwan by it grieb'd me much,
To tink no tidings came,
I hunt de woods both day and night,
To find poor Mary Blane.

I often ask'd for Mary Blane,
My Massa he did scold,
And said you saucy nigger boy,
If you must know she's sold.
If dat's de case she cannot live,
Thro' out a weary life,
Oh let me die and lay me by
My poor heart broken wife.

Superficial differences between this version and the others show
an effort to refine and expand the basic idea. "I once did know" of the
first verse changed to "I once did love" strengthens the emotion.
Replacing the "pretty" with the symbolic "yaller" as a descriptive
adjective shows the early use of the lightened skin color as symbolism
for greater beauty.

Changing the location from Louisiana to Virginia is a minor point
inasmuch as both are Southern; of greater significance is the failure, in
the Fiot-Mayo edition, of the protagonist to marry the heroine:

> When fust I saw her lubly face,
> My 'fections she did win,
> And oft I hasten to de place
> Where dwelt my Mary Blane.
> We liv'd together many years,
> And she was still the same,
> In joy and sorrow, smiles and tears,
> I lov'd my Mary Blane.

The manner in which Mary disappeared also reveals a curious reluctance on the part of songwriters to admit the realities of slavery:

> Unto de woods I went one day,
> A hunting ob de game,
> De Indians came unto my hut
> And stole my Mary Blane.

In "The New Mary Blane," Guernsey offers a more plausible explanation:

> De white man come into my house,
> And took poor Mary Blane.

With the blame being shifted from the "nigger" to the "Indian" as the culprit in Mary's abduction, it is refreshing candor to find that the real villain is a white man. But this sole example of naming the white man as the person responsible for this crime was too close to reality to last. Reprints of "Mary Blane" alternate between the blame being placed on the "Nigger" or the "Indian" with the white man guiltless.

Comic representation of the "happy plantation slave" with the added love interest follows the same general format as the sentimental type. Nostalgia for the South and the maternal connotations are included—but as comedy. The primary differences between the two types are found in the characteristic callousness of the comic representations as opposed to the naivete of the sentimental. The coarse, cutting humor of the comic type found favor with audiences despite these apparently contradictory elements. The most incredible fact emerging from the study of the comic songs on this subject is that audiences—and subsequent historians—could be so conditioned as to assume that the real-life black could have had any part in the production of such songs as "Whoop De Doodle Do,"[40] sung by Dan Emmett "with thunders of applause":

> Simon had a son born,
> Whoop de doodle do,
> Simon had a son born,
> Whoop de doodle do,
> Simon had a son born,
> You'd think she was a daughter,
> Yaller Sal, de Georgia gal,
> An' de big buck in de water.

The elements of the formula for the sentimental songs are present within this song, but the meaning is clearly worlds away from the emotional surface pity of the sentimental type.

Other comic representations were less splenetic in content, perhaps because the subject itself was recognized as undeserving of such treatment; yet the basic insult managed to survive. "The Jolly Raftsman"[41] adopts a posture of ingenuousness which approaches the preposterous:

> I was born in ole Virginny
> And my little gals name is Dine,
> She always told me the prettiest nigger,
> Was Dandy Jim ob Caroline.
>
>> My raft is by the shore,
>> She's light and free,
>> To be a jolly raftsman's
>> The life for me.
>> And as we glide along
>> Our song shall be,
>> Dearest Dine, I love but thee.
>
> Cum, oh cum wid me, my dearest Dine,
> You shall go to de eastern states,
> Where you can tend my oyster cellar,
> You can hurry up de cakes.
>
> A gemblum come from de Alabama;
> To steal my pretty little Dine from me,
> So den I taut I'd take her wid me,
> To de nordern country.

> When we got dere she was lubly to see,
> De berry next day she was wedded to me;
> So now bofe voices togedder agree,
> We lib in de sweetest harmony.

Successful escape to the North and marital bliss were unusual fare for minstrel songs; more often, the Northern adventure yielded frustration and a strong desire to return to the South, and marriage ended in separation. Comic songs could allow such aberrations since the whole matter was presented as a joke, as in another example, "Lovely Rosanna; or, Clem Tanner's Bride":[42]

> I'm a gwan back to de old plantation,
>   Away down Louisiana,
> De garden ob de whole creation,
>   And de home ob my dear Rosanna.
> But a long time past, since I braced her last,
>   And my lub is running ober,
> But I ain't got far, I'll soon be dar,
>   Den I'll be in de highest kind ob clover.
>
>   Oh, lobely Rosanna, I'll be at yer side,
>   And I'll nebber rest till de parson's blest
>   Clem Tanner and his bride.

"Clem" adhered to formula in returning to the South; but the song does not recount how successful was his anticipated marriage.

Almost as a burlesque, James Sanford's "Missy Lucy Neale"[43] fits the mold of the comic "carry-me-back" with added love interest:

MISS LUCY NEALE

> I was born in Alabama,
>   My master's name was Meal,
> He used to own a yellow gal,
>   Her name was Lucy Neale.
>
>   Oh! poor Lucy Neale,
>   Oh! poor Lucy Neale,
>   If I had her in my arms,
>   How happy I would feel.
>
> Miss Lucy she was handsome,
>   From de head down to de heel,
> And all de niggas fell in love,
>   Wid my pretty Lucy Neale.

> She used to go out wid us,
>   To pick cotton in de field,
> And dar is whar I fell in love,
>   Wid my pretty Lucy Neale.
>
> I asked Miss Lucy would she have me,
>   How glad she made me feel,
> When she gave to me her heart,
>   My pretty Lucy Neale.
>
> My massa he did sell me,
>   Because he thought I'd steal,
> Which caused a separation,
>   Of myself and Lucy Neale.
>
> . . . .
>
> Miss Lucy she was taken sick,
>   She eat too much corn meal,
> De doctor he did gib her up,
>   Alas! poor Lucy Neale.
>
> One day I got a letter,
>   And jet black was the seal,
> It was de announcement ob de death
>   Of my poor Lucy Neale.

The text of "Miss Lucy Neale" does not demonstrate the humor of the song unless the musical accompaniment is added. A somewhat similar situation occurs with another song of the same type, Joseph Murphy's "Lou'siana Belle,"[44] which directs the performer to render the piece "alla niggerando." The humor becomes more direct in the last two verses, as the protagonist rhapsodizes:

> Dere's Dandy Jim ob Caroline,
> I knows him by de swell,
> Tryin' to come it mighty fine,
> Wid de Lou'siana Belle.
>
> Dere's first de B and den de E,
> And den de double LL;
> Anodder E to the end ob dat,
> Spells Lou'siana Belle.

The circle representing the relationship of the sentimental "carry-me-back" in all its forms with the comic types can be closed with the rollicking "Massa's Old Plantation," written by D. Loughery and set to music by Harry Lake.[45] This comic "carry-me-back" has all the elements of the sentimental "carry-me-back" except the lachrymose illusion of pity. Here, the deceit is complete. Words and music are combined with consummate skill to picture a "happy plantation slave" who fulfills Hughes' romantic image of the "happy warrantee;" a picture so far removed from reality that the imagination is strained to think that it could have been credited by reasonable persons on either side of the Mason-Dixon line. However, the incredible output of such songs leaves no other conclusion.

MASSA'S OLD PLANTATION

When I was little and very young,
My heart wid joy was glowing,
And happy were de days I spent,
Wid all de darkies hoeing,
Old massa he was very kind,
And missus she was kinder,
I wish to see dem all again
In good old Carolina.

    Hurrah, Hurrah, for massa's old plantation,
    Hurrah, Hurrah, I'm going back again,
    Dere's not a spot on all de earth
    Nor yet in all creation,
    Dat's half so near dis darkies heart,
    As massa's old plantation.

Dere I left my yellow gal,
De sweetest in all nature,
I often dream I have my arms
Around de lovely creature;
I'll never leave my love again,
My own, my sweet Alvania,
She is de belle of all de South,
De pride of old Car'lina.

Dere's de place where fun am good,
And darkies hearts am lightest,
And when de banjo gins to tum,
De gals eyes am de brightest,
Dere's coons and possums plenty dere
In eb'ry swamp and hollow;

And massa's dogs can scear dem up,
De darkies den will follow.

Farewell to roaming now,
I'm done wid dis dat's sartin,
And when I sing you dis here song,
For massa's home I'm startin,
Oh how old massa den will smile
And missus face will brighten,
De darkies all will welcome me,
And den my heart will lighten.

The protagonist of this model of mendacity had effected a self-cure, perhaps, of that dread slave disease which had been discovered only a few years before by the respected Southern physician, Dr. Samuel Cartwright. He found that "Drapetomania," or the disease of the mind which causes the slave to run away, was cured by "whipping the devil out of them."[46]

The love song which provided "carry-me-backs" with their love interest stemmed directly from the archetypical "Coal Black Rose" and in due course developed its own set of cliches. The genre was one of the mainstays of the minstrel repertoire and literally thousands of songs of pseudo-black love appeared. In its simplest form and in its associations with the Southern Cavalier myth, the love song proved one of the most durable of all types of songs with black subjects. The crudity of the "coon song" of the 1890's and the suggestiveness of the black female's sexuality of the 1920's, seen in the "Red-hot Mama" of the "hotcha" song types, all derive from the love song of the period under discussion.

As with the "carry-me-back," the love song fell into two broad categories of sentimental or comic representations. The sentimental love song, as might be expected, bespoke a deep and enduring affection which would have been less demeaning to the black image had the approach been based on something more substantial than myth. The comic representation of the black female, on the other hand, made few pretentions of serious intent and presented to the public a black female who was hardly a flattering model.

Many comic love songs emphasized physical attributes of the black female implying that ugliness was a desirable quality. The blackness which was abhorrent to most whites was occasionally presented as a physical feature demanding a comic solution, or at least apology, as in "Brack Ey'd Susianna":[47]

> I been to de east, I been to de west,
>   I been to Souf Car'lina,
> And ob all de gals I lub de bes,
>   Is my brack ey'd Susianna.
>
> She's brack, dat's a fac,
> She's brack, dat's a fac,
>
> I been to de east, I been to de west,
>   I been to Souf Car'lina,
> And ob all de gals I lub de bes,
>   Is my brack ey'd Susianna.

Soon after the establishment of the pseudo-black love song, the "coal black" of the female began to adopt a lighter shade in many of the songs. She became "lasses" (molasses) in color; or more frequently "yaller," as has been seen in "My Heart's In Mississippi," "Mary Blane," "Miss Lucy Neale," and so on. Among the reasons for albescence of the black female subject might be counted a natural or assumed attitude of loathing for blackness itself, especially in its association with evil and filth. Extreme darkness did not enhance the association of the female with the South where womankind was regarded as lily-white, helpless, and pure. In addition, the sexual implications of the love theme may have led the performer—who was, after all, white underneath his burnt cork—to reserve his highest praise for beauty that was nearer his own color. With only a few exceptions, in any event, the general rule developed in the love song: the lighter the color, the greater the beauty of the female subject. The color of the female associated with the South became so light, in fact, that by the second decade of the twentieth century, she was often completely white. Even in those instances where the color remained "yaller," many listeners of the twentieth century did not realize that the subject of the song, as in the case of the 1950's revival of "The Yaller Rose of Texas," was a black female.

The desirability of the "yaller" female can be seen in "Will No Yaller Gal Marry Me":[48]

> All the gals are getting married, dropping off on every side—
> Ah, I fear too long I've tarried, seeking, sighing for a bride—

Seeking, sighing for a bride;
Listen now, all darkey beauties, I am handsome as you see—
Will no yaller gal marry, marry, will no yaller gal marry me.

There is no flaw in the Rose of "The Yellow Rose of Texas."[49] In this love song, the pride expressed for the locality takes second place to the female, diluting somewhat the "carry-me-back" spirit. The sheet music version of "The Yellow Rose of Texas" lists the composer only as "J.K." and the original title reads "Yellow," instead of the commonly cited "Yaller," which leads to the presumption that the intent to demean the black was somewhat less than usual. The words seem to bear this out; but the song is, nonetheless, contributory to the overall picture of the black as a stereotype:

THE YELLOW ROSE OF TEXAS

There's a yellow rose in Texas, that I am going to see,
No other darkey knows her, no darkey only me,
She cried so when I left her, it like to broke my heart,
And if I ever find her, we never more will part.

CHORUS: She's the sweetest rose of color,
     this darkey ever knew,
    Her eyes are bright as diamonds,
     they sparkle like the dew,
    You may talk about your Dearest May,
     and sing of Rosa Lee,
    But the yellow rose of Texas
     beats the belles of Tennessee.

Where the Rio Grande is flowing, and the starry skies are bright,
She walks along the river in the quiet summer night;
She thinks if I remember, when we parted long ago,
I promis'd to come back again, and not to leave her so.

Oh! now I'm going to find her, for my heart is full of woe,
And we'll sing the song together, that we sung so long ago;
We'll play the banjo gaily, and we'll sing the songs of yore,
And the yellow rose of Texas shall be mine for ever-more.

Not all the "yaller" females were so gallantly treated in song. The tendency to make the virtues and physical appearance of the female subject an object of humor can be seen in "The Yaller Gal With A Josey On":[50]

> Her form was round, her step was light—
> But, wan't her bustle heavy?

later, the fact that the blushing black was of a somewhat different shade than her blushing white counterpart does not pass without comment:

> She blush'd quite blue, and then she said,
> "You're quite a dandy, John";

The difficulties of married folk are common fare in songs of English-speaking people all over the world; but here, as in other songs of marriage among the blacks, the implication is strong that the marriage contract was of slight importance:

> I married her that very day,
> A week we lived in clover;
> But soon my lov'd one ran away
> With Joe the cattle drover.
> And now she troubles me no more,
> Good lor!—I'm glad she's gone,
> For she was the taring yaller gal
> That had a josey on!

This compares to the final verse of "Will No Yaller Gal Marry Me?" in which the protagonist, after having vowed to "swim de wide Atlantic" in order to win the love of his woman, declares:

> All is over, I am married, what a hasty fool was I—
> Where's the end of all creation, let, oh, let me hither fly—
> Help! oh, help me, Mister Lawyer, cut the rope and set me free,
> I will sell myself forever, if you will unmarry me!

Statements such as these could hardly be expected to enhance the images of the black as a family man, nor of his wife as constant companion and faithful helpmeet.

Facets of the stereotyped black female image began to assume the character of clichés in the minstrel songs. The comic representation of the female was incomplete without some mention of grotesqueness associated with the black. In *The Negro Forget-me-not Songster* alone, there are more than twenty songs which make reference to physical malformations of the black female, especially her feet, which seemed to fascinate songwriters by the size of the heel as well as the overall length. "Jumbo Jum" states this sentiment in general terms:

> Oh, she looked so very fine,
> She was the real superfine;
> Of all the wenches that I meet,
> I never seed one wid such feet.

Another way of suggesting that the black female's foot was extra large is found in various versions of "Lucy Long":

> She leaves a strong impression
> Wherever she does go;
> Her footsteps mark the gravel,
> As easily as snow.

and:

> Oh Miss Lucy when she trabbles,
> She always lebes a mark,
> Ob her footsteps on de grabble,
> You can see dem in de dark.

The heel's length was the main attraction, however, as seen in "Way Down South In The Alabama":

> Before I left we danced two reels,
> De holler ob her foot war back ob her heels.

"Julina Johnson" was somewhat more graphically portrayed:

> I took Julina from her home,
> And we trabled thro' the fields,
> She got fast in de ditch and could not get out,
> For de largeness ob dem heels!

One version of "Bowery Gals" contains the verse:

> Den we stopp'd awhile and had some talk,
> O we had some talk,
> O we had some talk,

> And her heel cover'd up the whole side-walk,
> As she stood right by me.

"Ginger Blue" ingenuously informs the listener that the outlandish foot was common to male blacks as well as the black female. A spoken dialogue addresses itself to the description of the female:

> I golly, I tell you wot, dare was one nigga wench wat
> had such almighty big feet dat wen she gan to dance,
> dey had to open de back door, to let her heels go down
> into de cellar. Whew!

Two verses touch upon the same phenomenon as applied to the male:

> As I was gwan down town,
> De other day,
> And tinking about nothing in particular,
> I come across a nigger,
> Wat cut a mighty figger,
> I golly you tink he was a tickler.
> He swelled in de middle,
> And spread at de heel,
> But he couldn't come de busterations science
> Ob walk chalk, Ginger Blue, etc.
>
> De niggas in dis place,
> Count on dere handsome face,
> But dey can't trick de niggas in Virginny,
> Dar noses are too flat,
> And dere wool is curled too much,
> Like de deck of de ship from ole Guinea.
> Dey put dere feet in small shoes,
> But it's all no use,
> For de toes will push up de nigga's heel,
> When they walk chalk, Ginger Blue, etc.

Negroid facial features, as may be noted in the above example, were natural objects of ridicule in the minstrel songs. Usually, the joke revolved around a general description which included color, disposition, food predilections, and at times, even the voice, as in "In De Wild Rackoon [sic] Track":

> I hab crossed de Mississippi,
> I hab kissed de black gals lippy,
> But de happiest time war in ole Carolina,
> When dis nigga fall in lub wid a gal named Dinah.
>
> Her lips war white, her eyes war bright,
> Her voice war berry clear,
> Her lips war big, she could sing like a pig,
> Her mouth stretched from ear to ear.

Additional verses of "Old Dan Tucker" reveal that:

> Oh, Sarah Lovelip is a beauty,
> Her sooty 'plexion 'zaxtly suit me,
> De black ob her face it shine so bright,
> Dat it puts de candle out at night.
>
> I won my sweetheart at a hustle,
> She has got old nature's bustle,
> Goose egg eyes as white as natur,
> And a nose just like a roasted tater.

Tony Winnemore sang, "with great and unbounded applause," a parody on "Old Dan Tucker" entitled "Mrs. Tucker," in which the female black is presented as a composite of unattractiveness:

> Mrs. Tucker is big and fat,
> Her face is black as my old cat,
> Her eyes stick out, her nose sticks in,
> Her under lip hang ober her chin.
>
> Mrs. Tucker is juss eighty-nine,
> Her hair hangs down like oakum twine,
> Her face so black, it shines in de dark,
> Her eyes shine like a charcoal spark.
>
> . . . .
>
> She came home drunk, to bed she reel,
> She put her night-cap on her heel,
> She blows out de light, and shut her eyes,
> And snore away until de sun does rise.
>
> Mrs. Tucker's heel so long,
> She ploughs de street as she goes along,

> De city marshal say one day,
> When she goes out she must say.

In "Gray Goose and Gander," however, the female scold is seen starkly contrasted with the sentimental image which is central to the "carry-me-back":

> When I war a single feller,
> I lived in peace and pleasure,
> But now I am a married man,
> I'm troubled out of measure.
>
>> Den look kere, den look dare,
>> And look ober yander,
>> Don't you see dat old gray goose,
>> A smiling at de gander.
>
> Ebery night when I go home,
> She scolds or its a wonder,
> And den she takes dat pewter mug,
> And beats my head asunder.
>
> My old wife war taken sick,
> De pain ob death came on her,
> Some did cry, but I did laugh,
> To see de breff go from her.
>
> Saturday night my old wife died,
> Sunday she war buried,
> Monday was my courting day,
> On Tuesday I got married.
>
> My old wife has gone abroad,
> Some evil spirit guide her,
> I know she has not gone to church,
> For de debil can't abide her.

The widespread belief among whites that the black had a characteristic odor found expression in songs about the black female. In "Ginger Blue," this notion appears as:

> Wid de nigga wenches ob de inhabitation
>> De gals looked well,
>> My eyes what a smell. . . .

Part of the justification for slavery rested on the argument that only the African black was biologically suited for the role. It was presumed that he was endowed with a superior strength and resistance to diseases of the South. While the majority of songs touching upon this assumption were those concerning the male black, the black female was occasionally mentioned in this regard. In one of the many versions of "Lucy Long," entitled "De Rale Lucy Long," the composer endows "Lucy" with a truly enviable strength:

> Oh, she is a fair darkey, ob de rale fust stock,
> And wid her head and shoulders she could split a block.

This particular "Lucy" was also a menace to her lovers through her unusual strength and a matching tendency toward violence:

> Oh, I kotch you toder morning, hanging by an injin rope,
> Because Miss Lucy cut you like a cake o' brown soap.

The examples cited to this point demonstrate how far minstrelsy's songwriters had come in promulgating the stereotype of the black female; it was a popular subject which, with constant reiteration, assumed the aura of established truth. The great number of sheet music and broadside editions of this type of song lends considerable support to this thesis. Of the multitude of broadsides on the subject, "What A Heel She's Got Behind Her"[51] leaves little to the imagination concerning the features of the female:

> Down in de hills ob Indian,
> I loved a sylph so sable,
> Her skin was black as oak-tan,
> And her breff was sweet as an apple.
> Her legs was straight as grape vine limbs,
> Dat round a stone fence twine, sar,
> And folks cried when dey seen her shin,
> "What a heel she's got behind her."
>
>> Sing, tramp it, locomotive shin,
>> All creeping insects mind her,
>> Or else you'd wid de earth cave in,
>> By de heel she's got behind her.

The remainder of the song is a rather drawn out account of various disasters resulting from encounters with the oversized feet of the subject.

It is impossible to cite the hundreds of sheet music examples with the female as the butt of the joke, but "Gal From The South"[52] by L.V.H. Crosby serves to sum up her qualities:

GAL FROM THE SOUTH

Old massa own'd a coloured gall [sic]
He bought her at the south,
Her hair it curl'd so bery tight,
She couldn't shut her mouth,
Her eyes dey were so bery big,
Dey both run into one,
Sometimes a fly lights in her eye,
Like a june-bug on de sun.

    Yah, ha, ha; yah, ha, ha,
    De gall from de south,
    Her hair it curl'd so bery tight,
    She coudn't [sic] shut her mouth.

Her nose it was so bery long,
It made me laugh, by gosh,
For when she got her dander up,
It turned up like a squash,
Old massa had no hooks or nails,
Nor nothing like ob dat;
So on dis darkey's nose he used
To hang his coat and hat.

One morning massa gwain away,
He went to get his coat,
But nedder hat, nor coat, could find,
For she had swollow'd both,
He took her to a tailor's shop,
To hab her mouth made small;
De lady took in one long breath,
A swollow'd tailor and all.

By way of contrast, Henry Howard Paul's "She's Black, But That's No Matter,"[53] sung by Edwin P. Christy, stands as one of the most amazing products of the period, in that the total effect is one of true affection for the black female, an attitude held by such a microscopically few people that the failure of the song was assured. The literature of the minstrel stage fails to yield another example such as this, and the song itself is rare in sheet music collections today.

SHE'S BLACK, BUT THAT'S NO MATTER

My Dinah, dear me, she's as beautiful quite,
As a star that shines calmly at the close of the night,
A voice like a siren, a foot like a fay—
"She's just such a gal you don't meet every day."

Spoken. But she's black!

> I know she is, but what of that,
> You'd love, could you look at her,
> I'd have her just the way she is,
> She's black, but that's no matter.

She lives on the banks of a bright flowing stream,
In a cabin that might have been built in a dream,
Surrounded by roses, and woodbines, and leaves,
"That twine and climb lovingly up to the leaves."

Spoken. But she's so very black!

> I know she is, etc.

If ever I marry this dark color'd maid,
You'll believe in the truth of what I have said;
I love her because her complexion will keep,
"And they say that all beauty is only skin deep."

Spoken. But she's black!

> I know she is, etc.

Beneath the surface of this farrago of songs depicting the black female runs a strong suggestion of sexual anxiety which existed as an impassable, invisible deterrent to social interaction between white and black. The open mention of sex was taboo for songwriters, of course; but the greatest fear whites held concerning blacks—racial mixing—was a constant theme of varying intensity not only in the songs of the female black but in the entire genre. The "yaller" of the songs depicting the black woman could hardly be the result of racially pure mating, but it was a recognition of a fact of life.

It has been mentioned that the lightened color of the black female in song served as a more acceptable image in her connection with the

South. Still, the repugnance for blackness felt by most whites as an ingrained response, and the obvious sexual appeal of the female of the vanquished race added a dimension which produced mixed results. Slavery could be—and was—justified in principle among the pro-slavery forces not only through historical, scriptural, and socio-economic expedients, but on the grounds of race. The feeling was strong that racial mixing, or "amalgamation," would pollute pure Caucasian races and worse, would weaken the very foundation of slavery. How then to recognize in song the undeniably powerful sexual attraction of the black female? Songwriters answered the question in the main by simply making her whiter—"yaller."

The concept of the master as all-powerful over the destiny of the black female put her at a disadvantage, however, and surrounded her with an allure which proved irresistible to a considerable number of white males. Social proscription in all its forms was incapable of preventing great numbers of children of mixed parentage being born without a visible father, to the great discomfort of many white wives. Thus, Henry Hughes's picture of "warranteeism" as racially pure was more imaginary than real as he proclaimed:

Amalgamation of races is systematically suppressed. Caste for the purity and progress of races is actualized. The purity of the females of one race, is systematically preserved.[54]

The songwriters attempted to resolve the problem of the attractiveness of the black female through another artifice: the implication that her allure was primarily directed toward black males. The white male was, with the exception of "She's Black, But That's No Matter," seen as holding himself above such matters as association with the female black. Her vanity and other female characteristics were fully exploited as comedy in relationship to the black male, as seen in "De Nigga Gal's Dream; or, I Loved Coon Still De Same,"[55] a parody on Balfe's "I Dreamt That I Dwelt In Marble Halls":

DE NIGGA GAL'S DREAM
I dreamed dat I libed in hotel halls,
Wid silvery pans at my side,

And ob all de buck niggas dat sarv'd in dem walls,
Dat I was de pet an' de pride.

I'd wittals ob all kinds, boiled an' roast,
An' dishes too many to name,
An' I also dreamed what charmed me most,
Dat I lobed *Coon* still de same.

I dreamed dat buck-niggas did sought my hand,
Each night I set on dar knee,
An' wid busses dat no poor wench could stand,
Dey *Spouted* dar hearts to me.

I dreamed dat one nigga hug me more close,
Brought sassage and oder roast game,
But I also dreamed what charmed me most,
Dat I lobed *Coon* still de same.

The black female in song had more than the usual aspirations attributed to females in general. She, along with the black male, wanted to associate with whites of the opposite sex. The black was seen as striving for equality through association either with white values or, even more comical to songsmiths, associations with whites themselves. This was expressed in song in a manner which reflected negatively on the white liberal as well as the black, exemplified by "De New York Nigger":[56]

When de Nigger's done at night washing up de china,
Den he sally out to go and see Miss Dinah,
Wid his Sunday go-to-meetings segar in his mouth-a,
He care for no white folk, neder should he ought to,
His missy say to him, I tell you what, Jim,
Tink you gwan now to cut and come agin.

He walk to de Park, an' he hear such mity music,
A white man he did say enuff to make a dog sick,
He turn round to see who make de observation,
An de sassy whites laugh like de very nation,
Jim was in de fashion, so he got into a passion,
'Cause de damn white trash was at him a laffin.

Jim cut ahead an tink he never mind 'em,
White folks got de manners—he tink he couldn't find 'em,
He walk a little furder an tink he die a laffin,

To see his Dinah walkin' wid Massa Arfy Tappan,
Ole Bobolition Glory, he live an' die in story,
De black man's friend, wid de black man's hourii.[57]

The apparent disdain shown by the black male protagonist for whites and white values was, of course, a thinly disguised admonition by whites that the black's "place" was with his own kind. But a more important feature of this song is the attempt to discredit the anti-slavery movement through the implication that its leaders found ready access to the favors of the black female.

A deeper, more subtle reference to the relationship between the white male and the black female can be found in the frequent mention in song of how Southern blacks were conceived by the whites' sticking their "toes" in the ground. One verse of "Camo Kimo"[58] relates:

In South Carolina the niggers grow,
If de white man only plant his toe,
Water de ground with 'bacca smoke,
And up de niggers head will poke.

The identical verse appears in other songs, such as "The Old Pee Dee."[59]

While the sexual interest between the white male and the black female could command considerable attention in song, the attraction of the black male to the white female was evidently too horrible to contemplate except in a few isolated instances. One verse of "Long Tail Blue," it will be remembered, comes directly to the point with:

Jim Crow is a courting a white gal,
And yaller folks call her Sue (etc.).

While more or less explicit references can be found concerning the attraction of the white male for the black female, the black female for the white male, and the black male for the white female, there is yet to be found a concrete example in which the white female expresses sexual attraction for the black male. This greatest of all racial fears held by whites was evidently too ghastly for direct expression in song. Perhaps the nearest to this unthinkable notion in song is the euphemistic, highly tenuous "The Blackbird,"[60] wherein the female protagonist—presumed to be white by the choice of words and the absence of pseudo-black dialect—bemoans her lost love. This white woman is not an American, however, for the listener is assured again and again that the affair took place in England, where such alliances might conceivably occur.

THE BLACKBIRD

It was on one fine morning for soft recreation,
I heard a fair damsel making a sad moan,
Sighing and sobbing with sad lamentation,
Saying my Blackbird most loyal has flown.

My thoughts they deceived me, reflection it grieves me,
And I am o'er-burden'd with sad misery;
But if death should blind me, as true love inclines me,
My Blackbird I'll seek out wherever I be.

Once in fair England my Blackbird did flourish,
He was the chief flower that in it did spring,
Fair ladies of honor his person did nourish,
Because that he was the true son of a king.

But, O, that false fortune has proved so uncertain,
That caus'd the parting between you and me,
But if he remain in France or in Spain,
I'll be true to my Blackbird wherever he be.

In England my Blackbird and I were together,
When he was the most noble and gen'rous of heart,
But woe to the time when he arrived there,
Alas! he was soon forced from me to part.

In Italy he beam'd and was highly esteemed,
In England he seems but a stranger to me,
But if he remain in France or in Spain,
All blessings on my Blackbird wherever he be.

But if by the fowler my Blackbird is taken,
Sighing and sobbing will be all the tune,
But if he is safe, and I'm not mistaken,
I hope I shall see him in May or in June.

The birds of the forest, they all flock together,
The turtle was chosen to dwell with the dove,
So I'm resolved in fair or foul weather,
Once in the spring to seek out my love.

Oh, he is all my treasure, my joy and my pleasure,
He's justly belov'd though my heart follow thee,

How constant and kind, and courageous of mind,
Deserving of blessings wherever he be.

It's not the wide ocean can fright me with danger,
Although like a pilgrim I wander forlorn,
For I'll find more friendship from one that's a stranger,
More than from one that in Briton was born.

Outright seduction of the female, while rarely mentioned, was never an interracial affair. The rather graphic description contained in "Dinah Doe"[61] is exceptional:

Oh down in Indiana woods,
Whar color'd angels grow,
Dar I fust track'd a darkey gal,
Her name was Dinah Doe;
Her shape was like a sheaf ob corn,
Her step was like de Roe,
An' my heart an' heel was beating,
To follow Dinah Doe.

I foller her thro' flow'ry woods,
Each step she walk more slow—
An' when she peep'd behind, I thought
The stars had dropt below;
For her eyes were like de risen moon,
When daylight out does go,
An' my heart an' heel was beating,
To foller Dinah Doe.

While looken round, she bumped a tree,
An' backward down she go,
I catch her in dese trobbing arms,
As an eagle catch a crow.
Oh she trembled like a color'd lamb,
Out in a storm ob snow,
An' my heart it beat de banjo,
When I hold sweet Dinah Doe.

I prest de wound, I kiss her lip,
And she revived not slow;
Her teeth showed like white grains ob corn,
Laid in a double row.
An' her breath was like de summer wind,

> Dat on de clover blow,
> Oh she vowed dat night to 'lope wid me,
> De charming Dinah Doe.

The male black in song was normally pictured as even less gallant than the seducer of Dinah Doe. He was no less ardent, but the image presented on the minstrel stage contained other facets of supposed black character decidedly less attractive in nature, some of which have been noted earlier. His relations with women were marked by excessive jealousy and a belligerence which often belied his readiness to abandon his lady on the slightest whim. These traits can be traced directly back to "Coal Black Rose" through countless examples. Imagery of this type was counterbalanced through additional presumed characteristics such as buffoonery, cowardice and, of course, the picturing of the black males as physically unattractive.

The younger, more virile black male presented the most obvious threat to the institution of slavery and racial purity. He was therefore singled out for treatment as the repository of the most undesirable characteristics attributed to blacks in general. This treatment was directed not at the sentimental picture of the happy plantation slave, as in the "carry-me-back," but at the very heart of the black character. Its aim was to wound, distort, or even destroy the image of the black as a human.

The presumed combative spirit of the black, it must be remembered, was cause for real fear among whites. Diminishing their fears through popular song was only part of the elaborate political, social, and economic structure which attempted to keep blacks out of the mainstream of American life. A glimpse of this larger scheme of things can be seen in such totally unexpected sources as the unique, "Philadelphia Riots," a song of considerable length written on the 1844 riots between Protestants and Catholics in the Kensington section of Philadelphia.

In Philadelphia, as in many larger cities during this period, relations between blacks and whites were often marred by violence.[62] The normal pattern for interracial strife in Philadelphia was attack by whites on blacks after some real or imagined threat of black violence. Overwhelming power of the white factions precluded the outcome of all such riots, which perhaps explains why the unnamed author of

"Philadelphia Riots" chose to cast his song in pseudo-dialect and
to give it the facetious subtitle: "I Guess It Wan't De Niggas Dis
Time."

Sung to the tune, "It Will Neber Do To Gib It Up," "Philadelphia Riots" consists of nineteen verses and choruses which itemize
the details of the event. The first verse and chorus contain the main
points of interest to this study, however, and little is gained by quoting
the entire song.

PHILADELPHIA RIOTS, or
I GUESS IT WAN'T DE NIGGAS DIS TIME[63]

Oh, in Philadelphia folks say how,
Dat Darkies kick up all de rows,
But de *riot* up in *Skensin'ton*,
Beats all de darkies twelve to one.
   An' I guess it wasn't de niggas dis time.
   I guess it wasn't de niggas dis time,
   I guess it wasn't de niggas dis time, Mr. Mayor,
   I guess it wasn't de niggas dis time.

At the individual level, black aggressiveness appeared in song in
the forms of jealousy, braggadocio, bullying, and the like. Jealousy
was presented in essentially unchanged manner from its first
appearance in "Coal Black Rose," as seen in "Katy Dean,"[64] or the
extended "Who's Dat Nigga Dar A Peepin'?"[65] This latter example,
written and performed by J.H. White, utilizes spoken dialogue and
song to depict the male as a jealous lover, dominated entirely by brute
passion:

WHO'S DAT NIGGA DAR A PEEPIN'?

Oh, here I cum jist fur to sing,
'Bout dis and dat, and de oder ting;
Oh, I am gwaine for to tell you all,
How I rose in lub, and how I did fall.

Spoken: But first ob all, fore I spress myself on de kashion, I shud
like to know—

Who's dat nigga dar a peepin'
Who's dat nigga dat I see,
Who's dat nigga dar dat's peepin'
Say who's dat nigga dat I see.

Oh, I fell in lub wid Miss Dinah Crow,
And her teeth was like de clar grit snow;
An her eyes like dem beams dat shine from de moon,
Sharper dan de teef ob de possum or de koon.

Spoken: Yes, you see dis nigga first exprised herself by seeing
her promulgating herself up an down Chesnut Street,
persipitating dat foot ob hers up so high dat when it dropt it war
death to all creepin' insects, and den wid de poet I slcaimed—

Who's dat nigga dar a peepin' etc.

Oh, I went dar one ebening kording to rule,
And dar I was exprised to see a nigga squatting pon de stool;
Dar was Massa Zip Coon squatting down by de fire,
Singing dat song ob "Ole Vurginny Neber Tire."

Spoken: Yes, indeed, dare de nigga was, dares no 'sception in
dat, and as soon as dis nigga lit his eye 'pon him, dare was quite a
constervation 'mongst us niggas, kase I axed Dinah if she would
jist 'spress herself openly 'pon de raison and inform dis nigga—

Who's dat nigga dar a peepin', etc.

Oh, den us niggers you ort for to see,
Dar was me hugging him, and he was hugging me,
Oh, he bit me 'pon de arm and tore my close,
I fotch him a lick, and broke Miss Dinah's nose.

Spoken: Den, says I, jist look at here Miss Dinah, dat's de fects
ob your habbin more dan one nigga dressing himself to you at
one time; and now den, Miss Dinah, I shall leave you for de
present; but next time I sees any gemmem ob kulor sept myself, I
shant be under de discumgreeable necessity ob axing you—

Who's dat nigga dar a peepin', etc.

Oh, de next morning dey took dem for de mare,
Who taught dey had not acted fair,
So he sent dem down jist for thirty days apiece,
For kickin up a row, and brakin de police.

Spoken: Oh, Lord, lova, lova, ha, ha! Hush, honey, hush. De fus
ting I knew in de morning, dere Massa Zip was, poking he ugly
mug out ob Black Maria, and den you ort to hear dis child fling
out to him, and ax—

Who's dat nigga dar a peepin', etc.

Now ladies and gemmen my song is sung,
And I hope you all hab some fun,

If you want to hear a song dat will keep you from sleepin,
Hear "Who dat nigga dar a peepin'?"

Spoken: Yes, indeed; dares so much percipation in it dat it
probilates de promulgation ob all oder sentimations, and de only
spression dat you hear is—

Who's dat nigga dar a peepin'? etc.

In "Katy Dean," the protagonist limits himself to merely threatening his rival with:

I'll call that darkey out, I will, and kill him very dead,
I hear the bullets running through his huckelberry head,
And if she loves another man, I'll go and squeeze her wiz'n,
And if she'll not be mine, by gum, she never shall be hiz'n.

The black male in song was frequently pictured as incapable of
decisive action when confronted with a rival, as in "Dearest Belinda"
by S.A. Wells.[66] Searching for any excuse for interaction, the
protagonist equates the fickleness of his Belinda with her color in the
chorus and develops a solution in the final verse which would be quite
in keeping with modern times, a solution uncharacteristic of the songs
on nonblack subjects of the period in which it was written.

DEAREST BELINDA

Now blackmen come around me,
And listen to my song,
I'll sing you of a darkie gal,
Who in Kentuck was born,
She had such charming jet black eyes,
Her teeth dey shone like silver,
Dar was no gal in all Kentuck,
Compar'd with my Belinda.

Den I'm tap, tap, tapping at de winder,
Don't you hear me my dearest Belinda,
For I'll knock here no more so open your door,
For I know you'r as black as a cinder.

One night I went to visit her,
I tapped upon de door,
If I'd have known who was in dar,
I'd quit de house before.

> I ope'd the door, I looked around,
> It fill'd me with surprise!
> Dar sit my rival Count Mustache,
> I scarce believe my eyes.
>
> I left de house I felt so bad,
> I know not where I went,
> I thought I'd drown all in a drink,
> But I found I hadn't a cent.
> Belinda made me feel so bad,
> I wished my rival dead,
> My feelings got de best of me,
> And so I went to bed.
>
> In de morning when dis nigger wake,
> I tink ob all dat past,
> Belinda treat me very bad,
> But I found her out at last,
> I go and bid her den farewell!
> I'll see her not again;
> I since have found another gal,
> And loved her not in vain.

Picturing the black as reacting with irresolution in the face of problems requiring accepted standard responses was more compatible with the stereotype. He could be pugnacious on his own ground; but when faced with white authority, he was quick to retreat, as seen in "Run, Nigger, Run!":[67]

RUN, NIGGER, RUN!

> De sun am set—dis nigger am free,
> De colored gals he goes to see;
> I hear a voice cry, "Run, dad, fech you!
> Run, nigger, run, or de M.P.'ll catch you![68]
>
> Run, nigger, run, de M.P.'ll catch you!
> Run, nigger, run, tum a du daddle da!

Spoken: Oh! you ought to seen me dressed dat day. I had a pair ob dese United States gaiters, hem-stiched behind, made ober at Blackwell's Island; and den I had on dat pink snuff-colored coat, and den I had on dat green white satin vest, together wid a hickory cane, wid a gold brass feller on de bottom. Oh! dar wasn't room enough dat day for me. I knocked de people off of de

sidewalk, and some of de time I got knocked off; but I got dar at
last, and rung de bell. She opened the door; then hung my hat up
on the floor. I set down by her side about an hour, telling her dat I
lubbed her, when all at once she swooned ober in de chair, and
exclaimed, "Look dar!" Says I, "Whar?" when I looked ober
t'oards the door, and there was a white man's face, peeping fro'
de crack ob de door; at the same time he exclaimed, "What, Mr.
Bones?"

Run, nigger, run, etc.

The remainder of "Run, Nigger, Run" describes the flight of the
beleaguered black and his inability to find sanctuary. At one point in
the spoken dialogue, the protagonist is caught by the heel:

Spoken: Yes, just like all the niggers, the heel is the biggest part
ob the foot, an' just as I jumped ober de fence, he coch me by the
heel, an' held me fast, an' sez, "I got you now . . . ."

Perhaps nowhere was the image of the black male delivered a more
damaging blow than in the picture of the black dandy. The desire to be
well-groomed and fashionably dressed was distorted in song to
represent ludicrous mimicry of white values and a presumption of
equality by blacks. Songwriters took pains to forestall any such
pretensions through such ego-shattering songs as "Dandy Jim From
Caroline,"[69] one edition of which carries on its cover a picture of a
mincing black fop (Figure 11).

DANDY JIM FROM CAROLINE

I've often heard it said ob late,
Dat souf Carolina was de state,
Whar a handsome nigga's bound to shine,
Like Dandy Jim from Caroline.

For my ole massa tole me so,
I was de best looking nigga in de country,
O, I look in de glass an found 'twas so,
Just what massa tole me, O.

I drest myself from top to toe,
And down to Dinah I did go,
Wid pentaloons strapped down behind,
Like Dandy Jim from Caroline.

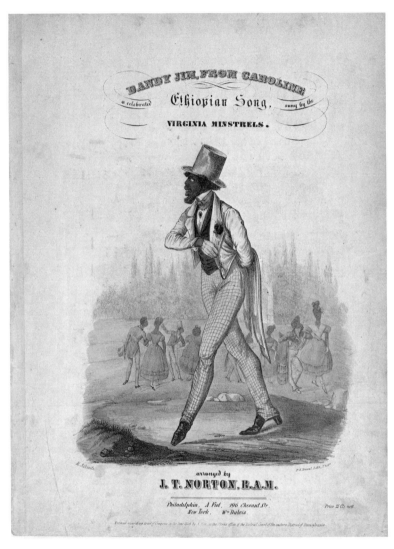

Figure 11

De bull dog cleared me out ob de yard,
I tought I'd better leabe my card,
I tied it fast to a piece ob twine,
Signed "Dandy Jim from Caroline."

She got my card and wrote me a letter,
An ebery word she spelt the better,
For ebery word an ebery line,
Was Dandy Jim from Caroline.

Oh, beauty is but skin deep,
But wid Miss Dinah non complete,
She changed her name from lubly Dine,
To Mrs. Dandy Jim from Caroline.

An ebery little nig she had,
Was de berry image ob de dad,
Dar heels stick out three feet behind,
Like Dandy Jim from Caroline.

I took dem all to church one day,
And hab dem christened widout delay,
De preacher christened eight or nine,
Young Dandy Jims from Caroline.

An when de preacher took his text,
He seemed to be berry much perplexed,
For nothing cum across his mind,
But Dandy Jim from Caroline.

Songwriters contributed heavily to the image of the black as inherently stupid. Songs of the black male were a favorite medium for carrying this facet of the stereotype, as exemplified by "Going Ober De Mountain,"[70] and the witless commentary on natural and Biblical phenomena, "Walk In The Parlor";[71] the natural ignorance assumed to be a common black trait was also mentioned as an integral part of countless songs, such as "Good Morning Ladies All" from Rice's "opera" *Oh Hush*,[72] and the "everlastin and unkonkerable screamer," "Pompey Smash."[73]

Intellectual pratfalls have long been staple items in American humor, thus it was inevitable that songwriters would emphasize the point in demeaning blacks, as "Pompey Smash" is inspired to declaim:

As I sing to folk now dat I tink is disarnin [discerning]
I'll tell you whar I cum from and whar I got my larnin,

I'm hot from ole Wurjinny, whar you fine all de great men,
An I'm Pompey Smash, one de principal statesmen,
I'm sekun bess to none, on dis side ob de sun,
And by de laud, I weigh widout my head half a ton.

Dis wurl's made ob mud an de Mississippi river,
De sun's a ball ob fox-fire, as you diskiver,
De moon's made ob cheese, and allus keeps a flyin,
De wurl stands still, while de sun keeps a guyin [going]
An de stars are ladies eyes dat round de wurl flies,
To gib us a little lite when de moon don't rise.

Now I've splain'd dese tings in a logigraphic manner,
I gib you a little touch of ole Wurginny grammar,
Dey say fotch and toat insted ob bring an carry,
An dat what dey call grammar, by de laud Harry,
And de Yankees all gues, but de French speak de bess,
For dey say *we mosheer*, when dey go to say yes.

The remainder of "Pompey Smash" devotes itself to a description of a fight between the protagonist and Davy Crockett, and a rambling commentary on current events:

Dis star storm[74] shows dat dar's someting bad a bruin,
An shows dat de niggers am on de brink of ruin,
For ebery single star, as it kum down a whizzen,
Says, Pompey Smash, here you see de fects ob abulishun,
We were kick'd from de sky, kase we tried to nullify
De laws ob de white folks, an so we hab to die.

This sinister observation indicates clearly how the song's author felt about the growing abolition movement and his willingness to connect his feeling with superstition surrounding the natural phenomenon of a meteor shower.

Rice's "Good Morning Ladies All" begins with an account of a coon hunt—also part of the stereotype—which takes six verses to relate. Stupidity is attributed to both father and son in this example, as the seventh verse abandons the hunt with:

Den I got a wife on Sunday,
Oh, Roley, Boley,
My son cum down a Monday,
An I neber seed a finer.

Wid a hida ka dink, ah, ah!
Oh, Roley, Boley,
Wid a hida ka dink, who dare?
Good morning ladies all.

Den I sen my son to college,
Oh, Roley, Boley,
Whar he got his sense an knowledge,
An growed up to a man.

His learning cost me a dollar,
Oh, Roley, Boley,
An now he is a lawyer,
An soon will be a judge.

The black male was seen as imbecile concerning even the more prosaic habits and occupations of man, as in "Going Ober De Mountain":

A nigger come from Arkansaw,
De biggest fool I ebber saw,
At mornin when dis nigger rose,
He put his mittens on his toes.

Dis nigger went to feed de sheep,
He gib em green tobacker leaf,
He went some water for to get,
And carried it in a corn basket.

He went to shell corn in de shed,
He shell'd his shins all bare instead,
He went to feed de horse at de barn,
He put himself in de trough for corn.

Ebery day when Sunday come,
He comb'd his head wid a horse jaw-bone;
He went to split some oven-wood,
And split himself up clar to foot.

With no less hyperbole than the above examples, "Walk In The Parlor" is nonetheless a more concise statement of the theory of the inherent imbecility of the black in that it devotes itself entirely to this theme. The song shows more technical competence, almost as though a pinnacle of perfection had been reached in the writing of inferior songs. Still, the arrogance with which the protagonist parades his ignorance in this instance reveals more of the crassness of the author than that of the subject.

WALK IN THE PARLOR

I'm right from old Virginny,
    wid my head so full of knarledge,
I never went to free school,
    or any odder college,
But I will tell you one ting,
    it is a certain fact,
I'll git you 'scription of de world
    in a twinkling of a crack.

So walk in, walk in,
Walk in to de parlor and hear de banjo ring,
And watch de darkeys fingers
While he picks it on de string.

Lightning is a yaller gal
    who libs up in de clouds,
Thunder is a brack man,
    and he can holler loud,
When he kisses lightning,
    she darts up in a wonder,
He jumps up and grabs de clouds,
    and dats what makes it thunder.

Noah built de ark
    and filled it full of sassage,
All de odder animals
    took a cabin passage;
De elephant he cum last—
    Noah said "you's drunk!"
"No" says he,
    "It took me all dis time to pack away my trunk."

O, Noah sent de bird out,
    to look for dry land,
When he cum back,
    he had de banjo in his hand,
I took up de banjo,
    and played 'em dis ere tune,
All the animals, 'cept de elephant,
    fell into a swoon.

Biblical allusions in the comic songs of the black subject sometimes mislead authorities into believing that these allusions are evidence of actual black influence. The line of descent of this phenomenon is easily traced to white origins in such examples as "Sambo's Address" and the catachrestical sermon of Charles Mathews (see Appendix I).[75] Perhaps the closest that any of the minstrel stage songs approached actual religious music is "Fi, Hi, Hi The Black Shakers" by Even Horn.[76] Considering the extraordinary body of Shaker sacred music, it is rather difficult to categorize "Fi, Hi, Hi," excepting the observation that it is psychologically incompatible with both black and Shaker expressions, while it remains entirely compatible with the minstrel stage expression.[77]

> FI, HI, HI
>
> Bress dat lubly yallar gal,
> De white folks call miss Dinah;
> Oh! pity me ye shakers all
> And tell me where I'll find her,
> She's gone away to Leb'non state
> To hoe de corn and bake de cake
> Massa says it is to late
> Let her go to Leb'non state.
>
> Fi hi hi lum i dum didle lum
> Fi hi hi ri tidle lum i dum
> Fi hi hi.
>
> And since she's gone and left me,
> I don't know what I'll do;
> I'll buy a rope and drown myself:
> Dat make her mad I know.
> She's gone away to Leb'non state,
> To hoe de corn and bake de cake;
> And Massa says it is to late:
> Let her go to Leb'non state.

Songs such as "Fi, Hi, Hi" and Emmett's "Jordan Is A Hard Road To Trabel" indicate that composers of minstrel melodies had not yet experienced or grasped the religious music of the black. There is little connection between the titular suggestion of religious intent and the textual content of minstrel songs until the period following the Civil War, when spurious black spirituals became a reigning fad in popular entertainment. During the period under discussion, however, these songs were devoted mainly to caricaturing the black through methods identical to the love songs, carry-me-backs, and other types.

"Jordan Is A Hard Road To Trabel,"[78] commonly credited to Dan Emmett, was widely copied, parodied, and imitated, on occasion by Emmett himself.[79] Its title belies the text; it is a song of the "Jim Crow" type with no religious connotations of any kind. Male prowess is lampooned through the familiar method of commentary on current events or the personal history of the protagonist. The eight versions used for this study lean heavily on foreign affairs, politics, and the slavery issue, which had been thrown open to international criticism by the publishing of Harriet Beecher Stowe's *Uncle Tom's Cabin.* As in the case of the "happy plantation slave" and carry-me-backs, the comparison of the lot of the slave in America with the industrial slaves of England and New England was irresistible:

> Poor Mrs. Beacher Stow, she thinks herself so brave,
> So she left her own country accordin',
> She went on too England for to see dere White Slaves,
> For to write about on t'odder side o' Jordan.[80]

or:

> Uncle Tom's Cabin never was written by mortal hands,
> It never was, and there's no use of talking,
> It was written long ago by Mrs. Harriet Beecher Stowe,
> When she lived on the other side of Jordan.
>
> Poor old Uncle Tom had a berry hard time,
> Tho' he asked Mrs. Beecher's toe's pardon,
> But she never will diskiver what a wicked thing she did,
> Till she tries to reach de odder side o' Jordan.
>
> Uncle Sam's Black Slave hab got a mighty hard time,
> But de "White Slave ob England" a more hard one,
> An' I radder do believe Uncle Sam comes out de best,
> An' he needn't fear de odder side o' Jordan.[81]

The various editions of "Jordan Is A Hard Road To Trabel" betray not only an unbending attitude in support of slavery, but an all-embracing chauvinism which excluded almost anything or anyone foreign:

> The Irishmen think that they can rule
> Over the American people according,
> But the Americans will show them what they will do,
> On this and the other side of Jordan.[82]

and:

> Let all the world know, that where ever we may go,
> Our Government will be ready in affording,
> Protection alike to all, both the great and the small,
> That hail from the Yankee side of Jordan.[83]

or:

> The spirits of fifty murdered Americans are crying for revenge,
> To de whole Yankee nation to go on,
> Staight off to Havanna their blood to avenge,
> And blow Moro Castle to de odder side of Jordan.[84]

Right-wing extremism seems rather peculiar fare for the entertainment of the masses, but the frequency with which this syndrome recurred in songs of this type indicates that the audiences of the 1850's found little inconsistency in mixing doctrine with pleasure. Quotation of the full text of Emmett's original version of "Jordan Is A Hard Road To Trabel" shows that syncretizing racism, nationalism, and hedonism could have been his intent from the outset; none of the versions which followed, at any rate, changed the formula to any degree of significance.

JORDAN IS A HARD ROAD TO TRABEL

I just arrived in town For to pass de time away
And I settled all my bisness accordin'
But I found it so cold When I went up de street
Dat I wish'd I was on de oder side ob Jordan.

> So take off your coat boys, and roll up your sleeves,
> For Jordan is a hard road to trabel,
> So take off your coat boys, and roll up your sleeves,
> For Jordan is a hard road to trabel I believe.

I look to the East, I look to the West
And I see ole Kossuth a comin

With four bay horses hitc'd up in front,
To tote his money to de oder side ob Jordan.[85]

David and Goliath both had a fight
A cullud man come up behind 'em
He hit Goliath on de head, wid a bar of soft soap
And it sounded to de oder side ob Jordan.

If I was de legislator ob dese United States
I'd settle de fish question accordin
I'd give de British all de bones and de Yankees all de meat
And stretch de boundary line to de oder side ob Jordan.

Der's been excitin times for de last year or two
About de great Presidential election
Frank Pierce got elected and sent a hasty plate ob soup[86]
To his opponent on de oder side ob Jordan.

Louis Napoleoan after all is emperor of France
And all Europe begins to tremble accordin
But the Yankees dont care for if with us he wants to fight
He'll wish he'd staid on de ober side ob Jordan.

The pseudo-black postured and fulminated; he strutted and blustered; his vanity knew no bounds as he pranced about on the minstrel stage. Laughter provoked by the caricature of his physical appearance, his love-making abilities, his outlook on life, in short, his entire character, was effective in stripping him of dignity. In song he was not a man; he was not even fully human.

One song concerning the black male, "A Nigger's Reasons,"[87] is a rather comprehensive picture of the character as seen through white eyes. Most of the facets of the stereotype are contained in this song, including the pointed reference in the final verse which presumes that all blacks harbor the desire to be white:

A NIGGER'S REASONS

Nigger man good reason hab,
    For ebery ting him doing,
Wedder it be work all day
    Or ebery night go wooing!
He dearly lub a pretty gal,
    Wid kiss her mouth to stop a,
But nigger lub himself de best,
    Cause him tink it proper!

Ching, ring, banjo goley, loo,
Ching ring banjo nigger,
Know well how take care himself,
'Cause number one a figger.

Times are growing bery bad,
    Through care, or Massa Cupid;
Some kill demselves acause dere mad
    And some acause dere stupid.
Nigger ne'er take in him head,
    And for de best perswashun,
He never kill himself at all,
    'Cause he no occasion.

Nigga lub new rum galore,
    But all in moderation;
For if him take a drop too much,
    May lose him sityvashun.
But should a friend invite him home;
    Afore him good tings putting;
Dere no objection, drink like mad,
    Acause it cost him notting.

He neber care for making love,
    Dat trouble neber move him,
Nigger man wid handsome face,
    Make ebery body lub him.
Him like a widder best wid cash,
    Dat not a chance to pass a;
'Cause when he de money tush,
    No care a dam for massa.

Him no like at all to cry,
    Sorrow make all crusty;
He tink it best to laugh all day,
    'Cause it make him lusty!
Nigger lub good living well,
    Starvation make him frightful—
Him like rump steaks and oyster sauce,
    'Acause 'em so delightful.

He'd like to be a gentleman,
    If he could live unhired,
Nigger man no like to work,
    'Cause it make him tired!

> Him tink it bore him debts to pay,
>   Though folks may say is not right,
> 'Cause for three months in de bench,
>   *Black* man come out all *wash white!*

The deep-seated fear of sexual attraction of the black male for the white female found expression in songs such as "A Little More Cider,"[88] which, incidentally, provided its own solution through the assumed egotism of the black subject:

> I love de white gal and de black,
> And I love all de rest;
> I love de gal for loving me,
> But I love myself de best.

It was one thing to have the black female courted by a white lover; it was quite another to see the white female become the love object of the black man. Apart from songs dealing with the ghastly possibility of interracial love, songsters of the period occasionally embellished their pages with illustrations showing mixed couples.

Songwriters were not above attacking their colleagues in the entertainment field with accusations of racial mixing. The great dancer, Fanny Elssler, was the object of at least two such songs: "Fanny Elssler Leaving New Orleans,"[89] and "The Serenade."[90] While the first of these songs deals with a black lover who mourns the departure of Elssler from New Orleans, the latter is an even more outrageous love song which slanders the race and Miss Elssler alike:

THE SERENADE (DUET)

He.   Oh, Miss Fanny, let me in,
        For de way I lub you is a sin;
        Oh, lubly Fanny, let me in,
        To toast my feet and warm my shin.

She.   Oh, no, I cannot let you in.

Both.   To toast your feet and warm your shin.

She.   Sam Slufheel when last we parted,
        You to me did prove false hearted,
        Whitewash Sal you went to see,
        And she ain't one bit better dan me.

NIGGA SONGS.

    Now tell me Joe if you love me.
He.   Dars none that I adore above thee,
She. My heart with love now is pealing,
He.   Oh! Moses how she works my feeling

He.   Oh! lubly Rose, dares my hand,
    No wench could have it in this land,
    You are my thoughts by day and night
    Oh! Moses, she's a beautiful sight,

    How I do adore the creature.
She. Moses, he's got a splendid feature.
He.   She's the only wench I ever see
She. He's stole my heart away from me.

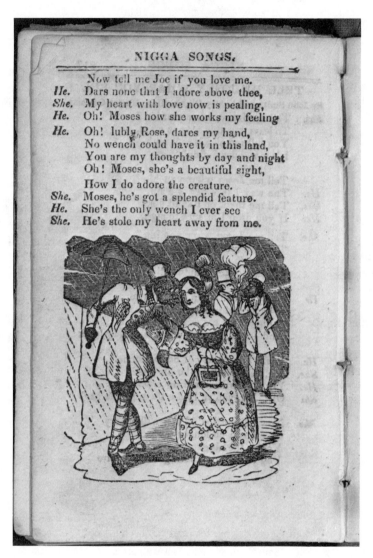

Figure 12

He. Oh, Miss Fanny, how I prizes,
   Lubly teeth and lubly eyeses,
   Your handsome Fanny Elssler feet—
   Growling music, also sweet.

She. My lub for you is so berry great,
   Dat it is a sin to make me wait,
   Sam Slufheel I ain't got no fine made, [maid]
   And tain't no use to slamanade.

He. Oh, when I set up oyster cellar,
   You shall wait upon de feller,
   Sell hot corn and ginger pop,
   You be de lady ob de shop.

She. Oh, Sam, if dat's de trufe you tell me,
   I shall wait upon de feller,
   Sell hot corn and ginger pop,
   I'll be de lady ob de shop.

   Oh, Sam Slufheel, you may come in.

He. Oh, Miss Fanny, I'se a coming in,
   For de way I lub you is a sin.

The male black was prevented from becoming too attractive as a figure in song by the same expedient followed in the songs about the black female: he was made physically undesirable. Not only was he an excessive drinker and given to fits of jealous rage; not only was he a slacker and a thief and a liar; not only did he presume to importance as a political pundit and philosopher—he was also physically repulsive.

There is little doubt that the grotesquery pictured in song was exclusively Negroid in the minds of white songsmiths. "A Life By De Galley Fire," a parody on "A Life On The Ocean Wave,"[91] is explicit:

A life by de galley fire,
A home in de good ole ship,
Whar de waves curl higher an, higher,
Like a nigger's under lip.

Or, in a silly parody on "The Old Granite State" entitled "De Oe [*sic*] Virginia State":[92]

> We're all real darkies,
> Our hair an lips am curled . . . .

The large, misshapen foot was not limited to the female blacks, as Rice's "New Oh! Hush!"[93] points out:

> Next I saw the coloured gemman,
> With such old Verginy feet,
> His heels were at the Coffee House,
> His toes on 'leventh street.

The widespread belief that the black had a characteristic odor was exploited by numerous songsmiths. Henry H. Paul's "Sam Of Tennessee,"[94] a parody on "Dandy Jim Of Caroline," is quite explicit:

> De niggas in Tennessee am proud,
> Dey look very handsome, but dey smell very loud.

In "Do Come Along Ole Sandy, Boy,"[95] there is an attempt to compare the physical characteristics of white and black:

> Niggers hair am berry short,
> White folks hair am longer,
> White folks dey smell very strong,
> Niggers dey smell stronger.

One version of "Ginger Blue"[96] contains spoken dialogue which equates the importance of the individual with the strength of his stench:

Says I, look here, Pete, I doesn't like to be cutting round that daughter of yourn, when Clem Grum is throwing his affections at her, besides he's such a consequential Nigga, you can smell him half a mile off . . . .

Allowing the male black a certain degree of virility, so long as it was kept strictly within the bounds of race, was a means of lessening the fear of mongrelizing the Caucasian race. This slight recognition of humanity in the black did not, of course, come as serious reflections on the black personality in song; it was seen as another comic possibility which also served the additional function of diminishing white fears of racial pollution by blacks. Black males were seen as animals with voracious sexual appetites that somehow had to be controlled. These appetites, many had convinced themselves, were directly aimed toward gratification at the expense of the purity of white womanhood. Chivalry demanded that the sanctity of the white female honor and purity be defended; still, the importance of masculine biological imperatives transcended racial boundaries and required some sort of resolution, regardless of whether it was treated as a serious or comic problem. Today, this matter might be regarded as male chauvinism; in the 1840's it was merely a matter of expedience.

"Who Dare?"[97] contains verses showing that the punishment for fathering children out of wedlock was thirty-nine lashes if the racial boundary were not crossed:

> Go down to momo Dinah's, what you tink we do, ah,
> We play upon de banjo, an dance a jig about, ah!
> Den I meet Miss Fillacy, corna ob de lane, ah!
> I asked her ain't you gwoin for to play de game, ah!
>
>> Dingee I otten dotten, ballio otten dotten,
>> Dingee I otten, WHO DARE?
>
> Den in six months time, oh, Fillacy get bigger, ah!
> An in three months arter dat, den comes a little nigga, ah!
> De chickey chimey born, an de massa say he mine, ah!
> An den for dat I get anoder thirty nine, ah!

The black was not answerable to God for his sins; the "massa" owned him body and soul. His sufferings, joys—his very being amounted to no more than a joke in the eyes of the writers of minstrel songs. Whites were secure in the belief that slavery and the separation of the races could continue forever, with the blacks enjoying an existence without care, as long as they kept their "place" and somehow convinced the whites that interracial sexual intercourse was not their primary goal in life. There is an almost wistful longing in the verse of "Old Dan Tucker"[98] which attempts to express these sentiments as though they originated with the black slave:

> White folks treat de niggers well,
> If dey do not cut too great a swell,
> And talk about amalgamation,
> Disgustin' ting to ebery nation.

And for the meddling whites who were agitating for the end of slavery, another version of the same song addresses a rather petulant remonstrance:

> There is some folks called abolition,
> Want to mend de nigger condition,
> If dey would let them niggers alone,
> The niggers will always have a home.[99]

The black represented on the minstrel stage was, in summarizing characteristics stressed through songs, sketches, and dances, unrecognizable as the actual black in bondage. Yet this image was disseminated and accepted internationally as the true black. Contradictions between myth and fact melted before the avalanche of songs depicting the "happy plantation slave," living on "de ole plantation," and whiling away the evening hours playing on his "ole banjo." It was an idyllic picture, enhanced by the addition of romantic love and sentimentality, which evoked a superficial pity as the slave pathetically beseeched his hearers to "carry-me-back" so that he could die in the locality which had provided such marvelous comfort in earlier days.

Images of the male and female were encumbered with strong sexual implications. Distortions of physical features were transformed into desirable qualities as part of the desperate, but needless, effort to demonstrate that racial purity was, in actuality, the desire of the black as well as the white. To clinch the argument, the black male and female were ridiculed to the point of utter destruction as viable human figures. The overwhelming majority of songs on these figures were demeaning; faults were held to be virtues, and values were made objects of shame as the crude humor of the minstrel performer obliterated any redeeming qualities possessed by the real black.

The vast number of successful songs in the minstrel repertoire helped form and solidify the white conception of the black. They contributed heavily to a stereotype which even today hinders understanding between races in America. This stereotypical black operated as an insuperable barrier to a realistic appraisal of true black character and, perhaps worse, provided itself with virtually limitless resources upon which its own traditions could be extended. Self-perpetuation of the degraded image of the black was thus assured.

The real black—slave or freedman—could only hope that enough truth would be contained in the black image constructed by whites to cause some favorable reaction in his behalf. But it was an unreasonable hope. Even the most ardent abolitionists were influenced to some degree by the image of blacks exhibited on the minstrel stage. It was useless to remind the American public of the time that while the blackface performer awakened each morning as a free white man the slave awakened to find himself still very much a slave.

Chapter Four

The Abolition Movement
versus Minstrelsy

To the abolitionists, slavery was an affront to God and man. Abolition of the slave trade in 1808 was expected to produce eventual emancipation of those in bondage as the system atrophied. The failure of this assumption was a blow to abolitionists who had been relatively moderate in their actions and speech, and many, largely as a result of the religious fervor engendered by Charles G. Finney's revival of 1824, intensified their attact on slavery. Some of the more determined members of the movement turned to direct action in order to express their discontent, helping slaves to escape to the North and working to prevent their capture and return to the South.

The South responded to the abolitionists by becoming even more rigid in its view that slavery was both morally and legally right. The rift between the abolitionist North and the slaveholding South grew progressively wider, marked by violence such as the killing of abolitionist Elijah P. Lovejoy at the hands of a mob in 1837.

The movement toward abolition reached crusading proportions in the 1830's, spurred in large measure by the stentorian trumpet blast of William Lloyd Garrison's entry into the anti-slavery movement. His fiery rhetoric destroyed whatever hope remained among abolitionists that slavery would die of its own accord.

Although militant abolitionism had existed prior to 1831,[1] it was Garrison's uncompromising attack that brought the South wide awake with alarm. The state of Georgia felt threatened enough to ram through their Senate a resolution offering a reward of $5,000 for Garrision's apprehension and conviction in a Georgia court. The Garrisonian slogan of immediate and unconditional emancipation was both the means and the ends of the radical abolitionists, and the South could feel the hot breath of total ruin for their "peculiar institution" through the relentless efforts of this firebrand.

Naturally, Garrison and other anti-slavery leaders were reviled in many minstrel songs of the day, as has been noted. Garrison responded by contributing lyrics for a number of hymns and songs, many of which appeared in Jairus Lincoln's *Anti-Slavery Melodies*.[2] His "Song of the Abolitionist" states the Garrisonian position quite clearly:

SONG OF THE ABOLITIONIST
(Tune: Auld Lang Syne)

I am an Abolitionist!
I glory in the name;
Though now by slavery's minions hissed,
And covered o'er with shame;
It is a spell of light and power,
The watch-word of the free;
Who spurns it in the trial-hour,
A craven soul is he.

I am an Abolitionist!
Then urge me not to pause,
For joyfully do I enlist
In Freedom's sacred cause;
A nobler strife the world ne'er saw,
Th' enslaved to disenthral;
I am a soldier for the war,
Whatever may befall.

I am an Abolitionist!
Oppression's deadly foe;
In God's great strength will I resist,
And lay the monster low;
In God's great name do I demand,
To all be freedom given,
That peace and joy may fill the land,
And songs go up to heaven.

I am an Abolitionist!
No threats shall awe my soul;
No perils cause me to desist,
No bribes my acts control;
A freeman will I live and die,
In sunshine and in shade,
And raise my voice for liberty,
Of nought on earth afraid.

Other men of letters joined the ranks of those contributing texts for anti-slavery songs. Music for the texts was drawn largely from existing hymnody and revivalist tunes, as well as popular song on nonblack subjects. It was not long before abolitionists adopted the position of Wesley—that the devil should not have all the best tunes— as they worked to arouse anti-slavery passions. Collections such as *The Harp of Freedom*[3] appeared with parodies, copies, and flagrant borrowings from the minstrel repertoire.

In most instances, borrowings from the minstrel repertoire proved to be no less demeaning to the black than the originals. These songs leaned heavily on the image of the degraded black as evidence of the evils of slavery—precisely the argument used by pro-slavery forces as "proof" of the inherent inferiority of blacks. Anti-slavery songs had not only to show the evils of slavery, they had to meet the dilemma of status accorded the black should he achieve freedom.

Not everyone within the abolitionist camp agreed that the freed slave was a social equal to the white, and anti-slavery songs approached this aspect of the problem gingerly. Out of the welter of songs depicting the horror of slavery, only a few dared to suggest that the black was the equal of the white. "Am I Not A Man And Brother?"[4] with words by A.C.L. placed the idea within the Christian context, thereby availing itself of whatever protection an attitude of sanctity could afford. Given even a haven such as this, the author still protected himself by using only his initials in the song credits. But "Am I Not A Man And Brother?" is nonetheless a remarkable statement for the times:

> Am I not a man and brother?
> Ought I not, then, to be free?
> Sell me not one to another,
> Take not thus my liberty.
>
> > Christ our Saviour,
> > Christ our Saviour,
> > Died for me as well as thee.

The answer to the thorny question comes in the final verse:

> Yes, thou art a man and brother,
> Though we long have told thee nay;

And are bound to aid each other,
All along our pilgrim way.

Come and welcome,
Come and welcome,
Join with us to praise and pray!

Of course A.C.L. wrote a companion piece, "Am I Not A Sister?"[5] which touched upon the lustful instincts of the slaveholder:

Am I not a sister, say?
Shall I then be bought and sold
In the mart and by the way,
For the white man's lust and gold?

Save me then from his foul snare,
Leave me not to perish there!

But the central problem, the status of the freed slave, was never fully resolved in abolitionist song. "There's Room Enough For All"[6] suggests rather vaguely that the answer could be found through removal of the slave without actually identifying the process by its correct title—deportation. "For Freedom, Honor, and Native Land"[7] mentions equality, although whether in reference to the relationship between black and white, or to white factions of the North and South, is not made clear:

Abuse of power will the free repel,
The flame of sedition they'll strive to quell;
Alike are they friendly to equal rights,
And hostile to anarchy's deadly blights.

The ultimate social status to be afforded the freed black was apparent to abolitionists as the weakest link in their chain of social reform. They risked losing support should they claim that the black was equal to the white; yet the black, if not the equal of the white, could find it difficult to strive for an improved, free life. John Pierpont, an abolitionist poet, attempted to offer the anti-slavery point of view in a hymn that could stand as a model of circumspection:

HYMN 1.[8]

We ask not that the slave should lie,
As lies his master, at his ease,
Beneath a silken canopy,
Or in the shade of blooming trees.

We mourn not that the man should toil;
'Tis nature's need, 'tis God's decree;
But let the hand that tills the soil,
Be, like the wind that fans it, free.

We ask not, 'eye for eye,' that all,
Who forge the chain and ply the whip,
Should feel their torture; while the thrall
Should wield the scourge of mastership.

We only ask, O God, that they,
Who bind a brother, may relent;
But, Great Avenger, we do pray
That the wrongdoer may repent.

Timorous as abolitionists might have been regarding the status of the freed slave, they became as a raging fire in their condemnation of the institution itself. By the middle 1850's, the stiffening attitude of the South had caused anti-slavery forces to turn from moral suasion, exemplified in song by the use of hymnody, to a more militant stance, as shown by increasing use of materials of the pro-slavery songsmiths. "Old Dan Tucker" was among the numerous examples of this practice; "Strike For Freedom And For Right"[9] is a world apart from the reasoned appeal of the preceeding example:

From the bloody plains of Kansas,
From the Senate's guilty floor,
From the smoking wreck of Lawrence,
From our Sumner's wounds and gore,
   Comes our country's dying call—
   Rise for Freedom, or we fall!

Not all songs derived from minstrel or sacred sources; a significant body of song was developed from sentimental ballad traditions having roots in the English ballad opera. These songs were neither hortatory nor particularly moralistic, at least in the sense of songs based on sacred music. In the beginning, these songs strove to evoke pity for the condition of the slave without attacking directly the institution of slavery, as in "The Desponding Negro," or "I Sold A Guiltless Negro Boy." Henry R. Bishop's "Pity The Slave," from his opera, *The Slave*,[10] is typical of the florid style which came to characterize later American efforts on the theme. Musically pretentious and lofty in sentiment, this approach nonetheless had substantial appeal and might have been, if it were possible to measure such things, more effective in the anti-slavery cause than the reasoned or the hortatory styles. These songs appealed to man's better instincts rather than trying to batter down his attitudes with logic or force. Consider the first verse of "Pity The Slave":

> Sons of Freedom, hear my story,
> Mercy well becomes the brave,
> Humanity is Britain's glory,
> Then pity and protect the Slave.

The British, of course, arrogated unto themselves a self-righteousness on the issue of slavery which infuriated their American cousins. Thus, the slaver in Henry Russell's "The Chase"[11] was on his way to Cuba, rather than the United States, when overtaken by the British man-of-war. Russell, after all, had an American career to consider!

"The Chase" deserves attention on other grounds, however. It is one of the few truly exciting songs in a genre usually encumbered by excessive emotionalism and rhetoric. Apart from the British attitude toward slavery, "The Chase" shows the undiminished pride of the British in their naval heritage as portrayed in song by Dibdin.

THE CHASE

Set ev'ry stitch of canvas, to woo the fresh'ning wind,
Our bowsprit points to Cuba, the coast lies far behind;
Fill'd to the hatches full, my boys, across the seas we go,
There's twice five hundred niggers in the stifling hold below.

A Sail! what say you boys? well let him give us chase!
A British Man-of-War, you say—well, let him try the race.
There's not two swifter vessels ever floated on the waves,
Than our tidy little Schooners, well ballasted with slaves.

Now stronger yet, and stronger still, came down the fiery breeze,
And even fast and faster sped the strange ship on the seas;
Flinging each rude and bursting surge in glitt'ring halos back,
And bearing high to heav'n aloft, the English Union Jack.

"Now curses on that Ensign," the Slaving Captain said,
"There's little luck for Slavers when the English bunting's
    spread.
But pack in sail, and trim the ship, before we'll captur'd be,
We'll have the Niggers up, my boys, and heave them in the sea.

Hoarse was the Slaving Captain's voice, and deep the oath he
    swore,
"Haul down that flag, that shot's enough, we don't want
    anymore."
Alongside dash'd the cruiser's boat, to board and seize the prize;
Hark! to that rattling British cheer, that's ringing to the skies.

"Up, up, with the Negroes speed'ly, up, up, and give them
    breath;
Clear out the hold from stem to stern, that noisome den is death.
And run aloft St. George's Cross, all wanton let it wave,
The token proud that under it there never treads a slave.

Pro-slavery elements in the Unites States were not in complete agreement with the sentiment expressed in the final line of Russell's song, as seen in the preceeding chapter. The attempt to utilize the ballad technique in America called for an approach on different grounds. Whereas opposition to slavery was seen in England as a national characteristic, the Americans viewed it as a matter of personal choice between two sides of an issue that was tearing the country apart.

This difference can be detected in "The Grave Of The Slave" written by a "Lady of Philadelphia" and set to music by the famous Philadelphia musician, Francis Johnson.[12] The obvious aim of this piece is to arouse the feelings of the individual; slavery as a national shame is not directly mentioned.

THE GRAVE OF THE SLAVE

The cold storms of winter shall chill him no more,
His woes and his sorrows, his pains are all oe'r;
The sod of the valley now covers his form,
He is safe in his last home, he feels not the storm.

> The poor slave is laid all unheeded and lone,
> Where the rich and the poor find a permanent home,
> Not his master can rouse him with voice of command,
> He knows not, he hears not his cruel command.
>
> Not a tear, not a sigh to embalm his cold tomb,
> No friend to lament him, no child to bemoan,
> Not a stone marks the place where he peacefully lies;
> The earth for his pillow, his curtain the skies.
>
> Poor Slave! shall we sorrow that death was thy friend
> The last and the kindest, that heaven could send;
> The grave to the weary is welcomed and blest,
> And death, to the captive, is freedom and rest.

Given that manumission of the Southern slave was an unreasonably difficult legal process, the proposition that death brought the slave freedom was not altogether a fabrication. On the other hand, it was an unacceptable notion when placed against abolitionist demands for immediate emancipation. The idea continued to influence songwriters for the opposing side in the slavery issue: minstrel songwriters used the "death equals freedom" theme in repeated instances, such as "Pompey's Grave"[13] and the well-known "Poor Old Slave,"[14] which tearfully reminds the listener:

> The poor old slave has gone to rest,
> We know that he is free,
> Disturb him not, but let him rest,
> 'Way down in Tennessee.

The attempt to incorporate the art ballad into the anti-slavery movement required a more direct assault on slavery's manifold injustices; yet abolitionist songwriters, perhaps because of their amateur status in a field dominated by professionals on the opposing side, were slow to grasp the need for imaginative songs which would animate the public toward their cause. As late as 1844, S.G. Fessenden provided a musical setting for "The Captive's Lament,"[15] the text of which was written by "a member of the Massachusetts Female Emancipation Society." This song is reminiscent of the earlier British ballads which depicted a slave so removed from actual experience as to be ludicrous.

THE CAPTIVE'S LAMENT

Oh! my country, my country, how long I for thee,
O'er the mountain, O'er the mountain far over the sea,
Far, far, far, far o'er the sea.

Where the sweet Joliba kisses the shore,
Say, shall I wander by thee never more,

Say, O fond Zurima, where dost thou stay
Say, doth another list to thy sweet lay
Say, doth the orange still bloom near thy cot?
Zurima, Zurima, am I forgot?

Under the baobab oft have I slept
Fann'd by sweet breezes over me swept
Often in dreams do my weary limbs lay
Neath the same baobab far, far away.

O for the breath of our own waving palm,
Here as I languish my spirit to calm,
O for a draught from our own cooling lake,
Brought by sweet mother my spirit to wake.

The slave depicted by this deplorable song was neither to be believed nor pitied. Far more efficaciously, the fabulous Hutchinson family entered the scene in 1843, and soon their success in the popular song field was carried over into the anti-slavery movement with such songs as "The Bereaved Slave Mother"[16] and the lengthy "Get Off The Track!"[17] The words and much of the music for the Hutchinson's songs were produced from within the group. This family was one of a number of such groups, but their pre-eminence in the field added to the significance of their staunch New England views against slavery.[18]

The cover of "The Bereaved Slave Mother" illustrates that most despicable aspect of slavery, the slave auction. The text is equally unsparing in its condemnation of slavery as the brutal story unfolds:

THE BEREAVED SLAVE MOTHER

Oh! deep was the anguish of the Slave Mother's heart,
When call'd from her darling forever to part;
So grieved that lone Mother, that heart broken Mother,
    In sorrow and woe.

The lash of the Master her deep sorrows mock,
While the Child of her bosom is sold on the Block;

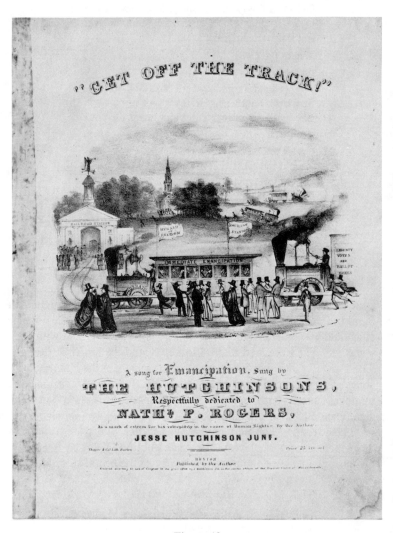

Figure 13

Yet loud shrieked that Mother, poor heart broken Mother,
  In sorrow and woe.

The Babe, in return, for its fond Mother cries,
While the sound of their wailings together arise;
They shriek for each other, the child and the Mother,
  In sorrow and woe.

The harsh auctioneer to sympathy cold,
Tears the Babe from its Mother and sells if for Gold;
While the Infant and Mother, loud shriek for each other,
  In sorrow and woe.

At last came the parting of Mother and Child,
Her brain reel'd with madness, that Mother was *wild*;
Then the *Lash* could not smother, the shrieks of that Mother,
  Of sorrow and woe.

The child was borne off to a far distant clime,
While the Mother was left in anguish to pine,
But reason departed, and she sunk broken hearted,
  In sorrow and woe.

That poor mourning Mother, of reason bereft,
Soon ended her sorrows, and sunk cold in death;
Thus died that Slave Mother, poor heart broken Mother,
  In sorrow and woe.

Oh! list ye kind Mothers to the cries of the Slave;
The Parents and Children implore you to save;
Go! rescue the Mothers, the Sisters and Brothers,
  From sorrow and woe.

Here was the dramatic, searing indictment of slavery that could transfix audiences; it is difficult to imagine hearing this song and remaining neutral on the issue. Indeed, the Hutchinson Family caused violent reactions with their anti-slavery songs; the abolitionists were loud in their approval while the pro-slavery forces responded with boos and hisses.

One of their most effective abolitionist songs was "Get Off The Track," which combined the objective of emancipation with the mystery and romance of the Underground Railroad. The central issue, slavery, is barely mentioned in the text, as though the cause, and not its rationale or consequences, were the only point worth celebrating. Jesse Hutchinson, Jr. was the author of the text, and

Emmett's "Old Dan Tucker" provides the musical setting—a piracy
which the Hutchinsons accomplished with obvious relish.[19]

"Get Off The Track" is a purely hortatory song which seems to
lend importance to details of the moment in the abolitionist struggle
and minimizes the opportunity to produce a truly memorable song on
a vastly more intriguing subject, the Underground Railroad. The
stature of the Hutchinson Family within the anti-slavery movement
elevated the song to a position of public esteem that—taken on its own
merits—it did not deserve.

GET OFF THE TRACK

Ho! the Car Emancipation,
Rides majestic thro' our nation,
Bearing on its Train, the story,
LIBERTY! a Nation's Glory.
> Roll it along, thro' the nation,
> Freedom's Car, Emancipation.

First of all the train, and greater,
Speeds the dauntless *Liberator*,
Onward cheered amid hosannas,
And the waving of Free Banners.
> Roll it along! spread your Banners,
> While the people shout hosannas.

Men of various predilections,
Frightened, run in all directions;
Merchants, Editors, Physicians,
Lawyers, Priests and Politicians.
> Get out of the way! every station,
> Clear the track of 'mancipation.

Let the Ministers and Churches
Leave behind sectarian lurches;
Jump on board the Car of Freedom
Ere it be too late to need them.
> Sound the alarm! Pulpit's thunder!
> Ere too late, you see your blunder.

Politicians gazed, astounded,
When, at first our Bell resounded:
Freight trains are coming, tell these Foxes,
With our *Votes* and *Ballot Boxes*.
> Jump for your lives! Politicians,
> From your dangerous false positions.

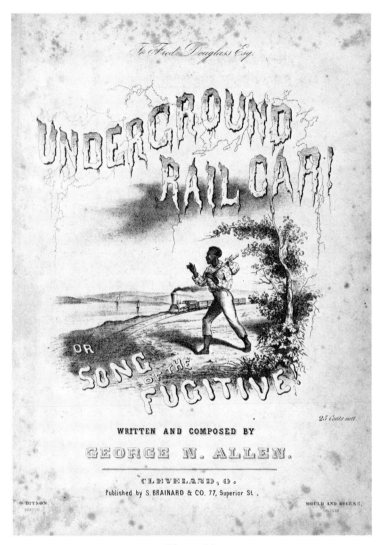

Figure 14

Rail Roads to Emancipation
Cannot rest on *Clay* foundation
And the *tracks* of *"The Magician"*
Are but *Rail Roads* to perdition,
  Pull up the Rails! Emancipation
  Cannot rest on such foundation.

All true friends of Emancipation,
Haste to Freedom's Rail Road Station;
Quick into the Cars get seated,
All is ready, and completed.
  Put on the Steam! All are crying,
  And the Liberty Flags are flying.

The remaining four verses continue in the same breast-beating vein without expanding the ideas sufficiently to warrant citation here. The contribution of those who repeatedly risked their lives in the operation of the Underground Railroad, as well as the courage of those who availed themselves of its services, make "Get Off The Track" something of a disappointment as a tribute. In the following decade, the organization was served in rather superior fashion by "The Underground Rail Car! or, Song Of The Fugitive," with words and music by George N. Allen.[20] While the musical accompaniment for "The Underground Rail Car!" is drawn from the minstrel tradition, the words reflect considerable depth in comparison with "Get Off The Track."

THE UNDERGROUND RAIL CAR,
or SONG OF THE FUGITIVE

I'm on my way to Canada, a freeman's rights to share,
The cruel wrongs of Slavery I can no longer bear;
My heart is crushed within me so while I remain a slave,
That I'm resolv'd to strike the blow for Freedom or the Grave!

  O Great Father! do thou pity me.
  And help me on to Canada where the panting slave is free!

I've heard that Queen Victoria has pledged us all a home
Beyond the reach of Slavery, if we will only come;
So I have fled this weary way, my guide the bright north star—
And now, thank God, I speed today in the Underground Railcar.

  O old Master! why come after me—
  I'm whizzing fast to Canada, where the panting slave is free!

> I now embark for yonder shore, sweet land of liberty,
> The vessel soon will bear me o'er, and I shall then be free;
> No more I'll dread the auctioneer, nor fear the Master's frowns,
> No more I'll tremble lest I hear the baying of the hounds.
>
> > O old Master, 'tis vain to follow me,
> > I'm just in sight of Canada, where the panting slave is free!
>
> Yes! I am safe in Canada—my soul and body free—
> My blood and tears no more shall drench thy soil, O Tennessee!
> Yet how can I suppress the tear that's stealing from my eye,
> To think my friends and kindred dear as slaves must live and die.
>
> > O dear friends, haste and follow me—
> > For I am safe in Canada, where the panting slave is free!

The Underground Railroad was an object of scorn on the minstrel stage. A rambling commentary on pseudo-Negro philosophy and religion, "Dan Rice's Original Few Days"[21] ends with the observation:

> De Railroad dat's *underground*,
> > Few days,
> In Canada I can be found,
> > I's guan home.
> De white folks say dat I must come,
> > Few days,
> De whites and nigs dar are one,
> > For I guan home.

Abolitionist songs were all but eclipsed by the outpouring of songs which accompanied the dramatized versions of Harriet Beecher Stowe's literary bombshell, *Uncle Tom's Cabin* (1852). These songs were distinguished from other anti-slavery songs in attacking slavery on specific, rather than general grounds. Incidents and characters of the dramatized novel provided subjects for the staggering flow of sentimental, comic and descriptive songs which embellished stage versions of Stowe's work.

It is said that passage of the Fugitive Slave Law was the incident which impelled Stowe to produce *Uncle Tom's Cabin*, and that the major characters were drawn from real life.[22] Tom himself was purportedly based on the model of Reverend Josiah Henson, whose deep faith and remarkable loyalty to a harsh master provided an example of incredible self-effacement. But the novel, and certainly the songs accruing to its stage versions, perpetuated stereotypical images of the black as surely and effectively as did any minstrel performance. Stowe was not an avowed abolitionist when she wrote her book, nor did she have significant knowledge of slavery or the South. Yet her work was both praised and damned on these very grounds. Europeans, largely ignorant of the situation, accepted hers as the voice of authority on the entire subject.[23]

The influence of *Uncle Tom's Cabin* in aiding the anti-slavery movement must not be minimized however. Its sales rivalled those of the Bible and catapulted the horror of American slavery into the consciousness of the entire world. Perhaps the best measure of Stowe's novel is the violent reaction it produced in her Southern contemporaries. Not only was the book banned throughout the South and anti-Tom literature issued, but on one occasion Mrs. Stowe received a package containing an ear severed from some unfortunate slave.[24] More importantly, *Uncle Tom's Cabin* threw the South into a defensive position from which it has yet to emerge.

Uncle Tom on stage had little in common with his characterization in the novel. The story was twisted to suit the purposes of the adaptors, who in many cases recognized and exploited comic features as commercial windfalls. Not covered by copyright in these instances, Mrs. Stowe never received royalties from this artistic parasitism, characterized by Stern as "the entertainment business at its worst."[25] Despite a few serious efforts at capturing the essence of the novel in the adaptation of *Uncle Tom's Cabin* for the stage, Harriet Beecher Stowe and any vestiges of social accountability were largely overlooked in the headlong scramble to pluck fruit from her tree of success.

The songs connected with stage productions of *Uncle Tom's Cabin* suffer from the same ambiguity as the plays; it is not always clear whether the excessive sentiment was meant to be taken seriously or as a joke. Assessment of intent in this regard sometimes requires a judgment based on the overall performance and style of the composer of a particular song. Thus, we can be fairly certain that the psalmodist and teacher Isaac Baker Woodbury was in earnest with his "Uncle Tom's Lament For Eva." Woodbury has been described as a gentle person whose ill health foreshortened a promising career, and it was not his practice to write comic songs.[26] The edition of "Uncle Tom's

Lament For Eva" used in the present study does not indicate that it was intended for any stage production, and it is possible that the song was meant to honor the novel instead.[27]

The words of "Uncle Tom's Lament For Eva" seem excessively sentimental by today's standards but are, in fact, quite in keeping with the genteel spirit of its day. What is more of an anomaly is the association of the florid utterance of the text with the speech of Tom, pictured in the novel as a semiliterate slave.

UNCLE TOM'S LAMENT FOR EVA

The sun arose in beauty;
The birds caroled their song;
Sweet flowers sent forth their fragrance,
And decked the verdant lawn.
But sad my heart was breaking,
No gleam of sunshine there,
All, all was drear and darkling,
No comfort, e'en in prayer.

For 'twas the morn they laid you,
Dear Eva, in thy grave,
E'en now my heart is breaking,
O God, in pity save.
Thou knowest human weakness,
Thou knowest human wo;
O take me to those mansions
Where heavenly waters flow.

There, 'mid seraphic beings,
I'll meet my darling one,
And join with her in singing
Amid that heavenly throng.
Forever and forever
Our swelling songs shall rise;
O take me to those mansions
Far, far beyond the skies.

Again the sun in beauty
Arose in cloudless dawn;
Again sweet flowers in fragrance
Bloomed gaily o'er the lawn.
But Uncle Tom ne'er heeds them
He's joined the angel throng,

> And strikes his harp immortal
> To Eva's heavenly song.

Another song based on the same incident in the novel is "Uncle Tom's Glmipse [sic] of Glory,"[28] with words by "Eliza" and music by Frank Howard. Howard, who is not to be confused with the actor-producer George C. Howard (q.v.), was a self-taught performer on several instruments. His real name was Delos Gardiner Spalding, and he led a rather nomadic life until he settled in Chicago in 1853 at age twenty.[29] "Uncle Tom's Glmipse of Glory" is probably a serious effort, although there is much to commend this song to Jones' criticism of Howard's songs when he stated that they "became popular though not of a high order."[30]

The "glimpse of glory" refers to that part of Eva's death scene in which Tom explains to Miss Feely:

"The Lord, he sends his messenger in the soul. I must be thar, Miss Feely; for when that ar blessed child goes into the kingdom, they'll open the door so wide, we'll all get a look in at the glory, Miss Feely."

The excessive piety of the "Eliza" text removes the incident from the realm of worldly experience, however, and leaves a bloodless, sanctimonious perversion of black religious belief.

UNCLE TOM'S GLMIPSE OF GLORY

Gently, as fadeth the glad light of day,
Little Evangeline passeth away;
No more her feet through the flowers will roam,
Slowly but surely she neareth her home.

Now all her loved ones she calls round her bed,
And gives each a curl from her fair, drooping head;
And bids to remember to meet her above,
And Him who so loves them, forget not to love.

Why seeks the veranda, the good Uncle Tom,
And leaves his own cabin though midnight has come?
He knoweth the Bridegroom ere long will be here,
And watcheth and waiteth till he shall appear.

For O, when he cometh and taketh his own,
He knows, while the gates shall be wide open thrown,
He may catch, of the world without sorrow or sin,
A glimpse of the glory, as Eva goes in.

The first, and perhaps most successful, version of *Uncle Tom's Cabin* to reach the stage was written by George L. Aiken for the actor-producer George C. Howard. Howard's wife played Topsy and her daughter, Cordelia Howard, became famous as Eva. G.C. Germon was the original Uncle Tom in the cast, the only part he played during the rest of his life.[31] George Howard was something of a songwriter in addition to his other talents, and he produced songs for the play, including "Uncle Tom's Religion," for Germon, and "Oh! I'se So Wicked," for his wife.

"Uncle Tom's Religion"[32] is more faithful to the original conception of the main character of the novel than the preceding examples. The text, in dialect, does not attempt to forge credentials by adopting the speech mannerisms of an Oxonian, and the beliefs expressed by this Tom are, by comparison, far more credible. The musical accompaniment, on the other hand, retains the overwhelming sentimentality that threatens at any moment to degenerate into outrageous buffoonery. Although "Uncle Tom's Religion" is lacking in those qualities which make memorable songs, it would be remembered that it was produced to serve a function on stage and not presented as a single piece of great musical value.

UNCLE TOM'S RELIGION

Far away from wife and children,
Still I plod my way along,
Massa Clare has gone to Eva,
Leaving friendless poor old Tom.
Yet with trust and strength in heaven
I remain a faithful slave,
When de whip to me is given,
I'll think of him who died to save.

Shall I turn against my brother,
Raise the hand of cruelty,
No, we must love one another,
Den we'll get where all am free.
Patience here I'll go to glory,
There is comfort for the slave,
When de lash makes dis flesh gory,
I'll pray to him who died to save.

Good bye Chloe, farewell children,
Poor old Tom you'll see no more;

Mind be good and hab religion,
'Twill bare you to the faithful shore.
Do not weep nor shed tears bout me,
Suffering's over in de grave,
But at de glorious resurection,
We'll meet with him, who died to save.

Howard's "Oh! I'se So Wicked"[33] opened a vast, new, and potent
subject for the exploiters of the black in song by establishing the figure
of the mischievous black child as a lovable, yet exasperating,
stereotype. "Oh! I'se So Wicked" was the unquestioned model for
songwriters who subsequently produced thousands of songs of the
type and thereby molded the figure into a firm American stereotype.
The character of Topsy was a sure-fire popular hit in the play as in the
novel; the song could hardly have failed.

OH! I'SE SO WICKED

Oh, white-folks I was never born,
Aunt Sue, raise me on de corn,
Send me errands night and morn,
Ching a ring a ring a ricked.
She used to knock me on de floor,
Den bang my head agin de door,
And tare my hair out by de core,
Oh! cause I was so wicked.

> Black folks can't do naught they say,
> I guess I'll teach some how to play,
> And dance about dis time ob day,
> Ching a ring a bang goes de break-down.

Oh! Massa Clare, he bring me here,
Put me in Miss Feeley's care,
Don't I make dad [that] lady stare,
Ching a ring, a ring a ricked,
She has me taken cloth'd and fed,
Den sends me up to make her bed,
When I buts de foot into de head,
Oh! I'se so awful wicked.

> I'se dark Topsy, as you see;
> None of our half and half for me,
> Black or white its best to be,
> Ching a ring a hop, goes the break-down.

Oh! dere is one, will come and say,
Be good Topsy, learn to pray?
And raise her buful [beautiful] hands dat way,
Ching a ring a ring a ricked?
'Tis LITTLE EVA, kind and fair,
Says if I'se good I will go dere,
But den I tells her, I don't care,
Oh! aint I very wicked?

    Eat de cake and hoe de corn,
    I'se de gal dat ne'er was born,
    But 'spects I grow'd up one dark morn,
    Ching a ring a smash goes de break-down.

Music publishers on both continents rushed "Uncle Tom" songs into print as the dramatized novel evidenced its remarkable staying power. From London, for example, whole collections appeared, such as *Jefferys' Edition of Uncle Tom's Cabin Songs* by the composer-author-publisher, Charles Jefferys. Songs appeared with vividly illustrated scenes from the story, and many songs began to aspire to greater heights than a mere stage functionalism. Stephen Glover's setting of Jefferys' "George's Song of Freedom" recalls the *Sturm und Drang* of an earlier era with mighty leaps in the melody and a carefully worked out accompaniment that must have presented a formidable challenge to pianists of the day.

Details of the drama and the novel were altered at will in many of the songs; thus, for example, "Eliza's Flight"[34] pictures Eliza gaining safety when she reaches the Ohio shore, whereas the novel leaves her and her loved ones in danger until they find sanctuary in Canada:

    The mother gains the further shore,
    Her babe is on her breast,
    The race is past, the peril o'er
    One moment is she blest!

Perhaps the most preposterous scene in Stowe's creation occurs with the death of St. Clare, Eva's irresponsible father. He rejects the physician's offer to fetch a clergyman and asks Tom to pray for his soul. The scene is complicated through knowledge that St. Clare has promised Tom his freedom without assurance through legal means that this would happen. It is likewise antithetical to the main premise of the novel to show sympathy for a slaveowner, regardless of what lovable qualities he might possess. The many songs on this scene are consistent in their overblown sympathy for the well-intentioned but shallow St. Clare. Typical of songs on this scene, M.A. Collier's "Death of St. Clare"[35] is an emotion-laden picture of interracial love which flies in the face of the author's own conscious prejudices, revealed through association of whiteness with goodness and the awe with which Tom's religious impulse is regarded by even a white person. It is easier to understand the anguish of Tom at the death of Eva than it is to visualize the same emotion at the death of one who has left unfulfilled his promise of manumission. Yet the author unblushingly flounders through the incredible scene with:

DEATH OF ST. CLARE

Wo! wo was stamped on the bondman's brow,
But not for himself he wept;
His master lay on the death couch low,
And its shadows had o'er him swept.
Life's full warm tide—it was ebbing fast,
And the lord he had loved so well,
Are passing away—but that look he cast,
Its meaning, O who can tell.

Mournful in death's sad hour he turned
To the far off spirit-land;
But dimly the light within him burned,
Where, where is the guiding hand!
He gazed once more on the slave's dark face,
The soul to its depths was stirred,
And what shall win for the dying grace,
But of prayer, the hallowed word!

And that meek bondman is bending low,
And breathes from his heart of love,
Such thoughts of prayer for the dying flow,
As are sent from the Lord above.
Nearer and nearer that lowly one
To God the petition brings—
And his words of prayer to the great white throne
Ascend on the spirit's wings.

And the soul of his master to him is given,
And sweet peace is shed abroad,

In both, as the earnest and pledge of heaven,
The gift of a present God!
And the pale, pale hand of the dead is twined
With the hand of the dark-browed slave;
As low on the death-couch his lord reclined,
There was granted a power to save!

The unparalleled and apparently unstoppable success of *Uncle Tom's Cabin* evoked depreciative responses from pro-slavery minstrel songwriters, as noted in the previous chapter. The examples which have been discussed were sniper shots aimed mostly at criticism of slavery resulting from the novel; other songsmiths unleashed full attacks on the novel and its author, attempting to discredit both through song. In 1860, Dan Rice published "Uncle Tom's Cabin," a tasteless, sniggering impression of Tom, which Rice sang in his "original"play, *Southern Uncle Tom's Cabin*.[36] Rice's "Uncle Tom's Cabin" was sung to the tune of "Wait For The Wagon" and relates what might happen to the black upon his manumission.

UNCLE TOM'S CABIN

Now listen while my story with plainess I relate,
Of my strange adventures among the Nordern States,
Dey tried to make me b'lieb 'em, and said dey lub'd me well,
And jes' as good as white man, in eb'ry thing but smell.

But gib me de plantation,
Gib me de plantation,
My Jenny Mules to dribe;
Den wait for the wagon,
And we'll all take a ride.

Dey called me brudder Thomas, an' said you're quite secure,
An' locked me up to prove it, till I broke down de door,
I asked them for some money, an' what d'ye tink dey said?
Why, you must be crazy fellow, jes' trabel on ahead.

I show'd 'em my diploma, but it was no sort ob use,
Dey said I was de gander and Debby was de goose!
I says you all am robbers, dat decent people fleece—
An' dey put me in de calaboose for 'sturbin of de peace.

I trabel'd round de country an' felt dat I was free,
For I was cold and starvin' from de elbow to de knee,

> But Massa hab forgib me, an' I know dat all am right,
> Tho' if (to audience) it gibs *you* pleasure,
>   I'll run off eb'ry night.

It was Harriet Beecher Stowe herself, however, who was most viciously attacked. The scandal accompanying her acceptance of almost $20,000 collected in England and presented to her on her first visit there provided a windfall to composers with Southern sympathies. Her claim that these funds had been used to educate several former slaves was never substantiated, and the whole affair was enshrined in a song, the scatological "Aunt Harriet Becha [sic] Stowe."[37] Its author, Charles Soran, and the composer, John H. Hewitt, could scarcely conceal their glee at having discovered the chink in the armor of the crusader.

Soran was not particularly noteworthy as an historical figure, but John Hill Hewitt, son of James Hewitt, has been called the father of the American ballad. He became the principal composer of the Southern Confederacy which was established less than a decade after the appearance of this song. Despite his musical skill, he was a chronic loser, but he never abandoned his musical career.[38]

"Aunt Harriet Becha Stowe" was written for Kunkel's Nightingale Opera Troupe, with the dedication:

Respectfully dedicated to the estimable wife of Ex-President Tyler, and the other patriotic and Union loving Ladies of Virginia, who so justly rebuked Lady Sutherland and the Ladies of England for their uncalled-for meddling in the affairs of the people of the United States.

Soran's text is hardly a credit to Southern concepts of chivalry:

AUNT HARRIET BECHA STOWE

> I went to New York city, a month or two ago,
> A hunting for dat lady, Aunt Harriet Becha Stowe;
> I see'd de Abolitions, dey said she's gone away,
> Dey told me in this city it was no use to stay.
> She take away de dollars, and put 'em in her pocket,
> She laid her hand upon it, and dar she safely lock it,
> Dey said if Massa come for me, den dey would quickly meet,
> Dey'd make a lion of me, and gib me 'nuf to eat.

> Oh! Oh! Oh! Aunt Harriet Becha Stowe!
> How could you leave de country
> And sarve poor nigga so.

Dey treated dis here child, as doe I was a Turk,
Den tole me for to leave dem, and go away to work;
I couldn't get no work, I couldn't get no dinner,
And den I wish dis Fugitive was back to ole Virginny,
Oh! when I was a picanin, Ole Uncle Tom would say,
Be true unto your Massa, and neber run away,
He tole me dis at home, he tole me dis at partin'
Ned, don't you trust de white folks, For day am quite unsartin.

Ole Massa's very kind, ole Missus' gentle too,
And much I love my Dinah in ole Virginny true,
Now I'll go back and stay dar, and neber more will roam,
Lor bress de Southern Ladies, and my ole Southern home!
But don't come back Aunt Harriet, in England make a fuss,
Go talk against your Country, put money in your puss;
And when us happy niggers you pity in your prayer,
Oh! don't forget de *WHITE SLAVES* dat starvin ober dare!

Now de rules of dis here house don't 'mit of an encore,
So afore we go just listen, I'll sing you one verse more;
Aunt Harriet Becha Stowe, She tried to see de Queen,
But Victoria was too smart for her and could not be seen.
She den went o'er to France, and tried to come it dere,
But de Empress and de Emperor, know'd 'xatly what dey were,
So de best way to fix it and hab it understood,
Is dat she left her Country for her own country's good.

> Go go go Aunt Harriet Becha Stowe,
> I'se glad you left de Country
> And don't come back no more.

The implacable forces that were relentlessly driving the nation toward civil war led some minstrel performers and songwriters to attempt the role of mediators in the dispute. While their minstrel stage fame gave them influential voices and forums, their position was weakened by their unbending support for an imagined status quo which unrealistically presumed that the slavery issue could be resolved if people would only stop arguing about it. They adopted a hand-wringing attitude toward the divisiveness rampant between the North and the South without ever recognizing the simple fact that the

Southern position was indefensible. Further, the minstrel stage never fully realized its own role in the establishment of stereotypes of the black in the minds of Americans; thus, its influence in mollifying sectional antagonisms was undermined by its own beliefs and actions.

Minstrel stage composers had attacked abolitionism in song; they had pictured the black in the most unfavorable light; now, as the opposition began to state its case in militant terms, they adopted a position of querulous disbelief that the United States would tear itself apart over slavery. Their Frankenstein monster had turned on mankind and they, in total misunderstanding of the situation, reacted with hostile dismay at the uncontrollable events taking place before their eyes.

Political commentary, a feature of minstrel songs from the outset, became common as the opposing sides paired off for the inevitable showdown. The vote in the 1856 Presidential election was dominated by the slavery question, and political songs took direct aim at both the candidates and their positions on slavery. Stephen Foster's "The Great Baby Show; or, The Abolition Show"[39] attacked the newly formed Republican Party and its nominee, John Fremont, in a smirking commentary that does little to bolster Foster's image as the gentle genius of "Ethiopian" songs.

> On the seventeenth day of September, you know,
> Took place in our city the great Fremont show;
> They shut up the factories and let the schools out,
> For the children will all vote for Fremont, no doubt.
>
> They had "gemmen of color," to join in their games,
> And jokers and clowns, of all ages and names,
> They had pop-guns, and tin pans, and all kinds of toys,
> And a very fine party, all made up of boys.
>
> Now is it not kind in these good simple souls,
> To amuse all the children with antics so droll?
> To shut up their house, and spend so much money,
> To black up their faces, drink grog, and be funny?

But Foster's best effort for pro-slavery politics came with his "The White House Chair"[40] written for the same campaign. National unity was seen in this song as being threatened by those who would elevate blacks to positions of power should the Republicans win the election:

THE WHITE HOUSE CHAIR

Let all our hearts for Union be,
For the North and South are one;
They've worked together manfully,
And together they will still work on.

> Then come ye men from every State,
> Our creed is broad and fair;
> Buchanan is our candidate,
> And we'll put him in the White House Chair.

We'll have no dark, designing band,
To rule with secret sway;
We'll give to all a helping hand,
And be open as the light of day.

The abolitionists, however, replied to this type of appeal with scathing broadsides against pro-slavery candidates; if unity were to be achieved at the expense of foregoing their demands for an end to slavery, they were having none of it. Songs such as "Down With Slavery's Minions,"[41] written by E.W. Locke and sung to the tune of "Old Dan Tucker," blasted any person or institution supportive of slavery.

DOWN WITH SLAVERY'S MINIONS

Rouse ye, freemen, from your slumbers;
Seize your arms and count your numbers;
Now's the time for deeds of bravery,
Freedom grapples now with Slavery.

> Down with Douglas, Pierce and Shannon,
> Down with Slavery and Buchanan!
> Freedoms traitors—sing their dirges,
> Long and loud as ocean surges.

In the halls of Congress pleading,
On the fields of Kansas bleeding,
Brothers true as steel implore us—
"Join the fight and join the chorus!"

Mark the flag of Slavery's minions—
"Bludgeons versus Free Opinions!"
"Rule or Ruin!" "Compacts Broken!"
"Choke Free Words, before they're spoken!"

> Are we cowards now to falter?
> Have we naught for Freedom's alter?
> Shall our forces by division,
> Reap defeat and bold derision?
> Never! Never! all are ready!
> Every column marching steady;
> True as were our sires before us,
> Marching steady to the chorus!

The passage of the Kansas-Nebraska Act in 1854 had reopened the question of slavery in the Louisiana Territory and turned Kansas into a battlefield where pro-slavery forces and abolitionists fought what might be considered the first skirmishes of the Civil War. "Bleeding Kansas" entered the vocabulary of songwriters in both camps, each attaching its own interpretation to developments in the emerging state. From the minstrel stage came "Dat Gets Ahead Of Me,"[42] which stated the minstrel stage position:

> How is it so much time is spent
>   By Congress members now,
> In quarrels, fights, and long debates,
>   With one continual row?
> Why don't they hold their noisy tongues,
>   If they want Kansas free?
> Why can't de people's votes decide?
>   Dat gets ahead of me.

Nothing, of course, would have suited abolitionists better than to have abided by the will of the people in settling the matter of slavery in Kansas. Through deceit or sheer stupidity, the author of "Dat Gets Ahead Of Me" neglected to mention that anti-slavery forces *had* won the election in Kansas in 1856, but their decision had been nullified by Buchanan, who sided with the pro-slavery government of Kansas under Lecompton.

Agitation by abolitionists continued to erode the patience of minstrel performers who doubtlessly considered themselves self-anointed authorities on the black question. Even on the brink of actual hostilities, songs emanating from the minstrel stage maintained the position exemplified by a verse taken from "There's Nothing Like It":[43]

> The Abolition men they preach 'bout settin' niggers free,
> I think they'd better hold their tongues and let the niggers be;
> They only want to coax them off, then leave 'em all alone,
> But the niggers are contented as long as they've a home.

On the eve of the Civil War, it became clear to even the most thickheaded minstrel performer that a national catastrophe was in the offing and that they, along with everyone else, would soon be forced to choose which side held claim to their loyalty. Some still clung to the hope that their position in the public eye would allow them to act as mediators; thus, from Philadelphia's Academy of Music the famous Dan Rice addressed himself to an audience made up, in part, of a large delegation of medical students from the South who were returning home in protest of anti-slavery feelings then prevalent in that city. A mixture of anti-abolition sentiment and apology to the sensitive Southerners, Rice's speech drew glowing praise from the press the following day:

In the course of the evening, Dan Rice made a strong Union and Conservative speech, abandoning for once the role of the humorist, and delivering a plain, matter-of-fact oration, as becomes a citizen, that brought down the house with thunders of applause. As a resident citizen of Philadelphia, he . . . begged his young friends then present not to be rash or hasty in jumping to a conclusion, or imagining that the fanatical principles broached by the few were the sentiments of the many . . . .[44]

Having assured his audience that fanatical abolitionism should be left to the purging effect of the "sober, common sense of the people," which had "come to the rescue of the many against the impotent attempts of the few would-be disturbers of the public peace," Rice then spoke of solutions for the problems which were dividing the country:

. . . when the North and the South thoroughly understood each other, and the great community of interests which bound them, all fanatical attempts to dissever them would be laughed to scorn.

Whether Rice was merely trying to adopt the role of peacemaker out of basic decency or patriotism, the fact is clear that he neither understood the fundamental dynamics of the situation unfolding about him, nor did he perceive that he had, through his professional activity, contributed enormously to the difficulties himself. He cannot be singled out for blame, of course, yet his speech is remarkable in its revelation of attitudes of the minstrel show profession with respect to the slavery question. His allusions to familiarity with Southern life and the "gayety of the Negro in his plantation home" are a measure of Rice's self-delusion concerning actual conditions in the South, not to mention his inability to see that the stereotypical "happy plantation darky" was no longer relevant.

Rice further demonstrated the minstrel performers' characteristic insensitivity to the humanity and dignity of blacks by treating these matters in his speech as though they were comedy:

Speaking of his colored friends, he alluded to having built a place of worship for them, and conceived that as long as they obeyed the laws of this great Union, and the sovereign State in which they lived, they had as much right to all the enjoyments of humanity as white folks; and further, that white folks were just as good as colored folks as long as they behaved themselves (A sentiment which elicited much merriment, whilst his kindly allusions to the blacks were invariably received with tumultuous applause by the Southern students).

Perhaps it is unfair to single out Rice for censure: he was, after all, a victim of decades of repeated myths concerning blacks and slavery. His life had been devoted to the perpetuation of those myths which created such comfortable illusions for audiences and himself. But now that the dream was falling apart, the ghastly interior of a society which condoned slavery was being revealed, and the voice of the comic had the ring of impending disaster rather than the sonority of wisdom. Finally, Dan Rice was not alone. His views represented the norm among his colleagues as he deplored the current state of affairs in his "Things That I Like To See":[45]

> I would like the North and South to leave slav'ry alone,
> And stand by the Union unto the last stone;
> To settle the question by war, blood and vice,
> Is like burning your house to scare out a few mice.
>
> I'd like moderation all parties to sway,
> And slavery would dry up and soon blow away . . . .

Chapter Five

Civil War

The Civil War has been aptly named "the singing war." Both Northern and Southern armies marched off to battle with songs on their lips. The mere fact that so many of these songs are familiar today, after more than a century, attests to the intrinsic musical value and emotional power of much of this body of music. More memorable music came out of the Civil War, perhaps, than any other period of American history. In many instances, however, excellent melodies were used as settings for execrable texts on black subjects. Composers had perfected their craft in meeting the demand for morale-boosting melodies, but lyricists found it impossible to rid themselves of attitudes prejudicial to blacks. Deplorable words set to outstanding tunes was frequently the result.

Songs of the Civil War under consideration here fall into three broad and sometimes overlapping categories: the hortatory songs designed to foment enthusiasm for the military and political aims of either side; the songs concerned with the central issue of the war—the black; and those songs which carried on established traditions without conspicuous reference to the war or its issues.

It is almost an article of faith among students of Civil War songs to begin their deliberations with a discussion of "Dixie,"[1] Daniel Decatur Emmett's minstrel "walk-around" which served the Confederacy as a war song and subsequently as the musical symbol of the South. It was a product of the North and originally had no bearing on the war. Emmett wrote "Dixie" in 1859, simply in answer to the need of Bryant's Minstrels for a new number on their program. Emmett adopted the "carry-me-back" theme in its comic form to supply the text for his lively melody.

"Dixie" proved to be one of America's all-time hits and, as is often the case, gave rise to a number of legends about its creation. A considerable portion of these legends were contributed by Emmett himself. He, like "Daddy" Rice and his fanciful stories of the creation of "Jim Crow," gave out stories in later life which were largely the result of retrospective invention rather than accurate descriptions of what probably—or indeed possibly—were the details of the genesis of "Dixie."[2] Over the years, the imaginations of the faithful supplied what was lacking in the apocryphal tale.

Although it was known throughout the South prior to the Civil War, "Dixie" became permanently associated with the Southern cause through its performance at Jefferson Davis's inauguration as the Confederate President in 1861. After the Southern defeat, "Dixie" remained as the most tangible reminder that the South, although beaten, had not relinquished any of the basic tenets which had comprised its rationale for separatism. The South had lost the war, but none of its ante-bellum ideals.

Consanguinity of "Dixie" and racism is inherent in the original purpose for which the song was written. Association with the Southern Confederate cause emphasizes its racist mold as both words and music assumed meanings far beyond anything conceived by Emmett. Today, the performance of "Dixie" still conjures visions of an unrepentant, militantly recalcitrant South, ready to reassert its aged theories of white supremacy at any moment; it does not bring to mind the image of the slave's longing for the happy plantation envisioned in the original text. This is why the playing of "Dixie" still causes hostile reactions—after more than one hundred and ten years have passed since it was first heard.[3]

The greater part of the Civil War editions of "Dixie" were hortatory, with little or no reference to the black in the texts. It is for this reason that the 1860 Firth, Pond edition is cited. Compared with texts of the many other "carry-me-backs" in the minstrel repertoire, the overwhelming popularity of "Dixie" might seem difficult to explain. The text is well within established practice and the music distinguished primarily by its coherent form and the brassy impudence of the melody. It is only when the song is taken as a whole that an understanding of "Dixie's" conquest of the public is possible.[4]

DIXIE'S LAND

I wish I was in de land ob cotton
Old times dar am not forgotten;
    Look away! Look away!
    Look away! Dixie Land.

In Dixie Land whar I was born in,
Early on one frosty mornin,
  Look away! Look away!
  Look away! Dixie Land.

Den I wish I was in Dixie,
Hooray! Hooray!
In Dixie Land, I'll took my stand,
To lib an die in Dixie,
Away, Away, Away down south in Dixie,
Away, Away, Away down south in Dixie.

Old Missus marry "Will-de-weaber,"
Willium was a gay deceaber;
  Look away! &c—
But when he put his arm around 'er,
He smiled as fierc as a 'forty-pound'er.
  Look away! &c—

His face was sharp as a butchers cleaber,
But dat did not seem to greab 'er;
  Look away! &c—
Old Missus acted de foolish part,
And died for a man dat broke her heart.
  Look away! &c—

Now here's a health to the next old Missus,
An all de galls dat want to kiss us;
  Look away! &c—
But if you want to drive 'way soorow,
Come and hear dis song to-morrow.
  Look away! &c—

Dar's buck-wheat cakes an 'Ingen' batter,
Makes you fat or a little fatter;
  Look away! &c—
Den hoe it down an scratch your grabble,
To Dixie land I'm bound to trabble.
  Look away! &c—

Curiously enough, the south, which stood to lose its cherished
institution of slavery should the North win, had very little to say about
blacks in its songs. Songs published in the South during the Civil War
were generally those which championed the cause of states' rights:
rallying cries exhorting all true Southerners to defend the South

against Northern "tyranny." Sentimental songs were also popular—
either produced by local talent or pirated from Northern sources. But
slavery, the real heart of the conflict, was hardly ever mentioned
excepting in those minstrel songs reprinted from existing materials
favorable to the South.

The catalog of Louis Grunewald, who published in New Orleans
during the war, listed only a single song of the minstrel type in 1865,
Billy Emerson's "Sassy Sam" which ridiculed the efforts of former
slaves in aiding the Union cause. As will be seen in subsequent
examples, this subject was already outdated when it appeared in the
South, which would seem to indicate that earlier editions exist,
although none as of this writing has been found.

SASSY SAM

Oh I'm sassy Sam, a Southern nig' as you can plainly see
I was born among the Sugar-canes, some miles from
      Point Coupee;
My master used to wallup me, so I cut my sticks and ran,
And the soldiers they got hold of me and made me contraband.

    Oh if you listen white folks,
    I'll please you if I can,
    For I am a bully nigger
    And my name is sassy Sam.

I then put on a uniform and drilled at all occasions,
And called myself a Corps d'Afrique and learned to cook
      my rations,
But soon I found it would not pay; the greenbacks were
      not plenty,
So down I went to New Orleans to deal in Cakes and
      Candy.

But soon I burst, and gave up shop and changed my avocation,
And then bought out a shoe-black stand in a very fine location,
Now gents if you nees some blacking done, just come right
      to my stand;
Three doors from the St. Charles Hotel you'll find me Sassy
      Sam.

Other Northern minstrel favorites pirated in the South during the
Civil War included "Kingdom Coming," "The Yellow Rose of
Texas," and several Foster songs.[5] Billy Emerson, whose real name
was William Emerson Redmond,[6] was a Northern composer as were

the others copied in the South; whether these composers approved of the practice is impossible to state with certainty.

Even those songs complaining of conditions in the Confederate Army, or "Corn-fed" Army, as they termed themselves, refrained from mention of blacks. "Short Rations,"[7] with its doleful lament over the Spartan existence imposed by the exigencies of war, never once places blame for the army's troubles at the door of blacks.

Perhaps the question of why the black appeared so seldom in Southern music of the Civil War period can be partially explained by the patrician philosophies which dominated Southern life. There was certainly no dearth of composers capable of producing such songs. Aristocratic behavior, on the other hand, demanded a strict avoidance of anything which tended to elevate the servant to the level of the master; equality on any point was a concept that was antithetical to the entire social structure of the South. It was hardly necessary to spell out the terms or implications of the unwritten social code; it was accepted as natural that the ruling class should rule and the servant class should serve. No Southern gentleman could unbend far enough to enjoy a hearty laugh at himself or his way of life and retain the dignity of power which he was certain came to him by the will of God. Slavery to the slaveholder was no laughing matter.

It was no accident that the Confederacy was built on the idea of rule by a despot, checked only by the will of the states. It was the myth of paternalism in action, a system designed to benefit a select few at the expense of the many, whether black or white. Under this system, the black was seen as subhuman and as chattel—unworthy of notice in song or anywhere else.

The concept of the slave as property influenced Northern thinking as Union leaders struggled to cope with the problem of numbers of slaves that came under Northern control through the fortunes of war. The slaves who came into the Union camps were called "Contrabands," a term which came into general use after May 23, 1861, when General Benjamin Butler decided that slaves belonging to the Confederates were to be considered as contraband of war—just as other captured war materiel.[8] This step has been interpreted as the first move toward legal emancipation of the slaves; they achieved freedom by being considered as property—contraband of war.

The reaction of songwriters to the phenomenon of the black contraband was mixed. Many viewed it as another comic windfall, while others, particularly the abolitionists, took it as a fitting subject for serious song. The best result of Northern whites' contact with the contraband, however, was that now, for perhaps the first time in American music history, whites could observe, hear, and record the black musical experience. It was at this point in history that America discovered that the so-called "Ethiopean" song of minstrelsy was a fabrication of white showmen, and that actual black music had beauty far in excess of anything heretofore heard on the stage.

Many of the escaping slaves made their way to Fortress Monroe, where General Butler had first decreed them contraband. The chaplain assigned to the contrabands, Rev. L.C. Lockwood, was profoundly affected by the ex-slaves' singing and undertook to bring it to the attention of the world. This music was too exotic for white ears, however, and it was deemed essential to edit the music rather than admit that unfamiliarity with the genre confounded white musicians. Thus the actual music of the black entered the mainstream of American song, bowdlerized, "corrected," and altered to suit the purposes of the time, but with enough original vitality and beauty to mark it as peculiarly black.

Lockwood introduced the haunting "Go Down Moses" in 1861, in a highly altered version entitled "The Song of the Contrabands. O! Let My People Go."[9] The "corrections" made by Lockwood and Thomas Baker, who arranged this grand spiritual for publication, almost obliterated the original. The further encumbrance of the song with extraneous verse and a parody, "The Lord Doth Now To This Nation Speak,"[10] are distractions which in no way enhance the work. Despite all the meddling, "The Song of the Contrabands" is still recognizable as "Go Down Moses," a testament to the inherent strength of the original.

While the unique qualities of this new music were obvious, and although the transcribers' sympathies were probably with the blacks, it is still evident through the efforts to refine this music for white audiences that blacks were considered as inherently inferior people incapable of producing music on a par with that of the whites. The readiness with which the melodies were emasculated and the willingness to concoct ridiculous parodies could easily be taken as musical stupidity if it were not for the fact that through such crudities a new musical horizon was opened to the world. But were it not for the great strength of those noble melodies, they might well have perished under the heavy hands of their admirers.

THE SONG OF THE CONTRABANDS
"O! LET MY PEOPLE GO"

The Lord by Moses to Pharaoh said:
O let my people go!
If not, I'll smite your first-born dead,
Then let my people go!

> O! go down, Moses,
> Away down to Egypt's land,
> And tell King Pharaoh,
> To let my people go!

No more shall they in bondage toil,
O let my people go!
Let them come out with Egypt's spoil,
O let my people go!

There are eleven verses of "The Song of the Contrabands" which Lockwood maintained had been sung for some nine years previous. Most of the text is similar to the verses quoted, but at least one, the tenth, has about it the unmistakable earmarks of proselytizing Northern abolitionism:

> O let us all from bondage flee,
> O let my people go!
> And let us all in Christ be free,
> O let my people go!

At the risk of sounding an unjust criticism, it might be well to remember that there is irony in the call of Christianity to the "heathen" black: it was this same argument which had been used in the enslavement of blacks during the colonial period. The abolitionists were not content to leave "The Song of the Contrabands" in its original state, however. They had an exciting item and they knew it—"The Song of the Contrabands," transformed into "The Lord Doth Now to this Nation Speak," was entirely devoted to the abolition theme of militant response to slavery. Laudable as those ends might have been, this parody of such a grand monument to black song could hardly have produced words to dignify the melody.

THE LORD DOTH NOW TO THIS NATION SPEAK

The Lord doth now to this nation speak,
"O let my people go!"
The bruised reed ye shall not break,
O let my people go!

> Then go down, freemen,
> Away down to Dixie's land,
> And tell Uncle Sam
> To let my people go!

No more shall they in bondage bleed,
O let my people go!
Oh! men of state, this message heed,
O let my people go!

Haste freemen, 'till the sea you've crossed,
O let my people go!
Their chains shall in the deep be lost,
O let my people go!

Go freemen, say to Abraham:
O let my people go!
If not, I'll smite the best in your land,
O let my people go!

Like Abraham of old we pray,
O let my people go!
That faith and works God's wrath may stay,
O let my people go!

Save freemen, save, our land from stain,
O let my people go!
Go say to Congress yet again,
O let my people go!

God's hand hath opened freedom's door,
O let my people go!
From sea to sea, from shore to shore,
O let my people go!

The cry of blood ascends to Heaven,
O let my people go!
As unto them, to you be given,
O let my people go!

Go say to Stanton, Seward and Chase,
O let my people go!
Lift up a poor down trodden race,
O let my people go!

Go say to Smith, Welles, Blair and Bates,
If you let my people go;
Peace shall return to the Rebel States,
O let my people go!

But, if you will not let them go,
Oh! now a warning take,
Old England sure will be your foe,
She'll smite from sea and lake!

Fear not Jeff. Davis, nor his host,
O let my people go!
The great Rebellion shall be crushed,
Soon as my people go!

Blacks escaping into the Union camps presented something of a problem as to how to care for them and what to do to provide employment for them. They were set to work at various menial tasks at first. The obvious solution of allowing black males to fight in their own behalf in a war that was of overriding concern to them only occurred to Union leaders later and over violent objections of many Northerners.

"To Canaan; Song of the Six Hundred Thousand,"[11] one of the hundreds of hortatory songs of the North, mentions the role of blacks in the earlier days of the war:

What troupe is this that follows,
All armed with picks and spades?
These are the swarthy bondsmen,
The iron-skinned brigades!
They'll pile up freedoms breastwork,
They'll scoop out rebels' graves,
Who then will be their owner,
And march them off for slaves.

There is little similarity between the vigorous denunciation of the South contained in "To Canaan," which promises to "blow before the heathen walls the trumpets of the North" and to "break the tyrant's scepter," and the product of two other zealous abolitionists, Mrs. E.A. Parkhurst and Lucy Lovell, in which the contraband in song is a conglomerate of white prejudices. Without meaning to belittle the two good ladies' effort, their "Little Joe, the Contraband"[12] depicts a

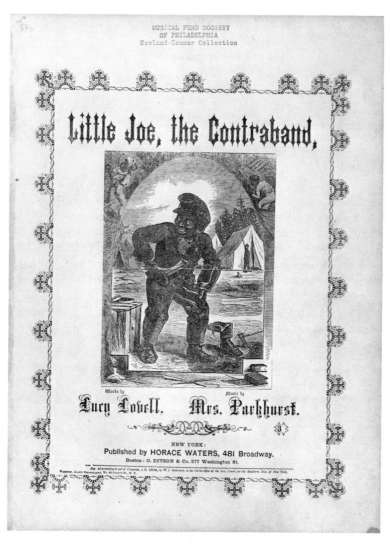

Figure 15

fawning, scraping figure who could only be described as thoroughly demeaning to the black image. Even the cover of "Little Joe, the Contraband" pictures the subject as a truckling bootblack, lacking in those vigorous qualities which the genteel New England ladies might have found at variance with their preconceptions. This is a prissy song with words in the standard pseudo-black dialect of the minstrel stage.

LITTLE JOE, THE CONTRABAND

And who are you, my merry boy,
    With blacking brush in hand?
Oh, I's a happy darky, sah!
    I's Joe, de Contraband.
I's born in ole virginny, sah,
    In a hut on massa's land;
And dere's where Joe lib seben years,
    Afore he's Contraband.

Dey sole me way from my mammy den,
    To a wicked massa, too;
An' dere I's kick'd and cuff'd about,
    An' heaps ob work to do!
I neber seed my mammy, sah,
    'Till time I feel her hand
Right on my shoulder, one dark night,
    She say "we'm Contraband!"

Wake up, Joe! Daddy's here! we's come
    To carry you away!
We'll run an' fine de Linkum folks
    Afore de break ob day!
I rub'd my eyes, an' when I know'd,
    O, den I clap'd my hands!
I wanted so to shout hurray!
    Hurrah! we'm Contrabands!

But mammy say, "be quiet Joe!"
    An' dad he tuk me den
Right on he back. We runned all night,
    An' foun' de Linkum men.
Dem Yankee folks am bery kind
    We couldn't hardly stand;
Dey let us rest, dey gub us food;
    Dey'm good to Contraband!

An' now we works, and gets de pay!
    We owns ourselves! We's free!
We's gwine to hab a house some day,
    To lib in! Yas we be!
My daddy fights for Uncle Abe,
    Mammy works on de land,
Dis chile, he bracks de gemmen's boots,
    Becase he's contraband.

I's gwine to school! Dat lady dar
    Said she'd tell little Joe
All about dem pretty letters, sah,
    In de little book, you know!
Brack boys can larn to read, sah, now!
    I knows de w'ite folks planned
Dem pretty books, wid pictures in,
    To larn de contraband.

De preacher, he am dat nice man,
    Joe hearn 'im preach one day,
If any body want to be good,
    He'll show 'em all de way.
He say, you leab off lie an' 'teal!
    You keep de Lord's commands!
An' dat's what we's agwine to do,
    We is, de contrabands!

'Spec massa Linkum come some day,
    Make all de brack folks free;
Who'll massa hab to hoe de corn,
    Dat time, instead ob we?
Ole massa neber get us here!
    How tall de niggers stand!
I's just as good as w'ite folks now!
    Hurrah! I's contraband!

The contraband was depicted as a comic figure by most professional songwriters of the Civil War period, as they exploited white fears that the emancipated slave would demand—and overzealous abolitionists would grant—equality with whites. The tendency was to exaggerate the problem in the popular songs, many of which showed the blacks not only living at the expense of whites, but expecting whites to become the servants of the freed slaves. This was no idle fear

Figure 16

among great numbers of whites, whether Southern or Northern. Even "Little Joe" could be heard to say, "I's just as good as w'ite folks now." This sentiment was utilized by numerous composers as a reminder to whites that only evil could come from recognition of the black as a member of the human race.

No better example of the white fear of emancipation can be found than Frank Wilder's "Uncle Sam's Hotel,"[13] a song which reached both Southern and Northern audiences. In a single stroke, Wilder plumbed the depths of the anxieties which dominated whites in their relationships with blacks, anxieties which eventually wrecked Reconstruction efforts in the years following the Civil War. Although gross exaggeration was one of the mannerisms of such songs, it must be reiterated that much of the white public held notions as fully exaggerated on the subject of emancipation. To them, "Uncle Sam's Hotel" was no more than a statement of fact.

UNCLE SAM'S HOTEL

I's took rooms for de season—I's cuttin' quite a swell,
I's stoppin' at a tavern—de United States Hotel.
Ole Uncle Sam's de landlord—we eat and drink our fill—
And de wisdom ob de measure is, dar's nuffin for de bill!

> Oh, hi O Dinkum Darkey,
> De white trash can't afford
> To take rooms at de tavern
> Whar de cullud gentry board.

De possum it was lubly but we've better grub dan dat;
De hoe-cake it was 'niffcent, de rackoon sweet an' fat;
But 'possum, 'coon, and hoe-cake—I bid you all farewell!
You wo'dn't suit de S'iety at Uncle Sam's Hotel.

> Oh, hi O Dinkum Darkey,
> Oh don't you hear de bell!
> It's ringing for de boardahs
> At Uncle Sam's Hotel.

And don't you know de boardahs! de accomplished Dinah
        Crow—
De scrushiatin' Pompey, and de gallant Mistah Snow;
And all ob de "born equals," no matter whar dey dwell,
Are goin' to be boardahs at Uncle Sam's Hotel.

> Oh, hi O Dinkum Darkey,
> Oh berry sure I am,

> De best of all de taverns
> Is kept by Uncle Sam.

De scrushiatin' Pompey, when he sits down to dine,
Just hear him call de waitah, to fotch along de wine!
And see de little white boys a helpin' Mistah Snow,
And bringin' chicken fixin's to de lubly Dinah Crow!

> Oh, hi O dinkum Darkey,
> I's cuttin quite a swell,
> I's took rooms at a tavern—
> De United States Hotel.

It's a mighty big old tavern, dat United States Hotel!
It has sixty thousand boardahs, and it 'commodates 'em well;
It has room for all of Dixie, an 'spect dey'll al be here,
Wid dar wives and piccaninnies, 'for de endin' ob de year.

> Oh, hi O Dinkum Darkey,
> We have no bills to pay,
> Dey charge 'em to de white trash,
> I hear de landlord say.

Oh take de mattock, white man! de shubble and de spade—
We boardahs hab no work to do, we all hab quit de trade!
But fore you pay de board bills, you'll hab to tub and sweat,
And wish you wasn't white trash, a t'ousand times I'll bet!

"Ole Shady," also calling itself "the song of the contraband," is said to be of slave origin.[14] It is counted the work of an ex-slave, D. Blakely Durant, who served in the Union headquarters as a cook during the seige of Vicksburg. Benjamin R. Hanby, composer of the well-known "Darling Nelly Gray," provided the musical setting for "Ole Shady." Granting that "Ole Shady" is perhaps authentic black song, there is still a very noticeable white influence in editorial "corrections." There is a vast difference between "Ole Shady" and the previous example, however. The disparagement of freedom is conspicuously absent, as the protagonist proclaims:

> Oh! yah! yah! darkies laugh wid me,
> For de white folks say Ole Shady's free,
> So don't you see dat de jubilee
> Is a coming, coming,
> Hail mighty day.

"Ole Shady" attempts to allay fears that the freed slaves only wanted to live at the expense of whites:

> Good bye hard work wid never any pay,
> Ise a gwine up North where the good folks say,
> Dat white wheat bread and a dollar a day
> Are coming, coming,
> Hail mighty day.

The joy of the slaves' first experience of freedom contrasts sharply with the canard set forth in song toward the end of the war to the effect that slavery constituted the preferred way of life for the black.

"Skedaddle" was a term coined during the Civil War to describe flight from the thick of the action; it was naturally used repeatedly by songwriters to humorously depict the flight of black, as well as his former master, who usually went the opposite direction. One of the several "skedaddle" songs, "The New Skedaddle,"[15] was by R.D. Scott, possibly a pseudonym for Henry Clay Work.[16] Work was reputedly a fierce abolitionist and Union patriot who nonetheless could produce radiantly cheerful songs on the minutiae of the momentous events then taking place. While such songs were doubtless of great value as morale-builders, and although they lacked the merciless sting of most songs of black subjects, Work's songs did little to dispel the false images of blacks.

THE NEW SKEDADDLE

> I'll sing you now de last new song
>   I heard down in Secessia;
> I'll change de words a little mite,
>   And hope dey won't distress you,
> Twas Gen'ral Price fus' pitch'd de tune
>   "Ole Ben" struck in sonorous;
> While Ployd and Polk took up de strain,
>   And all jined in de chorus.
>
>   We hear it by night, we hear it by day;
>   On foot or in de saddle;
>   Dey used to sing de Dixie song,
>   But now, "Skedaddle," "Skedaddle."

De rebels dey am husky boys,
    Quite fond of tune and rhyme, sah,
Dey sing dis one to double quick,
    While toes and heels keep time, sah.
De darkeys too, dey lub to sing,
    And so be in de fashion;
De way dey promulgate dis ting
    Skedaddle am a passion.

Secesh and contrabands unite
    Like brodders all before us,
Dough one go souf, de oder norf,
    Tis all to dis same chorus.
De locomotives cotch de tune,
    De steamboat as dey paddle;
And keep dar wheels a goin round
    To dis same tune Skedaddle.

Jeff Davis wants to learn de song,
    De Richmond papers tell us;
But dar's no music in his soul
    I know dey're try'n to sell us.
Den darkeys run, and darkeys sing
    "Skedaddle" am de chorus;
We'll nebber fear, but always keep
    De norf star right before us.

Work's greatest contribution to this type song was his "Kingdom Coming,"[17] reputedly his first song in pseudo-black dialect. The use of the dialect, plus the broad implication of "the servant becoming the master" as a recurring theme, are enough to question the depth of his commitment to abolitionist concern for the welfare of blacks, except that few abolitionist songs were any better in this regard. If one can disregard the offensive manner of the words for the moment, the musical setting which Work composed for "Kingdom Coming" must certainly rank as one of the finest examples of American popular song. But whether slander is excused on the basis of an excellent musical setting remains a moot question.

KINGDOM COMING

Say, darkeys, hab you seen de massa,
    Wid de muffstash on his face,

Go long de road some time dis mornin',
        Like he gwine to leab de place?
He seen a smoke, way up de ribber,
        Whar de Linkum gumboats lay;
He took his hat, an' lef berry sudden,
        An' I spec he's run away!

        De massa run? ha, ha!
        De darkey stay? ho, ho!
        It mus' be now de kingdom comin'
        An' de year ob Jubilo!

He six foot one way, two foot tudder,
        An' he weigh tree hundred pound,
His coat so big, he couldn't pay de tailor,
        An' it won't go half way round.
He drill so much dey call him Cap'an,
        An' he got so drefful tann'd,
I spec he try an' fool dem Yankees
        For to tink he's contraband.

De darkeys feel so lonesome libing
        In de log-house on de lawn,
Day move dar tings to massa's parlor
        For to keep it while he's gone.
Dar's wine an' cider in de kitchen,
        An' de darkeys dey'll hab some;
I spose dey'll all be confiscated
        When de Linkum sojers come.

De ober-seer he make us trouble,
        An' he dribe us round a spell;
We lock him up in de smoke-house cellar,
        Wid de key trown down de well.
De whip is lost, de han'cuff broken,
        But de massa'll hab his pay;
He's ole enough, big enough, ought to known better
        Dan to went an' run away.

In April, 1862 Lincoln's proposal for emancipation of slaves in the District of Columbia became law, and Henry C. Work celebrated the event with his "Uncle Joe's 'Hail Columbia!' "[18] Work approached this subject somewhat more seriously, which may account for the fact that it is musically less exciting. The protagonist is cast as an aged slave who has only lived to see this day and is now willing to pass on to glory knowing that freedom has at last come to his people. The pseudo-dialect is not the only flaw in the piece, however; the assumption that freedom had arrived was premature and, in any case, applied to only a small portion of the total slaveholding regions of the United States.

Certain passages and expressions in "Uncle Joe's 'Hail Columbia!'" suggest that Work was unsure of himself or under pressure to finish the song. When Work writes "Dis is what our faders fought for," as an example, we cannot be sure if he was aware of the actual struggles of slaves who fought valiantly and long to gain their freedom, or that he was merely repeating rhetoric that had been standard fare in white patriotic song for more than fifty years. A more fitting tribute to such an important milestone in the abolition of slavery might have been expected; but there are sympathetic stirrings in the chorus:

> RING DE BELLS in eb'ry steeple!
> Raise de Flag on high!
> De Lord has come to sabe his people—
> Now let me die.

Work was a prolific composer, and his output during the Civil War was aimed almost exclusively toward promoting Union and abolitionist goals. His was a fertile imagination which could turn a trifle into a song. His "Grandmother Told Me So"[19] places the appeal to patriotism and the cause of emancipation in the mouth of a child, shown on the illustrated cover, declaiming to the American eagle:

> American Eagle! hysterical bird!
> Oh, flap your wings and crow!
> The slaves are embellished—
>   yes, that's the word,
> For Grandmother told me so!

"Wake Nicodemus"[20] came rather late in the war and revived the theme of the aged slave whose great desire is to be a witness to emancipation. In this song, Work pictured a Negro of some character and a situation more dramatic than that of "Uncle Joe's 'Hail

Columbia!' " Understandably, "Wake Nicodemus" survived much
longer than the latter song.

WAKE NICODEMUS

Nicodemus, the slave, was of African birth,
    And was bought for a bagful of gold;
He was reckon'd as part of the salt of the earth,
    But he died years ago, very old.
'Twas his last sad request—so we laid him away
    In the trunk of an old hollow tree.
"Wake me up!" was his charge, at the first break of day—
    Wake me up for the great Jubilee!"

    The "GOOD TIME COMING" is almost here!
    It was long, long, long on the way!
    Now run and tell Elijah to hurry up Pomp,
    And meet us at the gum-tree down in the swamp,
    To wake Nicodemus today.

He was known as a prophet—at least was as wise—
    For he told of the battles to come;
And we trembled with dread when he roll'd up his eyes,
    And we heeded the shake of his thumb.
Though he clothed us with fear, yet the garments he wore
    Were in patches at elbow and knee;
And he still wears the suit that he used to of yore,
    As he sleeps in the old hollow tree.

Nicodemus was never the sport of the lash,
    Though the bullet has oft cross'd his path;
There were none of his masters so brave or so rash
    As to face such a man in his wrath.
Yet his great heart with kindness was filled to the brim—
    He obeyed who was born to command:
But he long'd for the morning which then was so dim—
    For the morning which now is at hand.

'Twas a long weary night—we were almost in fear
    That the future was more than he knew;
'Twas a long weary night—but the morning is near,
    And the words of our prophet are true.
There are signs in the sky that the darkness is gone—
    There are tokens in endless array;
While the storm which had seemingly banished the dawn,
    Only hastens the advent of day.

Henry Clay Work was a formidable figure in the history of popular song in America. As a musical propagandist for the causes he espoused, there were few who could excel or even match him. The major fault in his work was the same lack of firsthand knowledge of the black that flawed the work of all his contemporaries. There is evidence that his publisher, George Frederick Root, was exposed to the sacred music of the black on at least one occasion, although there is no indication that this exposure influenced his own composition.[21]

George Frederick Root, also a prolific composer of popular song, published his own songs, at times under pseudonyms such as "Wurzel," the German term for "root." His style was accommodated to the times; he produced sacred music, hortatory songs, and pseudo-black songs. His "De Day Ob Liberty's Coming"[22] explores the same subject as Work's "Uncle Joe's 'Hail Columbia!' "

"De Day Ob Liberty's Coming" contains a thought that was new, however: the slave in this song begged for a chance to join the conflict being fought in his behalf. Blacks had been refused this opportunity when they had volunteered for service after the fall of Fort Sumter and were allowed to take arms in support of the Union only after great political pressure and the exigencies of war demanded it.

Congress had authorized the use of black troops in 1862, but Lincoln mandated that blacks would be used as laborers—not as soldiers. The Navy accepted blacks, but they could achieve no higher rank than "boy." In the meantime, "De Day Ob Liberty's Coming" was proclaiming a very real black wish:

> White folks let us help ye trou,
>   De day ob Liberty's comin', comin',
> We can fight and die for you,
>   De day ob Liberty's comin'.

The impulse to use contrabands as soldiers was based on both the abolitionist aim of freedom for blacks and difficulties encountered in raising sufficient numbers of white troops. Few Northern whites felt that it was wise to arm blacks or that they were capable of becoming fighting men. It was widely assumed that they lacked both the intelligence and courage to be soldiers. While the notion of black ignorance and incompetence had appeared in song, the idea of cowardice as a black trait was less developed. The Christy Minstrels had featured black fearfulness in a parody on the "Phantom Chorus" from Bellini's *La Sonnambula*,[23] which began:

> Look yar Sir! as slowly comes de night:
> Den dese poor darkies am almost friz'd wid fright: . . .
> Tis true indeed Sar!
> Tis true indeed Sar! tis de debil or some
> Bugaboo dat goes about at night.

There was also the parody on "The Haunted Spring," an Irish ballad by Samuel Lover, entitled "Haunted Well"[24] by Nelson Kneass, wherein an attempt at exploitation of presumed black fear of the supernatural produced an inferior song. These songs were too few and unconvincing to fix the stereotype, but the idea was by no means dead. Fear was revived during the Civil War as one of the many undesirable traits that songwriters depicted—sometimes unwittingly—as characteristic of the black soldier.

William Shakespeare Hays produced a song of the black soldier that sums up most of the white anxieties concerning emancipation and arming of ex-slaves. "Nigger Will Be Nigger"[25] is a monumental insult to both the black and to reality; blacks were not only anxious to join the Union ranks but fought as valiantly as any white when allowed to do so.

NIGGER WILL BE NIGGER

Oh! If you listen to my song, I'll sing a little story,
About a Nigga size o' me, dat use to lib in glory,
I run away from Massa—leff de little ones wid Dinah,
When de bottom ub de Union tub fell out in Norf Car'lina.
Spoken: Yes I did.

I see'd de muss a bilin', an' I put de hoe away,
"Oh! we gwine to whip de Yankees," so I heard ole Missus say,
"An' dey gwine to free de Niggas" but dey'll nebber
Cum it quite,
Kase, a Nigga will be Nigga, dey kin nebber make him white.

I got down to New Orleans, Ole Massa was forgatten,
A sojer man he cum along, an' sot me rollin' Cotton,
At night I axed him for de pay, he tole me take my lip in,
He tuck me to de Calaboose, an' dar I cotch a whippin.
Spoken: Well, if dey didn't dey mos?

I look at him a little while, an' den he look at me,
An' tole me to go to—Washington, an' dar dey'd set me free,
I ax him for to gim me pass, he said he couldn't write,
Oh! a Nigga will be Nigga, dey kin nebber make him white.

Dey run me to de Steamboat, wid finger on de triggers,
You ought to see de Scatteration den among de Nigga's,
Some jump'd in de scuttle hole—an some o' dem did shiver,
An' half a dozen drown dey selves, by jumpin' in de ribber.

Spoken: Dey was fools fo' dat.

I was 'mong de Captur'd an' dey gib a gun to me,
An' tole me for to follow dem, an' dey would set me free,
Dey dress me up in Sojer close—dey didn't fit me right,
Kase a Nigga will be Nigga, you kin nebber make him white.

Dey put me in de black brigade—de Kernel he was drillin',
An' told de "fust American" ob de blood dey'd soon be Spillin'
De Nigga's eyes was bottom up—dar teeth begin to rattle,
He tole 'em not to trod upon each others heels in battle.

Spoken: You ought to see dem Nigga's heels.

Dey sent us out upon a Scout—an' we each had a gun,
De Rebels made a dashin' raid, you ought to see us run,
An' I'm satisfied de Niggas would rather *run* dan fight,
Kase a Nigga will be Nigga, you kin neber make him white.

De Nigga's good fo' throwin' dirt—an' purty good at bitin',
Dey'd better let de "Western boys" go in an' do de fightin',
Dey nebber run in battle yet, but when dey pull de trigger,
Dey go(t) one eye upon de reb—de toders on a Nigga.

Spoken: None o' dat for me.

Day may put us on de "bumgoats" or run us on de shore,
You may shut 'em up in bress works, dey'll allers find de door,
You may rub an' scrub 'em allors, an' dey will be black as night,
Kase it neber was intended dat a Nigga should be white.

William Kiernan's scurrilous "I Am Fighting For The Nigger"[26] bluntly states the feeling, widely held in the North, that blacks were hardly worth the bloody struggle that was taking place in their behalf:

I AM FIGHTING FOR THE NIGGER

I calculate of niggers we soon shall have our fill,
With Abe's proclamation and the nigger army bill.

Who would not be a soldier for the Union to fight?
For, Abe's made the nigger the equal of the white.

> Go in for the nigger,
> The sweet scented nigger,
> The woolly-headed nigger,
> And cream colored moke.

Each soldier must be loyal, and his officers obey,
Though he lives on mouldy biscuit, and fights without his pay;
If his wife at home is starving, he must be content,
Though he waits six months for Green-Backs, worth forty-five
      per cent.

If ordered into battle, go in without delay;
Though slaughtered just like cattle, it is your duty to obey;
And, when old Jeff Davis is captured, paid up you may be;
If you do not mind the money, don't you set the nigger free.

Moreover, if you're drafted, don't refuse to go,
You are equal to the nigger and can make as good show;
And when in battle, to the Union prove true:
But don't the nigger is as good a man as you.

Three for Honest Abe, he will be a great man yet,
Though he has loaded us with taxes, and burdened us with debt;
He often tells us little jokes, when pocketing our pelf,
And, at last, has made the nigger the equal of himself.

Guard well the Constitution, the Government and laws;
To every act of Congress don't forget to give applause,
And, when you meet the Rebels, be sure, and drive 'em back,
No matter if you do enslave the white man, you liberate the
      black.

Stephen Foster's contribution to the type was "A Soldier In De Colored Brigade."[27] The insult was the same but with a more polished technique:

> Old Uncle Abram wants us, and we're coming right along,
> I tell you what it is, we're gwine to muster mighty strong.
> Then fare you well my honey dear! now don't you be afraid;
> I's bound to be a soldier in de colored brigade.
>
> > A soldier! a soldier, in de darkey brigade!
> > I's bound to be a soldier in de colored brigade.

The text of "A Soldier In De Colored Brigade" reflects a degree of uncertainty concerning its own point of view. The song is unquestionably aimed toward ridiculing the black soldier, yet there are verses which, taken alone, might suggest a favorable attitude toward blacks in the armed forces. The fifth verse, on the other hand, is an attack on abolitionist aims that reveals something more than the mere desire to write a comic persiflage on the black soldier:

> Some say dey lub de darkey and dey want him to be free,
> I s'pec dey only fooling and dey better let him be.
> For him dey'd brake dis Union which de're forfadders hab made,
> Worth more dan twenty millions ob de Colored Brigade.

> Dan millions! Dan millions ob de darkey Brigade,
> Worth more than twenty millions ob de Colored Brigade!

"Abraham's Daughter"[28] is another of the professionally produced songs belittling the role of the black soldier in the Civil War. Attributed to Septimus Winner,[29] "Abraham's Daughter" became a great hit owing to its subject or, perhaps more likely, its technical and musical superiority over others of the type. Much of the affront to black manhood and the efficacy of blacks as troops lies in the cover illustration of "Abraham's Daughter." The text covers a variety of subjects, including the mock inspirational song of the black "Fire Zou, Zous," an attack on British sympathy for the Southern cause and an accolade for McClellan. Leaving aside those verses on subjects of no concern to the present study, an examination of the text shows little of the attitude of the composer on the question of the black soldier. Indeed, that the troops in this instance *are* black is discovered primarily through the cover illustration, and only secondarily through such textual references as "Zou-Zou," or Zouave, the term applied to volunteers of several regiments patterned after French infantry corps recruited in Algeria from the Zwawa tribe.

At the Battle of Milliken's Bend, a black soldier took his former master prisoner, an incident which might have influenced Henry C. Work's "Babylon Is Fallen!"[30] The innuendo and outright hostility characterizing most of the songs about the black soldier to this point in our study are missing in this piece, although use of the pseudo-black dialect and the "servant will be master" theme do little to enhance the black image. The publishers claimed that some singers preferred

"Babylon Is Fallen!" to the tune for which it was the intended sequel, "Kingdom Coming," stating that: "It certainly becomes more and more appropriate as the strongholds of the South fall into our hands, and the soldiers of "African descent" join in the fight."[31] Considering the self-congratulatory attitude of the publishers and the topic of the song, indications are clear that in the abolitionist's opinion at least one of their goals had been reached.

BABYLON IS FALLEN!

Don't you see de black clouds
Risin' ober yonder,
Whar de Massa's old plantation am?
Nebber you be frightened—
Dem is only darkeys,
Come to jine an' fight for Uncle Sam.

Look out dar, now!
We's a gwine to shoot!
Look out dar—don't you understand?
Babylon is fallen!
Babylon is fallen!
And we's a gwine to occupy de land.

Don't you see de lightnin'
Flashin' in de canebrake,
Like as if we gwine to hab a storm?
No! you is mistaken—
'Tis de darkey's bay'nets,
An' de buttons on dar uniform.

Way up in de cornfield,
Whar you hear de tunder,
Dat is our ole forty-pounder gun;
When de shells are missin',
Den we load wid punkins,
All de same to make de cowards run.

Massa was de Kernal
In de rebel army,
Ebber sence he went an' run away;
But his lubly darkeys,
Dey has been a watchin',
An' dey take him pris'ner tudder day.

We will be de massa,
He will be de sarvant—
Try him how he like it for a spell;
So we crack de Butt'nutts,
So we take de Kernel,
So de cannon carry back de shell.

Regardless of abolitionist views on the matter of black freedom and equality in being allowed to fight, the songwriters of the minstrel stage remained skeptical of the ability of blacks as soldiers. Dan Emmett's "The Black Brigade"[32] echoed sentiments expressed in "Nigger Will Be Nigger" and Foster's "A Soldier In De Colored Brigade" with the implication that conditions in the North had reached a point of desperation now that the black—by common consent a coward and self-seeker—was accepted into the armed forces.

THE BLACK BRIGADE

Dar's someting rong a brewin';
  Gwine to jine de Union.
Dar's somting rong a brewin',
  Hy-ro! we go!
We're on de brink ob ruin;
  Gwine to jine de Union,
Ah, ah, ah, ah!
  De boys from Linkum Land.

Den harness up de mule,
Be careful how ye whip,
An' mind your eye,
Sam Johnson am de nigga Gin'ral,
We're de Brack Brigade,
Why don't ye let her rip?
Jeemeses Ribber
Massa Greely, O!

We am de snolly-gosters, (Repeat)
An' lubs Jim Ribber oysters.

We're gwine to fight de South, O, (Repeat)
All by de 'word ob mouth,' O.

To fight for death an' glory, (Repeat)
Am quite annudder story.

Old John Brown dey strung 'im, (Repeat)
As high as Haman hung 'im.

I'll take my boat an' paddle, (Repeat)
For freedom will skydaddle.

After the black soldier had taken his place in the thick of battle and proven his worth as a soldier, sympathetic songwriters tried to find ways of supporting him in song. The result was often quite the opposite of the intention, as can be seen in a brace of songs written in 1864 by individuals with reputations of being favorable to blacks. "Dey Said We Wouldn't Fight,"[33] with words by Mrs. M.A. Kidder and music by Mrs. Parkhurst, attempts to refute arguments against the use of black soldiers with the same methods employed by those who ridiculed the idea. What the two well-meaning ladies accomplished was the production of a superlatively bad song with a ghastly pseudo-black dialect, a combination making it one of the most demeaning songs issued during the Civil War.

DEY SAID WE WOULDN'T FIGHT

Dey said we wouldn't fight,
Kase we's born so awful black,
Kase we's lazy from de cranum to de toes,
But dey'll find dese darkies some
When de rebel sojers come,
If dey'll keep us well in powder for de foes.

    Hi! ho! boys, we's a gwine home,
    Hi! ho! now for de fray,
    Yes, when de work is done,
    We's all a gwine home,
    And Abraham, we's longin for de day.

We's fitin for de flag
Dat is floatin ober head,
And we's left our piccaninny's home to cry,
But we'll neber leabe de field
Till de [we?] make de rebels yield,
And we's drefful sure to do it bye and bye.

Put de baccy in de pipe,
Put de powder in de gun,
And dese darkies in de foremost ob de din,
Den we'll put de foe to rout,

For we'll smoke de rebels out
While dese chilen tote dere bag and baggage in.

Oh some hab gone away
To de army ob de Lord,
And dey lef dere gun and knapsack way behind,
But dey'll neber see em more,
Ober on de oder shore,
When de blessed land ob liberty dey find.

If any of the ostensibly favorable songs could have done less for the black image than "Dey Said We Wouldn't Fight," it had to be the other example in this pair, the brutally direct "Sambo's Right To Be Kilt"[34] dedicated to the notion that whites would be altogether happy to let the blacks do all the suffering and fighting to save the Union. "Sambo's Right To Be Kilt" was written by Charles Graham Halpine under the pseudonym, "Private" Miles O'Reilly, and set to music by Samuel Lover. It is, according to Silber, the attempt of Halpine to defend the action of his superior, General David Hunter, of mustering into the Federal Service one of the first troops of black soldiers.[35]

Regardless of Halpine's motives in writing the song, "Sambo's Right To Be Kilt" appears to be an accurate appraisal of sentiments held by many whites: rancor against blacks that was nearly always on the verge of exploding into white rage as it did in the example of "I Am Fighting For The Nigger." But one must marvel at the tastelessness of such expressions coming from sources seemingly faithful to the ideals of radical abolitionism. The logic—or wisdom—of appealing for white recognition of the inherent worth and dignity of blacks through such contrived banalities as "Dey Said We Wouldn't Fight" and "Sambo's Right To Be Kilt" is not easily deduced, especially as the fake-Irish protagonist of the latter song proclaims:

Some tell me 'tis a burnin' shame
To make the naygers fight;
And that the trade of bein' kilt
Belongs but to the white:
But as for me, upon my sowl!
So lib'ral are we here,
I'd let Sambo be shot instead of myself,
On evry day in the year,

On evry day in the year, boys,
And in evry hour in the day;
The right to be kilt I'll divide wid him,
And devil a word I'll say.

In battles wild commotion,
I shouldn't at all object
If Sambo's body should stop a ball
That's comin for me direct;
And the prod of a southern bagnet
So ginerous are we here,
I'll resign and let Sambo take it,
On evry day in the year,
On evry day in the year, boys,
And wid none 'iv your nasty pride,
All my rights in a southern bagnet prod,
Wid Sambo I'll divide.

The men who object to Sambo,
Should take his place and fight;
And it's better to have a nayger's hue
Than a liver that's wake and white.
Though Sambo's black as the ace of spades,
His fingers a trigger can pull,
And his eye runs straight on the barrel sight,
From under his thatch of wool,
On evry day in the year, boys,
Don't think that I'm tippin' you chaff,
The right to be kilt we'll divide with him boys,
And give him the largest half.

Even though sympathetic to the cause of abolitionism, the composer who adopted the mannerisms or technique of minstrelsy in order to extol the black soldier risked having his effort misunderstood, or even mistaken, as the work of the opposition. Worse, on those few occasions in which pro-slavery minstrel melodists attempted to compliment the black soldier, admitting the necessity and efficacy of his contribution to the war, the endeavor was vitiated by the virtual world-wide acceptance of the contrived black imagery of the minstrel stage. Applied to the phenomenon of the black soldier, this tradition-building process made tributes into insults, as in "I'm One Of The Black Brigade":[36]

Ring de bell and boom de gun,
Make way for freedom's car,
For ebery cullered mudder's son,
Am gwine to gine de war,
Dey can't obfusticate de Souf
Widout de nigger's aid,
So tumble in, ye cullered folks,
And join de Black Brigade.

We're gwine down to take de Souf,
And ride em on a rail,
De white folks try to win de day,
But de nigger nebber fail;
Dey'll think John Brown am coming down
To make annudder raid;
So tumble in, ye cullered folks,
And join de Black Brigade.

Considered apart from their musical settings, songs about the black soldier and the contraband show little variation, whether inspired by abolitionist zeal or by professional ambition. By way of example, the difference between the choruses of "I'se On De Way" by George Frederick Root[37] and Dan Emmett's "Road to Richmond"[38] is too slight to show that Root favored the abolition cause, while Emmett had built his career out of demeaning blacks.

The chorus of "I'se On De Way:"

Hail! all hail!
I'se gwine to de Union ahmy,
Hail! all hail!
I'se on de way.

is almost identical with that of "Road to Richmond":

All hail! All hail! for we are under way.
Under way, under way,
Yah! we belong to de Union Army . . . .

The remainder of the two songs reveal some differences, of course, and a distinction could be made in the motivation of the black in Root's song, in which the ex-slave is "gwine" to join the army, whereas Emmett's protagonist already belongs to the organization; but the point remains that the technique in both instances is the same, and the black, alas, does not escape the bonds of his stereotypical image. Uncharitable though such a judgment might seem, the Civil War songsmiths, regardless of their personal convictions in the matter, never produced a suitable tribute to the black contraband or the black soldier.

Militant abolitionists clamored for Lincoln to show more vigor in the emancipation of slaves, while other Northerners insisted that the war was being fought in order to save the Union and that freeing the slaves would be the height of folly. To the abolitionist, slavery was what the war was all about. Some felt that it was perfectly legitimate to confiscate Southern property—including slaves—as a military expedient, while to set those classed as contraband alongside the white man as free men with equal rights was going too far. The black, according to this view, might become a freedman, but not a free man.

The view that preservation of the Union was the paramount issue in the Civil War was reflected in thousands of songs, as could be expected. Most of these made little mention of the black while emphasizing the need to "crush all traitors," as John M. Loretz's "Uncle Sam, What Ails You?" asked in 1863:[39]

> Uncle Sam, wake up! wake up!
> Sure, courage never fails you,
> See the fiendish Rebels come!
> Uncle Sam, what ails you?
> Quickly, then, put forth your strength,
> Crush these heartless traitors,
> Put your foot down, firmly on
> The necks of Union haters.
>
>> Come then, Uncle Sam, wake up!
>> Since courage never fails you,
>> Crush all traitors, North or South!
>> Uncle Sam, what ails you?

It is the second verse, however, which indicates the extremes deemed vital for the subjugation of the South and reveals, at the same time, that the black was not much of a consideration beyond his value as Southern property:

> Confiscate their stocks and farms,
> Do it with a vigor,
> If it will our Union save,
> Confiscate the 'Nigger!'

Other songs, such as "Hoist Up The Flag,"[40] made the point plainer:

> We'll fight for the Union, but just as it was,
> Nor care what Secesh or Abe-o-lition does;
> We'll stand by the flag, the sword and the gun,
> To save from dishonor the land of Washington.

It was certainly not an oversight on the part of Unionists, who expressed in song the wish to reunite the states, to minimize the central role of the black in the war; great numbers of Northern whites were quite willing to allow slavery to continue in the South if that would bring the country together once more. Lincoln held a similar view as he responded to an editorial by Horace Greeley: "My paramount object in this struggle is to save the Union, and not either to save or destroy slavery."[41]

The prospect of facing the consequences of winning the war was viewed with little enthusiasm by many Northerners, who envisaged millions of ignorant and penniless free blacks demanding equality should slavery be ended. Confiscation of a rebel slaveowner's property was one thing—but emancipation of all the slaves evoked nightmarish images of caring for vast hordes of people totally unequipped to manage for themselves.

As might be expected, songsmiths set to work building images that would resolve the problem of emancipation as it affected whites. Reviving the "happy plantation darky," songwriters offered the thesis that freedom, and the war being waged on its account, were in actuality threats to the security enjoyed by blacks under slavery. This incredible theory was reiterated time after time during the Civil War, always as the expression of black feelings. Naturally, the fears and tensions of whites were infinitely calmed upon hearing the pseudo-black protest that the war and abolition placed him at an extreme disadvantage and that it shouldn't continue on *his* account. "Young

Eph's Lament"[42] is an example of this type song which appeared early
in the war and remained popular until events settled the issue in 1865.

YOUNG EPH'S LAMENT

Oh whar will I go if dis war breaks de country up,
　　And de darkies hab to scatter around,
Dis dam bobolition, 'mancipation and secession
　　Am a going to run de nigger in de ground!

　　　　De bobolition here, de secession dare,
　　　　And neather one nor t'other of 'ems right,
　　　　But one says dis, de oder says dat.
　　　　And dey both got de country in a fight,
　　　　But what can a poor nigger do.

Now what is de use ob dis jangulating fighting?
　　Botheration to de country so forlorn?
Why don't they tend to business, making boats and building
　　　　railroads?
　　While de niggers raise de cotton and de corn.

　　　　But Massachusetts dar and South Carolina here,
　　　　Disturb dis happy Union wid de growl,
　　　　One says dey shall, de oder says dey shant,
　　　　And Uncle Sam has got to stand it all,
　　　　But what can a poor nigger do.

Oh I wish de white folks ob dis great confederation,
　　Would only quit der quarrells and der fight,
And stop dar cannonading, marching, shooting and bombarding,
　　And be willing for to use each oder right.

　　　　For its very plain to see dat de end would be,
　　　　Dat dae'd know each oder better dan before,
　　　　And dae'd make up der minds, dat in all future times,
　　　　Dey would not go and do it any more,
　　　　And dat's what I want dem for to do.

What a deuc'd shame it is dis sesession revolution,
　　Am a useing up de bussness ob de land!
While trade an navigation, merchandizing, speculation
　　Hab very nearly come to a stand;

　　　　De crops won't be grow'd, de meadows won't be
　　　　　　mow'd,
　　　　'Kase dar's nobudy left for to tend 'em,

> Dar's a scarcity it seems, ob cabbage peas an beans
> 'Kase dar's nobudy home for to send 'em
> Den what's a hungry nigger goine to do.

The downright absurdity of having the black protagonist vacuously expressing concern that the war disrupted "trade and navigation, merchandizing [*sic*], speculation" is an assault on the intelligence of the listener, as well as an insult to the black. In spite of countless real-life affirmations of the slaves' craving for freedom regardless of its consequences, the ease with which the ideas contained in "Young Eph's Lament" captured the imaginations of the free, white North indicates a deep widespread desire to erase the unpleasantness caused by the war.

In other words, the white wish for peace and unity demanded an apology from blacks for having caused friction and disunity. "Young Eph's Lament" gratified that wish although whites had to invent their own propitiation, ventriloquized by their contrived "happy plantation darky."

Fear of the emancipated slave established in the minstrel songs continued almost as a reflex, to judge by the amount and the unvarying poor taste shown by the examples. Typically, the songs dwelt upon the presumption of black inferiority without ever attempting to justify or validate the claim. It was an article of faith among minstrel songwriters that black was inferior to white, as in "The World's Topsy Turvy":[43]

> The world is topsy-turvy as ev'ry one knows,
> We're starving our neighbors and feeding our foes,
> And Greely and Beecher, both of the same pack,
> Would have us say *white* is the same thing as black.
> Forever and ever you may argue in vain,
> But the world's topsy-turvy and the people insane.

Another feature of this viewpoint, the fear of the political potential of the freed black, emerged in "Adolphus Morning-glory,"[44] an inferior minstrel song written by J.B. Murphy and set to music by David Braham, then only twenty-five years old.

> Next week I'm going to married be
> To charming Mariana
> And then my name will live in fame and story,

For I'm going to run for congressman
Way down in Alabama
That's where you'll find Adolphus Morning-glory.

The abolition songwriters seemed incapable of devising a suitable response to the attacks voiced from the minstrel stage. Perhaps they were not themselves certain of the consequences of emancipation, beyond the ending of a great evil. A smattering of songs of the "Am I Not A Man And Brother?" type suggested rather timidly that slavery was bad because the blacks were human; but abolitionists never developed an attack sufficiently broad in scope to refute pro-slavery spokesmen on the minstrel stage. They might have launched attacks on slavery as economic, social, and political stupidity in addition to its immorality and inhumanity; they might have shown through song more of the legal and scientific arguments against the institution; a song which could focus attention on the beneficial results of elevating the black to a position of equality with whites was needed—but it was not written.

Abolitionists produced what they doubtlessly felt was the most effective argument against slavery that could be put forward at the time, and the victorious conclusion of the war proved them right in a sense. But, although they subdued the slavemasters, they could not conquer false images of the black. Perhaps it is unfair to expect more from the abolitionist songwriters than the unquestionably sincere efforts of such writers as Work, Parkhurst, Root, and others. Among the obviously earnest works concerning the emancipation of slaves are two songs with texts by John Greenleaf Whittier, "Song Of The Negro Boatman,"[45] and "We Wait Beneath The Furnace Blast."[46] Both songs contain the basic virtues and faults of most abolition music: they attack the evil of slavery without offering much to improve the image of the freed slave. In these songs, however, one can sense that Whittier is under no illusions concerning the true feelings of white Americans toward the black at the time.

"Song Of The Negro Boatman" is in three parts: the first, entitled "Port Royal, 1861," sets the scene of activity behind the Union lines and describes the boatmen whose song comprises the second part. The final section of "Song Of The Negro Boatman" is an epilogue in which Whittier expresses a deep concern for the fate of the blacks and indicates, in thoughtful tones, that the "hapless race must shape our good or ill."

SONG OF THE NEGRO BOATMAN

(I)
Port Royal, 1861

The tent-lights glimmer on the land,
    The ship-lights on the sea;
The night-wind smooths with drifting sand,
    Our track on lone Tybee.

At last our grating keels outslide,
    Our good boats forward swing;
And while we ride the land-locked tide,
    Our negroes row and sing.

For dear the bondman holds his gifts
    Of music and of song;
The gold that kindly Nature sifts
    Among his sands of wrong.

The power to make his toiling days
    And poor home-comforts please;
The quaint relief of mirth that plays
    With sorrow's minor keys.

Another glow than sunset's fire
    Has filled the West with light,
Where field and garner, barn and byre
    Are blazing through the night.

The land is wild with fear and hate,
    The rout runs mad and fast;
From hand to hand, from gate to gate,
    The flaming brand is passed.

The lurid glow falls strong across
    Dark faces broad with smiles:
Not theirs the terror, hate, and loss
    That fire yon blazing piles.

With oar-strokes timing to their song,
    They weave in simple lays
The pathos of remembered wrong,
    The hope of better days,—

The triumph-note that Miriam sang,
    The joy of uncaged birds;
Softening with Afric's mellow tongue
    Their broken Saxon words.

(II)
Song of the Negro Boatmen

Oh, praise an' tanks! De Lord he come
    To set de people free;
An' massa tink it day ob doom,
    An' we ob jubilee.
De Lord dat heap de Red Sea waves
    He jus' as 'trong as den;
He say de word: we las' night slaves;
    Today de Lord's freemen.
        De yam will grow, de cotton blow,
        We'll hab de rice an' corn:
        Oh, nebber you fear, if nebber you hear
        De driber blow his horn!

Ole massa on de trabbels gone;
    He leab de land behind;
De Lord's breff blow him furder on,
    Like corn-shuck in de wind.
We own de hoe, we own de plow.
    We own de hands dat hold;
We sell de pig, we sell de cow,
    But nebber chile be sold.
        De yam will grow, de cotton blow,
        We'll hab de rice an' corn:
        Oh, nebber you fear, if nebber you hear
        De driber blow his horn!

We pray de Lord; he gib us signs
    Dat some day we be free;
De Norf-wind tell it to de pines,
    De wild-duck to de sea;
We tink it when de church bell ring,
    We dream it in de dream;
De rice-bird mean it when he sing,
    De eagle when he scream.
        De yam will grow, de cotton blow,
        We'll hab de rice an' corn:
        Oh, nebber you fear, if nebber you hear
        De driber blow his horn!

We know de promise nebber fail,
    An' nebber lie de word;

So, like de 'postles in de jail,
  We waited for de Lord:
An' now he open ebery door,
  An' trow away de key;
We tink we lub him so before,
  We lub him better free.

    De yam will grow, de cotton blow,
    He'll gib de rice an' corn:
    So nebber you fear, if nebber you hear
    De driber blow his horn!

(III)

So sing our dusky gondoliers;
  And with a secret pain,
And smiles that seem akin to tears,
  We hear the wild refrain.

We dare not share the negro's trust,
  Nor yet his hope deny;
We only know that God is just,
  And every wrong shall die.

Rude seems the song; each swarthy face,
  Flame-lighted, ruder still:
We start to think that hapless race
  Must shape our good or ill;

That laws of changeless justice bind
  Oppressor with oppressed;
And, close as sin and suffering joined,
  We march to Fate abreast.

Sing on, poor hearts! your chant shall be
  Our sign of blight or bloom,—
The Vala-song of Liberty,
  Or death-rune of our doom!

Coalescence and interdependence of black-white welfare was a premise rarely heard in song, and it may be taken as a mark of Whittier's wisdom and courage to have made it the subject of this lengthy song. His "We Wait Beneath The Furnace Blast" reverts to the standard practice of abolition songs in its frontal assault on slavery as immoral and unjust—a "poison plant" that must be rooted out regardless of the cost in suffering to the nation. The "purifying fire" of the Civil War is justified if it achieves the goal of ending slavery, but black characteristics are not cited as part of the reason for doing away with the "ancient evil."

Lincoln's Emancipation Proclamation evoked an outpouring of songs which erroneously implied that all slaves were now free. Of course, the Emancipation Proclamation applied only to those states in rebellion against the Union at the time, but most songs overlooked this detail in announcing the arrival of the "year of jubilee." This glorious event had been anticipated in 1862 with "Year Of Jubilee; or, Kingdom Has Come" by "Sambo."[47]

YEAR OF JUBILEE; or, KINGDOM HAS COME

I come up Norf, on a little bender,
   Left Missus at home wid no one to tend her,
Ole Massa's gone, I dunno whar to;
   Sambo pretty sure he don't much care to.

    Den sound de horn, beat de drum,
    De year ob Jubilee am come.
    Sound de horn and beat de drum,
    De year ob Jubilee am come.

Met Gen'ral Bloaregard, on my way here,
   He told me dat I had better stay dere;
He said, up Norf, dey would skin and eat me,
   Dat was a yarn dat a little beat me.

He said he had just whipp'd Gen'ral Buel,
   Grant and Wallace, all three in a duel,
I axed him den, why was he running away?
   Sambo, says he, dat question ain't fair play.

Oh, times down South am getting quite rotten,
   Ile's so berry scarce, they have to burn cotton,
I left dat land ob oppression and gas,
   And roam de free Norf without nary a pass.

Molasses Junction was a big scarecrow,
   Nigh its wooden guns nobody didn't dare go,
But when McClellan got a good ready,
   De Southern gentry seemed quite unsteady.

Abraham Lincoln and Emancipation,
   De two tallest tings in dis tall nation,
Hurrah den boys, let us still be merry,
   Kingdom has come boys, we've good times berry.

The following year the Emancipation Proclamation took effect,[48] and many songs celebrated the occasion with more enthusiasm than skill, as " '63 Is The Jubilee," a song written by J.L. Greene and set to music by D.A. French.[49]

'63 IS THE JUBILEE

Oh darkeys hab ye heerd it,
 Hab ye heered de joyful news:
Uncle Abra'ms gwine to free us
 And he'll send us where we chuse;
For de Jubilee is comin,
 Don't ye sniff it in de air:
And sixty three is de Jubilee,
 For de darkeys eberywhere.

  Oh de Jubilee is comin,
  Don't you sniff it in de air:
  And sixty three is de Jubilee,
  For de darkeys eberywhere.

Ole massa, he hab heerd it,
 Don't it make him awful blue,
Won't ole Missus be a ravin
 When she finds it comin true;
Specs dar'll be a dreffle shakin,
 Such as Jeffy cannot stand,
Cause kingdom kum is a movin now,
 And a clawin tro' de land.

No more we'll work for nuffin,
 But we'll own a little farm,
And no more dey'll sell our chil'en,
 But we'll keep 'em all from harm,
And no more we'll pick de cotton,
 And no more we'll feel de lash,
We'll shout, and drum on de ole banjo,
 'Till we break it all to smash.

Dar'll be a big skedaddle,
 Now ole sixty three hab come,
And de darkeys now, will holler,
 'Till dey make de country hum.
Oh we tanks Ole Uncle Abra'm,
 Yes we brees [bless?] him day and night,
And pray de Lord bress de Union folks,
 And de battle for de right.

While both the minstrel stage and the abolitionists varied greatly in their approach to emancipation, the slave himself was overjoyed at the prospect and expressed his joy in songs of great beauty and strength wherein pain was intermixed with gladness. None of these songs suggested concern for the political or social position of the ex-slave—only the ineffable happiness of freedom. No thought was given that could have been construed as a threat to the stability of white society; nothing was contained in the songs that was designed to arouse the manifold fears that white songwriters were debating at every turn. The white American public could have—were it not for propagandists on either side of the black issue—taken great comfort in such black songs as "No More Auction Block For Me":[50]

> No more auction block for me,
> No more, no more!
> No more auction block for me;
> Many thousand gone.

Unfortunately, the American public chose to regard the freed slave as both a political and a social threat. The black, figured in campaign songs of the 1860 and 1864 elections, precedented by songs of former campaigns, such as Foster's "The Great Baby Show" and "The White House Chair" which were written for the Buchanan campaign of 1856. Foster, incidentally, was an ardent Democrat with no love for abolitionism. Thus, his strongly pro-Union "Better Times Are Coming" of 1862 appears as something of an anomaly within the body of Foster songs of pro-slavery sentiment.[51]

"Honest Old Abe," written for Lincoln's 1860 campaign by D. Wentworth and set to music by "A Wide Awake,"[52] puts the question of slavery in terms designed for maximum embarrassment to the Union's political foes, without apparent concern for the effect on black imagery produced by such expressions as:

> Our foe is divided and rent, boys,
> They're going to ruin quite fast,
> Let them down on their knees and repent, boys,
> And "own up" the "nigger" at last.

It was the Democrats, however, who in 1864 played most heavily upon white fears of emancipation as they utilized scare imagery of blacks and abolitionism in aiming for Lincoln's political jugular. The

Little Mac Campaign Songster, published by E.P. Patten (New York, 1864), contained, in addition to campaign songs, an advertisement for the racist booklet entitled "Miscegenation: The Republican Theory of the Blending of the Races, applied to the American White Man and Negro." This booklet had appeared late in 1863 and was made to resemble the thought of some overenthusiastic abolitionist who saw the nation's ills resolved through racial intermarriage. Actually, "Miscegenation" was the work of two New York newspapermen, David Goodman Croly and George Wakeman, who hoped to discredit the Republican party through exploitation of the most deeply seated fear, black equality.[53]

The songs in the *Little Mac Campaign Songster* differed from the pamphlet only in their approach: they attacked Lincoln, abolitionism, and the black directly, without suggesting or implying that the ideas upon which the songs were based had any origin outside the Democratic party campaign strategists. In "We're Bound To Beat Old Abe," anti-Lincoln feelings are generated by linking him to the black:

> Old Abra'm's race is run,
> He's gliding over the dam;
> Oh! hear the niggers' mournful cry,
> Our Father Abraham.

> Old Abe is growing worse,
> Things look so mighty queer,
> He sold himself for the niggers,
> No Union for us here.

And further, in a "Campaign Song," sung to "Yankee Doodle":

> Attend, while we unite and sing
>   Of this mismanaged nation,
> And show you how we're crushed beneath
>   Whole mountains of taxation.

>> Let young and old—let every one
>> Unite against Abe Lin-*king*;
>> For since the day he took the helm
>> The Ship of State is sinking.

> We're taxed to pay three million men
>   To subjugate our neighbors;

> We're taxed to elevate the blacks
> Above their useful labors.

MacClellan was propounded as the man to right the wrongs besetting the country, as in "To The Rescue":

> With "Mac" in the van, we'll all, as one man,
> Set our heels on the neck of the radical clan;
> For we're all to the rescue, our country to save
> From black abolition and ruin's foul wave.

Stephen Foster was erroneously credited with one of the MacClellan campaign songs which set a new low in scurrility, "Little Mac! Little Mac! You're The Very Man":[54]

LITTLE MAC! LITTLE MAC! YOU'RE THE VERY MAN

> Little Mac, little Mac, you're the very man,
> Go down to Washington as soon as you can,
> Lincoln's got to get away and make room for you,
> We must beat Lincoln and Johnson too.
>
> > Hurrah, hurrah, hurrah!
> > Sound the rally thro' the whole United States
> > Little Mac and Pendleton are our candidates.
>
> Democrats, Democrats, do it up brown,
> Lincoln and his Niggerheads won't go down,
> Greeley and Sumner and all that crew,
> We must beat Lincoln and Johnson too.
>
> Abraham the Joker soon wil DISKIVER,
> We'll send him on a gun boat up Salt River,
> Scotch caps and military cloaks won't do,
> We must beat Lincoln and Johnson too.
>
> Southern men come again, Little Mac's a trump,
> He'll restore the Union with a hop, skip and jump,
> With nigger proclamations full in view,
> We must beat Lincoln and Johnson too.

The period from 1861 to 1865 was dominated by songs related to the war with varying emphasis on the black as the central subject. Some songs, however, were produced of the type that had furnished material for the ante-bellum minstrel stage—songs that made little mention of the war or the issues involved. These songs lacked the excitement of great events then taking place and, in the main, merely perpetuated existing stereotypes.

Sentimental songs on black subjects became even more maudlin than before the war, surpassing, if it were possible, the abolitionists' tearful inanities. "The Blind Slave Boy, or Come Back To Me, Mother"[55] by J. William Suffern is an example of sentimentality that exceeds all bounds of good taste but, while the incident is credible enough, the story is rendered impotent through overblown verbosity. "The Blind Slave Boy" appeared near the end of the war, suggesting perhaps a bid for increased sympathy for the freed slaves; but the song's background—Suffern's motivation for writing this particular piece—may never be known.

THE BLIND SLAVE BOY; or, COME BACK TO ME, MOTHER

Come back to me, mother! why linger away
From thy poor little blind boy the long weary day?
I mark every footstep, I list to each tone,
And wonder my mother should leave me alone,
There are voices of sorrow, and voices of glee,
But there's no one to joy or to sorrow with me,
For each hath of pleasure, and trouble his share,
And none for the poor little blind boy will care.

My mother, come back to me, close to thy breast,
Once more let thy poor little blind one be press'd;
Once more let me feel thy warm breath on my cheek,
And hear thee in accents of tenderness speak,
Poor blind one! no mother thy wailing can hear,
No mother can hasten to banish thy fear,
For the slave owner drives her o'er mountain and wild,
And for one paltry dollar, hath sold the poor child.

Ah! who can in language of mortals reveal
The anguish that none but a mother can feel;
When man in his vile lust to mammon has trod,
On her child who is stricken and smitten of God,
Blind, helpless, forsaken, with strangers alone,
She hears, in her anguish, his piteous moan,
As he eagerly listens, but listens in vain,
To catch the lov'd tones of his mother again.

The sentimental song offends primarily because it, more than any of the other types, pointed up the wide discrepancies between ideology and practice; it offered pity that proved to be a sham in cold reality. Moreover, the sentimental song called for pity for a race who needed much more tangible responses from the whites as freedom was achieved. Whereas hortatory songs could be expected from the abolitionists in time of great stress on their ideals, and comic songs as well as the songs of self-styled patriots could be expected to attack or defend those ideals, the sentimental song expresses a hopeless partisanship that never was shared by more than a handful of whites at any time.

The North, which had fostered the myth of the "happy plantation darky," now found itself in real life engaging that myth in a battle to the death. While comic representations of blacks could be rationalized as typical American humor directed toward American foibles and folly, the sentimental song had gained stature as a serious matter. To create the image of a black totally satisfied with his existence as a slave, and then to take arms to destroy that image, left the sentimental songwriter with no place to stand. Thus, sentimental songs such as "Cloe Bell,"[56] presented a somewhat unsure picture of the "happy plantation slave" and his "good massa," but retained the death of the slave's mate, as the composer T. Brigham Bishop struggled with what had become a rather perplexing technical problem.

Bishop resolved his dilemma by eliminating the pseudo-black dialect and by hurrying through the "carry-me-back" idea; most of the song is devoted to the grief felt by the protagonist after the death of the loved one. It was a fairly good try, but the myth was just as strong as ever as "Cloe Bell's" lover soulfully declaimed:

> When spring first dawn'd upon the lea,
> And scatter'd flowrets o'er each dell,
> Then dear old massa gave to me
> My Georgian bride sweet Cloe Bell.
>
> Where birds are singing, sweetly singing,
> Far, far away within a southern dell,
> There my heart is ever clinging
> To the grave of my sweet Cloe Bell.

It is not necessary to quote the remainder of the song in order to perceive that the sentimental song of the "carry-me-back" order lacked the distinguishing marks of the pre-war model. This song merely put black people in white situations, a sign that either the form had been drained dry of new ideas or, more probably, that society had advanced to new situations which made the form obsolete.

Comic songs on black subjects, however, continued to appear, although in smaller numbers, owing to the intrusion of themes related to the war. Despite this diversion of emphasis, the standard minstrel stereotypes flourished in songs that perpetuated ante-bellum black images as though the events of earth-shaking importance to blacks and whites alike were not taking place at all. Assumed black characteristics were unaltered excepting for a noticeable improvement in the manner of presentation: many of these songs reflect a smoothness—or "slickness"—that represents growing mastery of the craft of popular song composition. At the same time, this very "refinement" of such songs weakened them. They showed even less of the black than had their predecessors and unwittingly set the stage for the decline of the minstrel show in American entertainment.

One of the more popular songs of this type, "Sally Come Up"[57] by Frederick Buckley, was plagiarized in England by E.W. Mackney and T. Ramsey. Dave Reed popularized "Sally Come Up" in the United States, and Mackney performed the same function in England. Lithographed portraits of both men in blackface adorn their respective version's cover.

Buckley's song combines the "while massa's away, the darkies play" theme with that of the love song, with a rather obvious result of a supposedly typical black outlook on life and love, characterized by frivolity. The Mackney version differs only in the addition of verses describing the physical features of "Sally" in the backhanded terms of the original. Quoted in full, the Buckley version reads:

SALLY COME UP

Massa's gone the news to hear,
And he has left de Overseer,
To look to all de Niggers hear,
While I make love to Sally.
　She's such a belle,
　A real dark swell,
　She dress so slick and looks so well,
　Dar's not a gal like Sally.

Figure 17

Sally, come up! oh, Sally go down!
Oh Sally, come twist your heel around,
De old man he's gone down to town,
Oh, Sally come down de middle.

Monday night I gave a ball,
And I invite de Niggers all,
The thick, the thin, the short, the tall,
But none come up to Sally.
  She's such a belle,
  A real dark swell,
  She dress so slick and looks so well,
  Dar's not a gal like Sally.

De fiddle was play'd by Pompey Jones,
Uncle Ned he shook de bones,
Joe he play'd de pine stick stones;
But I made love to Sally.
  She's such a belle, etc.

Sally has got a lubly nose,
Flat across her face it grows,
It sounds like thunder when it blows,
Such a lubly nose has Sally!
  She can smell a rat,
  So mind what you're at;
  Its rader sharp although its flat,
  Is the lubly nose ob Sally!

Additions in the Mackney version are:

Dar was dat lubly gal, Miss Fan,
Wid a face as broad as a frying-pan;
But Sally's is as broad again—
Dar's not a face like Sally's!
  She's got a foot
  To full out de boot,
  So broad, so long, as a gum-tree root,
  Such a foot has Sally!

Sally can dance, Sally can sing,
De cat-choker reel, and break-down fling:
To get de Niggers in a string,
Dar's not a gal like Sally!
  Tom, Sam, and Ned,

Dey often wish me dead;
To dem both all tree I said,
Don't you wish you may get my Sally?

Dave Reed sang another song describing the black female, "Nancy Fat,"[58] for which he wrote the words. The first verse of "Nancy Fat" is a declaration of unbounded love for a woman with few defects; but the second and third verses amplify the description in an emerging picture of ugliness typical of ante-bellum minstrelsy. The fourth, and final, verse merely expresses the joy of anticipated marriage to "Nancy Fat."

Although "Nancy Fat" appeared two years after "Sally Come Up," it is more representative of earlier songs of the black female, as seen in the first three verses and chorus:

O Nancy Fat she was a gal,
Fair and tall and slender,
The fairest gal I ever saw,
In all the female gender;
A lovely foot I know she had,
Into a boot to thrust,
Her ankles small were made for use,
To keep from it the dust.

O Nancy Fat,
What are you at,
I love you as no other,
O Nancy Fat
Get out of that,
With sweetness me you'll smother.

O Nancy Fat she had a mouth,
I cannot now describe it,
It opened like a safety valve,
When she wished to divide it;
And well I knows she had a nose,
And ev'ry body knows it,
The end of it just looks as if
The Brandy bottle froze it.

O Nancy Fat had two such eyes,
Like burnt holes in a blanket,
The inspiration from her soul,

> I took it in and drank it;
> She says this darkey am so sweet,
> She loves me like molasses,
> Dat small machine she calls her heart,
> Goes pit pat as it passes.

Other aspects of imagined black behavior, such as jealousy of the lover, male vanity, and so on, plus pseudo-black attitudes toward life, all found expression throughout the minstrel repertoire of the Civil War period. A fair representation of these types can be found in practically any songster of the times, as exemplified by *Buckley's Melodist* (Boston, 1864), or in reprints of pre-war favorites, as *The United States Songster* (Cincinnati, 1863).

"Go Away Black Man,"[59] among the songs sung by G. Swaine (or Swayne) Buckley, pointed up an assumed trivial black attitude toward male-female relationships. The verses describe the meeting, wooing, and wedding of "Busha Belle" by the protagonist while the chorus contains her response and the protagonist's reply to her singularly hostile attitude.

GO AWAY BLACK MAN

> As I walked out one moonlight night,
> I met a pretty gall, and her eyes shone bright,
> Her face was so black dat you couldn't see it well,
> And she was called the yaller Busha Belle.
> Says I young lady, may I walk wid you?
> What do you think was de answer dat she gave me?

> > Go away, black man,
> > Don't you come nigh me,
> > I'll burn you wid a chunk,
> > If I don't blow digh me.
> > > Ra-di inka da,
> > > Ra-di inka da,
> > > I never saw a yaller gall
> > > Could make me run away.

> We didn't talk much longer, when down the rain it fell,
> In a minit I up wid my cotton umberell,
> Says I, young lady will you lean upon my arm,
> And I pledge you my solemn appetite dat I mean no harm,
> So come young lady, may I walk wid you?
> Dis time a different answer now she did give me.

> Come along black man,
> I'll go along wid you now,
> Hold up your umberella,
> Or I'll get wet through now.
>   Ra-di inka da, etc.
>
> Now as we walked along, I don't know what we said,
> But de subject of matrimony it pop in my head;
> But what passed between us I'm not a gwine to tell,
> But next week I was married to yaller Busha Bell.
> We went to a parson, all to be wed,
> When he axed the lady's name, what do you think she said?
>
> Go away black man,
> Don't come nigh me,
> I'll burn you wid a chunk,
> If I don't blow digh me.
>   Ra-di inka da, etc.

R. Bishop Buckley, brother of G. Swaine, sang of the fickleness of the black female in "Crying Song":[60]

> Oh! I could tear dis wool, heigho!
> For love of charming Sue;
> Dat cruel color'd gal, heigho!
> Has split my heart in two,
> She promised once dat she, heigho!
> To me would married be;
> But now my money's gone, heigho!
> She says she won't have me.

"Buckley's Sleepy Song,"[61] written and composed by A. Sedgwick, set a new standard for delineation of the image of the lazy black. This standard was not surpassed for the next thirty years until the malevolent "coon song" explored the subject with a vengeance.

BUCKLEY'S SLEEPY SONG

> One morning very early,
> Old massa bid me rise,
> But 'twas no use, in vain I tried;
> I could not ope my eyes,
> And so it always is with me
> Throughout the whole day long—

I cannot dig, I cannot hoe—
I can scarcely sing this song.

> For he's so very sleepy,
> He could fain drop off his chair;
> It's not from work!
> It's not from fat!
> He's lazy everywhere, yaw . . .
> With sleep I do declare, yaw . . .
> He could fain drop off his chair.

Miss Luciana Dobson
Once on a time did say,
You handsome looking Darkey—
We'll wed, just name the day—
The day was fixed—the morning came,
The engagement I did keep,
But when the broom was to be jumped,
> or:
But when the Darkey said "Amen,"
Why I was fast asleep.

In Mexico while fighting,
One day with Gen'ral Wool,
I cut three en'mies heads off,
And did it mighty cool;
But the Mexicans they saw me,
Though fast I tried to creep,
They took and made me prisoner,
And they caught me fast asleep.

> But I'm (but he's) not so very sleepy now,
> I hope my song (he hopes our) song will take;
> Our patrons ere will find me (him)
> Ev'ry evening wide awake, yaw . . .
> I hope (he hopes) our song will take, yaw . . .
> Indeed I'll (he'll) try to wake.

The black dandy was updated from its earlier "Dandy Jim" imagery with "Daniel Crow,"[62] a song which followed the original formula faithfully in mocking whatever pride the black could muster for himself in the United States at that time. "Daniel Crow" can be taken as a reminder that blacks' status had not changed as a result of the war and that freedom most definitely did not guarantee social equality with whites.

DANIEL CROW

I once did know a Gembleman,
One of true Nigger blood;
In Carolina he war rais'd,
Among de cotton bud.
He war de pride ob all de land,
And when among de gals
Dat shew'd him tick lip face, dey cry'd
De hansum Gembleman.

    Dere goes he, de hansum Gembleman,
    Dere goes he, wid his Banjo and his Bones.

He war a pleasant feller, an'
Could sing a right good song;
An' when de gals dey spied him,
Dey all would round him trong,
An' when dat him would play a tune,
Dey'd make him sing again,
Dey'd cry an' screech like wild cats,
Here's de hansum Gembleman.

Dis Nigger he war mighty tall,
And had a wooly head;
Oh! 'pon my word, he dress'd so fine,
He here de fashion led.
Him coat it was a bright sky blue,
His trousers war a tan,
De white folk cry'd, when he dey view'd,
Sich a hansum Gembleman!

Viewed as a whole, black imagery in song became focused during the Civil War as abolitionist sentiment and pro-slavery feelings merged, crossed, and intermingled. Yet while the conflict produced the long-sought "jubilee" for the slave, the black image remained essentially unchanged in song, although many composers were trying unsuccessfully to alter that image. But the stereotype was more durable—too deeply ingrained in the American consciousness—than the hasty and feeble attempts to dislodge it. The black retained his psychological bonds despite having thrown off his physical chains.

Most songs of the Civil War period evince a lack of deeper sensibility for the events which occasioned them. Technically superior to their predecessors, and immensely prolific in their output, the songwriters could not imagine any alternatives to the clichéd black as a subject. Exceptions, when they did occur, appeared as merely silly aberrations that stamped their creators as radicals. In very few instances, authors and composers managed to demonstrate perceptiveness of the world-shaking events and the meanings these events generated. The point, stated differently, might ask the question: by what logic could avowed and presumably sincere abolitionists have produced such malign songs as "Sambo's Right To Be Kilt," or "Dey Said We Wouldn't Fight"? How, in the face of direct knowledge of refugee slaves, could the mythology of the Southern "happy plantation slave" persist if it were not thoroughly ingrained as an American truism?

The minstrel show began its decline during the Civil War as well, although the war cannot be solely blamed for diverting public attention elsewhere. There are subtler reasons for the decrement of the minstrel show during this period: public demand for fresh entertainment; boredom with the now painful subject of the slave. Paraphrasing McLuhan and Watson, there was awareness of events so terrible that jokes (or songs) ceased to be funny.[63] Songs on nonblack subjects began to infiltrate the minstrel stage, thus diluting the sinewy toughness and crudity that had made it so attractive to earlier audiences.

Another of the reasons for minstrelsy's general demise was that, during this period, those connected with the genre began to believe their own press-agentry—a most deadly self-delusion. The preface to *Carncross & Dixey's Minstrel Melodies* (pp. 5–6), in attempting to refute the assertions of Fanny Kemble and others to the effect that "America had no music," claims that "America *has* a National music . . . a style of Melody *peculiarly her own* . . . with a beauty, power and soul of *original* song." This characterization of minstrelsy's music is apt enough; the flaw consists in the following statements concerning the origins of this music:

By whom has marked and extraordinary character of American Melody and Song been discovered, developed, and made a source of inestimable pleasure and profit? We answer, by THE SONS OF ETHIOPEAN MINSTRELSY. It was they who first caught them floating on the plantation atmosphere . . . and gave them "a local habitation and a name."

At last the endless claims on covers of sheet music, such as
"Ethiopean Song" or "Plantation Melody" had borne fruit as self-
proclaimed experts on black music imagined that their pretensions
were indeed fact. No voice was raised to question the authority of
these claims, and thus another myth surrounding the American black
entered the heady realm of certified fact, although less than a dozen
songs out of the entire minstrel repertoire could be authenticated as
black.

The enormous guilt and bitterness engendered by the war—the
phenomenon of whites fighting whites for the benefit of blacks—was
explored more fully in song than in most subsequent histories. Only
the "true Southron" knows the blind, searing hatred that can be
roused by the playing of Henry C. Work's "Marching Through
Georgia,"[64] as it joyously vaunts Sherman's triumphal march to the
sea and proclaims in the second verse: "How the darkeys shouted
when they heard the joyful sound." It was bad enough to brag about
the destruction of Southern resistance and property, but the pretense
that the slaves were happy to be free ran entirely counter to the myth.
This was not just rubbing salt into the wound—it was heresy.

Northerners were serious too, as they attempted to soften their
own guilt feelings by promoting the idea that Southern rebels
welcomed the forced reunification of the country, as in "Massa,
Massa, Hallelujah! The Flag's Come Back To Tennessee!"[65] No
Yankee could guess the depth of Southern scorn at this song,
particularly the final verse's unlikely sentiment:

> Pompey, hold me on your shoulder,
> Help me stand on foot once more,
> That I may salute the colors
> As they pass my cabin door.
> Never more shall treason trail thee,
> Glorious emblem of the free!
> God and UNION be our watchword
> Ever more in Tennessee!

While Northern songsmiths were dreaming such dreams, the
Southern songwriters were at work producing songs with their own
version of the situation. "You Can Never Win Us Back," a "patriotic
song" written by a Lady of Kentucky,[66] provides a picture of Southern

feelings that is not only valid for the time in which it was written, but proved to be the prevailing Southern attitude for generations after the end of hostilities.

YOU CAN NEVER WIN US BACK

You can never win us back, never, never!
Tho' we perish in the track of your endeavor
Tho' our corses strew the earth that smiled upon our birth,
And blood pollutes each hearth stone for ever.

We have risen to a man, stern and fearless;
Of your curses and your ban we are careless;
Every hand is on its knife, every gun is primed for strife,
Every palm contains a life high and peerless.

We may fall before the fire of your legions
Paid with gold's murderous hire—base allegiance;
But for every drop that's shed, we will have a mound of dead,
And vultures shall be fed in your legions.

You have no such noble blood for shedding;
In the veins of cavaliers was its heading;
You have no such stately men in your abolition den
To wade through fire and fen, nothing dreading.

While there is no equivocation in this presentation of the typical Southern attitude, the black, it might be noted, is never mentioned, especially since the evocation of the "noble cavalier" myth could become tainted in Southern minds by association with blacks.

In case Northern sentimentalists might have missed the point, Southern attitudes toward the Union were made even more explicit in "O I'm A Good Old Rebel,"[67] a highly seditious song of unparalleled bitterness that nonetheless characterized true Southern feelings:

O I'm a good old rebel,
Now that's just what I am,
For this "Fair Land of Freedom"
I do not care AT ALL;
I'm glad I fit against it—
I only wish we'd won,
and I don't want no pardon
For anything I done.

Since this was the representation of the Southern white middle classes, the black question was allowed to creep in —but not as a direct ascription:

> I hates the Constitution,
> This Great Republic too,
> I hates the Freedman's Buro, [Bureau]
> In uniforms of blue . . . .

Hatred for the Freedman's "Buro" was not confined to mere song following the Civil War; it became part of the very fabric of Southern life and ultimately led to repression of blacks that was virtually indistinguishable from slavery.

Thus the Civil War ended with the North torn between remorse and vindictiveness, the South solidly beaten—and just as solidly defiant in the face of defeat, and the black facing a future laced with hazards in his struggle to alter or overcome an image that had taken Americans two hundred years to construct.

Chapter Six

From Reconstruction to the 1880's

Lee's capitulation at Appomattox on April 9, 1865, spelled the doom of the Confederacy and set the stage for a long and bitter struggle to make freedom for the ex-slave meaningful. Some abolitionists saw their task as finished with the passage of the 13th Amendment abolishing slavery, while others more correctly envisioned an even more difficult struggle to bring the black to a useful and dignified place in American society.[1]

The South responded to efforts on behalf of ex-slaves with its Black Codes, all of which placed the black in a position only slightly better than slavery. As stated by Konvitz:

Essentially what had not changed was the image of the Negro in the mind of the white man in the South: it was the image of someone who might be thought of as a freedman but never as a freeman.[2]

This attitude was shared by many Northerners who felt that the black, as President Johnson expressed it in vetoing the First Freedmen's Bureau act, could "protect and take care of himself."[3]

Thus racism replaced slavery as the dominant theme in black-white relationships, taking on proportions of a magnitude such that almost every event came to be viewed in terms of its racial implications.[4] Racists used every means to spread a hysterical gospel of white supremacy. Newspapers, pamphlets, speeches, poetry, and, of course, songs were among the ways in which whites were warned of the black threat. Whites had felt capable of controlling blacks under slavery; but now cultural and racial purity of whites was in jeopardy, and the nation was in danger of degeneration unless some means could be found to "keep the blacks in their place." Northern racists joined

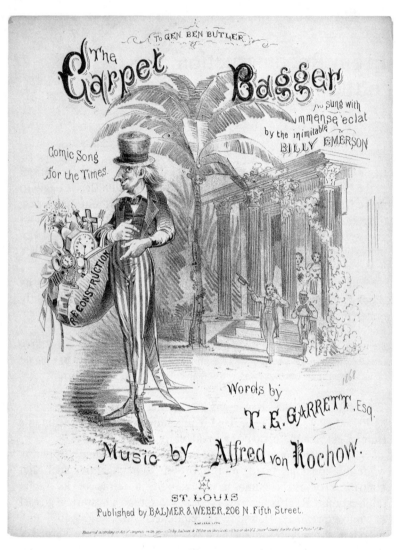

Figure 18

Southern demagogues in offering an endless stream of jeremiads on the black threat. Rational debate on the issue was impossible.

Passage of the first Reconstruction Act in 1867 intensified animosities between racists and radical Republicans and put both groups on a course which appeared to be headed directly back to open warfare. Whatever motivated the radicals—humanitarianism, politics, or simple revenge against the South—the racists viewed efforts on behalf of the black as sheer madness. Reconstruction, to the Southerner, was a bitter curse of Northern liberals, and the Yankee "carpetbagger" became an object of contempt throughout the South.

The carpetbagger's image as a rapacious opportunist bent on looting the South was vividly portrayed in "The Carpetbagger,"[5] a song which appeared in the year following the establishment of Reconstruction.

The illustrated cover of "The Carpetbagger" is designed to evoke maximum hatred for the subject; it shows the white carpetbagger making off with loot, including a crucifix, from a Southern plantation home. The bag containing the loot is labelled "Reconstruction," and the principal figure is dressed in the swallow-tail coat, striped trousers, and tall hat of the traditional "Uncle Sam" figure. Helplessly protesting Southerners, both black and white, are seen in the background. This cover, as powerful as a political cartoon, is amplified by the text:

> I'm a gay old Carpet Bagger!
> O! don't you understand?
> 'Mong the color'd folks I swagger
> Down in the cotton land.
> Now I got no eddication;
> Of brains I does not brag,
> But I owns a big plantation
> All in my carpet bag.
>
>> I'm a gay old Carpet Bagger!
>> O! can't you understand?
>> 'Mong the color'd folks I swagger
>> Down in the cotton land.
>
> In the North I was Nobody,
> O! don't you understand?
> Now I drinks my wine and toddy,
> King of the cotton land!

For I drives the old slave master;
He calls me scallawag,
While he cusses fast, and faster,
I fills my carpet bag.

I'm the loyal Carpet Bagger,
Who rules the cotton land;
I'm a happy scallawagger,
O! don't you understand?
For to Congress goes some mornin'
This curst old scallawag!
And I pays 'em back for scornin'
My loyal carpet bag.

But I hears a storm a comin'
O! yes I understand!
Now we'll get kick'd out for bummin',
Around this cotton land,
For I hears the nation's thunder;
We've lost our game of brag;
Now I'm off with spoons and plunder
All in my carpet bag.

"The Carpetbagger" was accurate in one detail: the "thunder" did indeed grow louder as Southerners fought to maintain white supremacy. The ultimate insult, liberal progress under Reconstruction, led to harsh reprisals against blacks and those concerned with their welfare. Murders, intimidation—any force by which blacks could be controlled—became customary means for white domination. Organizations such as the Ku Klux Klan were formed in order to enforce white supremacy. A barrage of racist invective obscured real advances under Reconstruction; but it is becoming more evident to modern historians that the "orgy of misrule" point of view was largely a polemic smokescreen covering maneuverings aimed at restoration of white rule.

Realizing that political support of the black depended upon the continued Northern presence in the South, radical Republican fervor waned, and in 1887 with the election of Rutherford B. Hayes to the Presidency, Reconstruction came to an end. Blacks were now left to whatever fate the Southern white decreed.

Abrogations of legal guarantees of black's civil rights went unnoticed and unredeemed as blacks saw whites making a mockery of freedom. Repression of blacks became the "American way" as each

state and locality of the entire country found their own methods for
putting the black "in his place." Not many whites were willing to
admit, as does the song "The Age of Wonders,"[6] that most of the
problem existed only in the mind:

> The North and South raised a question,
> Which neither should "see in that light,"
> Whether white man's as good as a nigger!
> Or nigger as good as a white!
> The matter was settled by fighting,
> For years they terribly fought,
> The result was, that white man or nigger,
> Was only a difference in thought.

Most of white America was more inclined to view the freed slave
as a threat. The boastful protagonist of "We'll March Around the
World"[7] had the ring of authority as he played upon fearful white
imaginations with:

> Now, white folks, listen unto me,
> While I sing a song to you,
> I'm going to tell you, yes I am,
> I left old Dixie one fine day,
> It was early in the morning,
> I left old missus to call in vain,
> And I never gave my old massa warning.
>
> > We'll work no more on the old plantation,
> > No, massa, not for you,
> > We'll march around the world to see all the gals,
> > And this is what we'll do.
>
> With my handsome face and musical voice
> I've travelled in search of fame,
> I never am going to work any more,
> Now who can dis darkey blame?
> Wherever I go it is my luck,
> To please the noble populace,
> So now you see I've settled down
> In this splendiferous metropolis.
>
> I'm going to love ev'ry pretty gal I meet,
> Yes, that's what this nigger means to do,
> I hope they will all love me in return,

> But that they are sure to do.
> I love them fair, I love them dark,
> I love them small and bigger,
> Now I am such a proper young man,
> Now who could help loving this nigger.

White fears of the freed slave had a strong sexual basis, as shown in "We'll March Around The World." Wood states: "Two fears underlay the racist outcry against miscegenation . . . the fear that the sanctity of white women would be lost, and the fear that the white race would be 'mongrelized.' "[8] Self-styled defenders of white womanhood placed every obstacle in the path of black freedom. In time, the black discovered that freedom for him was a travesty; his crime was not that he had been a slave, but that he was black. Those who recognized the basic injustice of this point of view wrote songs in which the name of Lincoln became associated with the cause of fairness in black-white relationships, as in "Lament For Lincoln":[9]

> White folks listen to the singing,
> Of the negro once a slave,
> Now made free by Father Abey,
> Who is resting in his grave.
> Of our much despised nation,
> Tongue could speak but mind was mute,
> Man denied us education,
> And then classed us with the brute.
>
> Say are we not fellow-creatures,
> Colors may be different; well,
> 'Tis not color, 'tis not features
> That the inward heart can tell.
> Brother man had long been cruel,
> To the skin of dusky hue,
> But gratitude is now the jewel
> Unto Lincoln's memory due.

Evoking Lincoln's name in connection with black freedom was part of the technique used by songwriters in building the hero-fantasies that obscured the martyred President's motives in freeing the slaves. Although Lincoln was unequivocal in his racial views, the radical Republicans needed an image of a Lincoln devoted to the cause of black freedom. Lincoln's image, therefore, took whatever cast necessary to advance the radicals' aims, while the black remained a political pawn.

During Grant's campaign for his first term in office, the opposition sang of political terrors to be expected from enfranchised blacks:

> Soon I'll cross the sea, a Congressman to be,
> I'll come back, clear the track,
> Don't you dare to look at me,
> Mr. U. S. G. is very fond of me.
>> Oh, my, Oh, my, he gib me lots of cash,
>> And now I cut a dash,
>> Oh, my, Oh git away you old white trash.[10]

Republicans tried to maintain their posture of favoring racial equality in their campaign songs. As late as 1880, they sang "Equal Rights To All,"[11] dedicated to "the Colored Republicans, true through every trial," in which black votes were solicited with: "O men of every soil and section, 'Gainst all treach'rous disaffection Band, and this be your election, Equal rights to all." Wrath was heaped upon "White Liners," "Chisholm Murderers," and the Ku Klux Klan in the Republican song, "Best Citizens Of Kemper County."[12] These groups were characterized as "Exponents of Satanic fury," part of a sectional conspiracy to deny the black his rights. In their "Battle Cry Of Freedom As Sung By the 'Solid South',"[13] this conspiracy was seen as including the very destruction of the Union:

> We will smash the Union boys, and establish slavery,
> Shouting the battle cry of Freedom,
> We will starve the Yankee soldiers, and tickle Liberty,
> Shouting the battle cry of Freedom.
>> 'Tis slavery forever, hurrah, boys, hurrah!
>> Down with the Yankees, up with the bars;
>> While we ostracize the loyal and murder thousands more,
>> Shouting the battle cry of Freedom.

Republicans adopted pious attitudes concerning black welfare:

> We know no line of color, nor section in our land,
> For no servile mark of bondage
>> of the cringing slave shall brand . . . .[14]

Democrats responded with "Ef De Party Wins,"[15] in which Republicans were pictured as using the black to further their own ends:

> Ef de party wins, den good-bye to my trouble,
> Good-bye to de brushes, and de whitewash too, say I,
> Tho' de bosses play'd dis solid darky double,
> Yet dey tell me now de lucky day am nigh.
> O! de white man used to say he worked for glory,
> But he allus 'pear'd to gobble up de pay,
> An' when 'lection time was ober, come de story,
> Mister Nigger he can call some oder day.
>
>> Stan' back, oh stan' back,
>> Ef de party wins,
>> His teeth now am shakin' in de cold;
>> But if he's not 'mong de "ins,"
>> Den, a warmin' ob his shins,
>> You can bet dere's been anoder darky sold.
>
> By de virtue ob de noble Constitution,
> Ebry fellow citizen am 'titled to his right,
> Tho' de ones for good luck, 'cordin' to my notion,
> Am de sort ob coons dat happen to be white.
> But de stormy days will go and be forgotten,
> An' de Jockey boys, dere backers, an dere kins,
> Surely will observe de "dark horse" am a trottin',
> Strait into de pasture ef de party wins.
>
> In de fields ob clover down in ole Virginny,
> Whar de shinin' waters ob de Rappahannock flow,
> Dar I used to dance, a jolly pickaninny,
> But its been a many weary years ago.
> O! ob all de spots on earth, dat was de section,
> Dat was sure to make a hungry nigger grin,
> But a better time am comin' wid de 'lection,
> For de party, den, I know am boun' to win.

Reluctance of the Republicans to vigorously enforce equality in the face of adamant opposition of the South amounts to nothing less than a betrayal of the black.[16] By 1888, the racial issue relinquished first place in campaign rhetoric to the issues of reform and corruption. Old antagonisms and loyalties persisted, however, and race lingered as a shadow over politics without assuming the importance of previous times.

The *True Blue Republican Campaign Songs for 1888* (Boston, 1888) devoted most of its space to charging Democrats under Cleveland with graft, fraud, and catering to Southern demands. Race was mentioned only in connection with Southern election frauds, as in "On The Louisiana Plan" (pp. 10–11):

> "Walk up and do your voting,
>   We'll not hinder you," they say,
> "For our double-barreled shotguns
>   Are forever laid away."
> "Walk up, my colored brother,
>   We'll not hinder any man,
> All the same we'll do the counting
>   On the Louisiana plan."
>
> They let the colored brother
>   Put his little ballot in,
> And they smile upon him blandly
>   When you see the count begin.
> But ev'ry vote is counted
>   For the Democratic man,
> And you bet he'll always get there
>   On the Louisiana plan.

From the black's standpoint, the entire Reconstruction period's politics could be summed up by the final verse of an earlier song, "In a Horn,"[17] with the reference to President Johnson altered to read virtually any politician of the two decades of Reconstruction:

> Ole President Johnsing's exackly de man,
>   He is in a horn, he is in a horn,
> He's gwine to do for us all dat he can,
>   He will in a horn, in a horn.

One of the more enduring and significant innovations in popular song of the Reconstruction was the exploitation of the figure of the black child. Derived from the character of Topsy, the stereotypical black child was seen as a mixture of insouciance, ignorance, incorrigibility, and a propensity for mischief and mishap. These qualities were balanced by a lack of real malice for the subject, as well as endowment of the stereotype with a certain degree of cunning and, at times, a convincing pathos.

The seeming inconsistencies of these characteristics gave rise to two distinct methods for treatment of the black child subject: the vision of the child as a black imp, or as the object of motherly affection. While the latter view produced a welter of lullabies and sentimental songs, the view of the mischievous "pickaninny" engendered a wide range of comic songs that were of incalculable influence in the overall black image held by whites during Reconstruction and after. White children were presented clockwork toys of blacks dancing, playing banjos, or being lynched; children's savings banks were available on baseball themes ("Dark Town Battery") or entertainment business subjects ("See Dapper Dan the Famous Coon Jigger").[18] The brainwashing effect of racial prejudice thus extended itself from the variety stage into the very homes of the American public, where the children received early training in considering blacks as objects of ridicule.

Septimus Winner adapted his "Ten Little Injuns" to the black subject in 1869, renaming it "Ten Little Niggers."[19] In this form, the song was pirated in England under the title "Ten Little Negro Boys"[20] with the explanatory note:

The popular song "Ten Little Negro Boys" is a great favorite with young people, to whom it affords a fund of amusement; nor does it lack the patronage of social gatherings, penny readings, & musical societies . . . .

The words of the two versions are not identical although the intent is, of course, the same in both instances. Winner's version is as follows:

TEN LITTLE NIGGERS

Ten little niggers going out to dine,
One choked his little self, and then there were nine;
Nine little niggers crying at his fate,
One cried himself away, and then there were eight.

> One little, two little, three little, four little, five little nigger boys:
> Six little, seven little, eight little, nine little, ten little nigger boys.

Eight little niggers slept until eleven,
One overslept himself and then there were seven;
Seven little niggers cutting up sticks,
One chopp'd himself in halves, and then there were six.

Six little niggers playing with a hive,
A Bumblebee kill'd one, and then there were five;

Five little niggers going in for law,
One got a chancery, then there were four.

Four little niggers going out to sea,
A red herring swallow'd one, then there were three;
Three little niggers walking in the Zoo,
A big bear cuddled one, and then there were two.

Two little niggers sitting in the sun,
One got frizzled up, then there was one;
One little nigger living all alone,
He got married and then there were none.

One little nigger with his little wife,
Liv'd all his days a happy little life;
One little couple dwelling by the shore,
Soon rais'd a family of ten niggers more.

The British "Ten Little Negro Boys" merely varies the circumstances leading to each disappearance; but the central idea was strong enough to survive all manner of reworkings, as J.W. Wheeler showed a generation later with his "Four Little Curly Headed Coons."[21]

By 1880, the songs with the black child subject had gained a solid hold on the imaginations of white songwriters. Considered technically, one of the better songs of the type was "Little Baby Joe,"[22] with words by "Brother" Gardner and music by M.J. Arthur. In this example, the insult to the black child is delivered by a protagonist cast in the role of a hard-hearted grandfather, a reversal of expected attitudes. This song might indeed be considered funny except for the racial insult:

Kase I'ze growin' old an' doan feel strong,
Dey put me in de cart an' drew me 'long,
Till I got down dar to my daughter Chloe,
Kase dey wanted me to see her baby Joe.
Dey axed me to kiss dat lump ob coal,
But I kep' him off wid a ten foot pole,
Kase I'ze read sumwhar dat babies bite,
An' dis little nigger war chock full o' fight.
    Oh, jist you hear dat baby howlin',
        Hi! yi! yi!
    Jist you see his mudder laffin',
        Te! he! he!
    Oh he's such a howlin' little nigger baby,
    I'd like to see him hangin' to a tree.

He am short an' fat an' six weeks old,
Dey hang to him like a lump ob gold;
His weight dey guess am 'bout ten pound,
An' he howls away wid a tin pan sound.
Dey gin him sugar an' fed him pap,
An' all went wild when he choked on a drap,
But I sot right dar an' I hoped he'd die,
An' sail up to heaben by a beeline fly.

Monroe H. Rosenfeld, using the pseudonym F. Belasco, produced "Hush, Little Baby, Don't You Cry,"[23] in which the image of the black child is confused with the practice of characterizing religious blacks as "children." The result is a song that is an incongruous mixture of pseudo-spiritual and unconvincing lullaby. The cover illustration is a caricature of a crying black child, while the text applies more readily to the adult black image. It is not difficult to perceive in "Hush, Little Baby, Don't You Cry" a thinly disguised warning to blacks that conformity to white expectations was the only way in which the black could enjoy peace on earth or in the hereafter:

No use for to weep and cry in de morn,
  You'll be an angel bye and bye,
Dig up de taters, hoe up de corn,
  You'll be an angel bye and bye.
Tie on de armor, armor of de Lord,
  You'll be an angel bye and bye,
Put on de helmet, swing on de sword,
  You'll be an angel bye and bye.

    Hush little baby, don't you cry,
    You'll be an angel bye and bye;
    Singing sweetly all the day,
      all the day, happy day;
    Hush little baby, don't you cry,
    You'll be an angel bye and bye,
    Softly, sweetly, gently sleep,
    You'll be an angel bye and bye,
      Don't you cry.

Ole Satan's a comin', don't you run,
Put on de armor, level up yo' gun,
Aim for his bosom, hit him in de back,
Keep on a shootin', keep him off de track.

Put on de robe and frizzle up yo' har,
Get out yo' ticket for de gospel car,

> Pin on de armor, armor of de Lord,
> Watch for de train, jump on board.

"Hush, Little Baby, Don't You Cry" was obviously written for the comic effect of viewing black religion as a childlike characteristic. Not all songs about the black child were as clear-cut with regard to intent. Harry C. Talbert's "Carolina We Name Dat Child"[24] could be taken either as a comic or sentimental song, depending on the manner of performance:

> Down the other end of old White Plain,
> And at Henrietta Jackson's home,
> We're to give a colored babe a name,
> Then drink cider that's never known to foam.
> How pleasant for the old folks,
> And the merry, laughing young mokes,
> A guessing names and telling jokes,
> At last they named the child.
> > Yes we did indeed!
>
> > Carolina oh, oh, we name dat child,
> > My goodness me, oh my,
> > Carolina oh, oh, we name dat child,
> > She's an Angel from the sky!
>
> With her Mamma she is nestled there,
> She is just as sweet as she can be,
> For she's got her Papa's coal black hair,
> Oh, dear Mama just dance her on your knee.
> We'll teach her Pigeon winging,
> You can hear our voices ringing,
> For the baby we are singing,
> We have named her Caroline!

Likewise, J.W. Wheeler's "We Couldn't Bring De Little Darky To"[25] purports to be a serious lament for a black child who "cotch de fever" and died in the cotton field. In the face of such vast quantities of music devoted to belittling the black image, one cannot avoid being skeptical concerning the motives of songwriters producing material designed to evoke sympathy for the figure of the black child. Perhaps it is more charitable to consider the sentimental treatment of the black child subject as a parallel to that of the white child subject during the period, inasmuch as kidnappings, runaways, death, and narrow

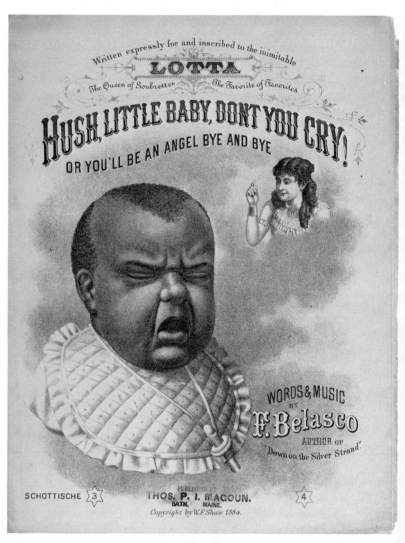

Figure 19

escapes provided plots for many songs about the children of both races. It cannot be denied, however, that the black child was more often than not the object of racially oriented humor.

Furthermore, plots were often distinguished by race in their resolutions, as in Theodore Robbins' "Rosebud of Virginia,"[26] a morbid song about the kidnapping of a black father's child. The piteous cry of the father goes unheeded as he tells his sad tale:

> I had a flower within my garden growing,
> A plant I cherished with a father's care,
> While all de darkies round dis spot were roving,
> To catch de sweets dat filled de desert air.
> I watched dis plant both day and night awaiting,
> And like her mother she was blythe and gay;
> One night I left her in bed a dreaming,
> And in de morning she was stole away.
>
>> Dey stole, dey stole, dey stole my child away,
>> Dey stole, dey stole, dey stole my child away,
>> Oh hear, oh hear my story, oh hear me I pray,
>> My heart, me heart is breaking,
>> For my child, my child dey stole away.
>
> [*Falsetto voice*]
> Hear dat voice.
> Hear dat voice.
>> I hear de wolves upon de hill,
>> I hear dem faint and fainter still,
>> I hear de wolves upon de hill,
>> I hear dem faint and fainter still.
>
> Oh! daddy's heart was sorrowed and dejected,
> I wandered forth upon de hills in vain,
> And ev'ry flower and ev'ry plant on me a shade reflected,
> My tears dey fell unto de ground like rain.
> De sun above looked down upon my sorrow,
> My heart had mostly burst its bounds in vain,
> My child was stole, was lost to me forever,
> I never saw that angel form again.

A song of this type could easily evoke tears from audiences of the 1870's, but the father was still alone in his grief.

Images of the adult black received more traditional treatment, altered, in the main, to reflect contemporary conditions. The "carry-me-back," for instance, advanced the absurd notion that ex-slaves, after their first taste of freedom, were nostalgic for their carefree life under slavery in "dear old Dixie." This preposterous myth perpetuated the mother image of the South as one of the enduring manifestations of white wishful thinking. Totally unmindful of reality, songwriters hammered out hundreds of songs on this theme and so fixed the idea in the American mind that even those black composers who attempted to enter the white world of popular song were forced to conform to the white conception of the "happy plantation slave" wishing to return to the sunny South.

Perhaps the best illustration of this phenomenon is James Bland's world-famous "Carry Me Back To Old Virginny,"[27] another of those songs of such popular power that it generated its own mythology concerning its creation. Despite attempts of historians to attribute the inspiration of "Carry Me Back To Old Virginny" to Bland's race and acquaintance with the south, the fact remains that he was a Northerner with hardly any knowledge of the locale of his song. What is indisputable is Bland's genius in imitating white song types. Ironically, he was largely unsuccessful in convincing whites that a black was qualified to represent blacks on the stage. Most of his work was done abroad or in all-black companies. Circumstances of Bland's life, as well as his known ambitions, suggest that "Carry Me Back To Old Virginny" was composed to advance himself in his profession—not to glorify the myth of the nostalgic ex-slave.

It is almost redundant to quote the text of Bland's great song; this is a song that must be viewed within the context of the history of the type. It represents a landmark in the development of a myth that only recently has come under question:

> Carry me back to old Virginny,
> There's where the cotton and the corn and tatoes grow,
> There's where the birds warble sweet in the springtime,
> There's where the old darkey's heart am long'd to go.
> There's where I labor'd so hard for old massa,
> Day after day in the field of yellow corn,
> No place on earth do I love more sincerely,
> Than old Virginny, the state where I was born.
>
> Carry me back to old Virginny,
> There's where the cotton and the corn and tatoes grow,
> There's where the birds warble sweet in the springtime,
> There's where this old darkey's heart am long'd to go.

> Carry me back to old Virginny,
> There let me live 'till I wither and decay,
> Long by the old Dismal Swamp I have wandered,
> There where this old darkey's life will pass away.
> Massa and missus have long gone before me,
> Soon we will meet on the bright and golden shore,
> There we'll be happy and free from all sorrow,
> There's where we'll meet and never part no more.

Some black composers found ways in which to minimize the impact of white mythology on their songs, at least in isolated examples. Sam Lucas presented the plantation slave as being uncharacteristically joyous over gaining freedom in his "De Day I Was Sot Free!"[28] Lucas's protagonist was further removed from the model in his noncommittal reference to his birthplace, an oversight that could have cost the song its popularity.

But Lucas had already rectified the matter through his singing of his own and other songwriter's compositions. One such piece was C.A. White's "Old Uncle Jasper"[29] which Lucas performed "with great success." White's conception of the "carry-me-back" did not vary in even the smaller details of the type:

> I was born in ole Virginny
> Where the fields of cotton grow,
> And de sugar cane de sweetest in the land,
> And de possum and de coon,
> Dey was always fat and good,
> And when de boys would kotch him dey feel grand.
> I hab trabbled o'er de land,
> Many times my heart's been sad,
> But I'se tried to make de most
> Of de good ole times I'se had,
> For de years are going fast,
> And I can't much longer roam,
> And so ole uncle Jasper's going home.

>> Den get up early in de morn,
>> I'se comin', comin',
>> Ring de bell and blow de horn,
>> And let me hear de banjo play,
>> Tell de old folks, one and all,
>> I'se comin', comin',
>> For I am so happy dat I sings all day.

When de war was done and gone,
Den I left my cabin home,
And I trabbled thro' de north, and thro' the west,
But of all de lands I'se seen,
And of all de place I'se been,
I like de land of sugar cane de best.
In de north it am so cold,
Dat de water freeze up hill,
And it makes de ole man shake,
Let him do whate'er he will,
But de good old sunny south,
Where de orange blossoms grow,
I lub dat good ole home, soon back I'll go.

Now good people one and all,
I shall have to say good-bye,
For de heart is sighing for de friends of yore,
And de older dat I grows,
Will de heart turn back de more
To childhood's home on ole Virginny's shore.
I is thankful to de Lord,
Tho' my time is drawing near,
Dat I've lived to see de things,
Of de great Centennial year,
And de 'mancipation day,
I hab lived to see dat too,
De happiest day de colored man e'er knew.

White reworked the "carry-me-back" theme numerous times during the 1870's. His "The Old Home Ain't What It Used To Be" (Boston, 1872) adheres to the formula as the protagonist exclaims:

Now the old man would rather liv'd and died,
In the home where his children were born,
But when freedom came to the colored man,
He left the cotton field and corn;
This old man has liv'd out his three score and ten.
And he'll soon have to lay down and die,
Yet he hopes to go unto a better land,
So now, old cabin home, good-bye.

And in his "I'se Gwine Back To Dixie" (Boston, 1874) the idea is even more unimaginatively expressed:

> I'se gwine back to Dixie,
> No more I'se gwine to wander,
> My heart's turn'd back to Dixie,
> I cannot stay here no longer,
> I miss de ole plantation,
> My home and my relation,
> My heart's turned back to Dixie,
> And I must go.

Reconstruction "carry-me-backs" differed from their ante-bellum counterparts in one important respect: the constant belittling of freedom's benefits and life in sections other than the South hint strongly that the North was feeling deep pangs of guilt over the destruction of the South and slavery. The spate of "freedom" songs that appeared immediately following the close of the Civil War contributed heavily to the notion that black freedom was a dubious trophy. At least three of these songs were published in 1866, two from the Northern press and one from the New Orleans publisher, A.E. Blackmar. This latter effort, "The Freedman's Song," was written by A.R. Watson and set to music by F.W. Smith. The text is entirely too long to quote in full, but the main point is that the protagonist, having lost the security and happiness of slavery, and despite his present, homeless, poverty-stricken state, is nonetheless adamant in his commitment to freedom. Yet he longs for former days, as exemplified in the penultimate verse:

> I dreampt last night ole massa come,
> And took us home with he,
> To de log cabin dat we left
> When fust dey sot us free,
> And dar I built de light'ood fire,
> And Dinah cook de yam,
> Dey say dat dreams are sometimes true!
> I wonder if dis am.

In the face of all misfortunes recounted in the verses of "The Freedman's Song," the chorus can only be classified as pure sarcasm:

> But den I'se flung away de hoe,
> To hab a juberlee,
> De rain may come, de wind may blow,
> But bress de Lord I'se free,
> But bress de Lord I'se free!

Granville Wood's "Free But Not So Happy"[30] is one of the
Northern expressions of the mixed blessing of black freedom. It, too,
is a lengthy description of a happy plantation life disrupted by
emancipation, with a protagonist longing for a return to the conditions
of slavery. The third and forth verses with the chorus illustrate the
point:

> And thus passed the time in a bright sunny clime,
>   'Till a stranger who said I was free,
> Came and took me away with him up north to stay,
>   But what is such freedom to me?
> Away from my home and my friends I must roam,
>   Of happiness always bereft,
> But I'll play as I go on my good old banjo,
>   It's all the companion that's left.
>
> When old age comes on and my work is all done,
>   Oh! who will care for me then?
> All tattered and torn, I've only to mourn,
>   And sigh for old Massa in vain!
> By and by death will come to welcome home,
>   And my last dying prayer shall be,
> That they'll lay me to rest in the spot I love best,
>   Away down in old Tennesee.
>
>> Happy, happy, happy and free,
>> Way down in old Tennesee,
>> Tho' now I am free,
>> I never shall be
>> So happy again as in old Tennesee!

"Freedom On The Old Plantation"[31] by the famous Irish bandmaster and composer, Patrick S. Gilmore, advanced the wholly
idealistic notion that freedom could be enjoyed by the ex-slave on the
very spot where he had been kept in bondage. Apparently in complete
ignorance of actual conditions, Gilmore's setting of W. Dexter Smith,
Jr.'s text amounts to a paean to expectations that were sincere and
noble, but beyond the capabilities of an America marred by prejudice.
Utilizing the call and response pattern, Gilmore's song extols the
virtues of freedom, work, and patriotism:

> Freedom, Freedom, Freedom on the old plantation,
>   Freedom, Freedom, Freedom ev'rywhere.
> Freedom, Freedom, Freedom on the old plantation,
>   Freedom, Freedom, Freedom ev'rywhere.

> Don't you hear the joy bells ringing,
>> Freedom on the old plantation,
> Don't you hear the freedmen singing,
>> Freedom ev'rywhere.
> Freedom to the great and lowly,
>> Heaven guard it—it is holy.
> Freedom, Freedom, Freedom ev'rywhere.

The second verse contains unrealities such as: "Free to speak and free to labor" or, "Free to live as man and neighbor." The final verse contains the ultimate irony: "No more chains, and no more crying." Somewhere between the fantastic naivete of "Freedom On The Old Plantation" and the sniggering sarcasm of "The Freedman's song" there was a real black, struggling to survive in a white world that seemed determined to oppose him regardless of what he did or where he turned.

Thus the notion that a functioning freedom existed, the myth of the freedman's longing to taste the blessings of slavery once more, and the standard formula of the "carry-me-back" were combined to produce a potent image of a black who was literally craving to remain at society's lowest level. Each Southern state had numerous songs proclaiming it as the very spot where the aged ex-slave wanted to spend his last days. Frederick Lyons's "I Wish I Was Back In Alabama"[32] sings out:

> I wish I was back in Alabama,
>> Where I used to hunt de coon,
> And dance wid ole Aunt Hannah,
>> By de light ob de silver moon.
> My heart never knew any sorrow,
>> 'Kase I always felt so gay,
> And I'm gwine back tomorrow,
>> To never come away.

The same ridiculous theme was given over to Georgia in "Trabling Back To Georgia"[33] which was written by Arthur W. French and set to music by Charles D. Blake:

> I'se trabling back to Georgia,
>> Dat good ole land to see,
> The place I left to wander,
>> The day that I was set free.

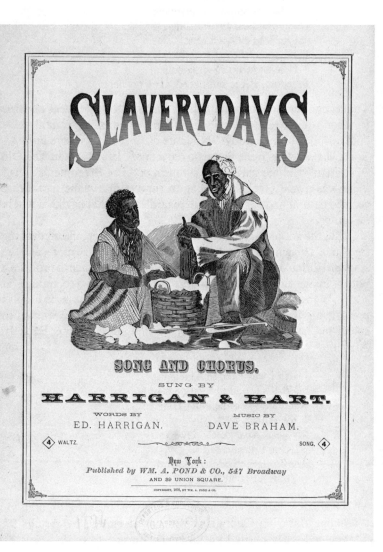

Figure 20

> I'se getting old and weary,
>   And tired of roaming too,
> So on my way to Dixie,
>   I'll say good-bye to you.

The myth of the South was being built anew as songwriters aligned themselves with the traditional Southern white viewpoint: Dixie was an earthly paradise and the natural home of the black. An occasional song endeavored to alter the formula without significant success, as was the case with "Slavery Days,"[34] a Harrigan and Hart song. This extraordinarily level-headed view of slavery violated the traditional euphoric concept of the "happy plantation slave" and, consequently, could not survive beyond the promotional efforts of the famous team that created it. The song deserves credit for good intent, even though the public saw fit to reject it. "Slavery Days" is a well wrought song that stands as a direct antithesis of the "carry-me-back" genre:

> I am thinking today
> Of dem years dat pass'd away,
> When dey tied me up in bondage long ago;
> In old Virginny State,
> It was dar we separate,
> And it fill'd my heart with misery and woe.
> Dey took away my boy,
> He was his mother's joy,
> From a baby in de cradle we him raise;
> Oh, dey put us far apart,
> An' it broke de old man's heart,
> In dem agonising, cruel slav'ry days.
>
>> Dey never comes again,
>> Let us give our praise to him,
>> Who looks down whar de little children play;
>> So ev'ry night and morn,
>> We will pray for dem dat's gone,
>> In dem agonising, cruel slav'ry days.
>
> Still my mem'ry will steal o'er
> To dat dear old Cabin floor,
> When de shadow of de sun came peeping in;
> At night, when all was dark,
> We would hear de watch dog bark,
> And we'd listen to de murmur of de wind.
> It seem to say to me,

"You people must be free,"
For de happy time am coming, Lord be prais'd!
For then we would weep and moan,
For our souls was not our own,
In dem agonising, cruel slav'ry days.
I am very old and feeble,
And our life am nearly done;
I have travell'd in the roughest kind of road;
Thro' sickness, toil and sorrow,
I have reach'd de end at last,
And I'm resting by de wayside wid my load.
Forget now and forgive,
Has always been my guide,
For dat's what de golden Scripture surely says;
But our mem'ry will turn roun',
When our souls dey were tied down,
In dem agonising, cruel slav'ry days.

The mawkish Dixie myth, by contrast, was so firmly implanted in the American consciousness that it was not always necessary to spell out the fact that the South was the sole location to which the freed slave wished to return. No song expresses the desire to return to the North, for example. In the ideal "carry-me-back" it was understood that the ex-slave meant Dixie when he expressed homesickness, as in "I Want to See The Old Home":[35]

I've wandered very far away
From the clime where I was born,
And my poor heart has been so sad,
Dejected and forlorn;
No master kind, to treat me well,
To cheer me when in pain,
I want to see the cotton fields,
And the dear old home again.

    Oh, the good old days are pass'd and gone,
    I sigh for them in vain;
    I want to see the cotton fields,
    And the dear old home again.

I'm left all sad and lonely now,
When my days are very few,
My wife and children both are gone,
I don't know what to do;

Old master too, he may be dead,
His hair was turning gray,
Oh! let me see that good old home,
Before I pass away.

When I was free, I left that land,
Where the days are bright and fair,
Where Missus spoke to me so kind,
When I was bow'd with care;
I left that home no friends to find,
My heart was fill'd with pain,
Oh! take me to that good old home,
To see it once again.

The protagonist of the "carry-me-back" was generally represented as very old and feeble. The lack of apparent threat in this figure allowed a certain amount of sympathy to be drawn from the audience; the younger, more active black male was seen quite differently inasmuch as he represented to white minds a real danger to society and to the white female in particular.

With emancipation and subsequent efforts to secure some measure of equality for blacks, many felt fearful that the ex-slave might seek revenge for the wrongs he had endured. Social equality would, the whites reasoned, open the door to black vengeance through pollution of white womanhood. As stated by Wood:

If there was one thing that was behind the white man's resistance to social equality it was the obsession with the issue of sexuality, especially as it related to the white woman. In the South, virtually every racist action could be justified, in the long view, on the grounds that it perpetuated, exalted, and, indeed, sanctified the myth of white womanhood.[36]

Wood goes on to explain that the ending of slavery exposed white feelings of sexual insecurity and emphasized fears that black men were endowed with superior sexual powers. Attempts to minimize the threat of the younger male black took shape in song as comic ridicule. Older songs were reprinted and newer types explored. In these songs a counterthreat can be detected; the black would be tolerated only so long as he stayed in "his place." This threat was seldom explicit, but clothing the message in humorous innuendo and placing the message in the mouth of a spurious black protagonist was effective—to white minds, at least.

Among the retrospective songs which presented the black male along ante-bellum lines, "Gay and Festive Nig,"[37] as sung by Frank Kerns, has its protagonist declare:

> I'm a gay and festive nig, and I do what I'm a mind to
> I'll sing my song and dance my jig whenever I'm inclined to;
> I doesn't fear de white folks, for wid dem I never bother,
> So I never gets into a row wid one thing or de other.
>
>> The scrape me up a lively jig,
>> Just while I get a chance, oh!
>> For I'm a gay and festive nig,
>> To throw you up a dance, oh!
>
> The darks are getting now-a-days to think dey're high falutin,
> The gals put on their winning ways and skirmish round galutin;
> But I don't think I'm going to spile it; wid em I don't bother,
> So I'll just look on and smile at one thing and de oder.
>
> This country's good enough for me to live and laugh and die in,
> And to better it I plainly see there is no use in trying;
> So I will sing and dance away, with politics won't bother,
> For I find I'm better off by half in one way or de other.

This song, particularly the last verse, reveals an idealized black that could have only been constructed by a white mind. The first verse establishes the "happy, singing darky" that is reinforced in the chorus. The second verse shows that the protagonist finds contemporary blacks striving for social parity with whites, a development that he as something of a philosopher deplores. The final verse shows that the status quo satisfies the protagonist; he is perfectly content to stay in "his place." Thus, the traditional stereotype of the "happy plantation slave" managed to survive the war that had destroyed whatever reasonable excuse had existed for its continuance. Slavery had fallen, but the image of the slave remained.

The "work all day, play all night" facet of the stereotype was reinvigorated with a number of songs dealing specifically with known or assumed musical predilections of the black. "Nigger In a Fit,"[38] with words and music by Andy McKee, is one such throwback. The imagery is that of pre-Civil War Southern life, with little to indicate that the institution that inspired it was nonexistent:

> After working hard all day, I have laid the hoe away,
> I'm the darkey that can make you laugh or cry,

> Kase I love to dance and sing, and to make the welkin ring,
> Kase I'se de happiest darkey from de state of old K.Y.
>
> Raise your voice and shout with glory,
> Listen to me I'll tell my story,
> I do not care a bit, just whether I stand or sit,
> As I go by you hear dem cry "A nigger in a fit."

John T. Rutledge's "De Banjo Am De Instrument For Me"[39] is typical of the hundreds of songs written about black musical prowess. The text leaves the impression that the protagonist is well along in years, but the cover illustration is that of a much younger, stereotypical black.

> I likes de ole piano, an' I likes de fiddle, too,
> An' de ole guitar makes music mighty sweet,
> I listens to de ladies when I've nothing else to do,
> Case their mellow voices never can be beat,
> But when de twilight falls around my dear ole cabin door,
> O 'tis den my heart feels happy, gay and free,
> I sits and picks de banjo, and I sings de ole songs o'er,
> Case de banjo am de instrument for me.

The inherent musicality of the black is one of those features of the overall stereotype that is harder to disprove than to prove: to demonstrate that the black is possessed of musical ability in about the same proportion as any other race or group carries in itself a certain degree of racism, intended or not. This facet of the stereotype worked to the advantage of blacks in many instances, yet there remains a noticeable amount of servility in the image of the black's singing, shuffling, dancing, and playing for the socially superior white audience. While it might serve to individuate the protagonist, it is not possible to view the musical black of this period as being in an enviable position in society. "The Acrobatic Nigs,"[40] by way of example, exploits the theme of the musically skilled black, but it is doubtful that the image evoked is one designed to enhance the complete black stereotype:

> Oh! dancing is a happy occupation,
> No matter whether dancing reels or jigs;
> But if you want to see a big sensation,

Cast your optics on these acrobatic nigs.
We learn'd our dancing down in Alabama,
Where all de darkies sing and crack their jok's;
But if you want to burst yourself with laughter,
Watch de motion ob dese Indian Rubber mokes.

Saul Ser-Trew's "Dar's Music in Dese Shoes"[41] is even less flattering:

O I'm a genuine bulgine,
    Old Virginny nigger,
And just come out before you all,
    To show my style and figure,
To sing and dance is my delight,
    The white folks to amuse,
And when I throw these feet of mine,
    There's music in these shoes.

        Oh Lord bless you white folks
        To drive away the blues,
        There's nothing like the music,
        That's in this darkey's shoes.

When this darkey's work am over,
    Then he is in clover,
Among the nigger wenches all,
    He am the gayest lover,
And at the darkey fancy ball,
    No fiddles do they use,
They all keep time and dance around,
    The music in these shoes.

To the piano and fiddle,
    White folks dance and figure,
But the tinkling of the banjo,
    Am just what suits this nigger,
And when he shakes his heel and toe,
    Let 'em play what they choose,
They couldn't hold a candle to,
    The music in these shoes.

The ladies as they pass me,
    Scrutinize his figure,
And say before they never saw,
    O such a gallus nigger,

> The milk that's in the cocoanut,
> Am what this darkey does,
> I golly there's a whole brass band,
> The music in these shoes.

Space prevents the fullest exploration and study of the musical black feature of the stereotype; but the above example suggests a link between the musical and sexual prowess of the black, a motive that is of importance in the investigation of the type. This connection exists in many of the songs dealing with the musical black, as in "Lively Sam"[42] by Maurice Stransky:

> Oh, I'm a nig that ain't afraid,
> To show what I can do,
> No doubt you'd like to see me sha [de?]
> And twist my heel and toe,
> Now white folks pay attention,
> And I'll show you how its done,
> I come from old Kentucky,
> And I'm always in for fun,
> For my name is Sam-u-el,
> And I always feel so well.
>
> > I am a happy darkey,
> > And what I do is right,
> > I always feel so lively,
> > And could dance from morn 'till night.
>
> At the fancy ball the other night,
> A yaller gal, named Nance,
> Walked up to me, and with a bow,
> Said, "Are you engaged to dance?"
> I looked at her with some surprise,
> But merely answered "No,"
> Then didn't we fly around that room
> On the light fantastic toe.
> For my name is Sam-u-el,
> And I always feel so well.

Fred Lyons's "I Always Takes De Cake"[43] brings to the dancing black stereotype still other features: the novelty of the cakewalk, and the older theme of male rivalry. The cakewalk is another of the

musical characteristics assumed to have originated upon the plantations with the slaves dancing before the master for the prize of an
actual cake. Research indicates that the cakewalk might well be as
much the invention of the imaginative commercial songwriter as it is a
folk expression of plantation society: it is striking how many of the so-
called cakewalks are of white origin. In any case, "I Always Takes De
Cake" is typical of the countless songs of the black male egotist, who
flaunts his prowess unreservedly and behaves precisely as whites
expected him to:

I ALWAYS TAKES DE CAKE

I'se gwine to sing a little song of a high ton'd colored affair,
And I is one of the darkies dat partisipated there,
We danc'd all night and had a time 'till day began to break,
To see which dandy darkey was a-gwine to take de cake.
We balanc'd to our pardners; we danc'd around de floor;
And such a funny dancing I never saw before.
Oh! one darkey danc'd upon his head, his name was Dandy Jake;
But when I danc'd off on my ear, dey said I took de cake.

Den I always takes de cake, just for de ladies' sake,
I almost die a laughing when I think about dat cake.
Den I always takes de cake, just for de ladies' sake,
I almost die a laughing when I think about dat cake.

I den took down de banjo' so softly I did play,
De ladies dey all gathered round to hear its gentle lay;
One smiling said to the other, "Such music he can make!"
And den I heard dem softly say, "Why he always take de cake,"
One darkey den got jealous; he said I was no good;
He hit me 'cross my noggen wid a great big chunk of wood,
Oh! den I began to show my teeth, at him I make a break;
For it's no matter what I do, I always takes de cake.

Braggadocio is the principal theme of "Alabama Sam,"[44] a song
which presents the black male's prowess in insufferably boorish style:

I come from Alabama,
  My name is Sam-u-el,
The white folks call me Sam,
  And that suits me quite as well,
'Most everything I spy,

Though I look so jolly green,
To take me in, 'tis all my eye,
For you'll find me all serene.

Oh, such a genius,
You never yet did see,
North, East, South, or West,
There's none comes up to me.
I'm a modern nonpareil,
The white folks say I am,
The pride of all creation,
Is Alabama Sam.

I come up to New York City,
My fortune for to make,
By golly it nearly broke their hearts
The fair ones to forsake.
Amongst them all I was first chop,
A regular darkey swell,
A taxation nigger I was called
By every yaller belle.

Stereotypical appetites of blacks changed in the Reconstruction period from the prevailing "possum" or "coon" to a craving for ham. "De Ham Fat Pan"[45] and "Good Sweet Ham"[46] compare the former favorites with current preferences in typical fashion. In "De Ham Fat Pan," four verses and two choruses are required to explain the protagonist's insatiable hunger for ham, a predilection that could adequately be described in a far shorter time:

Oh, good ev'n to you, white folks,
I'm glad to see you all,
I'm right from old Virginny,
Which some people say will fall,
You may talk about ole massa,
But he am just de man,
To make de niggers happy,
Wid de Ham Fat Pan.

Ham fat, ham fat, zig a zag a zam,
Ham fat, ham fat, frying in de pan,
Oh, roll into de kitchen, fast boys as you can,
O, rooksey, cooksey, cooksey, I'm de Ham Fat Man.

"Good Sweet Ham" is closer to the established formula for such songs, however:

> You may talk about good eating,
>> Of your oysters and your chowder'd clam,
> But it's when I'm awful hungry,
>> Then just give me good old sweet ham;
> Now some folks may differ with me,
>> But their talk 'tis nothing but a sham,
> For to touch this darkie's palate,
>> Oh! just give me good old sweet ham.
>
>> Old ham it is the meat,
>> For it is always good to eat;
>> You may bake it, broil it, fry it or boil,
>> But still it is always sweet.
>
> If you want to see good living,
>> Just go down to the cabins 'mongst the palm,
> And it's there you'll see the children,
>> Greas'd all over with old sweet ham;
> Now the possum is good eating,
>> When it's cook'd with taters call'd the yam;
> But there's nothing yet that suits me
>> Just as well as good old sweet ham.
>
> Now my song is almost ended,
>> And you all know who this darkey am,
> For the boys have all nick-nam'd me,
>> By them calling me old sweet ham;
> I am going back to the old home,
>> There to pass my life away in calm;
> And if you should hear I'm dead,
>> Then just lay it to old sweet ham.

Nonsense songs provided a vehicle for expressions of contempt for the black character, as they had in the past. The attractions inherent in the nonsense song, apart from the excitement generated in audiences, lie in its ability to show the black protagonist as revealing his own defects, and to convey the strong implication that the message was genuine. Thus, the nonsense song, "Shew Fly, Don't Bother Me" passed into the minstrel repertoire as a genuine black song sung by black troops in the Civil War, although the published date is 1869.[47]

But "Oh! Sam"[48] by Will S. Hayes, in somewhat the same manner as "Oh! Susanna," is calculated to reveal peculiarities of the American black through portraying him as humorously illogical without resorting to the onomatopoetic gibberish that marked so many songs of the type.

OH! SAM

Oh! Sammy, put dat banjo down, O Sam!
You good for nuffen lazy houn', O Sam!
Drive de dog in, out de rain,
Milk de cows for Liza Jane;
Liza's got de hoopin' cough,
De ole man's drunk in de stable loff.

    Oh! Sammy, just you put dat banjo down,
    De hog's in de garden rootin' up de groun',
    De mule am dead, an' de hoss am sick,
    Come here, Sam, I want you quick—
    you hear me, O Sam!

De coon an' possum settin' on de limb, O Sam!
I eats so much it make me slim, O Sam!
O, I can't get married any more,
Or slide wid Liza on de cellar door;
De wind blows hard and it's gwine to rain;
Stuff dat hat in de winder pane.

Oh, de roof it leaks, an' de chimley smokes, O Sam!
Hold up your head like udder folks, O Sam!
Pull your har down on your head,
Pour more 'lasses on your bread;
Send you off to go to school,
An' you come back home a bigger fool.

Ole Nelson's blind an' fell in de well, O Sam!
Aunt Hannah's got a big sick spell, O Sam!
An' de calf laid down for to catch his breff,
An' de dog he barked himself to deff;
De cow run off, an' de well run dry,
An' Liza's blind in her off-wheel eye.

I got maried de udder day, O Sam!
My wife got mad an' run away, O Sam!
I tried to make her "come to taw,"
I laid my han' on her lower jaw;

> She run straight home to stay wid her mudder,
> An' leff me lookin' around for anudder.

The atavistic approach to the black male subject shown in the examples thus far indicates that songwriters were severely limited with respect to black imagery. The "carry-me-back" and the "happy plantation darky" were hardly fresh viewpoints, and the methodology was little changed from pre-war examples. Textual material merely reflected current events rather than offering new imagery.

The proliferation of fraternal societies following the Civil War offered songwriters a new avenue of attack on the black character, however. Black organizations attempting to emulate their white counterparts, with their elaborately uniformed drill teams and paramilitary attitudes, were perfect foils for comic song. The pomp of these societies' display during public holidays and other occasions immediately evoked a picture—enormously amusing to the white audience—of blacks' using this means to enhance their prestige in a ludicrous and hopeless gesture.

Fred Wilson's "Then The Band Played"[49] places its protagonist in the role of a member of the band of a pseudo-military organization and, while no direct mention of blacks appears in the text, the cover illustration leaves no question concerning the song's intent; it is one of the most unflattering caricatures of the black yet encountered in the literature.

"The Full Moon Union"[50] describes the black fraternal organization as seen by whites:

> The noble order of full moons,
>   Descendants of old Ham,
> Dey recognize dere brethern wid
>   De secret word Baram;
> All dressed in full regalia,
>   Hibernians give us room,
> And please stand clear, don't interfere,
>   With a full grown colored man.
>
>   The first degree all bend your knee,
>   And then cross ev'ry hand,
>   The head you dip, den give the grip,
>   The password Ireland.
>   Oh, on your ear, den on your eye,

And all march around de room,
Imitate the darkies
In de order of full moons.
When de little stars are sleeping,
All in de evening afternoon,
It's dar you'll see a nigger peeping
Out from that red and gorgeous moon.

We hold a monster barbeque,
We're going to kill a calf,
Our lunar sacrifice it is;
There mist'ry, don't you laugh.
This auspicious occasion it
Am held next year in June,
Oh, we invite de satelites,
Connected with the moons.

De object of this order now
Am not to study stars,
But prevent Irish people from
A-riding on de cars;
It seems extraordinary, but,
Dere isn't any Coon
But what am a luminary in
A half a quarter moon.

"The Colored Grenadier,"[51] with words and music by Johnny Carroll, is even more explicit in picturing the black member of the paramilitary organization as motivated by desire for self-aggrandizement:

Now gaze on me and you can see
A warrior staunch and true,
With my white cockade I'm out on parade,
And to sing and dance for you.
Ah! All the other nigs are jealous,
And of me they have great fear,
But the ladies smile at the dashing style
Of this colored Grenadier.

I'm the Color'd Grenadier,
I have no dread or fear,
To please you all tonight it is my glory.
When the band begins to play,

I gayly march away,
And vanquish all the foes that come before me.

My style and regimentals are
  The talk of all the town,
And my rivals stare, for they're all aware,
  I'm a nig of great renown.
Ah! And the ladies when I'm passing,
  For me they all give a cheer,
Throwing kisses sweet, and boquets so neat,
  At this dashing Grenadier.

The formula thus established, dozens of songs appeared on the theme of the black paramilitary organization. With each contribution to the type, it became clear that in this instance, as in older established types, whites were reminding blacks that attempts to enter the mainstream of American society by emulating white institutions would prove unsuccessful, and every effort would be made to destroy those endeavors through ridicule. Although the threat was never overtly expressed, the songwriters confirmed it implicitly through attacking the image of the black members of the organization or the image of the organization itself. The image became rigidified in a very short time with the result that the idea seemed older than it actually was.

"The Bolivar Blues"[52] draws freely on black imagery to picture the black along standard lines:

Oh! here we come, with bang of drum,
  De pets, de "Bolivar Blues,"
Gay warriors from South Avenue V,
  De brunette corps, de boss are we;
Besides de gun and rifled sword,
  Its razors we can use;
De pop of cannon's music
  To de trusty "Bolivar Blues!"

Dress Right!
Mark time!
Johnson keep your hoofs a movin'.
Guide Right!
Wheel her round!
My! but ain't dis movement soothin'.
'Bout arms!

Halt! Face!
Keep de Captain always shoutin'.
Heels out!
Toes in!
As we tramp along.

Jest watch de pace, observe de grace,
    Of ev'ry "Bolivar Blue,"
De "Skids" and "Gingers" can't compare,
    Dey bust deir ranks in black despair;
Jest see de gait of Captain Slate,
    A sight dat's bad to lose;
And hear him shout, "Fall in and out,
    My trusty "Bolivar Blues." "

Heads up!
Eyes out!
Wonder what dem gals are sayin'.
Tramp! Tramp!
Tramp! Tramp!
Dat's de tune de band's a playin'.
For—ward!
March! Al-
dough we're shinin' and perspirin'.
Pre—sent!
Shoulder Feet!
In de trusty Blues.

J.P. Skelly's "The Dandy Coon's Parade"[53] differs little from "The Bolivar Blues." The common publisher for the two songs, plus the similarity of texts, suggests that perhaps Skelly wrote both. The main distinction of "The Dandy Coon's Parade," if it can be classed as a distinction, is the use of the term "coon" to signify black. The term had been used frequently, of course, as a foreshortened form for "raccoon"; it also served as a nickname for the Whigs during the 1840's; but the 1880's saw its emergence as a slang term signifying black exclusively. The expression, "coon song," came to mean songs of a comic nature on the black subject during the decade which followed.

"The Coons Are On Parade"[54] offers nothing new to the type excepting the dance or reception held as the climax of the holiday. The imagery of the black ball, characterized by unrestrained emotionalism, orgiastic behavior, and the pretension became established as a distinct type. In "The Coons Are On Parade," however, an artificial reserve can be detected in the strained politeness of the text, especially in the final verse:

> We'll give a grand reception
> At our armory way up town,
> The supper will be conducted by
> The wife of Captain Brown,
> The hall nicely decorated,
> The table grandly laid,
> The way things was eat we'll never forget,
> When the coons came off parade.

The fullest development of the black member of paramilitary organizations theme came at the hands of the great triumvirate of the entertainment business of the period, Harrigan, Hart, and Braham. The differentiating factor in their humor lies in the broad range of their lampoons of American institutions, however. Burlesques of both white and black institutions came from Harrigan and Hart, with Braham providing compositions for the acts. From their inception in 1871 as typical song and dance acts, the Harrigan and Hart shows developed into elaborate productions combining elements of minstrelsy, vaudeville and musical theatre.[55]

Edward Harrigan and Tony Hart, both Northeasterners, were blackface minstrels at the beginning of their partnership, while David Braham, Harrigan's father-in-law, was born in London.[56] The concentration of their efforts in Northern surroundings makes their "Slavery Days" (see pp. 267–268) something of an anomaly; but their *Skidmore Guards*, the medium through which their lampoons of black paramilitary organizations took place, were completely compatible with the groping, boisterous expansionary period. It is hardly coincidence that the two groups which provided the main source of physical labor for America's expansion—the black and the Irish—should also provide a main source for the contrived humor of Northern urban society. Harrigan, Hart, and Braham served somewhat the same function that "Daddy" Rice had served in the early days of minstrelsy: a cohesive example that could be emulated by colleagues in exploiting the full potential of the black subject.

"The Skidmore Guard"[57] serves as a prototype of the profusion of songs on the black paramilitary theme by Harrigan, Hart, and Braham. It is not strikingly different from songs of the same type by other composers, although the reference to "coons" in the chorus might be noteworthy in its historical context:

> We represent de members of
> De noble colored troops,
> Who march about de streets of York,
> In French imperial suits,
> Black pantaloons and yaller stripes,
> And helmets trimmed with blue,
> De wenches shout when we turn out
> On South Fifth Avenue.
>
>> Nobby, airy, light as a fairy,
>> Music playing sweet and gay,
>> Hats a-waving, we're parading,
>> Marching down Broadway. Umph.
>> Talk about your Mulligan Guard,
>> Dese nigs dey can't be beat,
>> We march to time, we cut a shine,
>> Just watch dese darkies' feet,
>> De left foot first, de right foot follow,
>> De heel down mighty hard,
>> Ten platoons of dandy coons,
>> March in the Skidmore Guard.
>
> Dar's Mister Brown, de waiter man,
> To de Astor House hotel,
> He's sargent in de second Brigade,
> Division Company L,
> He's six foot high, he carried de flag,
> So noble, proud and gay,
> He took de prize for marching out
> On 'Mancipation day.
>
> Dar's Adjutant General Lem Primrose,
> And Parson Simpson's son,
> De envy of de yaller gals,
> With boquets on der guns,
> Dey look just like a circus horse,
> When de band's a playing loud,
> For elegant style and sweet hair ile,
> Dem darkies lead de crowd.

> We never hire a German band,
>   Italians carry a can
> Of lemonade dat's fresh and sweet,
>   For ev'ry colored man,
> Dey follow up de Regiment,
>   Mackrony in de rear,
> And when dey get obstropulous,
>   We bounce dem on dar ear.

Harrigan, Hart, and Braham had by 1879 developed this idea fully and had incorporated it into important parts of their other productions. "The Skids Are Out Today,"[58] incorporated into the Harrigan play, *The Mulligan Guard Chowder*, is expanded by the addition of choruses from other popular songs. Apart from this, the song is indistinguishable from others of the type except, perhaps, the pointed reference to the self-aggrandizement portion of the formula:

> White folks are mighty jealous;
>   Look out den on de flank;
> Dey turn dar noses way up,
>   At ev'ry darkey rank:
> For skillful Revolutions,
>   And Tic Tack, ev'ry way;
> Bye-Law and Constitutions,
>   De Skids are all O.K.

"The Skidmore Fancy Ball"[59] expands the social function element of the formula into an entity in its own right:

> Oh, here we go so nobly oh! de Colored Belvidere,
>   A number one, we carry a gun,
>   We beat de Fusileers.
> You talk about your dancers when we hear the cornet call,
>   We wing and wing, de dust we sling,
>   At de Skidmore Fancy Ball.
> Now right and lef, just hold your bref,
>   We're bon ton darkies all,
> De fat and lean get in and scream
>   At de Skidmore Fancy Ball.
>
>   Oh, halleluyah, glory, oh,
>   Now balance down the middle,

I tell you what gue hah! it's hot,
Like gravy in de griddle;
All forward four, all on de floor,
Jest spread out through de hall,
Oh, every Coon's as warm as June
At the Skidmore Fancy Ball.

De supper's served at one G. M. by Brown de Catoroar,
Fat Turk and Goose, oh cut me loose,
Just lem me in de door.
De char's reserved for ladies' umberellas in de hall,
Dar's ettiquette in every set,
At de Skidmore Fancy Ball.
Den hands around, keep off de ground,
We're bon ton darkies all,
Get in and sail, do hold your trail
At de Skidmore Fancy Ball.

Oh every hat dat dey get at, dis Colored Coterie,
Will cost a half, you needn't laugh,
Oh help de Millishee.
We're gwine down to Newport just next summer in de fall,
So follow suit and contribute,
At de Skidmore Fancy Ball.
Oh waltz away, and mazurka,
We're bon ton darkies all,
Sweet Caledone, it gives a tone
To de Skidmore Fancy Ball.

The black celebration theme was successfully used in conjunction with the black female figure as well, as in "Clara Jenkins' Tea,"[60] a forerunner of a type which placed the older black female figure in the familiar role of provider of oral and sensory pleasure. Along with the mother image of the "carry-me-back," the imagery of the celebration theme furnished raw material for the "mammy" and "auntie" types which proliferated from the 1890's through the 1940's. "Clara Jenkins' Tea," however, confines itself to the characteristic female sociality of a rather primordial type:

Oh, now put on your Sunday clothes,
Get ready for the jubilee,

Dere's a mighty high time,
    When the clock strikes nine,
    Oh, do come along with me.
All Methodist and Baptist too, oh, my!
    Will sing about the old red sea;
De new church choir will sing a note higher
    At Clara Jenkins' socialistic tea.
Ladies, try this citron cake,
    Pass it round for goodness sake;
    Won't you try some lemon cream?
    Oh! yes, now don't be mean, Oh!

Now put on your Sunday clothes,
And get ready for the jubilee,
Dere's a mighty high time when de clock strikes nine,
At little Clara Jenkins' tea.

There is poor old Aunty Green, dear me,
    Her age it is just ninety four,
She's as lively as a kitten,
    Keeps a gettin' up and gettin',
    You can't keep her off the floor.
Dere's something in de old brown jug, look dar,
    Just yonder on the shelf, you see,
Don't let it go to waste, but give us all a taste
    At Clara Jenkins' socialistic tea.
Standing in the well so deep,
    Yes, indeed, a hundred feet;
    Will you be my loving queen?
    Go away, I'm just sixteen, Oh!

We'll go home when de sun does shine
    In de mornin', at de peep of day,
Isn't ev'rybody's sad,
    Cause ev'rybody's glad,
    Good Lord! how we'd like to stay!
Now colored gentlemen and ladies, all,
    Take a little kind advice from me,
Won't mention any name, but please to call again,
    When Clara Jenkins gives another tea.
Forfeit, all the gemmen, now,
    No, no, ladies, you'll allow,
    Dar's dat gal in velveteen!
    How do, sis? now don't be mean, Oh!

The relationship between male and female in song reflected whites' preoccupations and presumptions concerning black sexuality. The 1880's saw an intensified effort to establish the male as totally faithless and the female as unlovable. J.S. Putnam drew upon antebellum models of the "dandy" image in his "New Coon In Town,"[61] a song containing the portent of the so-called "coon song" of the next decade:

> There's a bran new coon in town,
>> He came de other day,
> A reg'lar la-de-dah,
>> Dat's what de girls all say;
> He dresses like a prince,
>> He wears a diamond ring,
> And in his snowy shirt-front wears
>> A great big cluster pin.
>
>>> New coon in town, new coon in town,
>>> New coon, he come de other day;
>>> New coon in town, new coon in town,
>>> A reg'lar la-de-dah, de girls all say.
>
> He well knows de game call'd "bank,"
>> He plays de queen to win,
> And at de game of "craps,"
>> He sneaks his queer dice in;
> He bets on ev'ry race,
>> He plays de ladies high,
> And ev'rywhere you go,
>> You can hear de boys all cry—

The "new coon" imagery became an instant favorite among songwriters. William Dressler composed a "Coon Schottische"[62] which incorporated melodies from "New Coon In Town" and "The Coon That Lived Next Door," another Putnam song. C.H. Sheffer drew upon Putnam's "new coon" in his "New Coon's Done Gone,"[63] a song demonstrating the black male's unreliability:

> New coon's done gone, left the other day,
> Broke all the yaller gal's hearts before he ran away;
> He told me that he loved me, on me he did dote;
> He borrowed my watch and chain, in the morning I got a note:

New coon's done gone, new coon's done gone,
New coon he left the other day;
Diamond, watch and chain; he took dat eight-ten train,
Dat new coon am done gone and run away.

New coon's done gone, what do you think he done?
Run away with a man's wife, the big, black son of a gun;
He was a gay deceiver, away from me he slid,
I heard he had eleven wives and fifteen nigger kids.

The talented black composer, Sam Lucas, contributed "The Coon's Salvation Army"[64] to the growing list of "coon songs." In this instance, Lucas drew upon the imagery of the military-fraternal, religious, and male character to produce a somewhat encyclopedic impression of supposedly Negroid behaviour. Lucas's true feelings concerning his songs demeaning his race may never be known, but at least one fact is certain: his songs are indistinguishable from their white counterparts. The imagery of "The Coon's Salvation Army" is white, not black.

De Coons am marching down de street
  And don't dey look just grand—
Dey'er all in uniform today,
  Dey hab a big brass band;
Just hear de drums a beatin'
  And de fifes and trombones play,
'Tis de coon salvation army,
  Dat's out in de streets today.

    'Tis de Coons' salvation army,
    Oh! see dem march along;
    Now blow de big salvation horn,
    Jes blow it loud and strong,
    'Tis de Coons salvation army,
    Jes' see dem march along;
    Oh! blow de big salvation horn,
    Now blow it loud and strong.

De Coons am falling into line,
  Wid hymn books all in hand—
Dey'er gwine to sing an pint de way
  To Cannan's happy land;
Ole uncle Jake hab got de book,

> He's searchin' for de text;
> And when de preachin am began,
> De debbil will get vexed.
>
> De melon patch am safe today
> No Coons am dar in sight,
> De chickens dey may roost in peace
> Wid in der coops tonight.
> For don't you hear de soundin' drum,
> De fifes and trombones play?
> Oh, de coon salvation army
> Am out in de street today.

Composers found in the "coon song" an effectual means by which the black image could be rendered impotent; in particular, the black male was psychologically castrated in this manner more efficiently (and eventually more brutally) than had been achieved up to that point by any imagery.

The same year in which "New Coon In Town" was written (1883) saw still another song, "Happy Colored Man,"[65] reflecting the bemused, rather doltish image of the old man. The chorus of "Happy Colored Man" is merely a rewording of textual material that had become common property among composers, but it also shows that those composers were unlikely to abandon a working (for themselves) formula.

> I am a happy colored man,
> And for short I'm call'd Black Sam,
> I've been living in the neighborhood for years;
> I never had a wife
> In the course of all my life,
> But once I courted pretty 'Cinda Jane.

The pitiable old man figure was joined by the "coon song," a newer, more vigorous attack on black masculinity, in order to displace or deny the authority of a true father figure. It is worthy of note that virtually none of these songs ever mentioned fatherhood, especially within the context of white conceptualization. This lack of a father image, indeed, was characteristic of the type.

By contrast, the black female image continued to vacillate between wantonness and offensiveness, or a motherly authority. The

"Old Aunt" was the hostess for parties, "jubilees," and teas, as seen in "Clara Jenkins' Tea"; she was also important as the social nexus of black culture, as seen in "How D'y Do, Aunt Susie?":[66]

> Oh! de bells dey rang when Massa went and died,
> Oh! how d'y do, Aunt Susie?
> And de darkies dey all holler'd and they cried,
> Away down South in sunny Georgia.
> Dey cried all day till dere eyes were very red,
> Oh! yes go tell the people Susie;
> Oh! dey cried so hard, took de wool all off dere head,
> Away down in de cotton land.

The younger black female received treatment in song along lines established before the Civil War. "She's Lovely As A Rose"[67] reflects the rather special American characteristic of an inability to view womanhood realistically:

> I'm gwine to sing a song,
>   I hope 'twill please you all,
> 'Tis of a yallah gal I met,
>   'Twas at the fancy ball.
> She was lovely as a rose,
>   Her eyes as black as coal;
> And when she gazed upon me
>   Oh! away my heart she stole.
>
>   Oh! she was such a charmer,
>   Oh! I had her for a partner;
>   She was lovely as a rose,
>   Her eyes as black as coal;
>   And when she gazed upon me
>   Oh! away my heart she stole.
>
> Her charms I will describe,
>   As I saw them at the ball,
> A boxing glove put in her nett,
>   And she wore a waterfall.
> She had a double-jointed thumb,
>   And a foot like a giraffe,
> And when she went to promenade,
>   She made the darkies laugh.

Ned Straight's "The Girl With The Coal Black Hair"[68] is more in keeping with the song technique of the period; the style of the genteel song is offset by a surprise ending that destroys the carefully built image of beauty:

> She was sweeter'n sugar cane,
> that cream color'd queen,
> She was the gayest creature,
> that ever yet was seen,
> She had a roguish eye,
> and her features were fair,
> Her lips were like red roses,
> and coal black was her hair.
>
>> They all did say, she was so very gay,
>> There were many lovely beauties,
>> That made the people stare,
>> But the prettiest one among them all
>> Was the girl with the coal black hair.
>
> It was on one moonlight night,
> we went to a ball,
> She wore her richest dresses,
> and her largest waterfall,
> She showed her pretty foot,
> in such coquettish style,
> And won the hearts of every one,
> with her bewitching smile.
>
> When the ball was done,
> in a buggy we did hop,
> And as I drove the horse along,
> the question I did pop;
> Says she go 'way you nigger,
> how dare you ax me that,
> When I'se a female suffrage
> mancipation ristocrat.

The technique of dialogue between the male and the female served to delineate supposed black character as it had in the past; the team of Hogan and Hughes performed G.W.H. Griffin's "I Really Shall Expire"[69] with "great success," to use their own expression:

> Woman: Oh, Augustus, don't be jealous, now,
>   You know I'm not to blame.

Man: Why I saw you walking arm in arm,
            With a darkey with a cane.

Woman: I tell you he's my cousin,
            Come on from Washington.

Man: If that's the case I'll not get mad,
            But take it all in fun.
            You are my heart's desire.

Woman: Oh, dear, I shall expire.

Both: We're a lively pair of Colored folks,
            And what we say is true;
            "French Ballet" troupes are in the shade,
            When we put down the shoe.

Man: We does our shopping on Broadway,
            Just like the poor white trash.

Woman: The clerks all roll their eyes on us,
            When we put down the cash.

Man: The white gals then turn up their nose,
            And say we put on airs.

Woman: But I tell them to shut up their mouths,
            And mind their own affairs.

Man: For you are my heart's desire, etc.

Man: I took her to the concert room,
            To hear Parepa sing.

Woman: The doorkeeper he put on airs,
            And would not let us in.

Man: I told him we were Arabs,
            From the burning desert shore.

Woman: Says he your hair is curled too tight,
            I've seen such nigs before.

Man: For you are my heart's desire, etc.

The open mention of sex was taboo, yet the prissiness of the age did not prevent salacious hints of the black female's sexual attraction. The white conception of the black female, the "forbidden fruit" image, merely made her irresistible. Songwriters of the 1870's and 1880's could only suggest the supercharged sexuality of the black female; later decades saw her emerge as the "red hot mamma" that fixed her in the minds of whites as an easy sexual prospect—imagery that preserved intact the sacred position of white womanhood.

The unrestrained enthusiasm of the protagonist in "Susan's Sunday Out"[70] needs no forthright expression of intent, as the chorus reveals an attitude influenced by obvious charms beyond mere physical beauty:

> Oh! Gemini crikey! Blow me tight!
> I always dance and shout.
> It fills my heart with great delight
> When it's Susan's Sunday out.

To remind the hearer that the white view of black womanhood is the subject of the song, "So Near Sighted"[71] relates a "horror" resulting from racial mixing:

> To meet my sister, once I went,
> Down to the railroad station;
> As the engine stopped, on the train I hopped,
> Quite filled with expectation,
> I caressed her sitting on the bench,
> And soon I was affrighted;
> For I found I'd kissed a nigger—female,
> From being so near sighted.

The cover illustration of "Good Bye My Honey, I'm Gone"[72] (Figure 21) is as graphic in describing the black female's character as is the text. This illustration focuses upon elements of generally accepted stereotypes as well: razors are pointed up as a particularly Negroid defense; chickens fly to the four winds; and the white policeman is pictured as pondering whether a black domestic quarrel is worth his intervention. Indeed, the text is hard pressed to match the insult manifest in the cover; its seven verses and chorus tell a meandering tale of infidelity that, given such an uninspired protagonist, should have been a foregone conclusion:

> I had a girl, and her name was Isabella,
> She ran away with another colored feller,
> And my load was all the stronger,
> And I couldn't stay no longer,
> Good-bye, my honey, I'm gone.
>
> Good-bye, my honey, I'm gone, yes, yes,
> Good-bye, my honey, I'm gone, yes, yes,

Figure 21

And she gave it to me stronger,
And I couldn't stay no longer,
Good-bye, my honey, I'm gone.

One day in de middle ob de month ob Januyear,
I rolled my dearie in my arms for to soothe her,
But her heart was with another,
And she wouldn't let me love her,
Good-bye, my honey, I'm gone.

I thought this girl was the nicest little daisy,
Till a dude came along from the roller rink so crazy,
And I hollered for a copper,
But he said he couldn't stop her,
Good-bye, my honey, I'm gone.

I had a girl and she was a little dilly,
Freddy came along and knocked her very silly,
And I hollered for a copper,
But he wouldn't run to stop her,
Good-bye, my honey, I'm gone.

I forgot to tell you her name was Mary Walker,
She wore the pants till she couldn't wear 'em shorter,
And I hollered for a copper,
But he said he couldn't stop her,
Good-bye, my honey, I'm gone.

This funny girl was a dandy little runner,
Her name was Belva Lockwood, but the White House was a
        stunner,
And I hollered for a copper,
But he said he couldn't stop her,
Good-bye, my honey, I'm gone.

I know a man and he tried to coin a dollar,
His name is Uncle Sam and he ought to get the collar,
For it isn't worth a dollar,
And the ninety cents was holler,
Good-bye, my children, I'm gone.

The songs of the Reconstruction period reflect a groping for ways
in which the black could be visualized as a free member within a white
society. Many songwriters were either unable or unwilling to recognize the human dignity of freedmen and resorted to atavistic forms

such as the "carry-me-back" in apparent disregard of the new status of blacks. Others attempted to update older forms in order to reflect current conditions, while some searched for new formulas. It was, in many respects, a period of great indecision on the part of songwriters; yet out of this period came the one truly significant—in terms of vulgarity, affrontiveness, and magnitude—new development in treating the black subject in song: the pseudo-spiritual. The sheer size of this body of material dictates special study, to which the following chapter has been devoted.

Chapter Seven

The Pseudo-spiritual

The actual music of the black, described by Whittier as "the gold that kindly Nature sifts among his sands of wrong," became known to white America on a significant level through the exigencies of the Civil War. Contrabands were among the first to impress whites with their strange new music, so utterly unlike the "Ethiopean" deceits of minstrelsy. Added emphasis was gained for the blacks' own music following the Civil War through highly successful tours of singing groups such as the Jubilee Singers of Fisk University and groups from Hampton and Tuskegee Institutes. The work of missionaries in studying black music provided an opening wedge into academic recognition.

Theodore Seward's observation that "the critic stands completely disarmed" in the presence of the black melodies[1] confirms the novelty of this music; but the white critic was still unable to grasp the fact that this was the true music of the black, while the songs of minstrelsy were not.[2] Perhaps the distinction between black religious and secular song and the slander of the minstrel song escaped the students of black music because they had accepted the latter as authentic; or they might have been misled by their enthusiasm and religiosity into believing that anything labelled "Negro" was a manifestation of the true black. Whatever the reasons, the fact remains that these people, fervid though ill-equipped for such a gigantic mission, brought awareness of the blacks' own music to a public that had heretofore been ignorant of it.

Commercial songwriters had no difficulty in perceiving the vast appeal of the "new" black music, however, and lost no time in exploiting it. In their hands, the unquestioned sincerity of the spiritual's cry from the depths of the black soul became a tawdry, derisory desecration of the original; all the sublime expression of the black's innermost being was transformed into a ridiculous triviality that was in every sense as degrading to the imitator as to the imitated.

Since many of these commercial imitations of the spiritual were presented as "plantation songs and choruses," or as forms within existing minstrel practice, it has been necessary to invent a term to facilitate discussion. For the present study, the term "pseudo-spiritual" has been chosen to designate the imitation spiritual, although, admittedly, the term does not convey adequately the contempt which the form merits.

Actually, the form, or type, was not new. The asinine pseudo-sermon documented by Charles Mathews in the 1820's and Dan Emmett's crude lampoon, "Jordan Is A Hard Road To Trabel," attest to the willingness of entertainers to abandon even rudimentary good taste in their eagerness to slander the black. But the pseudo-spiritual played no significant role in minstrelsy until the true spiritual came to light. To the commercial songsmith, the pseudo-spiritual represented a new "gimmick," or a fresh point of departure in his slander of the black. No other race or nationality, it is worthy of note, has ever had its religiosity attacked through popular song in the same manner or to the same degree as did the black.

Some commercial and other songwriters, it is true, did occasionally try to capture the authentic black in the pseudo-spiritual. One way in which the intent of the composer can be assessed is through study of the cover illustration of the sheet music. Those that are textually more serious are apt to have a correspondingly serious cover or no cover illustration at all. Those pseudo-spirituals that were designed to elicit laughter, on the other hand, often had grotesque caricatures that emphasized the demeaning texts. Illustrators frequently signed their work, an indication not that they were unconscious of the insult they were perpetrating, but that they were quite proud of their contribution to the crushing of the black ego.

For the present study, the pseudo-spirituals have been arbitrarily divided into three categories: camp meeting songs, tocsins, and salvation songs. All of the pseudo-spirituals were essentially alike; they differed mainly in the mechanics of carrying the message of the text. The protagonist was cast as a preacher, a member of the congregation, or as one relating a personal religious message. Underneath it all, the message remained the same: "be a good nigger, don't complain, and you'll find a reward in heaven."

The pseudo-spiritual was generally filled with misconceptions which whites had assumed to be typical of the black. The catachrestical protagonist was a standard feature. The misconstruction and misinterpretation of biblical homilies are common. But the main feature of the pseudo-spiritual is the evocation of an image of ludicrous attempts by less than human blacks to emulate white religious practices; it is the picture of a race hopelessly entrapped by a different, ruler race engulfed by laughter at the sight of its victim's struggles to escape the bondage of prejudice. The pseudo-spiritual was enormously satisfying to whites who needed reassurance that they were still superior following emancipation.

In distinguishing the arbitrary categories of the pseudo-spiritual, it should be remembered that characteristics of one type might be present in any of the others. The camp meeting type is usually a hortatory song which urges sinners to seek salvation through repentance. The protagonist is ordinarily cast as a preacher who sometimes is more concerned with the peccadilloes of his flock than he is with larger issues of Christianity. Attendance at the meeting is a matter of overriding importance and is encouraged by reminding the congregation that generally unrestrained behavior is permitted.

Tocsins are those songs which deliver the threat of punishment for sinning. Here too, the protagonist might be cast as an authority figure such as the preacher. It must be remembered that his is no viable authority figure, but an overblown, self-righteous image castrated through ridicule.

Salvation songs deal with personal salvation following death and the anticipation of full participation in heavenly glory, untouched by the prejudices of a hate-filled world. In its original form as the honest expression of the real spiritual, this theme contained much of the essential beauty of black music; in the hands of commercial songwriters, the earnest hope for salvation carried beneath the surface a thinly concealed threat aimed toward keeping blacks "in their place." Of the entire range of the middenheap of song known as the pseudo-spiritual, the salvation type is without question the nadir of vulgarity.

In all types of pseudo-spiritual, words become strongly associated with symbolic behavior. "Golden," "white," and "silver" are associated with virtue; travelling, whether by "chariot," "gospel raft," or other means, symbolizes staying with one's own kind as the black sinner wends his way toward his heavenly reward. Articles of clothing become symbols of the adoption of faith; putting on the "silver slippers" or the "golden robe" is the same as accepting Christ's word. "De Old Camp Meetin" by A.C. Sedgwick[3] is a lengthy example of a typical camp meeting song. The imagery of the text, emphasized by the cover illustration, and the urgent call to embrace a rather hazy notion of Christianity indicate that the song was certainly meant for entertainment, and it is equally certain that the song was not meant for worship. The text, quoted in full, is as follows:

> Come, bredern git in de golden car,
>   Dar's room fo you an me up dar,
> Come set down on de anxious seat,
>   Kase sin am sour an 'ligion sweet;
> Put dem slippers on your feet,
>   When you walk along de golden street,
> And in dem angels put your trus',
>   Kase no room dar for to raise a dus'.
>
>   Den come an jine right now in de ban',
>   And take de sistern by de han',
>   We bound fo Glory in de happy lan',
>   Aint no sufferin dar, up dar.
>
> If you see Peter sleep at de gate,
>   Kase de night befo he was up so late,
> You needn't 'spect wid your load ob sin,
>   Dat you git past him an steal right in;
> Dey'l know you here and dey'll know you dar,
>   Kase de angels alway on de squ'ar,
> Dey'l hist you out ob dar lubly sight,
>   'Ef your full ob sin an your soul aint right.
>
> Shout! sing! kase de time am nigh,
>   When you put on wings for to fix to fly,
> An dem what prays an de loudest sings,
>   And de ones w'at wears de bigges' wings;
> Bredern, sistern, lif' your eyes,
>   An fix your gaze on de starlight skies,
> Kase de Lord am good an de Lord am kine,
>   'Ef you can't see it you must be bline.
>
> Don't set down, upon your seat,
>   But rise up bredern to your feet,
> An shout for glory till your sick,
>   An get dat 'ligion cure you quick;

Figure 22

Figure 23

> Good Lord dis meetin's all broke up,
>   Kase satin sent some sinful pup,
> Who'l go to hell wid all de res',
>   For handin' in a ho'nets nes'.
>
> Lif' up your voice in humble pra'r,
>   An let dem sinners ober dar,
> Forget dar 'ligion for a spell,
>   An wish dem ho'nets was in hell;
> Glory! Whoopee shoo, wats dat?
>   What am all you sinners at?
> Brudder Jeems pull down your ves',
>   An let dem fight dat ho'nets nes'.

"De Old Camp Meetin" has a cover illustration, a Thomas Hunter lithograph, which pictures the camp meeting as an amalgam of pretended sincerity and comedy. Pretensions appear in the deliberately overdrawn dress of the preacher and his flock. The men in the congregation are particularly overdressed, with swallow-tailed coats and silk top hats contrasted with the ragged dress of the children and the gaudy costume of the women. The scene is especially strange in its woodland setting. Overdressed males became a standard feature for the pseudo-spiritual sheet music cover early in its history. Indeed, the image became a lasting part of the stereotypical religious black male.

"De Camp Meetin' Fire Bell"[4] by M. Louis is an early example of the typical camp meeting scene as portrayed on the cover of the sheet music edition (Figure 23). The males, who predominate in this illustration, are much overdressed for the sylvan setting. The serious expressions on the faces of the preacher and congregation are also exaggerated for maximum comic effect. The illustration complements the inane mock sermon of the text:

> I heahs de alarm from de number one box,
>   Listen Sinnahs, listen!
> Hark! how earnis'ly de angel knocks,
>   De fire am hot an' hissin',
>
>   Angels tappin' at de conscience bell,
>   Heah it, heah it bangin',
>   Hit's a great big fire dey's habbin' in hell;
>   Dat's why de 'larm bell's clangin'.
>
> Flames is a burnin' up higher and higher,
>   Surprisin' an' surprisin',

You haf an' interest in dat fire,
   An' de flames is still a risin'.

     Dat's not de place whar de Ice-carts run,
     An' Watermelons are nowhere;
     A vale of woe an' not much fun;
     Oh! sinnahs dont you go dere.

A fire de ingines nebber git 'round,
   Sinnahs, bilin', fryin',
Where de Babcock stingshers can't be found,
   An' de ain't no use a tryin'.

     Jump when you hear dat warnin' chime,
     Jump up sinnahs, jump up!
     So do your do in a berry quick time;
     Now is de time to jump up.

"De Camp Meetin' Fire Bell" is, of course designed solely for entertainment; it describes itself on the cover as "The great end song and chorus" rather than proclaiming a more serious intent. It is somewhat more difficult to judge the intent of some other examples, such as the famous "Hear Dem Bells,"[5] were it not for the cover illustration which shows a comic black couple riding to glory in a chariot drawn by winged stallions. The song describes itself as a "jubilee song," but it is the cover illustration that removes whatever reservations one might have concerning the purpose of the song.

The chorus of "Hear Dem Bells" is familiar to anyone who has participated in group singing, but the verses are not as well known. Taken as a whole, the text is less sanguinary in its thrust at black religion, yet the song cannot be excused from criticism on the grounds that the wound it inflicts is less painful. The entertainment hall has never been the place in which religion can be properly expounded, so even the comparatively mild "Hear Dem Bells" must be considered as an integral part of the racial insult.

     We goes to church in de early morn,
      When de birds am a singin' on de trees;
     Sometimes dese cloes am werry much worn,
      But we wears dem out at de knees;
     At night when de moon am a shinin' bright,
      And de clouds hab pass'd away,
     Dem bells keep a ringin for de Gospel fight,
      Dat will last till de judgment day.

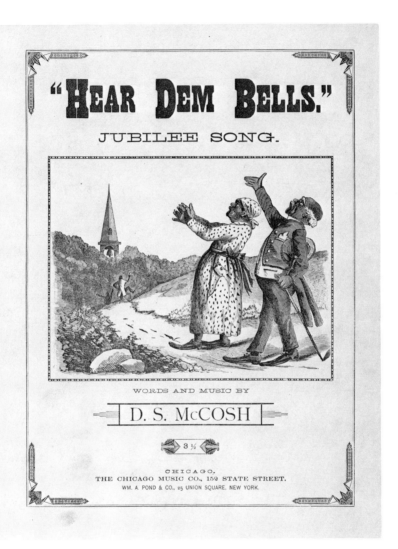

Figure 24

Figure 25

> Hear dem bells, don't you hear dem bells,
>   Dey's a ringin' out de glory ob de Lamb.
> Hear dem bells, don't you hear dem bells?
>   Dey's a ringin' out de glory ob de Lamb.
>
> De church am old, and de benches worn,
>   De Bible am a gittin' hard to read;
> But de spirit am dare as sure as you're born,
>   Which is all de comfort we need;
> We sing and shout, wid all our might,
>   To keep away de cold,
> Dem bells keep a ringin' out de Gospel light,
>   Till de story ob de Lamb is told.
>
> All day we work in de cott'n and de corn,
>   Wid feet and hands so sore;
> A prayin' for Gabriel to blow his horn,
>   So we don't hab to work any more;
> I hear dem chariots comin' dis way,
>   And I know dey's comin' for me,
> So ring dem bells till de judgment day,
>   And de land dat I'se gwine for to see.

The strong association of bright or light colors with virtue suggests an ideology of greater import than normal black concepts would require. White fears of black domination and eventual mongrelization of the races linger beneath the surface of this relationship, to be revealed occasionally in songs such as "Come Jine De Whitewashed Army,"[6] in which the black is pictured as not only desiring equality with whites, but hoping to actually *become* white through religion. Here again, the cover illustration is perhaps more precise than the text in demonstrating the point: a large, winged black woman with a bucket of calcimine and a brush is seen welcoming the "sinners" to step forward to accept religion and the reward of becoming white (Figure 25). Offensive though the text might seem, it is certainly mild in comparison to this illustration. The title, for example, contains an oblique reference to the Salvation Army that is not fulfilled in the text, but the cover illustration spells out the jape at the expense of this organization by showing a member of the flock holding aloft a banner with the words "Salvation Army" printed in bold letters. The text reads:

> Oh, don't ye heah de trumpet soun' a ringin' t'rough de lan?
>   An don't ye heah de loud salvation hymn?

Dere comes a great awakenin' to all de darkey ban',
  We're full o' gospel glory to de brim.
Come Uncle Pete, your poor ole feet am gettin' kinder slow,
  Come Hannah and Jemima jine de song.
Come right along aunt Chloe, get your angel robe so snowy,
  An' bring de pickaninnies all along!

    Come niggahs, quit yo' poutin',
    Salvation ev'ry body can afford,
    Put on a sweet expression,
    An' git inter de procession
    To jine de whitewashed army ob de Lord.

Come drop de half-done hoecake in de middle ob de fire,
  And leave de possum sizzin' on de coals,
Ye cannot tell what moment you's may suddenly expire,
  So hustle, niggahs, save yo' precious souls.
Come leave de shovel and de spade a stickin' in de groun',
  And drop de fiddle quick and drop de bow.
An' chil'en stop dat strummin', aint you niggahs never comin'
  Yes, quit yo' plunkin' on dat ole banjo.

Dar won't be no more slavin' in de regions up above,
  Dar won't be no more hoein' all de day.
We'll only hab to loaf aroun' a singin' songs o' love,
  An' on de harp we'll all learn how to play.
We each will wear a golden crown a shinin' on his head,
  An' wear a shinin' robe ob snowy white.
An' ev'ry pickaninny from Ca'lina or Virginny,
  Will sing plantation songs de live-long day.

The willingness of black composers to join in this white deprecia-
tion of the black religious impulse was taken as evidence of the
legitimacy of the pseudo-spiritual. It was, in actuality, proof of the
unyielding grip of white prejudices that dominated the entire field of
song production. The songwriting process was rigidified into a fixed
image of the black that had to be duplicated by any composer, regardless of the fact that being black might have constituted a qualification
for the production of real black music. Sam Lucas, for example,
repeatedly aped white models to produce inane pseudo-spirituals
such as "Dem Silver Slippers"[7] and "Put On My Long White
Robe."[8] Were it not known that Lucas was black, it would have been
difficult to determine the race of the writer of "Dem Silver Slippers,"
so closely does the song resemble the white model in every respect:

Dar's a mighty camp meetin' in de wilderness,
Of all denomination, with de Methodists,
The Baptists an' de Presbyterians
All together with the happy little ones;
Dar was ole Aunt Jemima an' Uncle Gabriel,
Singin', an shoutin' Hallelujarum,
Aunt Jemima got happy an' cut de Pigeon wing,
An' this am de song she did sing.

Just let me put on my silver slippers,
Just let me put on my silver slippers,
Just let me put on my silver slippers,
An' I'll never turn back no mo'.

One brudder said de Lord delivered Daniel,
One sister in de corner said yes he did,
Another brudder said whar was Immanuel,
Dat he wasn't delivered up too;
He was down by de water wid brudder Moses,
Huntin' de chillens ole closes,
When ole Aunt Jemima got happy again,
An' this am de song she did sing.

An' I'll never turn back no mo',
An I'll never turn back no mo',
I'm a ridin up in de Chariot
its so early in de morning
An I'll never turn back no mo'.

The mock sermon of the camp meeting type was a fertile ground for writers and composers of the pseudo-spiritual. In addition to the homilies and exhortations that were common to the type, Biblical stories could be twisted for comic effect; this device was also useful in demonstrating the total stupidity of the black preacher. No one could respect the black minister portrayed in Thomas P. Westendorf's "Dar's One More Ribber For To Cross,"[9] a song that effectively castrates the authority figure through ridicule.

Ole Noah, once he built de ark,
Dar's one more ribber for to cross;
He patched it up wid hick'ry bark,
Dar's one more ribber for to cross.

One more ribber,
And that ole ribber am Jordan,

> Dar's one more ribber,
> Dar's one more ribber for to cross.

He went to work to load his stock,
He anchored de ark wid a great big rock.

De animals went in one by one,
De elephant chewin' a caraway bun.

De animals went in two by two,
De rhinosceras and de kangaroo.

De animals went in three by three,
De bear, de bug, and bumblebee.

De animals went in four by four,
Ole Noah got mad and hollored for more.

De animals went in five by five,
Wid Saratoga trunks they did arrive.

De animals went in six by six,
De Hyena laughed at the monkey's tricks.

De animals went in seven by seven,
Says de ant to de elephant, who are you a shoving?

De animals went in eight by eight,
De come with a rush cause 'twas so late.

De animals went in nine by nine,
Ole Noah shouted cut dat line.

De animals went in ten by ten,
De ark she blowed her whistle den.

And den de voyage did begin,
Ole Noah pulled de gang-plank in.

Dey nebber knowed war dey was at,
Till de ole ark bumped on Ararat.

Tocsins, those pseudo-spirituals warning of the dangers of sinning and urging the sinner to follow the "straight and narrow," utilize the language and musical materials of the camp meeting type in striving for maximum comic effect. The principal difference between the two types can be stated in terms of the message contained in the text: the tocsin is normally concerned with an individual's behavior and salvation, whereas the camp meeting pseudo-spiritual is aimed at the entire flock. The tocsin also omits mention of the camp meeting as a social and religious event.

But tocsins sometimes present their messages to a collective group as though a spurious minister were addressing an imaginary black congregation. The thrust of the message is nonetheless personal; the tocsin is still a veiled warning to blacks who in real life caused so much white anxiety. "Ev'ry Day Gwine To Be Sunday,"[10] an "end song and chorus" by John T. Rutledge, addresses itself to both the individual and the group:

> Dere's a good time comin' for de niggers yet,
> Ev'ry day's goin' to be Sunday.
> Get your golden wings and don't forget,
> Ev'ry day's goin' to be Sunday.
> Niggers don't you worry, Massa's gone,
> Pick out dat cotton and shell dat corn,
> Good time comin' just as sure's you're born,
> Ev'ry day's goin' to be Sunday.
>
> Better times are coming, niggers skin your eye,
> Ev'ry day's goin' to be Sunday.
> Look out for dem angels, else dey pass you by,
> Ev'ry day's goin' to be Sunday.
>
> Dere's de sisters callin' on de oder shore,
> Ev'ry day's goin' to be Sunday,
> Grease your muscles niggers, for to pull dat oar,
> Ev'ry day's goin' to be Sunday.
> De tide am rough and de wind am strong,
> Fix yourself fo' to sing dat song,
> Work all together and it won't be long,
> Ev'ry day's goin' to be Sunday.
>
> When you hear Mr. Gabriel blow dat horn,
> Ev'ry day's goin' to be Sunday,
> Den de time am here just as sure's you're born,
> Ev'ry day's goin' to be Sunday.
> Fix yourself for to sail away,
> Pack your trunk fo' de broke ob day,
> Cause you ain't goin' to have no time to stay,
> Ev'ry day's goin' to be Sunday.

William Shakespeare Hays's "Keep In De Middle Ob De Road"[11] is similar to "Ev'ry Day Gwine To Be Sunday" in its exhortation of a diffuse audience. The point of interest—the "gimmick"—in Hays's song lies in its preoccupation with the manner in which the sinner reaches his goal—walking, in this case. Transportation to a

heavenly reward, whether walking, in a chariot, or by some form of
water craft, constituted one of the principal borrowings from the
actual spiritual, and was a constantly recurring theme in the pseudo-
spiritual. This, of course, was symbolic of leading the virtuous life in
expectation of heavenly reward, as well as a warning that stepping
over social boundaries would result in a very real earthly hell for
blacks. Great perspicacity was not required of blacks to fathom the
warning contained in the white tocsin, a voice which cautioned them
to behave in characteristic "Uncle Tom" fashion, clothed in a
pseudo-religious sophistry that would never, if believed, improve the
life of blacks. Indeed, the text of "Keep In De Middle Ob De Road,"
like that of other pseudo-spirituals, called upon blacks to submit to a
life-style that was fully as restrictive as slavery:

> I hear dem angels a callin' loud,
>> Keep in de middle ob de road.
> Dey's a waitin' dar in a great big crowd,
>> Keep in de middle ob de road.
> I see dem stand roun' de big white gate,
> We must trabble along 'fore we git too late,
> Fo' t'aint no use fo' to sit down and wait,
>> Keep in de middle ob de road.
>
>> Den, chil'ren, keep in de middle ob de road,
>> Den, chil'ren, keep in de middle ob de road,
>> Don't you look to de right,
>> Don't you look to de left,
>> But keep in de middle ob de road.
>
> I ain't got time fo' to stop an' talk,
>> Keep in de middle ob de road.
> Kase de road am rough, an' its hard to walk,
>> Keep in de middle ob de road.
> I'll fix my eyes on de golden stair,
> An' I'll keep on agwine till I get dar,
> Kase my head am bound fo' de crown to wear,
>> Keep in de middle ob de road.
>
> Come an' jine in de weary ban',
>> Keep in de middle ob de road.
> Kase we bound fo' home in de happy land,
>> Keep in de middle ob de road.
> Turn your back on dis world ob sin,
> Knock at de door an' dey'll let you in,

Kase you'll nebber git such a chance agin,
   Keep in de middle ob de road.

Dis world am full ob sinful things,
   Keep in de middle ob de road.
When de feet gits tired, put on de wings,
   Keep in de middle ob de road.
Ef you lay down on de road to die,
An' you watch dem angels in de sky,
You kin put on wings an' git up an' fly,
   Keep in de middle ob de road.

A closer examination of "Keep In De Middle Ob De Road" illuminates some of the darker implications of the text which, taken literally, would otherwise escape the student. The cover illustration is equally innocuous at first glance, but it must be considered alongside the text in order to establish the full implications of the song.

The cover illustration shows a weary black travelling down a dirt road through the woods, while overhead a band of white angels beckon him toward heavenly rest. It is a sentimental, almost sympathetic picture of white concern for the helpless black, a picture of an attitude that could give comfort to whites. Viewed differently, however, it is a picture of white paternalism that kept the black fixed in his role as a lonely outcast in an alien society.

The text reinforces the latter view, as the first verse clearly states that the black "sinner" must satisfy the urgent "callin' " of the white angel band as a prerequisite for entering heaven.

The chorus reiterates the warning to "keep in de middle ob de road," or to state the matter another way, "to act in accordance with the white Christian ethic" and to avoid conflict with white values.

This Christian ethic is the principal theme of the second verse, as the wasting of time and the conviction that the good in life comes as the result of suffering are combined with a belief that the end result of earthly suffering and strict adherence to doctrine lead to a heavenly reward.

The third verse extends the concepts of the second verse into a universal: *all* "good niggers" can enjoy the benefits that can be derived from accepting whatever the whites decide to hand them.

The fourth verse is both a recapitulation of the ideas that have gone before and a statement of the rather mystical notion that should the black supplicant falter in his journey, it is the white angel who will save him.

Seen in the light of this analysis, "Keep In De Middle Ob De Road" can be interpreted not only as a racist attack on the black religious impulse, but a rather pointed warning that a certain behavior was expected of blacks who hoped to receive benefits from their white benefactors.[12]

Most tocsins strove to elicit laughter along with delivering a message of white supremacy, however. Composers of pseudo-spirituals felt no constraints in their attack on black religion; at least there were none of the self-imposed restraints that made any attack on any other group unthinkable.

"Don't Take De Left Hand Road,"[13] with words by H.G. Wheeler and music by J.W. Wheeler, carries a typical message with the added presumption that blacks and whites would be equally blessed in heaven:

> When we get up to glory we'll stroll aroun' de street,
> Where all is peace and no police to drive us off dere beat;
> Where all de world am brudders, and get an equal show.
> Where darkeys of all colors are "washed as white as snow."

Monroe H. Rosenfeld's "Hustle On To Glory"[14] depicts the black sinner attempting to escape the clutches of the devil by catching a train, or "gospel car." The imagery of the cover illustration is ideationally and stylistically in advance of its time; the associations present in this illustration are those that became standard in the 1890's and lasted until after World War II. A traditional Satan, with trident and rising from flames, grasps the seat of the trousers of a fearful black who attempts to escape to catch a train supposedly bound for glory. A razor protrudes from the black's hip pocket and the Caucasoid features of the devil reflect a sardonic pleasure in the helpless struggles of his frightened victim.

Rosenfeld produced a considerable number of pseudo-spirituals, some of which are discussed later in the chapter. In general, Rosenfeld's songs mark the change from the indecisiveness of the Reconstruction period to the deliberate attack on the black collective ego in what came to be known as the "coon song." But Rosenfeld himself was groping for textual unity in his "Hustle On To Glory," as

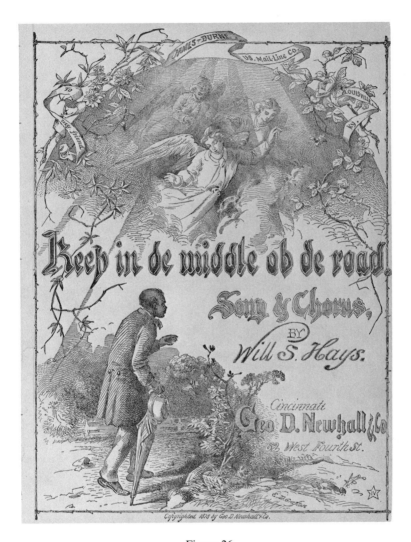

Figure 26

Figure 27

can be detected through his headlong pursuit of cleverness at the expense of making sense:

> Oh, way down on the shore of Sheol,
>   Take dat Hebenly road;
> I saw ole Bobby Ingersoll[15]
>   Take dat Hebenly road;
> With Satan hard he tried to fight,
>   Take dat Hebenly road;
> But Satan said: "I've got you tight,"
>   Take dat Hebenly road.
>
>> Hustle on, hustle on,
>>   If you want to go to heaven,
>>   You must take the train Eleven,
>> Hustle on, hustle on,
>>   If you want to go to heaven, hustle on.
>
> Now dar was Missus Langtry,[16] too,
>   Take dat Hebenly road;
> She said to Satan, I love you,
>   Take dat Hebenly road;
> But Satan said: "Oh, that's too thin!"
>   Take dat Hebenly road;
> "I guess I'll have to scoop you in,"
>   Take dat Hebenly road.
>
> Oh, my dear children, I could see,
>   Take dat Hebenly road;
> Ben Butler on ole Satan's knee,[17]
>   Take dat Hebenly road;
> Ole Satan said: "You're just my man,"
>   Take dat Hebenly road;
> And flipped him in his frying pan,
>   Take dat Hebenly road.
>
> I'd like to find the man so rude,
>   Take dat Hebenly road;
> Who made the thing you call the dude,
>   Take dat Hebenly road;
> The darling little luny dude,
>   Take dat Hebenly road;
> The poor, the persecuted dude,
>   Take dat hebenly road.
>
> Now, all you sinners, try to sing,
>   Take dat Hebenly road;

> Old Peter'll fold you in his wing,
>   Take dat Hebenly road;
> De train Eleven's standing dar,
>   Take dat Hebenly road;
> So mount dat joyful gospel car,
>   Take dat Hebenly road.

It is interesting to note Rosenfeld's reaching into the ante-bellum techniques to borrow the minstrel songwriter's practice of deflating the mighty by associating them with pseudo-black morality. Rosenfeld was one of the earlier expert song writers and song peddlers who gave "Tin Pan Alley" its name and character—indeed, it is generally agreed that it was Rosenfeld himself who first called the New York songwriting industry by that name.

Rosenfeld, who occasionally wrote under the pseudonym F. Heiser, was a shrewd man who instinctively knew the public appeal of a song, and he knew how to exploit that appeal. He lived his life with a flair, being fond of poker, women, and horseracing. He was also described, aptly enough, as a musical kleptomaniac.[18] His most popular works were not on black subjects, however; his fame rests on his syrupy songs of the 1890's such as "With All Her Faults I Love Her Still" and "Take Back Your Gold." The pseudo-spiritual, "Climbing Up The Golden Stairs," was, according to Spaeth, one of the songs which marked the real beginning of Rosenfeld's career.[19]

There is little doubt that "Climbing Up The Golden Stairs" was indeed popular; it was presented in several editions, including an instrumental version. The abrasive language of the text is a measure of Rosenfeld's blunt indifference to the sensitive nature of his subject. His characterization of the work as "the famous jubilee song," or later, as the "great jubilee song," is sheer puffery, and Rosenfeld knew it. But Rosenfeld was interested in selling songs, not expounding issues as he wrote:

> Come all you little niggers,
>   Now watch your cues and figures,
>   Climbing up de golden stairs,
> If they think you are a dude,
>   They will treat you rather rude,
>   Climbing up de golden stairs!
> Ole Peter looked so wicked,
>   When I ask'd him for a ticket,
>   Climbing up de golden stairs!

At the sight of half a dollar,
  He will grab you by the collar,
  And fire you up de golden stairs!
    Then hear them bells a-ringing,
    'Tis sweet, I do declare;
    Oh! hear them darkies singing,
    Climbing up de golden stairs!
Old Satan's not the dandy,
  To feed you on mix'd candy,
  Climbing up de golden stairs,
But he'll give you brimstone hot,
  And he'll choke you on de spot,
  Climbing up de golden stairs!
They'll lock you in the stable,   .
  Make you fight for Cain and Abel,
  Climbing up de golden stairs!
Old man Adam and his wife
  Will be there with drum and fife
  And march you up de golden stairs!

Go tell the Jersey Lily,
  The sights would knock her silly,
  Climbing up de golden stairs,
And tell John L. Sullivan,
  He must be a better man,
  If he'd climb de golden stairs!
Bob Ingersoll's respected,
  But is bound to be rejected,
  Climbing up de golden stairs!
Oh! you bet he'll kick and yell
  When they fire him into—well,
  Climbing up de golden stairs!

Water transportation seemed to many songwriters a singularly appropriate method for travelling to the promised land. Frank Dumont wrote "De Gospel Raft,"[20] characterized as a "plantation song and chorus," published with a cover illustration showing a ragged, frightened black adrift on a raft with sailboats in the background making no move to save him. Depicting the black as alone and friendless in a hostile sea is consistent with Dumont's witless text:

    I'm a going to cross de river on de gospel raft,
    Like Noah in de good ole ark,

Keep your candles all a burning, keep 'em burning all de time,
   Or you'll lose yourself and stumble in the dark,
Get your baggage on de craft, don't forget to get de check,
   For you've got to pay your passage right today,
Be sure de money's good, for de captain's eyes is sharp,
You can't sneak aboard and hide away.

  Hide away, hide away, hide away,
  Dar's no use in try'ng to hide away.[21]
  Get your baggage on de craft,
    Don't forget to get de check,
     You can't sneak aboard and hide away.

Now take warning little children, don't get fooled about de raft,
   For de opposition boats are running too,
But she's liable to bust the boiler any time at all,
   And cook you niggers all into a stew,
I'se got a private box and an op'ra glass to see,
   You sinners trying to buzz in at de door.
But they'll kick you down de stairs if you hasn't got de grace,
   If you come back they'll slap you on de jaw.

Let me tell you 'bout de army mister Pharo' did command,
   When he followed ole Moses long ago,
They was drownded in de water with their life preservers on,
   And de fishes had a jubilee down below.
Dar was Jonah was a fool and as stubborn as a mule,
   But de whale did make him quickly disappear,
Jonah den pulled out a razor and he cut de whale in half,
   And floated to shore upon his ear.

By the early 1880's, composers had refined their techniques for writing pseudo-spirituals, eliminating obvious defects of cumbersome texts and establishing a technically superior, thoroughly demeaning form. This refinement of technique can be seen in Stephen S. Bonbright's "Niggas Get On De Boat"[22] which has a more concise text for carrying its racial insult. The cover illustration of this song shows a group of black "sinners" attempting to escape a devil by climbing aboard a barge, while a beatific white angel looks on from above. The text reads:

  You can clim' dis way, you can clim' dat way,
   You can clim' up behind or 'fore;
  But you must get on Hebben's boat,
   Before it leaves de shore.

Figure 28

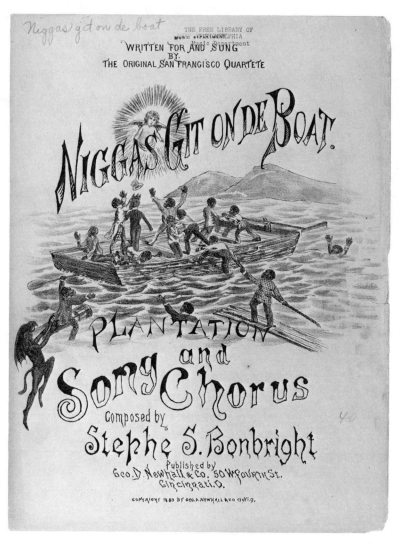

Figure 29

You may call on pa, you may call on ma,
  You can call on uncles or aunts,
But you can't wade if de boat goes,
  Rollin' up youah pants.
    Oh! Dingle, jingle, dingle, jingle,
      Heah de boat bell ringing;
    Dingle, jingle, dingle, jingle,
      Heah de niggas singing:
    Toot toot dingle, toot toot jingle,
      Jump on board I'm going,
    Don't stand around with common folks,
      But hurry on de boat.

You may live fah north, you may live fah south,
  You may live in de east or west;
If you ain't on de boat in time,
  You'd best pull down youah vest,
You will heah de horn, dat de angels blow,
  When de boat am ready to go;
You'd bettah hab your baggage checked,
  While you've got a show.

De gals wid de bangs an' boys wid high hats,
  Must all sit in de fohwad row;
Niggas will sit on high back seats,
  An' let dar burnsides grow.
You must all get on when de bell does ring,
  And don't you fall in de water;
Or you'll go back to dry youah clothes,
  Whar 'tis much hotter.

The portals of heaven, "the pearly gates," were prominent features of the pseudo-spiritual. "Swing Dose Gates Ajar,"[23] with words by Tom Merrie and music by William A. Huntley, is a tocsin dealing with blacks' conception of entering heaven, according to white suppositions. The cover illustration by Joseph Donaldson is a grotesque representation of ill-kempt, weeping black supplicants, one of whom is accompanying himself on the banjo. A ferocious small dog—white, of course— is biting the foot of the musician. The text contains strong racial allegations in the last verse, whereas the first two contain little more than the usual pseudo-spiritual trivia:

Oh, what will you do when de great day comes?
  Swing dose gates ajar,

When Gabriel's horn shall wake the tombs?
  Oh, swing dose gates ajar,
You must have a check or you can't get past,
  Swing dose gates ajar,
Ole Pete's got de keys an' he holds dem fast,
  Oh, swing dose gates ajar.

> Swing 'em open, honey,
>   Swing 'em wide and far,
> De bells will ring and angels sing,
>   Oh, swing dose gates ajar.
> (Chorus repeated)

Oh, what am you sinners a-gwine to do?
  Swing dose gates ajar,
You'll find ole Pete won't let you through,
  Oh, swing dose gates ajar,
Don't cry cause de golden gates won't fall,
  Swing dose gates ajar.
When Pete ain't around you can jump de wall,
  And swing dose gates ajar.

De white folks dey brag, but in days way back,
  Swing dose gates ajar,
Old Eve and Adam both were black,
  Oh, swing dose gates ajar,
Dey sinn'd 'gainst de Lord an' he showed his might,
  Swing dose gates ajar,
It skeered dem so bad dey bofe turned white,
  Oh, swing dem gates ajar.

Monroe H. Rosenfeld contributed at least one song to this theme, complete with illustrated cover containing all the elements of the stereotype, "Ring Dat Golden Bell."[24] The text of this Rosenfeld pseudo-spiritual is virtually identical to those mentioned earlier and does not warrant exposition; the illustration, on the other hand, is of interest because of the addition of the chicken as a Negrism. The cover illustration of "Ring Dat Golden Bell" offers a full range of stereotypical black religious images as seen by whites: hopeless struggles to enter an essentially white paradise; concentration on dress as a status symbol; the castrated authority figure vainly trying to support his flock as they struggle for admittance into heaven; plus the food predilections as symbolized by chicken and craven belligerence as symbolized by the razor. Although "Saint Peter" is in this instance

Figure 30

Figure 31

black, his white association is clearly indicated by his snowy robe and wings, as well as by the glee apparent on his face as he keeps the door closed against the desperate black crowd outside.

The salvation pseudo-spiritual can be considered the most demeaning to blacks of all the pseudo-spiritual types; it is not only a more direct expression of assumed black aspirations, but in many cases holds the irrelevant notion that the races enjoy equality only in heaven. The personal expressions of black religious faith are transformed by racial hostility in the salvation pseudo-spiritual, perhaps owing to the fact that they are presented as individual, rather than group beliefs. Will S. Hays's "Angels, Meet Me At The Cross Roads,"[25] for example, is not greatly different from other pseudo-spirituals, yet the protagonist's enunciation of his personal religious convictions in the manner considered Negroid by whites lends extra power to the insult. This view, it might well be noted, is directly contrary to that which holds that "Angels Meet Me At The Cross Roads" is truly a religious song,[26] an opinion hardly supported by the text:

> Come down, Gabriel, blow your horn,
> Call me home in de early morn;
> Send de chariot down dis way,
> Come and haul me home to stay, O!
>
> > Angels, meet me at de Crossroads, meet me,
> > Angels, meet me at de Crossroads, meet me,
> > Angels, meet me at de Crossroads, meet me,
> > Don't charge a sinner any toll.
>
> I'se libed for months, an I'se libed for years,
> Can't get used to my weepin' tears;
> Lost my way on de road in sin,
> Wake up, angels, pass me in, O!
>
> Plant my foot on de golden rocks,
> Put my money in de mission box;
> When I get dar, an you hear me call,
> Come on, den, for dar's room for all, O!
>
> Stand back, sinners, let me pass;
> I see de lane to de house at last;
> Come an' jine wid de angel band,
> We'll all git home to de happy land, O!
>
> Dem angels an't got long to wait;
> Dey's standing now at de golden gate;

> When we git dar, on de toder shore,
> Dey'll go inside, an dey'll shut de door, O!

It is evident by this text and Hays's musical setting that he was attempting to capture a true feeling of black spiritual practice. While the surface manifestations of the black music were given adequate attention, Hays missed the essence. Black attitudes as revealed in almost all spirituals view salvation as the responsibility of the individual, not something purchased at the small price of behaving in an acceptable manner. As a white songwriter, Hays was incapable of fathoming the distinction between his protagonist, who is demanding his reward for a piety that is really fake, and one of a real spiritual, such as that of "Swing Low, Sweet Chariot," who stands in grateful awe in the face of his deliverance.

Some salvation songs could not avoid being simply silly. The text of "Sunlight Of My Soul"[27] by James Maas suggests that the composer resorted to gibberish rather than try to understand the profundity of black religion:

> Gabriel on a hicory tree
> Hist up your attic windows,
> Shouting all that mercy is free,
>   Sinners go long.
> Grease your wings and slip up on high,
> Hist up your attic windows,
> Turn a summer-sault to the sky,
>   Sinners go long.
>
>   Oh! Josiah, I'll expire,
>   Wing your flight to heaven above,
>   Sinners go long.
>
> Rosy da da da,
> Pete da da da,
> Honey, darling, won't you love me long?
> Kiss me, da da da,
> Hug me, da da da,
> Love is strong as Samson and I tell you dat is strong.
>
> Rosey, posey pete weet,
> Honey's sour, you am sweet,
> I tell you, you am hard to beat,
> Sunlight of my soul.
>   Oh! Oh, my soul!

> Oh! Oh, my soul!
> Oh! Oh, my soul!
> Could not keep from loving her,
> The sunlight of my soul.

> Grab me, da da da,
> Clutch me, da da da,
> Lovey, Dovey, take me by de hand,
> Hold me, da da da,
> Scold me, da da da,
> We want to get a passport to de far off happy land.

The most that can be said for "Sunlight Of My Soul" is that it brings out the strong connection in white minds between black religion and unrestrained sexual expression. The common assumption that black religion was rooted in sensuality found expression even in the pseudo-spirituals written by black composers, although a less direct route was taken to accomplish the goal, as in James Bland's "Listen To The Silver Trumpet's Sounding,"[28] in which the protagonist declares:

> Listen to the silver trumpets honey!
> It makes us children feel so funny,
> When we hear the silver trumpets honey;
> Listen to the silver trumpets honey!
> It makes us children feel so funny,
> When we hear the silver trumpets sound.

Bland's most famous pseudo-spiritual was, of course, his "Oh, Dem Golden Slippers!"[29] which he had written before his "Listen To The Silver Trumpet's Sounding." And while sexuality is present, but not prominent, in "Oh, Dem Golden Slippers," it is worthy of note that Bland used the clothing "gimmick" for a sequel, "Golden Wedding," which did carry sexual implications. The two songs were, in fact, advertised together as a pair to be performed in tandem.

"Oh, Dem Golden Slippers" is almost too well known to require quotation in this study; yet it serves to illustrate the extent to which black composers adopted white images of the black in order to find success. It is an example of that curious mixture of black and white imagery which produced songs that were neither black nor white, but served to convince white songwriters that their own product was based on the real thing; meanwhile the black composer was convinced that debasing his own race was the key to personal success. There is a certain sadness in the imagery of "Oh, Dem Golden Slippers" as the black protagonist states, in puppetlike fashion:

> Oh, my golden slippers am laid away,
>   Kase I don't 'spect to wear 'em till my weddin' day,
> And my long-tail'd coat, dat I loved so well,
>   I will wear up in de chariot in de morn;
> And my long, white robe dat I bought last June,
>   I'm gwine to get changed kase it fits too soon,
> And de ole grey hoss dat I used to drive,
>   I will hitch him to de chariot in de morn.
>
>   Oh, dem golden slippers!
>   Oh, dem golden slippers!
>   Golden slippers I'se gwine to wear,
>   Bekase dey look so neat;
>   Oh, dem golden slippers!
>   Oh, dem golden slippers!
>   Golden slippers I'se gwine to wear,
>   To walk de golden street.
>
> Oh, my ole banjo hangs on de wall,
>   Kase it ain't been tuned since way last fall,
> But de darks all say we will hab a good time,
>   When we ride up in de chariot in de morn;
> Dar's ole Brudder Ben and Sister Luce,
>   Dey will telegraph de news to Uncle Bacco Juice,
> What a great camp-meetin' der will be dat day,
>   When we ride up in de chariot in de morn.
>
> So, it's good bye, children, I will have to go,
>   Whar de rain don't fall or de wind don't blow,
> And yer ulster coats, why, yer will not need,
>   When you ride up in de chariot in de morn;
> But yer golden slippers must be nice and clean,
>   And yer age must be just sweet sixteen,
> And yer white kid gloves yer will have to wear,
>   When yer ride up in de chariot in de morn.

Fred Lyons's "Hail Dat Gospel Tug"[30] shows the influence of pseudo-spiritual writing as practiced by Bland. Lyons saw blacks through white eyes, however, and his text is consequently permeated with white concerns:

Dar's trouble and hard times a knocking at my door,
  So I's gwine away to come back no more;
Den watch me cut a terrible shine,
  When I git on de gospel tug.
Den I must leave by de rising of de sun,
  So good-bye, brudder, for my work is done;
I will have sweet-meats of ev'ry kind,
  When I git on de gospel tug.

      Den hail dat gospel tug,
      We'se gwine from de harbor,
      Hail dat gospel tug,
      To bear dese children home;
      Den hail dat gospel tug,
      We'se gwine from de harbor,
      Hail dat gospel tug,
      To bear dese children home.

Oh! de whistle done blow, and de bell done ring,
  Den watch me spread my golden wing;
Dar's room for you and room for me,
  When I git on de gospel tug.
I run my best for to be on time,
  And git my check for de gospel line;
De ole folks weep and de young ones sigh,
  When I git on de gospel tug.

So good-bye, white folks, I bid you all adieu;
  Such a happy little band and a gallant crew;
I hate to leave you all behind
  When I git on de gospel tug.
If Satan fools about dat tug,
  I'll throw him over in de water ker-chug;
Den won't I spread my catfish mouth,
  When I git on de gospel tug.

"When Am You Gwine?,"[31] also by Lyons, is similar to the Bland formula, except that the repetitive refrain is omitted in favor of a spoken dialogue consisting of such 1880's side-splitters as:

      "Now dar am brudder Jonah,
      When am you gwine?"
      "Who, Me?"

"Yes, you."

All: "Ha, ha, ha!"

This level of humor doubtlessly contributed greatly to the decline of minstrelsy by 1890.

Jacob Sawyer, a black composer whose prodigious output attracted surprisingly little notice from historians, used the Bland approach in his "Put On De Golden Crown":[32]

> Good ebening white folks one and all,
>   I'se come to pay my custom call,
> Den cheer up my honey for I must go
>   To put on de golden crown.
> De jaybird chirps and de mocking bird sings,
>   De coons am a dancing de jing-o-fling,
> Den bye-bye, my honey, I'se gwine to fly
>   And put on de golden crown.
>
>   Den oh my, bye and bye,
>   Won't I shine when I get on high,
>   Put on de golden crown.
>
> Mary had an only Son,
>   De Jews and Romans had him hung,
> Den cheer up, my honey, I'se gwine to go,
>   To put on de golden crown.
> Den Hannah bile dat cabbage down,
>   And cook dem buckwheats good and brown,
> Den bye-bye, my honey, I'se gwine to fly
>   And put on my golden crown.

Unlike most composers of pseudo-spirituals, Sawyer seemed unsure of which direction to take; some of his productions were imbued with a simplicity and straightforwardness that approach the spirit of the true spiritual, while others doggedly follow the white formula writing at its inane worst. As an example of the former, his "My Lord Is Writin' Down Time"[33] is a tocsin possessing considerable power through insistent repetition of melodic and textual material:

> For he sees all you do,
>   And He hears all you say,
>   And my Lord is writin' down time.

He sees all you do,
  And He hears all you say;
  Yes, my Lord is writin' down time.
Oh! Hallelujah to de Lamb!
  My Lord is writin' down time,
De Lord is in dere giving a hand,
  My Lord is writin' down time,
For he sees all you do,
  And hears all you say,
  Yes my Lord is writin' down time.
He hears all you say,
  And sees all you do,
  Yes, my Lord am writin' down time.

Contrasted with this, Sawyer's "Blow, Gabriel, Blow"[34] could have been easily confused as the work of almost any white composer:

Darkies pray fo' de time draws nigh,
  Blow, Gabriel, blow,
We'll soon be mountin' up on high,
  Blow, Gabriel, blow,
Chicken coops you mus' leave alone,
  Blow, Gabriel, blow,
Or Satan'll cotch you shu's yous bo'n,
  Blow, Gabriel, blow.

The only element that differentiates "Blow, Gabriel, Blow" from other pseudo-spirituals is the rhythmic structure of the first part, which consists of two-bar phrases answered by one-bar phrases. This pattern, repeated four times, produces a lopsided gait that is unusual for a style rigidified by common practice into phrases of equal length. Indeed, this "error" is rectified in the chorus, which reverts to standard two-bar phrases for both the antecedent and the consequent.

Black composers who succumbed to the pressures to write pseudo-spirituals in the white manner reinforced the conviction widely held among whites that the black secretly wanted to become white, either through intermarriage or adopting white social values. They served to legitimize, to the white at least, the white approach to the black subject in song. The pseudo-spiritual's preoccupation with

light colors and their association with virtue tended to confirm these
notions. To carry the assumption a step further, the idea of a light-
colored paradise was intermixed with the Dixie myth, as can be seen
in George T. Pritchard's "On De Golden Shore":[35]

> I'se trabling back to ole Virginny shore,
>   Where I use to hunt de possum an de coon,
> And play de banjo round de cabin door,
>   As de pickanninies danc'd around de room.
> Dem good ole days will nebber come again,
>   My good ole wife Chloe am no more;
> Dey laid her to rest beneath the willow tree,
>   But I hope to meet her on de golden shore.
>
> > I'se coming, coming, yes, I'se coming;
> > Is dere no one to meet me at de door?
> > Ole Chloe am gone, an' de children eb'ry one,
> > But I hopes to meet dem on de golden shore.
>
> I'll nebber forget my dear old cabin home,
>   And de ivy green a growing round de door,
> Ole master kind and ole missus good and true,
>   But on earth I know I'll see dem nebber more.
> Dem cotton fields, where I used to work all day,
>   Are number'd wid de t'ings dat's gone before,
> I'll say good bye to ole Virginny when I die,
>   And meet my Chloe on de golden shore.

And in Charles Benedict's "I'll Be Dar":[36]

> Oh, come you sinners, go wid me,
>   Oh, I'll be dar,
> I'll take you down to Tennessee,
>   Oh, I'll be dar,
> Come and join de silver band,
>   Oh, I'll be dar,
> I'se gwine to fly to Canaan's land,
>   Oh, I'll be dar.

It has been noted that many illustrated covers of the pseudo-
spiritual sheet music editions were fully as demeaning as the textual
content of the song; there were other pseudo-spirituals with illustrated
covers that were misleading—although no less insulting. Through

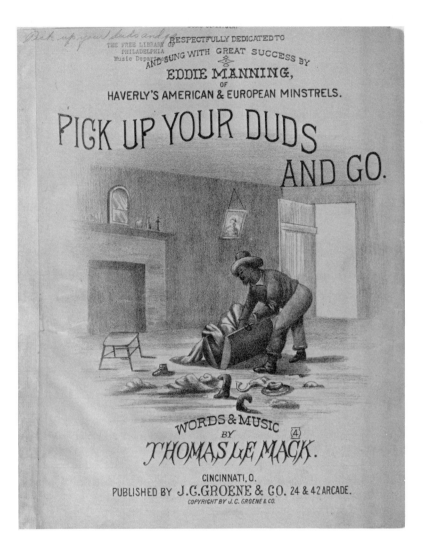

Figure 32

design or accident, these covers obscured the religious insult and led the viewer to expect some other aspect of the black stereotype within the text. "Pick Up Your Duds And Go"[37] by Thomas Le Mack has a cover illustration suggesting strongly that the song is concerned with a lover's quarrel; the text shows it to be another pseudo-spiritual, however:

> In this world of care and trouble,
>   There's heaps of strife and sin,
> For as soon as you are born, from that day on,
>   All your trouble does begin;
> So prepare yourself for the judgement day,
>   Save your pennies boys,
> Buy yourself a carpet sack,
>   Pick up your duds and go.
>
>   Then hurry on to glory,
>   Now children don't be slow,
>   When the roll is call'd on the judgement day,
>   Pick up your duds and go.
>
> And when you get up to heaven,
>   Mind now don't you get too gay,
> Or partic'lar 'bout your food, don't put on style,
>   Case de Lord don't like no dudes;
> 'Twas just there unhappy old saten liv'd,
>   Many years ago,
> He did sin and the Lord made him
>   Pick up his duds and go.

Monroe H. Rosenfeld, using the pseudonym F. Belasco, produced in 1885 his "I'se Gwine To Weep No More,"[38] which was issued with a rather misleading cover illustration showing a black infant with a grotesquely enlarged head, playing the banjo (Figure 33). This illustration has little to do with the content of the song, which is a typical Rosenfeld pseudo-spiritual loaded with topical comment and political satire.

Rosenfeld's "I'll Send You Down A Letter From De Sky"[39] carries a cover illustration on the sheet music edition that falls between graphic clarity and obscurantism; the cover shows a razor-carrying, chicken-stealing, fearful black being kicked by a mule into everlasting glory, which is indeed the gist of the song. But Rosenfeld

Figure 33

Figure 34

put this situation in the form of a pseudo-spiritual in the text, a technique that was somewhat unusual for the period and a departure from his own style. Composers of the following decades, however, would find in this type of pseudo-spiritual a rich new vein to exploit. Rosenfeld had joined the religious satire of the pseudo-spiritual with a loosely constructed ballad style to produce:

> De old man's got a heap of grief in his breast,
> O good children, weep;
> And he's waitin' for de sun to fall in de west,
> O good children, weep;
> Got on his robe and his velvet vest,
> O good children, weep;
> Gwine for to lay his ole bones to rest,
> O good children, weep!

> > Oh! Hannah, kiss your Daffy dear,
> > Kiss your Daffy dear,
> > Kiss your Daffy dear;
> > Oh, Hannah, kiss your Daffy dear,
> > And I'll send you down a letter from de sky.
> > And I'll send you, I'll send you,
> > I'll send you down a letter from de sky.

> Now de ole mule's heels cum up like a brick,
> O good children, weep;
> And downed de ole man quick and slick,
> O good children, weep;
> His shoes am torn and his crown all mussed,
> O good children, weep;
> And his teeth am black, and his coat all bust,
> O good children, weep.

> Now de angel's standin' on de big cross-cut,
> O good children, weep;
> And Ole Brother Satan is a sneakin' round de hut,
> O good children, weep;
> And he nebber speaks as he pass by,
> O good children, weep;
> For fear dat mule might catch his eye,
> O good children, weep!

> [*Refrain*]
> Up in de country where angels live and dwell,
> > Up in de fields beyond de sky;

> Up whar de banjo rings music to de bell,
>   I'll linger to live and nebber die;
> And I'll send you, I'll send you,
> I'll send you down a letter from de sky.

As the 1880's drew to a close, the pseudo-spiritual as typified by Rosenfeld's many works became the standard form followed by composers both black and white. Gussie L. Davis, one of the most talented black composers to enter the popular field during this period, adopted the white approach in his "Up Dar In De Sky,"[40] a pseudo-spiritual in direct imitation of the Rosenfeld model. "Up Dar In De Sky," subtitled "Sarah Jane Go Change Your Name," with all respect to the composer's talent, is a travesty of black music without the remotest propinquity for the real thing. It does not require great profundity to imagine the humiliation suffered by the composer who wrote:

> Darkies have you heard the news?
>   Up dar in de sky!
> I's gwine to shake these half sew'd shoes,
>   Up dar in de sky!
> Old aunt Hannah, how de do?
>   Up dar in de sky!
> I'm well, thank you, how is you?
>   Up dar in de sky!
>
>   Come here, black gal, come and kiss me,
>   Go 'way Mister Coon, I'm too shy.
>   In the evening I'm gwine to meet you,
>   I'm gwine to kiss you bye and bye.
>
> Oh, Sarah Jane, go change your name,
>   And don't you grieve and cry,
> I'll meet you when the moon is shining,
>   Up dar in de sky.
>
> Grease my head with mutton fat,
>   Up dar in de sky!
> My pigeon-tail coat and old plug hat,
>   Up dar in de sky!
> Good-bye honey, kase I'm gone,
>   Up dar in de sky!
> Gabriel's tooting on his horn,
>   Up dar in de sky!

The measure of this puerility might lie in a comparison of the pseudo-spirituals of serious intent which represented attempts to bring the essence of black music before discerning audiences. In the face of the flood of trivia produced by experienced and highly competitive songwriters, these few efforts of well meaning amateurs failed to draw much attention. Some of the serious attempts were inspired by accounts of the deep religious faith of the black, as in "The Bright Side! or, The Nearer I Draw To Jesus,"[41] which was based on an incident described by Dwight L. Moody:

"Just as the gray of the dawn in the morning the fold of my tent parted, and a black face peered in. It was old Nanny, a colored woman. Looking tenderly at me she said: "Massa, does ye see de bright side dis mornin'?" "No, Nanny," said I, "it isn't so bright as I wish it was." "Well, massa, I allus sees de bright side." "You do," said I. "May be you haven't had much trouble?" "Mebbe not," she said, and then she went on to tell me in her simple, broken way, of her life in Virginia, of the selling of her children, one by one, of the auction sale of her husband, and then of herself. She was alone now in the camp, without having heard from any of her kindred for years . . . ."

The song inspired by this incident is a sore disappointment. It conveys none of the profound sorrow of the black, nor does it show capability to even understand the deep agonies described in the story; it is merely a white revival-type song full of the commonplaces of bloodless religion. The raging fire of abolitionism can be said to have died an unprotesting and pathetic death with such songs as "The Bright Side" and its limp-handed platitudes:

> The nearer I draw to Jesus,
>   The brighter the sunbeams shine,
> The darker the cloud of sorrow,
>   The sooner comes light divine;
> The pathway most lone and dreary
>   Is often the safest way,
> Far over the roughest mountains
>   The fairest of valleys lay.
>
> The nearer I draw to Jesus,
> The brighter the sunbeams shine.
> The darker the clouds of sorrow,
> The sooner comes light divine.

> The closer I cling to Jesus,
>   The stronger in love I grow,
> When eyes have grown dim with weeping,
>   The happiest hours I know;
> When shadows are round my pathway,
>   And sorrow doth most abound,
> I know at the feet of Jesus,
>   The bright side is always found.

The remaining four verses of "The Bright Side" are almost identical to those cited and have therefore been omitted. None of the outrage so typical of the abolitionist songs appears in the song, as might have been expected from Moody's tale; indeed, there is no mention of the incident anywhere in the song.

The black spirit in song—absent in "The Bright Side"—is presented with slightly more understanding in George M. Vickers's "De Beacon Lamp Am Burning," notwithstanding the fact that it is a work designed for the stage rather than the pulpit. Quoting only part of "De Beacon Lamp Am Burning"[42] illustrates the lessening of the destructive tendency of most pseudo-spirituals:

> Oh, de beacon lamp tonight am brightly burning,
>   Lighting up de stormy sky,
> And we're safely onward sailing,
>   Glory, glory, port am nigh!
>
>   Let de dark clouds gather,
>   Let de white foam fly,
>   He am here, to give us cheer,
>   Who ruled de troubled sea in days gone by.
>
> Oh, de reefs ob Satan hide beneath de water,
>   Hark, how loud de breakers roar!
> Still de beacon light will guide us,
>   Glory, glory, safe on shore!

There is no comparison between "De Beacon Lamp Am Burning" and the true black spiritual; Vickers, no more than the other composers of pseudo-spirituals, did not capture the impressive and grandiose truth contained in the unblemished spiritual. There are no words, in fact, with which one can compare the true spiritual with the seemingly limitless middenheap of ill-concealed antipathy toward the black we have chosen to call the pseudo-spiritual.

There are several important insights to be gained from a consideration of the pseudo-spiritual, however. Perhaps the most significant fact to emerge from the study of pseudo-sprituals is that, in a nation that holds inviolability of religious belief as a founding principle, white fears of an emancipated black could so degrade popular thought that religious insults were even within the realm of possibility. A survey of popular music of America throughout its history fails to produce anything that compares with the demeaning pseudo-spiritual. Among the many songs ridiculing the Irish or Italians, for example, one searches in vain for a concerted attack on Catholicism as an assumed characteristic; none of the German dialect songs attacks Protestantism as a Germanic trait; religion, in short, has been shunned in popular song for every group except the black.

The breadth of insult inherent in the pseudo-spiritual is a measure of the extent of white fears and a measure of the lengths to which popular songwriters would go in attempting the destruction of black religion as a cohesive force. The pseudo-spiritual must be seen as more than merely a commercial type exploited by many songwriters; it was a musical assertion of white supremacy. American songwriters could hardly have conceived of a more cowardly thrust than to attack the black through his religious impulse. The prejudicial tissue that had been painstakingly built up through the years found the pseudo-spiritual a powerful ally in the effort to keep the black "in his place" at the lowest level of humanity.

Chapter Eight

From the Gay Nineties
Through the First World War

The period between 1890 through World War I is often characterized as one of progressivism in America—the so-called "Age of Reform." Industrialization brought about by the Civil War eventually transformed the United States from a rural into a predominantly industrial nation which came to be ruled by an aristocracy of wealth, men who not only controlled the economic life of the country but politics as well. The raw, savage power of giant corporations became a decisive influence in American society and placed the welfare of the millions in the hands of a financial elite.

Farmers and laborers suffered heavily under the yoke imposed by the economic system and, of these groups, the black members endured the worst of it. The sharecropping system which arose in the devastated South became a vicious trap for whites and blacks alike, since owners and sharecroppers both depended upon financial support of creditors who insisted on a single-crop operation.

Those blacks who managed to escape the sharecropping thralldom by moving North found a subtler, but no less effective, discrimination in industry. "Last hired and first fired" became a grim slogan with the bitter and enduring ring of truth. It seemed that the Negro could not find "his place" in any section of the United States.

Blacks found their legal freedom to be little more than a cruel hoax as the legislated guarantees at the state and federal levels were replaced by legal sanctions against political or social equality. Federal indifference to enforcement of laws designed to secure civil and political rights of the black created a void that was filled at the state level by the infamous "Jim Crow" laws. The prevailing attitude among the Presidents who followed Hayes was one of *laissez faire* or, at best, ambivalence in the face of wholesale denial of blacks' rights.

345

Blacks who protested were ruthlessly suppressed. Crying out against this madness, Frederick Douglass wrote:

> The sin against the Negro is both sectional and national, and until the voice of the North shall be heard in emphatic condemnation and withering reproach against these ruthless mob-law murders, it will remain equally involved with the South in this common crime.[1]

Authors wrote extensively on the "Negro problem" during this period. Lewis H. Blair's *A Southern Prophecy* (1889) suggested that the prosperity of the South depended on "the elevation of the Negro," a philosophy that was promptly dismissed as pure lunacy by Blair's southern neighbors. Thomas Dixon's *The Leopard's Spots* (1902) and Charles Carroll's *The Negro Is a Beast* (1900) were far more popular, inasmuch as they were among those works which viciously attacked the black. The "black peril" which motivated Dixon's book became the dominant theme of dozens of books as authors hastened to join the reactionary spirit of the 1890's.

Racism played a part in America's foreign affairs during this period as expansionist-minded leaders found themselves responsible for millions of dark-skinned dependents after the Spanish-American war. Despite a general mood of sympathy for their "little brown brothers," racist America struggled vainly against years of conditioned hatred for blacks as they tried to rationalize these new dependents—non-white, and worse, non-English-speaking—into the "American way of life." For once, racial prejudice in America worked to the advantage of the non-whites: the United States decided that Cuba and the Philippines were to be given eventual independence, a decision that rested as much on the inability to assimilate these hordes of non-whites as upon humanitarian grounds.

Denial of the full rights of citizenship to the inhabitants of the newly acquired territories supported and was supported by denial of the same rights to American non-whites. All too easily the white mind in the United States made a connection between the alien and the indigenous non-white, as leading entertainers sang:

> Der ain't no niggers since de war broke out;
> "I'm a Cuban now," you'll hear them shout . . . .[2]

Soldiers stationed in the Pacific islands taken from Spain—the "Black Islands," as they termed them—saw the islanders in much the same way as they saw American blacks. Of the Filipino the American soldier sang:

> Some claim they are a specie of human,
> They look like it in form, it is true,
> But in odor, morals and knowledge,
> The comparison to human falls through.
>
> For they are just as the Creator made them,
> And a pole-cat you know is the same;
> And a Gu-Gu will never be human,
> Though you call him a human by name.
>
> You are told he is your little Brown Brother,
> And the equal of thee and of thine,
> Well! he may be a Brother of yours, Bill Taft,
> But he is no relation of mine.[3]

The island female, on the other hand, evoked the sensuous image that had beguiled the white male for centuries; try as he might, the white American could not resist her charms despite the risk of being branded a "squaw man" and facing almost certain social ostracism. He sang of the "dusky maiden" in much the same way he had sung of "the yaller rose of Texas" years before:

> They'll play so soft for you,
> While dusky maidens will try hard to woo with
> Hmm, Hmm, Hmm, Hmm!
> It's worth your while on the South Sea Isle.[4]

The music business itself underwent fundamental changes during the 1890's. It became an industry of no mean proportions, turning out songs in a manner that approached mass production. New names appeared on the roster of publishers and newer, more aggressive techniques were developed in the marketing of songs. Literally tons of music flowed from Tin Pan Alley—music that probably more than any other entertainment medium reflected the spirit of the times. The exuberant cocksuredness of expansionist America found its best expression in its songs during this period. The songwriting business was itself transfixed and inspired by the heady example of the huge corporations that seemed impervious to failure.

Faddism became a dominant trait in the composition of popular song, with new rhythms, new dances, and new approaches to older material being developed, exploited and discarded in rapid succession. The period also marked the beginning of serious efforts to capture the black subject in art song, either as arrangements of black music or as ostensible attempts to utilize assumed Negrisms such as syncopation, dialect, and the like. The turn of the century in America saw the disheartening effect of having the black cheapened on both the serious and the popular stages.

Ragtime, often discussed but seldom understood, became a fad that endured as a reigning craze. The obscure beginnings of ragtime are accentuated by the disdain with which it was received in the academic world. The contribution of the black is unmistakable, yet the craze developed through exploitation by white composers and publishers. The contention that the black spiritual has connections with the secular profanity of ragtime is absurd, unless one accepts Goldberg's rather bold assertion that ragtime is "the release of the Negro from his own addiction to holiness."[5]

Despite the fumbling efforts of those who attempt to describe the elements of ragtime—form, melody, harmony, and so on—a glimmering of common sense can be discerned in their discovery that the comparison of ragtime with African music shows more differences than similarities.[6] In one of the tiny number of credible studies on the antecedents of jazz, Gunther Schuller comes out four-square for ragtime as a direct continuation of the march and the quickstep.[7] Inasmuch as the majority of published rags characterized themselves in this manner, it seems strange that it took researchers so long to notice.

The inadequacies of research in the area of ragtime is not to be construed as minimizing its contribution to America's cultural heritage; nor should the role of the black—or for that matter, white—composer be overlooked. Taken as a purely instrumental style, ragtime possessed a quality of excitement seldom equalled in the history of popular music; it was the addition of words to these pieces which altered the entire picture so far as this study is concerned.

Ragtime was primarily an instrumental, rather than a vocal art, despite implications to the contrary by Goldberg.[8] Stage presentation of the style demanded the addition of words and, since the origin of ragtime was supposed to have been among the blacks, the texts that were added—sometimes in an obviously forced manner—were on predominantly black subjects. Full-bosomed white female performers, corseted in what has been aptly called "armor plate," made their marks in the entertainment business singing these texts; their raucous "coon shouts" carried insinuations of black sexuality far more effectively than the same words sung by male performers.

The texts themselves became more openly insulting, with a materialistic cynicism that explored every conceivable facet of the black stereotype. Black composers joined in the heavy slander of their race, interpreted by Goldberg as "an engaging dash of self-criticism."[9] This characteristic white viewpoint was shared by publishers, who issued disclaimers such as: "Seems hard—but people will have coon songs— we must supply their demands and needs."[10] Publishers tried to justify coon songs with paltry arguments that implied that the "cullud bruder" enjoyed them as much as did the white. An advertisement printed on the turn-of-the-century hit, "If Time Was Money, I'd Be A Millionaire," stated:

If catching in a single phrase the most striking characteristic of a race may be considered a stroke of genius, then the author of this new hit may be set down fairly as, if not a genius, at least a writer of exceptional talent. A hearing of the song proves that the elements of humor which it contains serves to bring out the full strength of the good-natured satire on our "cullud bruder" with more force than could the pen wielded by the trenchant hand of the most able journalist. In plain English, "If time was money, I'd be a millionaire," hits off the average cullud man as we know him, so perfectly and, at the same time, so good naturedly, that even he will be bound to laugh as heartily at the story, and to hum the clever catchy melody with as much zest as will the "white fo'ks."

Sadly enough for the hopeful publishers of "If Time Was Money, I'd Be A Millionaire," there exists no evidence that blacks did indeed "hum the clever catchy melody," excepting perhaps under physical or economic duress. Such apologies were, of course, nothing more than the extravagances of press-agentry usual within the industry. Their main value lies in showing current attitudes of publishers actively producing material they knew full well to be offensive.

As stated, many popular instrumental rags were republished with added texts. Adam Geibel's "South Car'lina Tickle,"[11] originally conceived as a cakewalk, had words added to the final chorus somewhat as an afterthought:

> Come all yo' black coons,
> Come all yo' gals so shady,
> Put on yo' bes' style,
> Each gem'man bow to his lady!
> Swing out yo' right foot,
> An' tickle yo' lef' one too,
> Jus' hol' yo' breff,
> An' spread yo' seff
> Dat cake is in view, Car'lina.

A later printing of "South Car'lina Tickle" drops the characterization, "cakewalk," calling the piece by its more contemporary but certainly less flattering term, "coon song."

Kerry Mills's "Rastus On Parade"[12] followed the same plan of fitting words to the final section:

> When he is walking 'taint no bluff,
> He puts 'em in de shade,
> No use in talking, he's hot stuff,
> Is Rastus when on parade.

Mills was not one to stand on modesty in claiming to be the originator of the "characteristic cake walk march." As part of the advertising ballyhoo that accompanied the printed copy of his "Whistling Rufus,"[13] he makes his claim in direct terms:

Mr. Mills justly enjoys the distinction of being the originator of this peculiar style of two-step, nothing like it having been known until he wrote "Rastus On Parade." Since then there have been countless imitations of his unique style. The unprecedented popularity of Mr. Mills' compositions are so well known [*sic*] the world over as to render comment unnecessary.

"Impecunious Davis,"[14] a "characteristic two-step march, polka and cake-walk" by Mills, was published with descriptive notes which, along with the illustrated cover, portray the more demeaning aspects of the stereotypical black:

Davis lived in Black Creek, a small town on the Mississippi, just north of New Orleans. He was never known to have earned anything, and depended entirely upon the charitableness of the surrounding inhabitants for his existence; in fact, he considered that he was a child of Nature, and that the World owed him a living. . . .

Mills designed and copyrighted the cover illustration for "Impecunious Davis," which reveals a degree of interest in the commercial exploitation of the black stereotype that was noticeably above average. He wrote extensively and published numerous such songs, many of which became hits. His attitude toward blacks, revealed through music, lyrics, descriptive notes, and illustrated covers, is sufficiently well known to question the oft-repeated and widely believed story that his most popular piece, "At A Georgia Campmeeting,"[15] was written as a reaction against coon songs, which he considered demeaning to blacks. This, of course, is patent nonsense, for few would have been in a better position to have voiced effective opposition to the composition and publishing of coon songs than Mills, who was a leading figure in both fields at the time. The evidence suggests, on the other hand, that Mills, far from being opposed to coon songs on moral grounds, was one of the foremost exponents of the type and was among the first to put moral considerations aside when confronted with the prospect of great economic gain to be derived from exploitation of black stereotypes.

"At A Georgia Campmeeting" was one of the instrumentally conceived pieces to which words were added when it became evident that a popular hit was in the making. The text, also by Mills, derives from the pseudo-spiritual of the preceding decade; it shows that Mills was less interested in pointing a moral than he was in following precedent:

> A camp-meeting took place, by the colored race;
>   Way down in Georgia.
> There were coons large and small, lanky lean fat and tall,
>   At this great coon camp-meeting.
> When church was out, how the "Sisters" did shout,
>   They were so happy,
> But the young folks were tired
>   And wishing to be inspired
>   And hired a big brass band.

When that band of darkies began to play
  Pretty music so gay
  Hats were thrown away
Thought them foolish coons their necks would break
  When they quit laughing and talking
  And went to walking, for a big choc'late cake.
The old "Sisters" raised sand, when they first heard the band,
  Way down in Georgia.
The preacher did rare and the deacons did stare
  At the young darkies prancing,
The band played so sweet that nobody could eat
  'Twas so entrancing.
So church folks agreed
  'Twas not a sinful deed,
  And joined in with the rest.

Ragtime was popularized through association with almost anything that came to the composer's minds. Ragtime dances proliferated, each with its song describing and touting the step as the latest
craze. "First You Do The Rag, Then You Bombershay; or, That's
How The Rag-Time Dance Is Done"[16] is typical:

First you do the rag, then you Bombershay,
  Do the side-step, dip, then you go the other way,
Shoot along the line with a Pasamala,
  Back, back, back, don't you go too far,
Gaze into your baby's eyes. . . .

Old popular songs as well as so-called classics were revived by
"ragging" them in the current style. "Zip Coon" was given a new
lease on life in 1899 when Otto Bonnell reworked it as "Turkey In
The Straw," a "rag-time fantasie."[17] Bonnell's "fantasie" included
not only the music, but words appended to a final section:

Turkey'n the straw, Turkey'n the straw,
Turkey'n the straw, Turkey'n the straw,
The funniest thing I ever saw,
Is to play the same old tune and call it
Turkey'n the straw.

The success of these methods can be measured by the influence of
popular music of the period upon serious composers; for the first time

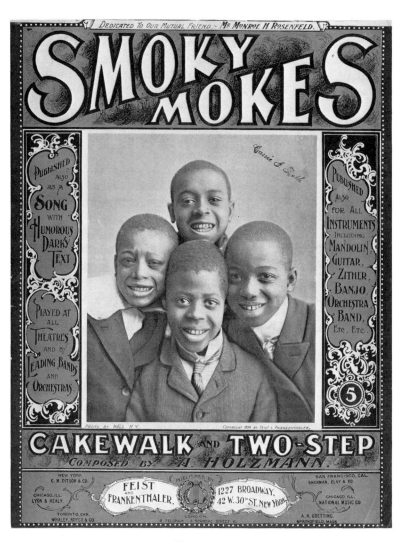

Figure 35

in recent music history, they embraced the stylistic features of popular music, at times under the erroneous impression that they were dealing with authentic folk expression, to produce works which attempted to transcend their humbler origins. Debussy's "Children's Corner," which he wrote for his daughter in 1906, contained the "Golliwog's Cake-walk," which utilized rhythms common to the American cake walk or rag. The American works of Dvořák were infused with the spirit, if not the content, of current popular styles and, while much has been written on the absence or presence of Americanisms in his "New World Symphony," little has been found in his String Quartet in F Major, Op. 96, to warrant the ignominious epithet, "Nigger" Quartet, by which it has been known. The main point to be made here is simply that European composers were captivated by surface manifestations of America's popular music and insufficiently acquainted with its demeaning qualities to make moral judgements on its use in their own creative efforts.

Cover illustrations adorning sheet music of the 1890's became more colorful and more insulting to blacks than at any other time in the history of American popular song. Almost every cover illustration published with songs about the black during this period constituted racial slander to some degree. Photographs of blacks became popular for use as cover illustrations. Even these carried strong suggestions of stereotypical appearance or behaviour. Rolling eyes, pursed lips, or suggestive winks were characteristic features of photographs allowed on sheet music covers, whether the subject were an actual black or a white performer in blackface (Figure 35).

Another factor contributing to the racial slander of ragtime was the ineluctable association made between the musical style and blacks in general. Whatever the black contribution might have been in this case, the relentless commercial exploitation of ragtime and associated styles was against the best interests of racial harmony. Blacks were stigmatized through the popular music of this period by a totally distorted image created for profit; if it were possible to measure vulgarity in music, the coon song would certainly represent the nadir.

The sheer magnitude of coon songs produced between 1890 and the end of World War I prevents the detailed description of more than the principal types along lines already established in this study. Creation of new types was not the distinguishing feature of this period; it was, rather, the culminating point in the development of types

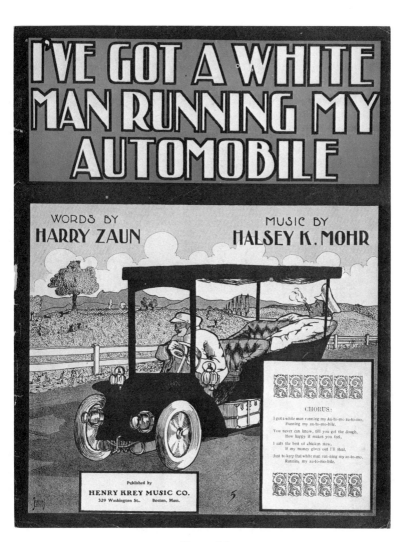

Figure 36

Figure 37

known to songwriters for years, the point beyond which songwriters could not go without sinking to a level of invective known only to radical hate-mongers.

The coon song put the figure of the black male under particularly heavy attack. Pictured as lazy, cowardly, faithless, given to excesses and vices, the male black figure in song had one characteristic that whites feared most: he wanted to be white.

The first chorus of John Queen's "Got Your Habits On" expresses the white anxieties directly:

> And when dey learn how to read and write
> why most of dem niggers just think they're white. . . .

Most often, however, the black male's longing to be white was expressed as a sort of covetousness of white values or standards, as though adopting the trappings of white society would cause albescence. "I've Got A White Man Running My Automobile"[18] and "I'm A Lucky Coon"[19] reinforce the fear that placing whites in positions inferior to that of blacks would undermine the whole structure of white society. Both songs carry cover illustrations showing a black man luxuriating in the rear seat of a car chauffeured by a white man, and the chorus of "I've Got A White Man Running My Automobile" reads:

> I've got a white man running my automo, automo,
>   Running my automobile,
> You never can know, till you get the dough,
>   How happy it makes you feel,
> I eats the best of chicken stew,
>   If my money gives out I'll steal,
> Just to keep that white man running my automo,
>   Running my automobile.

Naturally, the black man in song was seen as having designs upon white women. His prowess with females is seen in the chorus of "The Mormon Coon"[20] in which the bigamous protagonist declares:

> I've got a big brunette, and a blonde to pet,
>   I've got 'em short, fat, thin and tall,
> I've got a Cuban gal, and a Zulu pal,
>   They come in bunches when I call. . . .

The status associated with wealth (or the lack of it) was a basic element in the slander of the black male. When he had money, it was usually the result of good fortune in gambling or success at cheating; it was hardly ever the result of having worked honestly for it. A few songs saw black wealth as merely a dream, as expressed in Willie Wildwave's "I Was Certainly Dreamin'."[21] The key word in the title is "Certainly," for white dogma held that only fortuitous circumstance could bring wealth to the shiftless, ignorant black, excepting in dreams.

> I got aboard my private boat,
>   Smoking cigar which cost me one dollar note,
> Floating for hours on the briny deep blue sea,
>   We sailed up to my summer home for five o'clock tea,
> I sat me down ready to dine,
>   Just about to eat some cake and swallow some wine,
> When someone shook me, p'liceman said you'll have to roam,
>   Get out of this here ash-box ain't you got any home.
>
>   I was certainly dreamin'
>   While stars were a gleamin'
>   I'd a been awful wealthy
>   If the copper hand't woke me up.

Honest labor was an activity reserved for the unintelligent, according to the songs; endeavors to make money were usually proposed along lines set forth in "When A Coon Opens A Department Store":[22]

> What dis coon can do will prove to you,
>   Dat I'se forgot more dan some wise folks know;
> I'se hit upon a plan which will beat de baker man,
>   When it comes to making cakes, or raising dough;
> Dis quiet little scheme ain't no pipe dream,
>   No one's ever worked it out before;
> A skyscraper I'll buy, over ninety stories high,
>   Den I'll open up a coon department store.
>
> When dis coon opens his department store,
>   I'll be doing cake-walks 'long de polished floor,
> Sell ev'rything on earth for double what it's worth;

Figure 38

> Ragtime music furnished by a Ragtime Band;
> Dollar goods I'll mark a dollar ninety four,
> I'll have salesladies colored black and tan,
> A yelling "cash" all day, why, de coons can't keep away
> When dis coon opens his department store.
>
> Downstairs sporty nigs can play dere gigs,
> And lubricate dere pipes with Old Tom gin,
> Dreambooks at half price, rabbits' feet and loaded dice,
> And polka decks all marked to let you in;
> Fine razors will be dere for ev'ning wear,
> Corset sale for sizes fifty four,
> Don't care how much is spent, for coons always have a (s)cent,
> When I open up a coon department store.

Money fantasies dominate "The Coontown Billionaire,"[23] one of the dozens of songs in which the protagonist is shown as a caricature of the white moneyed class:

> I'm the Coontown Billionaire,
> I own in ev'ry trust a share,
> Have palace cars on ev'ry road,
> A gold keel on my pleasure boat,
> I own the largest hunting ground,
> Where bears with golden teeth are found
> My bank account is ten miles square,
> For I'm the Coontown Billionaire.

Every facet of white society had its "coon" counterpart, as though expression of the "separate but equal" doctrine through song would make the problem disappear. Thus, the blacks were given fantasy instead of opportunity; the accumulation of wealth or enjoyment of life's bounty was, for blacks, propounded in song in such preposterous terms as to render their real aspirations impotent and ridiculous. Rather than allow blacks to participate in activities considered exclusively white, songs on the various subjects appeared as though by an unseen guiding hand to provide a make-believe black counterpart. The typically white amusement parks that flourished at the turn of the century, for example, gave rise to "When The Coons Have A Dreamland Of Their Own" by Will A. Heelan and J. Fred Helf, with extra choruses by Ed Gardiner.[24] This lengthy song warrants complete citation for its thorough recital of white misconceptions of the black:

> You can jump aboard your trolleys bound for "Dreamland" if
> you choose,
> Get squeezed all out of breath,
> Get crowded most to death,
> But if white folks think that's dreaming, wake them up and spread
> the news,
> The coons are gwine to build a "Dreamland" too,
> 'Tisn't gwine to be no nightmare, there'll be nothing small or
> cheap,
> 'Twill be grand as anything that ever happened in your sleep,
> You'll think your sweetest dreams have all come true.
>
> We'll build it on the model of a great big chicken coop,
> A real French cut glass roof we'll introduce,
> We'll duplicate Niagara Falls in floods of chicken soup,
> The streams will all be watermelon juice;
> A dance hall with a diamond floor, and built of poker dice,
> All hand carved from the finest pork chop bone,
> And to light up all these sights,
> We'll have black electric lights,
> When the coons have a "Dreamland" of their own.
>
> You'll receive a million dark brown trading stamps as you come
> in,
> Our Ferris Wheel lays flat,
> We'll play roulette on that,
> You can float around "Ye Olde Mill" on the finest Holland gin,
> Real bunco steerers steering all the boats,
> 'Twill be nicer shooting crap than shooting chutes, you will
> agree,
> Just to get your numbers right will be our one grand policy,
> The slips will all be fifty dollar notes.
>
> You'll find our only barkers will be frankfurters, well done,
> Made from the best imported black and tans,
> Black eggs on egg plants growing with a chick in ev'ry one,
> Warm babies will have colored baseball fans.
> You'll see real black wool growing there from ev'ry darkey's
> head,
> All hoodoos are invited to stay home,
> And we'll have some black swans, I think,

Sailing 'round in India ink,
When the coons have a "Dreamland" of their own.

We'll have Jim Crow cars running ev'ry day to Dreamland's
    shore,
The passengers will dine on roasted pig,
All the trains will run on rag time 4-11-44,
And colored Doctors they can take a gig.
Instead of common boardwalks, we'll have cake walks ev'ry-
    where,
Coon shouters shouting through a megaphone,
Cotton fields a growing thick,
Ev'ry coon can take his pick,
When the coons have a "Dreamland" of their own.

The little pickaninnies will be picking liquorice drops,
Big blackfish swimming round in possum stew,
If any white man enters he'll be nabbed by colored cops,
And they'll proceed to turn him black and blue.
And all the colored babies will be togged in colored gown,
Swell colored moving pictures will be shown,
To keep up the color scheme,
We'll all eat jet black ice cream,
When the coons have a "Dreamland" of their own.

Coon gamblers they will have long suits with poker dotted vests,
And smoke big black cigars, two for a dime,
The coons will all wear diamonds made of hard coal on their
    chests,
Each guaranteed an eighteen karat shine.
We'll hand each coon a razor when he feels like cutting up,
If with your babe you wish to be alone,
Just keep it dark and spoon,
By the eclipse of the moon,
When the coons have a "Dreamland" of their own.

But Heelan and Helf managed to produce even greater racial
insult in their "Every Race Has A Flag But The Coon," which was
published by Joseph W.Stern in 1900. This song was based on the
theme of the black social or pseudo-military club that arose in the
Reconstruction period and, while the title alone is sufficiently degrading, the text is even more explicit:

The leader of the Blackville Club arose last Labor night,
 And said, "When we were on parade today,
I really felt so much ashamed, I wished I could turn white,
 'Cause all the white folks march'd with banners gay;
Just at de stand, de German Band,
 They waved their flag and played "De Wacht am Rhine,"
The Scotch Brigade, each man arrayed
 In new plaid dresses marched to "Auld Lang Syne."
Even Spaniards and Swedes, folks of all kinds and creeds,
 Had their banners except de coons alone;
Ev'ry nation can brag 'bout some kind of a flag,
 Why can't we get an emblem of our own?

> For Ireland has her Harp and Shamrock,
> England floats her Lion bold,
> Even China waves a Dragon,
> Germany an Eagle gold;
> Bonnie Scotland loves a Thistle,
> Turkey has her Crescent Moon,
> And what won't Yankees do
> For the Old Red White and Blue,
> Ev'ry race has a flag but the coon.

He says, "Now I'll suggest a flag that ought to win a prize,
 Just take a flannel shirt and paint it red,
Then draw a chicken on it, with two poker dice for eyes,
 An' have it wavin' razors 'round its head;
To make it quaint, you've got to paint,
 A possum, with a pork chop in its teeth,
To give it tone, a big ham-bone
 You sketch upon a banjo underneath,
And be sure not to skip just a policy slip,
 Have it marked four eleven forty-four.
Then them Irish and Dutch, they can't guy us so much,
 We should have had this emblem long before."

Destruction—or at least the severe crippling—of the black male's ego appeared to be a primary goal of the coon song. Human weaknesses were distorted, amplified, and presented as racial traits peculiar to the black. For example, it was widely held that all blacks gamble, and as a result, coon songs were full of allusions about blacks' addiction to gambling. Untold dozens of songs used the gambling theme as the central idea, as in "I Couldn't Stand To See My Baby Lose,"[25] characterized on the cover as "a Darktown expression of pride," which relates the story of the gambler's lady friend who stood behind the other players, relaying signals to her man to insure his winning.

"Gimme Ma Money"[26] by Nathan Bivins describes the typical gambling theme:

> Last night I went to a big Crap game,
> How dem coons did gamble wuz a sin and a shame,
> Coats and hats wuz layin' all over de floor,
> De house wuz crowded wid lots of toughs,
> Wid race horse touts wuz awful rough,
> One coon got broke and dese the words he said.
>
>> Gimme ma money,
>> Don't think you're funny,
>> Cause I'm a nigger,
>> You don't cut no figure,
>> I'm gambling for my Sadie,
>> Cause she's my lady,
>> I'm a hustling coon, and dat's just what I am.
>
> From der I goes to de Odd fellows Hall,
> To have a good time and dat wuz all,
> Another crap game wuz going on among a lot of touts,
> I shoots two bits dat's all I had,
> When I lost it of course dat made me mad,
> "Stop dat music" I began to shout.
>
>> Gimme ma money, etc.

Chicken, a food for which the black presumably had a hopeless addiction, replaced the "coon" of ante-bellum minstrelsy as the dominant food stereotype. Countless songs belabored this theme, with the assumption that the black rarely obtained this favorite dish by any means other than stealing. Further comedy was infused into the songs if the plot showed the thief being caught in the act. Thus the black was portrayed as a simpleminded gastronome and a thief.

This predilection for chicken, with implications of thievery is the theme of the "Chicken Song" from Klaw and Erlanger's production *In Hayti:*[27]

> Chicken's mighty sweet, nicest kind of meat,
> Chicken is the only bird that's really fit to eat,

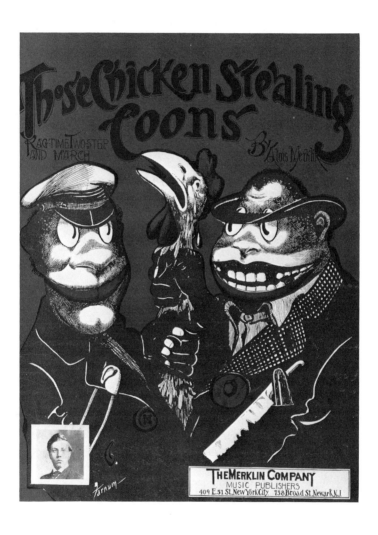

Figure 39

> Good old chicken stew, tantalizes you,
> Chicken is a dish that's only for the chosen few,
> On a moonlight night, chicken coop in sight,
> Always raises ructions with a black-man's appetite.

Imagery of the chicken stealing black seemed to appeal to Jean Schwartz, composer of the "Chicken Song." He had collaborated earlier with William Jerome to produce "Come Along With Me," a formula chicken thief song introduced "with great success" by Harry Bulger in *Noah's Ark*;[28] he also composed "Ramblin' Sam" to the words of Harry Williams. This inane song completes the imagery of the thief being apprehended with a disastrous denouement:

> Ramblin' Sam is the name of a man,
> Dat's been ramblin' all his life,
> Ramblin' in and a-ramblin' out of a various lot of strife;
> He rambled to a chicken coop and then he rambled in,
> Captured a fowl and it started to howl,
> But old Samuel just rambled with him.
>
> Ramblin', ramblin' Sam,
> Ramblin' innocent lamb,
> Hadn't any fear,
> Thought the coast was clear,
> When from the rear, let me tell,
> He heard the shot of a shell,
> Ramblin', ramblin' Sam,
> Fare-thee-well.

Charles Kohlman and Ed Gardiner exploited the chicken thief imagery in their "Appearances Dey Seem To Be Against Me"[29] in which they managed to interject an allusion to the Philippines, somnambulism, and watermelon thievery:

> A big black coon named Silas Jones,
>   While wrapped in slumber deep,
> Got out of bed one summer night,
>   Went walking in his sleep.
> He perambulated Darktown
>   For about an hour or more,
> Till he came to the meeting house
>   And walked right in the door.

It was the ladies' meeting,
 And the wenches gave one scream,
For Silas wore less clothing
 Than a native Philippine.
The racket brought the coons around,
 And they went for Silas "dead,"
They were just a-going to carve him
 When he woke up and said:

Appearances dey seems to be against me,
But I wants an explanation fo' to make,
I'se a "som'la'blust" what does things when I'se dreamin'
Dat I'd nebber dare do when I'se awake.
I know I'se in a dangerous position,
Excuse me do! a minute while I weep,
'Cause if I'se done any wrong I nebber know'd it,
An' I'se shuah I must hab done it in ma sleep.

This coon got off so easy,
 'Cause he did it in a dream,
It put an idea in his head,
 Each night to work a scheme,
He would "swipe" the neighbors' chickens
 And their melons by the score,
And Ev'ry time they'd "pinch" him
 Why he'd close his eyes and snore.

They caught him on a cloudy night
 Behind old Jackson's barn,
He had a bag of chickens
 And a melon in his arms,
Like a steamboat he was snoring,
 His eyes were shut down tight,
When they jabbed him with a pitchfork
 Then he yelled with all his might:

Appearances dey seems to be against me (etc.)

The stereotypical black thief was portrayed as a purely racial phenomenon, as seen in "Any Rags,"[30] a song in which the subject, Ragged Jack, will steal anything:

If you happen for to leave a thing out all night,
You get up in the morn and its gone from your sight;
You'll know then that Ragged Jack has been that way.

He's a very bad omen, people say.
He stole all his furniture, he stole his wife,
If he'd steal from his friend he'd steal yer life. . . .

And in "Fever's On,"[31] stealing is presented as a racial trait that could not be erased regardless of the efforts at reform made by the culpable subject:

Bill Johnson went one night to the church upon the hill
and listened to the good man preach and pray,
Bill had been a wicked coon, and he listened there until
He felt 'twas time to cast his sins away;
So when the parson called for souls, Bill shuffled up the aisle
And humbly at the alter there he stooped,
And Bill went home a singin' Hallelujah all the while,
Until he spied a lonesome chicken coop;
With an agonizin' look, this view of things Bill took:

Oh-h-h-h-h my! stealin' fever's on. . . .

Indeed, many songs, such as "Parson Johnson's Chicken Brigade,"[32] painted the preacher himself as the guilty party:

Parson Johnson am our leader,
He's de boss old chicken stealer,
An' he totes his razor an' he car's a gun;
If de chickens dey do run,
From de Parson's Chicken Brigade.

Stupidity, and a crudely drawn, loutish logic, were important elements of the black male image in the coon song. This imagery was exploited by the great black entertainer, Bert Williams, in his "I May Be Crazy, But I Ain't No Fool"[33] and numerous other songs. In "I May Be Crazy, But I Ain't No Fool," Williams declaimed:

I wonder why dat everybody always chooses me,
To sell things to and tell things to and give me sympathy;
You've heard what they hand farmer folks, well that ain't one,
        two, three,
With the fish tales and the gold bricks that they try to hand to me.

Well, I may be crazy, but I ain't no fool;
One and one always makes two is what I learnt in school;

'Cause I have known for many a year,
Well, I may be crazy, but I ain't no fool.

Now, me and a man once had a fuss and was to fight a duel,
They first said "swords," but I cried "No, I'm too good t'would
be cruel,
I think that pistols will be best" his seconds said, "they will,
Oh, yes, revolvers will just suit our friend there, Buffalo Bill."

Well, I may be crazy, but I ain't no fool,
I read all 'bout Buffalo Bill when I was goin' to school;
There's one thing that's a certainty,
He'll make no target out of me;
Well, I may be crazy, but I ain't no fool.

The effect of songs of this type was to stamp the black male as
weak-brained. In the songs, incapacity for rational thought and the
erratic behavior resulting from this defect were seen as racial characteristics. The comic possibilities of such views were endless, but
the final image is perhaps best summed up in "Nothin' From Nothin'
Leaves You,"[34] a song which puts the black male in the precise
category allotted by white society. Although the protagonist in this
song is a female castigating her man, her role could easily have been
assigned to the whole of society, in that the male black is seen according to the prevailing attitude: he was nothing.

You, Garfield Lee, listen to me,
There ain't no use talkin', man we can't agree,
You heard me say, you're in the way,
You better hunt a new henhouse to lay.
Go on now coon, give up that room,
If you don't somethin' will happen real soon.
What has you done, say! looka here, son,
You ain't done nothin' for none.

You walk like nothin' and you talk like nothin'
Nothin' seems to be your aim; (spoken: Doggone)
You look like nothin' and you act like nothin',
Nothin' and you are the same. (spoken: you fool)
You can't learn nothin' 'cause you don't know nothin',
I've forgot more than you ever knew;
And the only way I can figure you out
Is nothin' from nothin' leaves you.

I heard you said, since we've been wed,
When you married me you was out of your head,
Now take a walk add up your talk,
When you're thro' addin' your answer'll be naught.
One we were made, one we have stayed,
I am that one, while you've been mislaid.
I'm getting sore, just climb thro' that door,
Must I repeat once more?

　　You walk like nothin' (etc.)

The black male's legendary sexual prowess generated enormous quantities of music. The black lover was belligerent and had a mean jealous streak, yet he was constantly being cuckolded. In "Hesitate, Mr. Nigger, Hesitate,"[35] he warns his rival:

Hesitate, Mister Nigger, hesitate,
The way you carry on will never do,
Don't hang around my baby any more,
'Cause I doesn't ever interfere with you,
So if you think you'll steal my lady love,
My fighting powers don't you under-rate.
Just-a take this-a tip, I'm a givin' you now,
Hesitate, Mister Nigger, hesitate.

One of the most famous coon songs of the period, Ernest Hogan's "All Coons Look Alike To Me,"[36] shows the black male's relationship to his fickle lady:

Talk about a coon having trouble,
　I think I have enough of my own,
It's all about my Lucy Janey Stubbles,
　And she has caused my heart to mourn,
Thar's another coon barber from Virginia,
　In soci'ty he's the leader of the day,
And now my honey gal is gwine to quit me,
　Yes she's gone and drove this coon away.

She'd no excuse,
To turn me loose,
I've been abused,
I'm all confused,
Cause these words she did say:

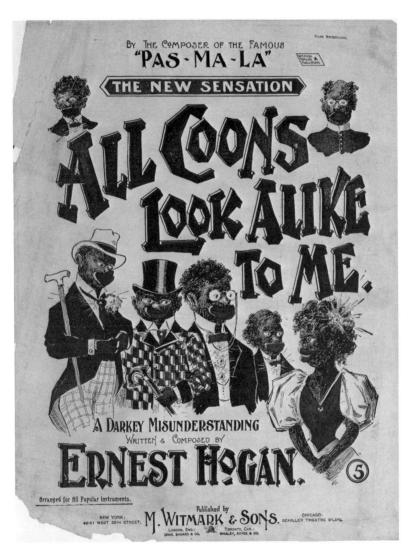

Figure 40

> All coons look alike to me,
> I've got another beau, you see,
> And he's just as good to me as you, nig! ever tried to be,
> He spends his money free,
> I know we can't agree,
> So I don't like you no how,
> All coons look alike to me.

It is said that Hogan heartily regretted having written "All Coons Look Alike To Me" because he felt it was demeaning to his race, and well he might. The song is interesting for reasons other than this, however: it became a model for many subsequent songs on the black male-female relationship, and it was one of the songs written by a black composer that seemed to compel white commentary. Both Ewen and Goldberg failed to detect racial slander in the song.[37] Witmark, the publisher of the piece, could find nothing vulgar in *any* of the coon songs they had published—including "All Coons Look Alike To Me."[38] This attitude was common among the white producers and performers of coon songs; it was not confirmed by the black community. But the cover illustration of "All Coons Look Alike To Me" reveals a truer picture of white attitudes than any of their pronouncements.

Hogan's hit was followed by many imitations shortly after its appearance; Flo Irwin shouted:

> Go away and leave me, I don't like you any more,
> You ain't got no money, what you hangin' 'round here for,
> No, I ain't your baby coon, I'se givin' you the laugh,
> For I'se got another nigger on ma staff.[39]

Imaginative songwriters added another element to the theme of black love gone awry: songs in which the male displayed uncontrollable jealousy. As by magic a new type was created—the bully. The belligerence of the black bully was that of an unthinking brute rather than a manifestation of manly strength; the bully was spoiling for a fight whether he were the aggressor or the aggrieved. The bully figure developed from a fusion of the imagery of the ostentatious black and the jilted lover. In this instance, the sexual implications were much stronger, however. Bully songs tried to convey and to dispel by humor the threat posed by the black male, who was, it was widely believed, possessed of superior sexual powers. The subject of these songs dominated his woman, exploited, and sometimes brutalized her. She never gained the upper hand. This is the theme of a perennial favorite, "Bill Bailey, Won't You Please Come Home,"[40] which is still heard today:

> On one summer's day, sun was shining fine,
> The lady love of old Bill Bailey was hanging clothes on the line,
> In her back yard, and weeping hard;
> She married a B. and O. brakeman,
> Dat took and throw'd her down,
> Bellering like a prune-fed calf, wid a big gang hanging 'round:
> And to dat crowd,
> She yelled out loud:
>
>> Won't you come home, Bill Bailey, won't you come home?
>> She moans de whole day long;
>> I'll do de cooking, darling, I'll pay de rent;
>> I knows I've done you wrong;
>> 'Member dat rainy eve dat I drove you out,
>> Wid nothing but a fine tooth comb?
>> I knows I'se to blame; well, ain't dat a shame?
>> Bill Bailey, won't you please come home?
>
> Bill drove by dat door in an automobile,
> A great big diamond, coach and foot-man, hear dat big wench
>>> squeal;
> "He's all alone," I heard her groan;
> She hollered thro' that door,
> "Bill Bailey, is you sore?
> Stop a minute; won't you listen to me?
> Won't I see you no more?"
> Bill winked his eye,
> As he heard her cry:
>
>> Won't you come home, Bill Bailey, (etc.)

The success of "Bill Bailey, Won't You Please Come Home" called forth imitations such as "I Wonder Why Bill Bailey Don't Come Home"[41] and "Since Bill Bailey Came Back Home."[42] Both of these songs appeared within the same year as the original "Bill Bailey," and both reaffirmed the degraded position of the black female before the fatal attraction of the black bully, as the chorus of "Since Bill Bailey Came Back Home" has her declare:

> Bill Bailey come home dis mornin' soon,
> I'm gwine to love him till I die,
> Makes no diff'rence to me how Bailey carries on,
> Everything he wants I'm gwine to buy. . . . .

Much of the black bully's contentiousness stemmed from an inordinate jealousy; he was quick to take offense when his lady showed interest in any other man, as in "Don't Butt In":[43]

> Ole Moses Green gwine to vent his spleen
> On a certain individual of color—
> Now he declares
> And he daily swears
> Dat he's gwine to prove dat he's a man of valor
> Dere ain't no doubt dat is came about
> On account of Miss Malinda, his intended;
> She went to walk,
> And she stopped to talk
> With another beau and Mose he got offended. . . . .

The bully figure contained a streak of cowardice, shown by "He's Up Against The Real Thing Now":[44]

> A real bad coon once came to town,
> Ev'ry body he met he'd knock down;
> At last he came across a coon as bad as himself,
> Says he, "You may be warm, but I'se pretty hot myself;
> I know you think that you'se all right,
> But you've either got to run, or stand and fight."
> Den dis coon pulled a gun, and aimed it at his head;
> And de bad man, he threw up both his hands and said:
>
>> I'm up against the real thing now,
>> I'm up against the real thing now,
>> I carved dem in de East,
>> And I shot dem in de West,
>> But I'm up against the real thing now.

The bully never understands his power over women. He placed this doubtful virtue on a plane just below his love of personal combat. "I'm De Coon Lothario"[45] has its protagonist immodestly proclaim:

> No gentleman o' color kin de fac' deny,
> Dat ah'm a perfic' terror wid de gals,
> When I walk abroad
> Pleasure I affo'd
> To all the female individuals. . . . .

Nor did the bully hesitate to declare his fighting abilities:

> I'm the toughest, toughest coon that walks the street,
> You may search the wide, wide world my equal never meet;
> I got a razor in my boot, I got a gun with which to shoot,
> I'm the toughest, toughest coon that walks the street.[46]

But the unquestioned paragon of bully songs remained the early favorite, May Irwin's "Bully Song," with words and music by Charles E. Trevathan.[47] The style and tone of virtually all subsequent bully imagery was set by this lengthy example.

> Have yo' heard about dat bully dat's just come to town,
> He's round among de niggers a layin' their bodies down,
> I'm a lookin' for dat bully and he must be found.
> I'm a Tennessee nigger and I don't allow,
> No red-eyed river roustabout with me to raise a row,
> I'm lookin' for dat bully and I'll make him bow.
>
> When I walk dat levee round, round, round, round,
> When I walk dat levee round, round, round, round
> When I walk dat levee round,
> I'm a lookin' for dat bully an' he must be found.
>
> I's gwine down the street with my ax in my hand,
> I'm lookin' for dat bully and I'll sweep him off dis land,
> I'm a lookin' for dat bully and he must be found.
> I'll take 'long my razor, I'se gwine to carve him deep,
> And when I see dat bully, I'll lay him down to sleep.
> I'm lookin' for dat bully and he must be found.
>
> I went to a wingin' down at Parson Jones'
> Took along my trusty blade to carve dat nigger's bones,
> Just a lookin' for dat bully, to hear his groans,
> I coonjined in the front door, the coons were prancing high
> For dat levee darkey I skinned my foxy eye.
> Just a lookin' for dat bully but he wasn't nigh.

Figure 41

I asked Miss Pansy Blossom if she would wing a reel,
She says, "Law, Mr. Johnsing, how high you make me feel."
Then you ought to see me shake my sugar heel.
I was sandin' down the Mobile Buck just to cut a shine,
Some coon across my smeller swiped a watermelon rin'
I drawed my steel dat gemmen for to fin'
I riz up like a black cloud and took a look aroun'
There was dat new bully standin' on the ground.
I've been lookin' for you nigger, and I've got you found.
Razors 'gun a flyin', niggers 'gun to squawk,
I lit upon that bully just like a sparrow hawk,
And dat nigger was just a dyin' to take a walk.
When I got through with bully, a doctor and a nurse
Wasn't no good to dat nigger, so they put him in a hearse,
A cyclone couldn't have tore him up much worse.
You don't hear 'bout dat nigger dat treated folks so free,
Go down upon the levee, and his face you'll never see.
Dere's only one boss bully, and dat one is me.

Encore

When you see me comin' hist your windows high;
When you see me goin' hang your heads and cry;
I'm lookin' for dat bully and he must die.
My madness keeps a risin' and I'se not gwine to get left.
I'm gettin' so bad dat I'm askeered of myself.
I was lookin' for dat bully, now he's on the shelf.

May Irwin's rendition of the "Bully Song" carried the ring of authority supported by her own avoirdupois as she shouted the song in the musical production, *Widow Jones.* Her imposing figure literally challenged the listener to deny the accuracy of the stereotype.

Any popular phrase or anything that had captured public fancy might be utilized as a "handle" or "gimmick" for another coon song. Interest in Spanish music resulted in "The Spanish Coon"[48] in which the tango is combined with the coon song in a rather forced relationship:

If evah I should start in to cry,
I'd cert'ny drown,
Oh! me, Oh! my.
There is a land that's fairer than this to roam.

(Spoken to musicians):
For God's sake, man, what you a-playin'?

Ernest Hogan and Will Accoe wrote "The Phrenologist Coon"[49] for Williams and Walker. Here, the inferiority of blacks was presented as a comic pseudo-scientific theory:

Now by us scientists 'tis often said,
If a coon has an egg-shaped head,
Means chickens he will steal!
And if his face looks like a frog,
And head shaped like a hog,
He can't keep a secret, he will squeal!
If his head's shaped like a melon,
It's no sign that he's insane;
But if his head looks like a bucket,
He's got water on the brain;
If his head's shaped like a razor,
You can bet that coon will cut;
If his head looks like a billy goat,
Beware! dat coon will butt.

The bullfrog imagery was the basis for "The Bullfrog And The Coon,"[50] introduced and featured in the 1906 production of *The Wizard Of Oz*. Sexual connotations are strong in the text, which describes the black lover conceiving the idea of using the example of the frogs' making love to arouse his own lady love. The suggestion of animalism is quite pronounced in this example as well. There was no hesitation on the part of white songwriters to delineate such imagery in connection with the black, however.

The male black figure was constantly pictured as a cowardly and preposterous military caricature during the entire period of expansionism in America. As imperialist sentiment grew and wars occurred or threatened, the question of black loyalty and courage reappeared in song. He was pictured as an ambivalent member of military organizations: when no fighting was involved and activities confined to public display, he was eager to belong, but the prospect of actual combat revealed him as a reluctant tyro or, more normally, as a rank coward.

The black male figure associated with pseudo-military organizations was developed from Reconstruction imagery and should be

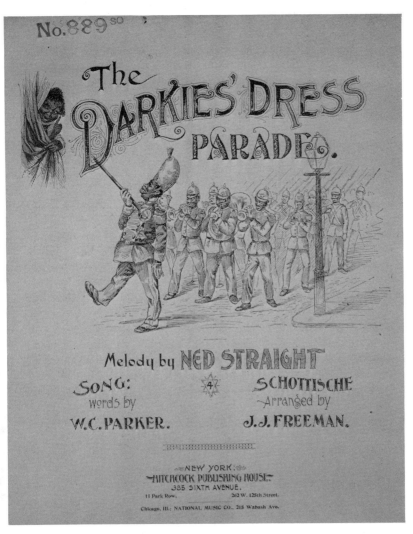

Figure 42

considered as merely a continuation of that type. H.G. Wheeler and
J.W. Wheeler, both active during the late 1880's, produced songs of
this type into the 1890's, such as "The Darkey Musketeers."[51] There
is little in "The Darkey Musketeers" to differentiate it from earlier
types, but it served as a forerunner of more elaborate efforts, such as
"The Thompson Street Cadets"[52] advertised as "the best coon march
song published."

> Did you ever see a nigger
> Who was feelin' any bigger
> Than the leader of the Thompson Street Cadets
> He can change a silver dollar
> But he cannot change his color
> This leader of the Thompson Street Cadets.

The black military figure was caricatured in many instrumental
pieces, usually called "characteristic marches and two-steps." The
illustrated covers of these pieces were reflections of popular attitudes,
as in S.R. Henry's "The Colored Ragamuffins" or his "The Colored
Major."[53] With or without words, the type maintained a steady
popularity throughout the period, counting among its favorites "The
Coons Are On Parade,"[54] the 1890's "The Coleville Coon Cadets,"[55]
and Dave Reed's hit, "De Leader Ob De Company B."[56]

President Wilson's view that "segregation is not humiliating but a
benefit" was a fine piece of casuistry that set the tone for both of his
terms and provided official sanction for strictures upon blacks which
grew harsher as the new century approached World War I.[57] Wilson's
high moral tone in foreign relations could not hide the shortsighted-
ness of his position concerning the American black. The action in
Mexico aimed at deposing Huerta and the punitive expedition against
Pancho Villa stemmed from Wilsonian righteousness—and nearly
plunged the nation into a fruitless war.

Naturally, Wilson's Mexican adventures evoked at least one song
demeaning to American blacks: "When The War Breaks Out In
Mexico I'm Going To Go To Montreal."[58] Sung by Sophie Tucker, it
eschewed the usual dialect and did not refer directly to the Negro, but
the illustrated cover left no doubt that the subject of the song is the
black male's cowardice.

Wilson's racial policies were reflected in Pershing's infamous
order to the French military mission stationed with the Americans in

World War I: the black troops were to be segregated and, above all, kept from white women.[59] The humiliation of this official attitude was not softened by such songs as "Nigger War Bride Blues"[60] which described the black soldier as "easy greasy breezy John." Interestingly enough, an identical song was produced from the same plates— including the cover illustration—with the sole alteration being the deletion of "Nigger" from the title.

Songs which attributed the black with fighting capability and patriotism did so in a curiously grudging manner; the older male figure, represented at times as the "uncle," was seen as willing and able to combat the enemy. Eddie Cantor introduced "When Uncle Joe Steps Into France"[61] to audiences in 1918:

> When Uncle Joe steps into France,
> With his ragtime band from Dixie-land,
> See the Soldiers swaying,
> When Uncle Joe starts playing a raggy ditty,
> So sweet and pretty,
> When they play the Memphis blues,
> They will use a lot of shoes,
> And fill them full of Darky gin,
> They'll rag their way right to Berlin.

Harry Carroll sang his "They'll Be Mighty Proud In Dixie Of Their Old Black Joe,"[62] in which the aged black shoulders his banjo and his gun and departs for France in order to "give the whole world liberty, just like Lincoln did for me." The principal contribution of the black to the war effort was, as represented in song, his presumed innate musicality.

Much of the imagery was openly absurd. The outrageous pun of "When The Boys From Dixie Eat The Melon On The Rhine"[63] was demeaning not only to the black but to the persons responsible for producing it.

Even the black who remained at home to work in the war industry was belittled in song. "Jefferson Brown,"[64] with words by Adrian Metzger and music by Gertrude Voorheis, pictured him as fearful of work in a munitions factory:

> Jefferson Brown left his home town
> For a job of twenty bucks a day and all found;

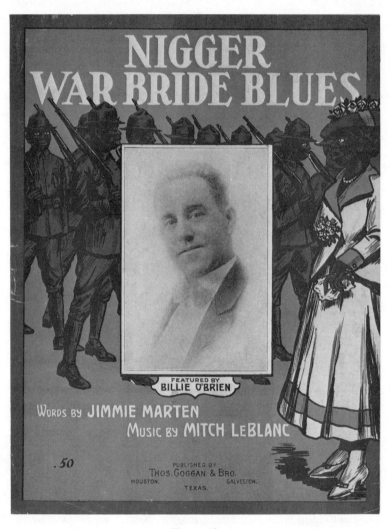

Figure 43

It looked all right as well it might
Till he found he had to handle dynamite.
Jefferson Brown he looked aroun'
A shaky feeling hit his spine and jiggled 'way down;
He sees the belles a-making shells,
Grabs his hat in panic and he loudly yells:

> Just keep your job, please, ah'm goin' away,
> No kind of money kin make me stay.
> No ammunition's in my ambition,
> Somethin' is tellin' me,
> Be on your way.
> May be a streak's in mah black and tan,
> This ain't no job fo' no cullud man.
> It's lots o' money but mah stummuck's funny,
> Ah'm a-goin' while the goin' am good.

Thus, the enormous contribution that the black actually made toward American participation in World War I was obscured and depreciated through song. The memorable songs of World War I were those depicting the patriotic fervor of the whites—not the blacks.

Black male imagery included, of course, refinements of types established by tradition. The preacher, already mentioned in "Parson Johnson's Chicken Brigade," developed into a durable type related to the types associated with the pseudo-spiritual. The authority figure, represented by the "preacher" or "deacon," was a total corruption of black religious manifestations; this figure propounded a phony morality while actively engaged in chicken-stealing, womanizing, drinking, or almost anything considered illegal or sinful during this period. Christianity through the lips of this preposterous creature was an insane compound of garbled Bible stories and superstition. Voodoo took over where conventional religion left off.

Courage was a quality conspicuously absent in the coon song preacher's character. "Mister Moon, Kindly Come Out And Shine"[65] offered the preacher's reaction to being the butt of a practical joke by young rowdies who followed him home in the wee hours of the morning, firing shots to test his bravery:

> Oh, Mister Moon, Moon, silvery moon,
> Kindly come out and shine,
> Do Mister Moon, Moon, come out soon,

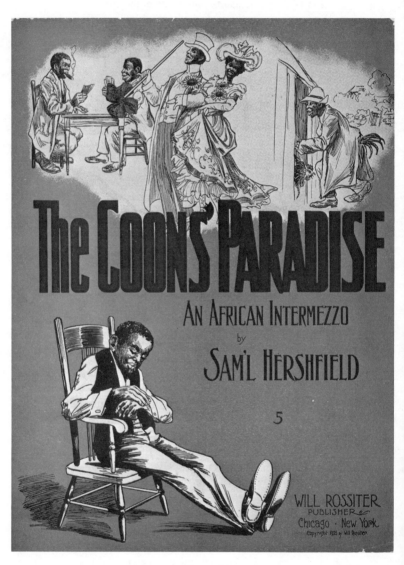

Figure 44

> My home I wants to find.
> I'm brave 'tis true, was never known to run,
> But the boys behind me with a gatling gun,
> Oh Mister Moon, Moon, silvery moon,
> Kindly come out and shine.

This fear motive was the basis of "The Preacher And The Bear"[66] which appeared in the year following "Mister Moon, Kindly Come Out And Shine." "The Preacher And The Bear" achieved popularity far beyond its worth as a song; it has maintained this popularity almost through the present day, being a veritable trademark of the late entertainer, Phil Harris.

> A preacher went out a hunting,
> 'Twas on one Sunday morn,
> Of course it was against his religion
> But he took his gun along,
> He shot himself some very fine quail
> And one big measly hare,
> And on his way returning home,
> He met a great big grizzly bear;
> The bear marched out in the middle of the road
> And he waltzed to the coon you see,
> The coon got so excited
> The he climbed a persimmon tree,
> The bear sat down upon the ground
> And the coon climbed out on a limb,
> He cast his eyes to the God in the skies
> And these words he said to him:

> > Oh Lord, didn't you deliver Daniel from the Lion's den?
> > Also deliver Jonah from the belly of the whale and then,
> > Three Hebrew children from the fiery furnace so the good
> >   books do declare;
> > Now Lord, if you can't help me, for goodness sake don't
> >   you help that bear.

> This coon stayed up in that tree
> I think it was all night,
> He says, "Oh Lord, if you don't help that bear
> Then you'll see one awful fight,
> Just about then the limb let go
> And the coon came tumbling down,

You should have seen him get his razor out
Before he struck the ground,
He hit the ground cutting right and left,
'Tis true he put up a very game fight,
Just then the bear hugged this coon,
He squeezed him a little too tight,
The coon he then lost his razor
But the bear held on with a vim,
He cast his eyes to the God in the skies
And once more he said to him:

Oh Lord, (etc.).

Bert Williams exploited the black preacher image in a series of "deacon" songs which showed, among other disrespectful attitudes, the unwholesome relationship between the preacher and women. "Somebody's Done Me Wrong"[67] pictures the preacher as a cuckold, and in one of the rare instances in which a father figure is mentioned explicitly, Williams sang "Pray For The Lights To Go Out,"[68] a song which directed the listener toward the sexual implications of black religion:

Father was a deacon in a hard shell church,
    'Way down South where I was born;
People used to come to church from miles around,
    Just to hear the Holy work go on,
Father grabs a sister 'round the neck and says,
    Sister won't you sing this song.
The sister tells the deacon that she didn't have time,
    Felt religion coming on.
Just then somebody got up, turn'd the lights all out,
    And you ought to heard that sister shout.

She hollered Brother,
If you want to spread joy,
Just pray for the lights to stay out.
She called on Deacon
For to kneel and pray,
You ought to heard that sister shout.
Throw'd up both hands and got way back,
Took two steps forw'd and ball'd the Jack,
She hollered Brother,
If you want to spread joy,
Just pray for the lights to stay out.

Father tried to quieten down his loving' flock,
   Call'd on all the saints above;
All that he could hear 'way down there in the dark
   Was baby, honey, turtle dove.
Deacon grabs his bible firmly in his hand,
   Pray'd to be show'd wrong from right.
Just then as if his pray'rs were answered from above,
   Someone got up turn'd on the light,
He feels himself a-slippin', grabs the first gal near,
   And she sings this sweet song in his ear.
      She hollered Brother (etc.).

"It's Nobody's Business But My Own,"[69] number six in the "deacon" series, shows the preacher defying the deacons who accuse him of scandalous behavior:

It's nobody's business but my own,
   What I do when my preachin's thru,
So refrain from "messin' " 'round my home,
   Leave me alone.
When a flock of sisters seek my door,
   You old jealous Deacons all get sore,
It's nobody's business but my own.

Many songs of this type were more direct in revealing the fraudulent preacher: "Shame On You"[70] by Chris Smith and John Larkins linked the preacher, obviously modelled on the central character in "Parson Johnson's Chicken Brigade," to chicken stealing:

Deacon Johnson was a preachin' to his flock,
   At a big camp-meetin' one day,
When a brother who was sittin' list'nin' to his text,
   Got angry and was forced to say,
"Brudder! how can you preach
   And expect to teach these folks how to be good?
When I saw you dis morn' 'bout two,
   Right in my chicken coop?
And any time a thief is round,
   My dogs commence to howl,
I caught you fair, but you declared:
   'You came to buy fowl.' "

> Jasper Johnson, shame on you!
> You can't preach and rob me too!
> You might fool me now and then,
> But you don't buy fowl at two A.M.
> I know what I'm talking about
> And I wants the people here to find you out;
> So they can all stand up and shout:
> "Shame on you!"

> Deacon Johnson tried his best to square himself,
>   'Fore the congregation that day,
> He was gettin' awful angry when he loudly said:
>   "Bout me you should not talk that way,
> Brudder! please don't abuse
>   Or ever accuse a full-fledged Christian man,
> I'm the deacon of this church
>   And one true son of Ham;
> The Good Book says: 'Thou shalt not steal!'
>   With me you'll all agree,
> As I passed by that brother's house,
>   That chicken followed me."

Superstition was represented by numerous songs based on the supposition that "Voodoo," or "Hoodoo," dominated black religion. The reasoning behind this assumption seemed to be that the black found Christianity inadequate during times of serious crisis and resorted to supplication of dimly remembered pagan gods; Christianity thus thrown off revealed the true, animalistic nature of blacks.

At times, it was not readily apparent that superstition was related to religion in song. "Dat Cross-eyed Hoo-doo Coon,"[71] sung by Josephine Gassman, is a song that dwells at length on the bully theme before finally revealing the nature of the "Hoodoo" curse:

> Dar's a Hoo-doo black coon in town
>   De gals call Rastus Jones,
> An' wid ma trusty blade in hand,
>   I'll carb dat nigger's bones.
> He's done gone an' won my lub
>   Ma baby, ma black dove.
> Dat buck-toothe ram, dat son ob Ham,
>   Dat Cross-eyed Hoo-doo Coon.

> Hoo-doo, dat Hoo-doo,
> Dat cross-eyed black coon.
> Wid face jes' like a big baboon
> An' eyes roun' like de moon.
> When I find dat nigger,
> Mah Jonah, ma HOO-doo

Spoken: What you gwine do wid dat wall-eyed, libber-lipped, number thirteen, rubber-neck Jonah?

> I'll carb him deep when we nigs meet,
> Dat Cross-eyed Hoo-doo Coon.

Patter: Question—How do you know dat coon's a Hoo-doo? Answer—How do I know? I knows! Mah buttons fall off, suspenders bust, lights go out, and de bones nebber come seben or eleben when dat wall-eyed, knock-kneed, pidgeon-toed, bandy-legged, snaggle toothed, libber-lipped, number thirteen, red-headed nigger wid de bad eye and yellow dog lopes 'roun'. Ob course he's a Hoo-doo!

Williams and Walker were nearer the norm for such songs with their "The Voodoo Man,"[72] in which the superstitious fears of both preacher and congregation debases and distorts their professed faith in Christian doctrine:

> One night in Souf Ca'lina at a gospel meetin' tent,
> Whar all de congregation heard the deacon preachin' Lent,
> They raised dere voices high in praise and shouted loud and long,
> 'Gainst chicken stealin' roustabouts and said 'twas very wrong,
> Upon the silence of the night dere rose a dismal moan,
> That raised their wool and made them wish that they were safe
>   at home,
> 'Twas then the deacon said confess yo' sinners all who can,
> Yo' rabbits foot youse needin' now for that's the Voodoo Man.

>   The Voodoo man will catch yo' sure,
>   Confess yo' sins, get gospel cure,
>   Now let us sing all those who can,
>   For that's the Voodoo man.

> Now Sally Jenkins raised her voice in accents very sad,
> O mister deacon pray for me I'se feelin' mighty bad,
> Youse shy some chickens for I called when yo' was far away,

Ma guilty conscience told me that I'd be found out today,
Beloved sister, you alone am guilty dat's a fact,
But I must have salvation for I lost de gospel tract,
I stole dat Possum from yo' coop, forgive me if you can,
For I'se a mighty feared I'se goin' with the Voodoo man.

Mock sermons were common themes in comic songs of the period. More than in the pseudo-spiritual of the Reconstruction period, these songs aimed for specific points in the attempt to catch the public fancy. The subject might be the distortion of a Biblical story such as the legend of Adam's fall, or it could dwell on some aspect of church experience. Bob Cole's "If Adam Hadn't Seen The Apple"[73] twists the doctrine of original sin into a ludicrous tangle of conjecture:

The apple tree it was the bummest in the garden,
There were choice and rarer fruit trees all around it,
No, Adam he then ev'ry warnin' was discardin',
Kept a rubberin' around until he found it,
He passed up all the cherry trees,
The pear trees, and the plum,
Until he found the tree that put poor mankind "on the bum,"
May be it was green persimmons that he ate, the sly old sneak;
If it was, it served him right,
He couldn't whistle for a week.

Songs dealing with church experience, such as Mills' "At A Georgia Campmeeting," were designed to make the very act of attending church a comic situation. "Sing Hallelujah!"[74] depicts a congregation utterly bored to sleep by the sermon, to be awakened by the irate parson, who shouts; "Will de congregation please stand up and sing Hallelujah!"

In "Parson Jones' Three Reasons,"[75] the congregation is chided for its penuriousness and lack of interest; in the chorus of the song the parson states his reasons for leaving:

Firstly there ain't no love in this congregation,
I haven't tied a knot since I've been here.
Secondly you all don't love your pastor—
Ain't had a cent of sal'ry in a year;
And thirdly I done accepted a call

As Chaplain of the penitentiary,
And I go to prepare a place for you all, Amen.

Pseudo-spiritual types suffered no decline during this time. Harry
Williams and Egbert Van Alstyne contributed "Camp Meeting
Time"[76] with a typical cover illustration of simple blacks listening
wide-eyed, sleeping, and courting while the chicken-stealing preacher
exorts them. Michael E. Rourke and Frank Palma wrote "Keep A-
Knockin,"[77] a pseudo-spiritual in the style of the older Reconstruction
types in both content and treatment:

> I'se gwine for to buy me a golden car,
>   Keep a-knockin', keep a-knockin';
> To carry me up to de land afar,
>   Keep a-knockin', keep a-knockin'

Few of these efforts could match Gussie Davis's "When I Do The
Hoochy-Coochy In De Sky"[78] with its cover illustration and text
offering a nonpareil insult to the black religious impulse:

> I ain't got no money and I don't need none,
> 'Cos I don't expect to stay here very long;
> An' old colored preacher by de name of Parson Brown,
> He used to sing to me dis good ole song:
> Says he, "I know you coons will stare
> When I fly up thro' the air,
> When I bid all of you black chromos good bye;
> I will raise a big sensation with the white population,
> When I do the hoochy coochy in de sky!
>
>> When you feel that funny feeling,
>> As it over you is stealing,
>> You will flop your snow-white wings and try to fly;
>> I know the angels they will giggle
>> When I do that awful wiggle,
>> When I do the hoochy coochy in de sky!"
>
> They'll turn the X rays on me when the music plays,
> So dat ev'ryone can see into the dance;
> I'm goin' to do de coochy seven thousand diff'rent ways,
> An' I'll knock the Midway people in a trance.
> Oh, I have got a big balloon

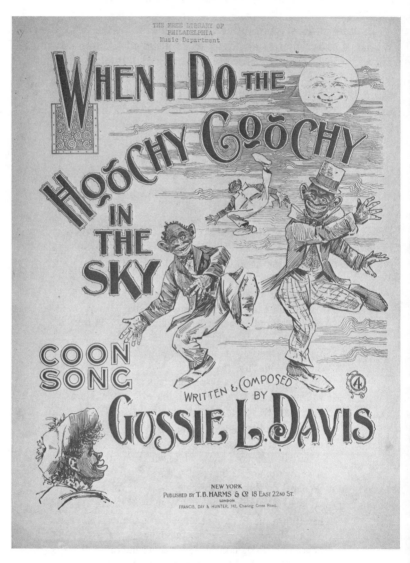

Figure 45

> With a seat for ev'ry coon,
> So now ev'ry nig must either go or die;
> Don't you listen to strange rumors, but go buy a pair of
> "bloomers,"
> For to do the hoochy coochy in de sky!

The figure of the black preacher was thus undermined by constant references to fraudulence, cowardice, superstition, philogyny, and intemperance. Religion itself was hardly ever recognized as a matter of real importance. Indeed, the sole exception found for this study to the accepted formula for such songs was "The Colored Preacher's Hymn,"[79] an obscure song that never achieved significant fame. This was understandable enough, considering the song's uncharacteristic reiteration of William Blake's idea—as stated in "The Little Black Boy"—that the skin is black but the soul is white. Although "The Colored Preacher's Hymn" echoes the attitudes surrounding Booker T. Washington's accommodation theories, it is, nonetheless, worlds apart from the ordinary song on themes of black religion.

Songwriters were ambivalent on the issue of racial pride. It has been demonstrated that many songs viewed the black as having aspirations to become white through emulation of white values. Yet there were songs in which blackness was counted—albeit rather defensively—a virtue. "Nigger, Nigger Never Die"[80] asserts an admirable sentiment within the context of the demeaning style of the period, almost as though the executioner were beseeching his victim to survive in order to be available for the next hanging.

> When I was a Pickaninny, my mamma sent me to school,
> She said, "Boy, you're old enough to go and learn the golden
> rule."
> At the Branch school where she sent me all the other Kids were
> white,
> Every morning noon and evening, with these Kids I had to fight,
> If at study I should whisper, someone would be sure to tell,
> When we went to play at recess, all the white Kids at me yell,
> Oh, Nigger, Nigger, never die
> Black face and a china eye,
> Mouth as big as a steamboat slip,
> India rubber nose and a liver lip;
> Eny, meny, miny, mo, catch a nigger by the toe,
> Nigger eat scrap iron, nigger chew gum.

The second verse of "Nigger, Nigger Never Die" relates the identical experiences occurring to the protagonist's son. Most songs were incapable of discovering racial pride within the black character, however. Except those songs in which the black was attempting to impress other blacks, the black was seen as desperately longing for whiteness. "Coon! Coon! Coon!"[81] is an example of this black-wishing-to-be-white syndrome that achieved virtual classic status in popular music:

> Coon! Coon! Coon!
>   I wish my color would fade;
> Coon! Coon! Coon!
>   I'd like a different shade.
> Coon! Coon! Coon!
>   Morning night and noon,
>   I wish I was a white man
>   'Stead of a
> Coon! Coon! Coon!

The relentless attack on black manhood was seemingly endless, a fact which inevitably gave rise to a song on the subject, "Everybody's Pickin' On Me,"[82] by Irving Lewis and Isabel D'Armond, in which the protagonist complains:

> Ev'rybody's pickin' on me,
> Gettin' sick of it as can be—

But if blacks expected any improvement in their treatment in song, they were doomed to be disappointed. Songwriters had no intention of abandoning the lucrative coon song craze by picturing the black in a favorable light. Indeed, the enterprising songwriting team of Sidney D. Mitchell and Archie Gottler saw the situation existing without change for at least fifty years in their "In 1960 You'll Find Dixie Looking Just The Same."[83]

The Dixie myth was a particular favorite of coon song composers; all of the sentiment and effeminacy of earlier types of carry-me-backs reached the highest point of development under the skillful hands of the professionals. The regional connection with the female figure was at last perfected; the female figure had become in many instances white. The motherly qualities of the Dixie image solidified into the

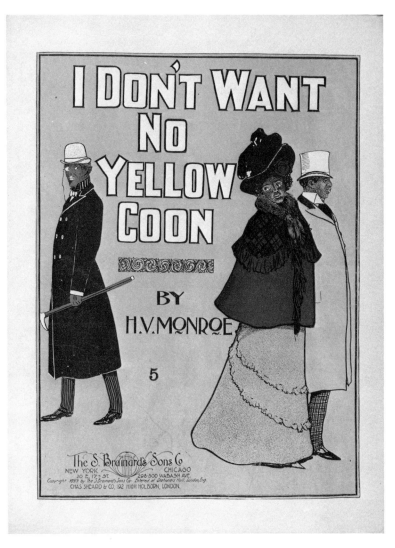

Figure 46

Figure 47

"Mammy" figure and provided the vehicle to fame for many performers, culminating in the early twenties with Al Jolson's tearful rendition of "My Mammy."

Dixie themes were worked and reworked as composers tried to achieve perfection in the type. Both Harry Von Tilzer and his brother Albert wrote songs entitled "Down Where The Swanee River Flows";[84] although there are superficial differences in the two pieces, they could easily have stemmed from identical sources, so common was the stereotyped South by that time.

The best songwriting names of the era are represented in numerous sallies into the Dixie theme: Richard Whiting wrote music for Raymond Egan's lyric, "Ain't You Coming Back To Dixieland,"[85] which was featured by Al Jolson; George Gershwin entered the field with his "Swanee,"[86] which became a permanent trademark of Jolson, who introduced it in *Sinbad.* "Swanee," as much as any other song of the period, became the prototype of the sweetly sickening sentimentality that characterized the final stage of association of Dixie with the mother image. The insistent rhythmic declaration of love for the South transcends the mere expression of homesickness and becomes instead an almost pathological yearning for a nonexistent region; it is the culmination of the mother-Dixie imagery that totally ignored reality.

But other well-known songwriters were also busy with the Dixie theme. Irving Berlin contributed a considerable number, among which were "When That Midnight Choo Choo Leaves For Alabam'" and "I Want To Be In Dixie,"[87] both of which lean on standard clichés for Dixie imagery. Jack Yellen wrote a lyric which was set to music by Charles Pierce and Jack Glogau entitled "Look Me Up When You're In Dixie,"[88] and Harry L. Lincoln set to music Reverend J.A. Patton's amateurish "My Southern Home."[89] Even Sigmund Spaeth tried his hand at the type with his lyric gem "Down South," set to music by William H. Myddleton.[90] Spaeth's imagery is identical to that of other lyricists as he conjures visions of balmy breezes, cotton blossoms, possums, cabin doors, pickaninnies, etc.

Utilizing the Dixie theme, an enterprising trio of brothers sang their way to temporary fame under the stage name of the Three White Kuhns, an obviously labored pun on the type of songs they featured. One of their songs, "Underneath The Cotton Moon,"[91] was written by Sam M. Lewis and George W. Meyer whose vision of Dixie is illustrated in the chorus:

> Watchin' and waitin' underneath the cotton moon,
> Watchin' and waitin' just to hear a wonderful tune,
> Where the buzz of the bee is a sweet melody
> The bird in the tree knows the right harmony,
> The leaves tod-a-lo to and fro
> Ain't you glad you're here "My honey dear"
> Mammy is sayin' pickaninnies go to bed,
> Mammy is sayin' "Cover up your kinky head,"
> That white out there ain't cotton, no,
> It's just the beard of Old Black Joe,
> That's wavin', yes wavin',
> Underneath the cotton moon.

As in the carry-me-backs of earlier periods, each state in the South was singled out for numerous syrupy tributes. Among these, Cal De Voll's "Alabama Lullaby"[92] is typical, as is "Hush-a-bye, Ma Baby," better known as "The Missouri Waltz,"[93] a Presidential favorite. The mother fixation of such songs is an embarrassment in today's psychologically oriented world; no present-day composer could ever face his public with words such as those of the chorus of "Missouri Waltz":

> 'Way down in Missouri where I heard this melody,
> When I was a Pickaninny on ma Mammy's knee;
> The darkies were hummin',
> Their banjos were strummin',
> So sweet and low. . . .

The stereotypical assumption of inherent musical ability of blacks was both sentimentalized and lampooned. Irving Berlin wrote an emotional "When It's Night Time Down In Dixieland,"[94] in which the apparent attempt to treat the black sympathetically is thwarted by the inability to discard the stereotype; but "Under Southern Skies,"[95] inspired by Lottie Blair Parker's play of the same name, is an even more explicit example:

> You'll hear the darkies singing,
>   The songs they love the best,
> You'll hear the banjoes ringing,
>   While the old folks rest.
> The pickaninnies dancing,
>   To see who'll win the prize,
> In the evening by the moonlight,
>   Under southern skies.

The connection between the twin myths of blacks' innate musicality and the sentimental Dixie imagery was given a more jovial, though no less stereotypical, treatment in "Alabama Jubilee":[96]

> You ought to see Mister Jones when he rattles the bones,
> Old Colonel Brown foolin' 'round like a clown,
> Miss Virginia who is past eighty three,
> Shoutin' "I'm full o' pep!
> Watch your step, watch your step!"
> One legged Joe danced aroun' on his toe,
> Threw away his crutch and hollered, "Let 'er go!"
> Oh, honey,
> Hail!
> Hail! The gang's all here for an Alabama Jubilee.

In a treatment derived from two popular hits of World War I, "Tipperary" and "There's A Long, Long Trail," "It's A Long, Long Way to Dixie"[97] evoked the Dixie myth as a means of exploiting the theme of the soldier longing for home. This was evidently stretching the point thin; the piece remained in well-deserved obscurity.

However, many songwriters of the time leaned upon earlier successes in trying to produce hits. Fleta Jan Brown, to name only one, recalled Stephen Foster with her "Back To The Old Folks At Home,"[98] a singularly unimpressive song distinguished only by the fact that it is among the carry-me-backs of the period in which the "old folks," by some mysterious process, have become totally white.

Albescence of the female black image in the carry-me-back, excepting the ubiquitous "Mammy," was virtually completed by the end of this period. "Coal Black Rose" had gone through the "yaller" of earlier times to become a white "My Dixie Rose"[99] or "Virginia Rose,"[100] if not in the text, then on the cover illustrations adorning most such songs.

For example, "Dixie, My Dixie Gal"[101] has a cover illustration that is unmistakably white, while the text is black:

> When de silv'ry moon am beaming, and de stars begin to peep,
> When de cabin light am gleamin', pickaninnies gone to sleep,
> Den I takes my good old banjo an' I tunes her up a bit;
> An' den I sings to Dixie, as de shadders pas' me flit:
>> Dixie! Ma Dixie Gal!
>> Ma little honey bee;
>> I ain't so personal

Figure 48

When I claims yo' loves no one but me;
Smile for me, baby mine,
Don't make yo' honey pine,
His heart am palpitatin',
Yo' so aggravatin',
Dixie! Ma Dixie Gal!

When de serenade am over, den I goes back home to bed,
Where I dreams of fields of clover, an' of Dixie's lips so red,
An' I dreams dat way 'till mornin' when I hears ole Mammy cry,
"Get up coon, day am dawnin'," an' de first thing dat I sigh is:
Dixie! Ma Dixie Gal! (etc)

The tendency among composers to make the female figure white in their representation of the South did not prevent the occasional reversion to black imagery to express the same message. Hughie Cannon's "Mason-Dixon Line"[102] is an example of this rather atavistic treatment with a cover illustration to match the text:

'Cross de river from Cincinnatti is de Mason Dixon line,
Dere is my only gal, she is my bestest pal and thinks dat I'm so fine.
Her name is Dixon, my name is Mason, won't dat be a funny sign,
When I wed dat gal across the Mason-Dixon line.

The norm for this period, however, was to portray the South in terms of the white female along lines shown by "She's Dixie All The Time"[103] in which the connection is made in both the cover illustration and the text:

She was born in old Kentucky,
She was raised in Tennessee.
Went to school in Alabama
Where she learned her A. B. C.
Then she mov'd down to Georgia when she was sixteen,
Spent vacation with her relation
'Bout a year or two in New Orleans.
She's been in ev'ry state in Dixie
'Cept the state of marriage bliss,
She takes a dip each morning in the Brandywine,
Hangs her clothes up on the Mason-Dixon Line.

> She was born and raised in Dixie,
> And she's Dixie all the time.

The comparison of Dixie to heaven on earth became more direct. Here again, the association of female or matronly qualities with the region was strong. Titles of the songs of this type are usually sufficient to describe the entire piece; Raymond Egan and Richard Whiting combined talents to produce "They Made It Twice As Nice As Paradise And They Called It Dixieland,"[104] and Gus Van and Joe Schenck set to music Jack Yellen's "Open Up The Golden Gates To Dixieland (And Let Me Into Paradise)."[105] The publishing house of Witmark offered in 1908 "Heaven Is Like Dixie After All" without naming the writer or composer.[106] The association of Dixie with heaven was, of course, infused into songs regardless of title, as in "When It's Cotton Pickin' Time In Tennessee,"[107] in which the protagonist confesses that the only reason he gambles is in order to win the money for a return trip to his particular Dixie heaven, in this case Tennessee, of course.

The strength of this imagery is shown by the fact that, as late as 1937, it was still being utilized in song. Irving Mills's production of the twenty-eighth edition of the *Cotton Club Parade* featured "Headin' For Heaven,"[108] which could easily have been written thirty years earlier, as the chorus repeats the same cloying list of Southern attractions:

> I'm headin' for heaven,
>   I leave tonight at seven,
> I'm headin' for heaven down South;
> Sweet music and laughter,
>   That's something to go after,
> I'm headin' for heaven down South.
> Oh, the moon shines bright in that land so heavenly,
> And the sweet part is the sweetheart waitin' for me.
> My Mammy, my Pappy,
>   I'm gonna make 'em happy,
> I'm headin' for heaven down South.

Perhaps the most enduring favorite of the times, however, was a song which put the listener somewhat on the defensive, making him feel somewhat guilty for not being Southern himself, if indeed that were the case. This was "Are You From Dixie?"[109] a carry-me-back that equated being a native Southerner with all the qualities associated with the South. While a convincing argument could be made concerning transference of regional qualities to individuals born in that region as typical of the Southerners' aversion to common logic, it must be remembered that this particular phenomenon was a whites-only situation; the cover illustration of "Are You From Dixie?" is quite specific in making the principals of the song well-dressed white Southerners.

Turning from the region to the female figure, there are two types that emerge clearly: the "Mammy" type, with unbounded capacity for love, understanding, and general qualities associated with motherhood; and the younger, sexually attractive though temperamentally repugnant female, whose motivation was usually some form of greed.

The younger female figure was, of course, the female counterpart of the "bully" figure, with whom she was often associated. This female figure could be presented in one of two general ways: if the song eschewed the sensual nature of the figure, the connection with the Dixie myth was ordinarily emphasized and the treatment over-sentimentalized; if, on the other hand, the figure was shown to be shrewish and grasping, the treatment was likely to be trivial and demeaning to concepts of black love.

In the former category, songwriters evoked an image of black love primarily as a vehicle for demonstrating the ideal of Dixie's enchantment. Sidney L. Perrin's "Mandy, Will You Be My Lady Love?"[110] put the lovers in Dixie, as though romance in the rest of the United States might be unworthy of mention:

> Way down in Dixie land among the pines of Tennessee,
> The mocking birds were cooing in their nest,
> Two little darky lovers sat behind a tall pine tree,
> Telling how they loved each other best.
> This darky belle was seated on a little wooden bench,
> And the little coon was kneeling at her feet,
> And then to her surprise,
> He gazed into her eyes,
> And these words to her he whispered soft and sweet.
> Mandy, will you be my lady love. . . .

This semiserious treatment of Negro love had tremendous usage among composers who considered themselves a cut above the ordinary songsmith. This theme became the basis for many songs that strove for status as artsong, exemplified by Adam Breede's "Mistah Moonshine," set to music by Charles S. Burnham:[111]

> Moonshine, moonshine, skippin' all aroun',
> Moonshine, moonshine, lightin' up de groun',
> Moonshine, moonshine, peepin' thro' de trees,
> Catchin' little niggers a-kissin' in de breeze.

And in one of the earlier "moon-June-spoon" songs, "Croon, Croon, Underneat' de Moon,"[112] the black lover sings:

> Won't you come, my love, won't you come, come soon!
> For my heart beats time to de old, old tune . . . .

A later version of this theme, "Wid De Moon, Moon, Moon,"[113] shows the futility of trying to elevate inferior lyrics by means of superior musical setting; little can be done to improve the sentimental words:

> I wonder is mah love in de sky wid de moon,
> Or is she down de valley wid roses of June?

The enduring favorite of this type of song was Caro Roma's "Can't Yo' Heah Me Callin' Caroline"[114] in which the region and the female figure are almost inseparable.

Treated as comedy, the black female differed only slightly from the "Coal Black Rose" of earlier fame. W.T. Jefferson's "My Coal Black Lady"[115] warned possible suitors:

> This coal black lady,
>   She is my baby,
> You cannot blame me,
>   No! no! no!
> 'Case I love her, so! so! so!
> Her color's shady,
>   But she's a lady,
> Don't trifle with my coal black lady.

The comedy treatment of the black female stressed her pretensions, vanities, and her greeds. She was seen as longing to change from black to white in order to gain status, as in "The First Wench Done Turned White,"[116] a "colored revelation" by Ed Rogers:

There's a lot of arg'mentation round the colored population,
'Bout Liza Green the wench that changed her color.
She has got the folks excited, but she seems delighted,
From a coal black she first changed into a yellow.
The colored folks despise her—they once did idolize her,
And thought she was really out of sight.
She's done gone shook her fellow, likewise her own real color,
She's the first wench that they've seen turn white.

    Says Miss Liza Green, you will seldom see
    Another wench that can change like me,
    Now I will happy be morning noon and night;
    No coal black coons will now be seen,
    A-walkin' round with Miss Liza Green,
    It ain't no use to argufy,
    I'm the first wench done turned white.

When this change made its appearance, colored folks then
        made a clearance,
They said whoever did it was to blame,
Now they cannot understand it, why a wench should so
        demand it,
Especially one who wears a colored name.
She's bought a dress to match it, with white they've had
        to patch it,
No other wenches with her can keep time.
All the coons that called her Liza, say from this [day?] out
        they'll despise her.
For she's bound to "draw the color line."

The assumption that black women saw whiteness as a desirable quality is evident in Williams and Walker's "She's Getting Mo' Like the White Folks Every Day":[117]

    She's getting mo' like the white folks every day,
    Tryin' to do jus' like 'em every way—
    Once she was stuck on calico patterns,
    Now all she wants is silks and satins,
    She's getting mo' like the white folks every day.

The grasping avariciousness of the female was the theme for countless songs; in "Every Day She Wanted Something Else" she was willing to strip her man of even his gold fillings in order to satisfy her greed: "Bill's teeth were filled with gold, she had them pulled and sold."[118] But as the male's money vanished, she sang, "When You Ain't Got No Money, Well You Needn't Come Around"[119] or make excuses, such as "I'll Be Busy All Next Week,"[120] although in this latter example the male ego was at least partially assuaged:

> An ebony tinted maid of affectation,
> Is loved by a gent of tawny hue,
> She gave him a standing invitation,
> Saying, "Call and I'll be always in for you."
> After she had spent most of his money,
> He said, "Don't leave me in this world alone,
> Could I call to see you once next week, my honey?"
> This excuse she offered in regretful tone:
>
>> Monday I'll be busy all the day,
>> Tuesday I'm going far away,
>> Wedenesday is the day that I study my French,
>> Thursday is for music, then you would intrench,
>> Friday I must paint a little bit,
>> Saturday in the dentist's chair I'll sit,
>> Sunday is for church, salvation I must seek,
>> I'm sorry, I'll be busy all next week.
>
> He easily hid from her his occupation,
> Till into jail they threw this maiden dear,
> For counterfeiting coins of this great nation,
> As the money that she took from him was queer.
> She was tried in court by judge and jury,
> She thought the tawny gent would come to speak,
> But he sent this note that drove her in a fury,
> "Good-bye, my gal, I'm busy all next week.

The female occasionally tried to reform her man, as in "Be Good Or I'll Quit You":[121]

> You'se got to be good or I'll quit you,
> Stop stealin' chickens kase dat a won't do,
> S'pose I'se a gwine to be the wife,
> Of a bad niggah all my life,
> So git religion an' cut out sin,
> All kinds of booze ah 'specially gin.
> You heah what I say an' I mean it too,
> Be good or I'll quit you.

More often, however, it was the wife or girlfriend who sinned against the male. When caught in her amorous peccadillos, the female invented excuses, as in "That's The Doctor, Bill!" sung by Marie Cahill in *The Boys and Betty*:[122]

> Mister William Brown, up in Blackville town,
> Loved a dusky belle named Sadie;
> She a fickle maid of copper shade,
> Used to work for an actor lady.
> When her work was through, ev'ry day at two,
> She received a railroad porter;
> But one day, Bill Brown chanced to come to town,
> And he slipped upstairs and caught her.
> William Brown couldn't understand
> Why this fellow held her hand,
> Until Sadie came to him and said,
> With a smile serene and bland.
>   That's the doctor, Bill . . . .

Or she might defy her man with the brutal truth, as in "He Used To Be A Friend Of Mine":[123]

> "Look here, Lize, who's that man you been talking to?"
> "None of your business, Mister Coon, now don't let him worry
>   you,
> For I don't see where you get your nerve to ask me such a
>   question as that,
> But if you really like to know,
> I'll tell you for a fact:
>   "Well, He used to be a friend of mine. . . ."

The female might also try to brazen out her infidelity with "Does You B'lieve Yo' Baby Or Yo' Eyes":[124]

> In Memphis town Mister Iv'ry Brown done had a lady love,
> She was the swellest gal in Tennessee.
> One day he thought he'd play a trick so he sent a spatch-o-graf.
> And said "I'll be home late don't wait for me."
> But he went to his baby's house an' bust right in the door,
> And there before his eyes as plain as day,

He saw her kiss anothah coon and when she saw de stuff was
     off
Why this is all that lady had to say:

"Now does you b'lieve yo' baby or yo' eye, eye, eyes.
I know dat you done took me by surpri-i-ise,
But I saw when you came in you was blin' from niggah gin,
Now does you b'lieve yo' baby or yo' eyes.

For all her fickleness and deceit, the black female was susceptible
to certain male blandishments. It has been seen that she suffered at the
hand of the bullying "Bill Bailey," but she could also be led astray by
other, more glamorous types such as the "actor who was painted like a
darky" in "I'd Leave Ma Happy Home For You":[125]

I'd leave ma happy home for you, oo, oo, oo, oo,
You're de nicest man I ever knew, oo, oo, oo, oo.

More often, however, she was coldly calculating with respect to the
type of man she sought. Clare Kummer's "A Rich Coon's Babe"[126]
expresses the thought concisely:

Yo' ain't de first dat's axed me fo' ma han',
I wants to marry if I can find de man;
But tho' I like yo' face, I ain't lookin' for a place
To cook an' take in washin', understand?
I ain't a-goin to marry just fo' love,
Dere's other little things I'se got to have;
You say I am a peach, but de fruit am out of reach,
Unless yo' got de money fo' to give.

   For I was raised to be a rich coon's baby,
   My mudder taught me fo' to be a lady;
   I don't know a-how to cook, or sew, or save,
   But you can hab me if you got de money,
   If you haben't I can't be yo' honey,
   For I'se only raised to be a rich coon's babe.

Dere's lots of girls dat marries do' dey know
De man ain't got a place to shovel snow,
Den dey can't understand why he didn't show his hand,
Why dere wasn't nuthin' in it for to show.
But as for me, I axes at de start,
Dat may be 'cause I hasn't got a heart,

> But I got dis little smile, an' to see it costs a pile,
> And its just a case of got de price or part.

This imagery came close to the view of the black female as a prostitute, or at least a mercenary vixen willing to forego true love for the sake of a bankroll.

Many coon songs showed the black male as a drunkard, but Billee Taylor's "Rastus It's Me!" switches the roles, making the female guilty of overindulgence:[127]

> Oh Rastus it's me—
> Won't you let me in?
> Oh don't you see—
> I have a little bit too much gin.

Open mention of sex has always been one of the unwritten taboos in commercial songs, but the coon song managed to show by implication and innuendo the insatiable sex drive of the black woman. "Make A Fuss Over Me,"[128] popular in the early part of the century, portrays the black female exhorting her beau to "come to life":

> There used to be in Tennessee,
>   A gal in swell society,
> She loved a coon who couldn't spoon,
>   Altho' he tried from morn 'till noon,
> At last she sighed, "Now man, you've tried,
>   To ask me for to be your bride,
> You've fussed and fussed, and I'll be cussed,
>   If you keep on my heart will bust,
> If I'm to be your wife,
>   You'd better come to life."
>
>   And, make a fuss over me,
>   Ain't it easy to see
>   I've an itching to be,
>   Sitting right on your knee,
>   That's my one longing plea,
>   If we're goin' to agree,
>   And you want me to love you,
>   Make a fuss over me.

The connection between sexuality and body temperature was not lost on songwriters; the "red hot mamma" of post-World War I fame had her beginnings in songs such as "I'se Got The Warmest Baby Of Them All":[129]

> You talk about your warm black babies,
> Say, I'se got one that will make your heart beat fast,
> And she's right from the state of Alabama,
> Where all those pretty gals dwell.

Part of the "hot" imagery derived from the stereotype of black dance, as in "Hotfoot Sue," an early example of the white conception of black dance cast in coon song style:[130]

> Hotfoot, de gal dat paces de cullud section,
> Hotfoot, de shinin' light o' de avenue,
> Hotfoot, de one possessor o' my affection
> I'se won dat black gal, Hotfoot, ma Sue.

Another part of the "hot" cliché applies to the general idea of uninhibited black fun, as in the venerable favorite, "A Hot Time In The Old Town,"[131] but the basis of such imagery was invariably concerned with the white conception of black womanhood.

An even less commendable song type grew out of the concept of blacks' uncontrollable behavior and the uncivilized manner in which they made love; there arose songs in which the black was psychologically exiled by associating him with the so-called "uncivilized" natives of Africa or other remote groups, or worse, by the thinly veiled implication that the black actually *was* a beast after all.

Cover illustrations of "cannibal" and "animal" songs were perhaps no more demeaning than those on most coon song covers, but they do offer strong support for the unwarranted cruelties of the texts. The text of "Cannibal Love,"[132] for example, is intensified by the sheet music cover illustration (Figure 49). Regardless of the intent of the creators of "Cannibal Love," their song must be seen as the result of years of prejudicial conditioning. The endless repetition of the notion that blacks were inherently inferior—less than human, in fact—bore fruit at last in song:

> Cannibal love,
> Cannibal love,
> With kisses dear I'll always greet you;
> Love you so that I could eat you.

Marie Cahill sang the "Hottentot Love Song"[133] which she featured in the musical production *Marrying Mary*, while Marie Marble

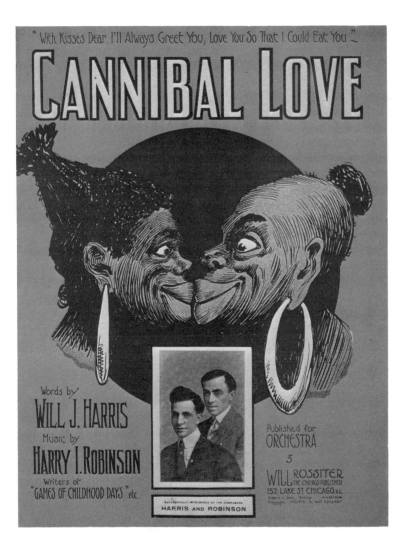

Figure 49

Figure 50

and Little Chip introduced "My Pretty Zulu Lu"[134] in Dunn and
Harlan's production of *The Man of Mexico*. "My Princess Zulu
Lulu,"[135] a "Senegambian love song" by Dave Reed Jr., was featured
in Klaw and Erlanger's production of *The Sleeping Beauty and the
Beast*. While these songs sustained the animalistic idea and a most
trivial attitude toward black love, it was "The Cannibal And The
Missionary,"[136] which appeared several years before any of the
others, that revealed basic white attitudes:

> A cannibal maiden loved too well,
> > A missionary good!
> And he loved her but dare not tell his love,
> > For this is how it stood:
> A clergyman he, and a cannibal she,
> > And their creeds were wide apart,
> And how could he take for sentiment's sake
> > A cannibal to his heart?
> Oh! 'twas a problem vexing, very,
> > For the cannibal maid and the missionary,
> In sooth it was, in sooth it was,
> > For the cannibal maid and the missionary.
>
> This cannibal maiden's love grew bold,
> > For she was a simple thing.
> And thus her love to her love she told:
> > "Oh, marry me, be my king!
> For I love you my sweet, well enough, oh, to eat,
> > It's a terrible thing, I know,
> But I must be your bride, or devour you fried,
> > Oh, I must, for I love you so!"
>
> He looked in the depth of her dark brown eyes,
> > With her wealth of love and trust,
> And cried in a flush of glad surprise:
> > "Ah, well, if I must I must."
> They were wed on that day, for 'tis ever the way,
> > That passion must conquer creed;
> And a happier pair, it's remarkably rare,
> > To discover it is indeed.
> And so 'twas settled nicely, very,
> > For this cannibal maid and the missionary,
> In sooth it was, in sooth it was,
> > For the cannibal maid and the missionary.

The condescending, sniggering attitude of the "cannibal" songs was hardly softened by black composers' contributions to the type; Bob Cole's "Under The Bamboo Tree,"[137] sung by Marie Cahill in *Sally In Our Alley*, merely added to the trivia with its chorus of inane babbling:

> If you lak-a me, lak I lak-a you,
>   And we lak-a both the same,
> I lak-a say, this very day,
>   I lak-a change your name. . . .

It was an easy change from the "cannibal" imagery to other jungle inhabitants, with unmistakable inference that the apes, monkeys, baboons, and so on were actually black subjects. This imagery was not without precedent; in the pre-minstrel 1830's an unknown songwriter produced "Monkey's Wedding,"[138] later to become famous as a college song widely known as "The Monkey Married The Baboon's Sister." This song, like its later counterparts, achieved the connection between the simian and the black by simply reiterating those parts of the stereotype that had been associated with the black. The description of the bride and groom in the second verse is that of similar songs on black subjects; the description, in the third verse, of the wedding feast emphasizes food associated with blacks; but the final verse, in which the music is described, leaves little to the imagination concerning the connection between black and primate:

> What do you think was the tune they danced to?
> "The Drunken Sailor"—sometimes "Jim Crow,"
> Tails in the way—and some got pinch'd too
>   'Cause they were to (sic) long.
> What do you think they had for a fiddle?
> An old Banjo with a hole in the middle—
> A Tamborine made out of a riddle,
>   And that's the end of my song.

The imagery of the "Monkey's Wedding" was virtually intact some eighty years later, when the re-emergence of the theme occurred on a significant level. "Monkey Land,"[139] "Down In Jungle Town,"[140] and "Monkey Doodle Dandy"[141] appeared within the space of three years. The pattern of each was the same: primates, behaving very much according to the manner ascribed to blacks, meet and marry. The association did not end there, however; there were "animal" songs on other assumed characteristics of blacks, such as "That Baboon Baby Dance"[142] which is merely a coon song with "Coon" and "Nigger" replaced by "Baboon." Given the vast quantity and strength of such imagery, plus the receptivity of audiences during that time, it is small wonder that some whites still believe that the black is possessed of a tail.

Some love songs achieved status as classics of popular expression. Howard and Emerson's "Hello! My Baby"[143] is still performed, as is "Put Your Arms Around Me, Honey,"[144] with words by Junie McCree and music by Albert Von Tilzer. Most audiences, and even performers, are unaware that the subject of these songs is black love. In "For Me And My Gal,"[145] the text is not explicitly black, but the performances were often done in blackface, as indicated by the sheet music covers. Other songs of this type were unquestionably black from the outset; "By The Watermelon Vine"[146] has the pseudo-dialect, stereotypical cover illustration, and subject matter, while "Li'l Liza Jane"[147] by Countess Ada De Lachau was presumed black by its title and text.

The figure of the older black female—the "Mammy"—did not often appear without regional connotations previously discussed. Among those songs which managed to portray the mammy image without mentioning the South is "Mammy Dear," an attempt at treatment of the subject on the level of art song, which shows the same cloying sentimentality of the cruder popular variety. The "Mammy" in this song is typical of the almost Oedipal concern shown by songwriters for mothers throughout the period; there is something revolting in the bathos of "Mammy Dear":[148]

> No one half so sweet could be
> As my old mammy dear;
> No one brings that joy to me
> I know when she is near.
> No one's smile is quite so bright
> None so quick the tear,
> No one prays for me at night
> But mammy dear!
>
> Never changing, steadfast, too,
> Is my old mammy dear;

One dear pal who's always true,
Her laugh I ever hear,
When her arms about me press,
Gone is every fear,
Magic's in the soft caress
Of mammy dear!

This figure was, of course, intimately tied to that of the black child. The lullaby became a favorite form for showing the black child as a lovable trifle, worthless except to the mother. The most famous lullaby of the period was Adam Geibel's "Kentucky Babe,"[149] which set the type for subsequent successes of Geibel and many others. Southern imagery, and the picture of the lovable "pickaninny," combined with the maternal imagery became an almost infallible formula for success. The lullaby was, at first hearing, convincing as treatment of the black subject with sympathy and understanding; but recurring terms, commonly used in the coon song, were used in order to reassure whites that not even the black infant was to be credited with human dignity. Nevertheless, some white performers felt that they were offering compassionate consideration to blacks in general as they sang:

Skeeters am a hummin' on de honeysuckle vine,
Sleep, Kentucky Babe!
Sandman am a comin' to dis little coon of mine,
Sleep, Kentucky Babe!

An even more forceful reminder that the child was worthless came in "Little No 'Count Coon":[150]

Bye low, bye low,
Doan yo' heah de night win' croon?
Bye low, bye low,
Bye low little no 'count coon.

Richard Henry Buck and Adam Geibel joined in an attempt to capitalize on the success of "Kentucky Babe" with a lullaby entitled "Little Cotton Dolly"[151] without achieving much beyond further demeaning of the black child. Here, the use of coon song imagery was predominant:

> Once dar was a baby coon, 'way down in Souf Car'lina,
> Coon! Coon! Coon!
> Daddy's name was Rastus, and its Mammy's name was Dinah,
> Coon! Coon! Coon!

Their "Pensacola Pickaninny"[152] was hardly an improvement:

> Is yo' gwine fo' to slumber, is yo' gwine fo' to sleep?
> Pensacola Pickaninny tell me!

The lullaby was a natural subject for those composers who strove for the finer expression of art song. W.H. Neidlinger produced several, among which his "Rockin' In De Win' "[153] aimed for the heights through use of lowly material:

> Sleep ma little baby Coon,
> Underneath de big roun' moon;
> W'en yo's in de tree a-swingin',
> Mammy jes can't keep from singin':
> Sleep ma little baby Coon.

Lily Strickland provided the musical setting for Van Zandt Wheeler's "Pickaninny Sleep-Song,"[154] which indicated in its first line the opinion that the black child was "jus' a liddle pickaninny," hence of lesser value than the normal white child.

    While the lullaby was designed ostensibly to lull the child to sleep, at least one art song attempted to show the reverse situation; Margaret Crosse's "Sleepy-Haid"[155] portrays the mother's efforts to awaken her child:

> Sleepy haid, oh, sleepy haid,
> Lil pickaninny snoozin' fas' in baid.
> Wake up lam', dat's what ah said,
> You'se a good foh noffin' lazy sleepy haid.

The ubiquitous fear that blacks secretly wished to become white appears in the lullaby frequently. "Mammy's Little Coal Black Rose"[156] develops this theme within the chorus:

'Cause you're dark, don't start a-pinin',
You're a cloud with a silver lining;
Tho' ev'ry old crow thinks his babe am white as snow,
Your dear old Mammy knows you're mighty like a rose;
And when the angels gave those kinky curls to you,
They put a sunbeam in your disposition too, that's true,
The reason you're so black I 'spose—
They forgot to give your Mammy a talcum powder chamòis,
So don't you cry, don't you sigh,
'Cause you're Mammy's little Coal Black Rose.

The idea is contained within the title of "Little Puff Of Smoke Good-Night"[157] and is the central theme of "Snowball Sammy."[158] Reference to the black child by such euphemisms as "Sunshine," "Smoke," "Snowball"—each term associated with whiteness—was a curious twist of logic that became commonplace in the songwriter's craft.

The projective mechanism by which songwriters attempted to show that both black males and black females harbored desires to be or to act white is fairly simple and straigtforward as compared to application of the same theme to the black infant. The black adult threatened white society through sexual and hierarchical ambitions; the black child, on the other hand, could hardly comprehend or enunciate such complex, sophisticated desires. To solve this problem, songwriters put the words in the mother's mouth to characterize the black child as white.

Moreover, songwriters could not escape a disposition to treat *any* mother-child relationship within the context of contemporary society, which considered motherhood sacrosanct. Tinctured by racial pre-judgments, the black lullaby and the "Mammy" song were a songwriter's trap; they called for sympathetic treatment whether the songwriter felt it or not. Thus the two types tended toward excessive sentimentality while retaining the attitude that blacks as a whole were inferior.

But deeper feelings were involved in songwriters' usage of white imagery to characterize the black child. The conflict between autistic thinking about black inferiority and the concept of motherhood were significant barriers to dealing honestly with the black child subject. It was a conflict that should not be minimized, for, as Allport shows, it is only with great difficulty that the prejudiced mind can handle differentiated categories—his reasoning is rigidified.[159] While it would be foolhardy to suggest that all songwriters of this period were hopeless bigots, it is safe to assume that the conditioning of society at that time produced a decided bias against the black. Songwriters who characterized the black child as white—calling him "Snowball," "Smoke," or whatever euphemism served for whiteness—may well have been indulging in over-compensation whereby the enemy is gratuitously endowed with worthwhile qualities. In a sense, it was a grudging compliment to the black mother; she knew her child was worthless, but she as a mother could love it although she still secretly wished it were white.

Songs which showed the child as old enough to attend school became rather preachy on the racial issue. The black mother in "Stay In Your Own Back Yard"[160] offers advice to her child that might easily be taken as indicative of current white attitudes:

> Lilac trees a blooming in the corner, by the gate,
>   Mammy in the little cabin door,
> Curly headed pickaninny comin' home so late,
>   Cryin' 'cause his little heart is sore;
> All the children playing 'round have skin so white and fair,
>   None of them with him will ever play,
> So Mammy in her lap takes the little weeping chap,
>   And says, in her kind old way:
>
> > Now honey, yo' stay in yo' own back yard,
> >   Doan min' what dem white chiles do;
> > What show yo' suppose dey's a gwine to gib
> >   A black little coon like yo'?
> > So stay on dis side of de high boahd fence,
> >   An honey, doan cry so hard;
> > Go out an' a play, jes' as much as yo' please,
> >   But stay in yo' own back yard.

The same sentiment is expressed in "Just Because I'se Black,"[161] although awareness and remorse for the prejudice displayed by the white children are unusual:

> From a schoolhouse romping,
>   Crowding close and bumping,
> Came a crowd of boys one day;

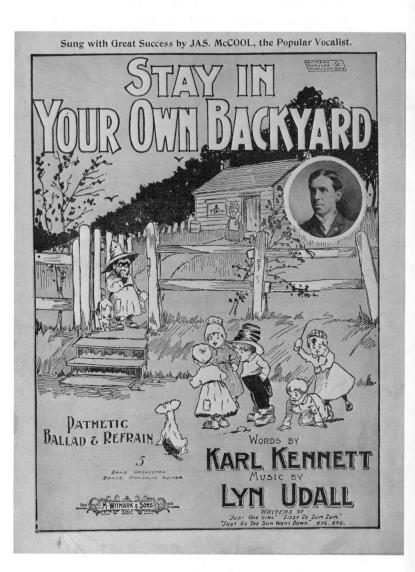

Figure 51

As a little nigger,
Short and frail of figure,
 Passed them on in silence
  till they blocked his way.
Said one lad, 'bit older
 Than the rest and bolder,
"From this coon-chap let us hide;
 He's too poor to walk with,
Far too low to talk with,"
 When the sobbing tot replied.

" 'Tisn't fair to tease me 'cause I'se black;
God loves me the same as you.
'Though to you mah skin is dark,
I've a white heart, froo' and froo'.
Let's be comrades always kind an' true,
Try to love each other, do;
Honor one another, too
But don't tease me just because I'se black!"

Soon the youngsters turning,
 Changing 'bout and learning
Of the mischief they had spread;
 Asked the tiny preacher
Who had been the teacher,
 That would put such sermons
  in his wooly head.
Spoke the child quite happy:
 "I got that from pappy"
While mah mammy made me pray;
 Just do like for white folks,
Yallah, black or light mokes
 Dat's de reason why I say:

" 'Tisn't fair to tease me" (etc.).

In other songs, black children were treated in precisely the same manner as were the adult black subjects. Black children's ignorance found expression in songs such as "Dat's De Way To Spell Chicken"[162] by Sidney Perrin and Bob Slater:

In a little country schoolhouse where de little darkies go
There is a pickaniny by de name of Ragtime Joe.
Now when it comes to spelling his ragtime brain works fast
He's de only well learned scholar dat holds his own in class.

One day de teacher call his class to spell one sort of bird,
Dat kind of bird was chickens—and they could not spell de word,
So de teacher called on Ragtime Joe to spell dat word to them,
He didn't hesitate a bit, this is how he began.

C, dat's de way to begin,
H, dat's de next letter in,
I, dat am de third,
C, dat's to ceason de word.
K, dat's a filling in,
E, I'm near de N'd [end]
    C-H-I-C-K-E-N,
Dat's de way to spell chicken.

The love song was exploited over and over again, using children as subjects. This theme reflected misconceptions concerning black sexuality, showing that even the small child was possessed of prowess far in advance of his age:

Two little piccaninnies sitting on a stile,
Billin' and cooing for a very long while;
Ole Mammy Jinny came a sneakin' 'long de fence,
Of course dose little niggers didn't have a bit of sense,
De stars were a blinking and de moon was shinin' bright,
Dey never saw dat niggar wench she kept right out of sight,
She listened to de kissin' on her face it brought a smile,
When dese words came from dat stile:

Honey, you'se ma lady love. . . .[163]

Every facet of the adult treatment of the black subject, in short, had its black child counterpart. The mischievous "Topsy" imagery was exploited in countless songs. This was to some extent counterbalanced by songs reminiscent of the limp-handed anti-slavery songs: Carrie Jacobs-Bond wrote what she chose to call "little songs of color," among which "Movin' In De Bes' Soci'ty"[164] is typical. In this song, the well-meaning Mrs. Bond propounds the notion—radical for the time—that the only difference between black and white is the unimportant consideration of color. While her motives are beyond question, her songs on the black are riddled with stereotyped thinking and atavistic technique, as can most readily be perceived by the terrible dialect used to convey black imagery.

It can be concluded then that the black child was treated in song along predictable lines: the helplessness of childhood conferred certain favored treatment, but apart from that, he was given little special consideration.

To sum up, the whole of black imagery in song during this period can be characterized as a peculiarly American form of misoxeny—for the black was still a largely unknown person in the United States, despite three centuries of life here. Even the efforts of black composers to portray their black brother in song left the character essentially unchanged.

Songs about the black were more brutally insulting than at any time following the advent of minstrelsy. The insult was often directed toward an individual without regard to effect; it is not difficult to imagine the extent of damage done to Booker T. Washington's image as a distinguished black leader by the scabrous "The Booker T.'s Are On Parade Today."[165] All of black America suffered the humiliation of "No Coons Allowed,"[166] as its warning "This place was meant for white folks, that's all" seemed to be an accurate assessment of the national mood. But the total character of the black, as seen through white eyes, was summed up in Martin Saxx's "He's Just A Nigger,"[167] the chorus of which began: "He's just a nigger, when you've said dat you've said all."

In short, the superimposition of an already misshapen black image through the medium of popular song further "distanced" the public from reality. It appeared that songwriters were not in the least concerned about the cumulative effect of their affront to an entire race; indeed, they and their publishers deluded themselves into the belief that their "cullud brudders" actually approved of the mountain of humiliation being heaped upon them.

Even the so-called art song efforts to capture black reality failed utterly because the true black identity had been entirely hidden and reshaped by countless thousands of less fastidious songs. Of all prior periods covered in this study, that of the 1890's through World War I must surely be counted as the most damaging to the black character and the true black image.

A measure of the efficacy of this distortion of black imagery can be seen in W.O. Carver's contribution to the *Encyclopedia of Religion and Ethics* (New York, 1961) concerning the religiosity of blacks, in which he states in all seriousness:

Evils most prevalent among the race and most harmful are indolence, theft, drunkenness, gambling, and sexual sins.

In the face of such an assault against the dignity of the black, the black entertainer Tom Fletcher could make the genial, but wholly inaccurate, observation that "before the end of the 1890 period, a large part of the malice and hatred toward colored people had softened."[168] Both the statistics on lynchings and the sea of musical invective of the times should have been enough to convince even the blinkered optimists that all was not well with the American black.

Chapter Nine

From the 1920's
to World War II

Roaring Twenties, Jazz Age, Prohibition Era—whatever it was called—the period following World War I was a spectacular and exciting episode in American history, characterized by extremes which eventually altered the very social fabric of the people. Older values came under attack from young Americans weary of the restrictions and taboos of society. Liberalism, represented by jazz, sexual freedom, and the general defiance of youth, was in direct conflict with the conservatism represented by such phenomena as the "Red Scare" of 1919–1920, Prohibition, and a resurgence of the Ku Klux Klan.

Society was tremendously affected by technological advances. The automobile alone created a revolution, and aviation began to shrink the boundaries of the country. The advertising business discovered Americans' tendency to substitute slogans for thought and thereby became a major industry. Through the use of mass media, advertising was capable of altering the tastes and desires of the nation. Exploitation of black stereotypical figures, such as "Aunt Jemima" and the "Gold Dust Twins," reinforced black imagery while selling millions of dollars worth of products.

Both radio and sound motion pictures contributed to the standardization of American life and habits and, at the same time, revolutionized the entertainment business. Neither field, however, made any attempt to portray the black in a role other than the accepted stereotype. Radio presented its version with such types as the enormously successful "Amos 'n' Andy," in which two whites, Freeman Gosden and Charles Correll, affected thick dialects to impose the imagery of bumbling, comical blacks; Eddie "Rochester" Anderson, as the servant of the comedian Jack Benny, recreated—without being aware of it, in all probability—the role of Mungo in Bickerstaff's *The Padlock*. This imagery was centuries old and thus considered "safe" for radio.

Motion pictures were far more effective in conveying the imagery of black inferiority than was radio, however. Not only were roles of blacks in accordance with the usual stereotype, but audiences themselves were often segregated. Following a practice developed by recording companies, some white motion picture producers made "race" movies with all-black casts in order to cater to black audiences.

The motion picture industry set the tone for its delineation of blacks during its infancy when D.W. Griffith's *Birth of a Nation* (1915) distorted historical fact to show heroic Klansmen defending white womanhood against blacks bent upon rape and murder. He further libelled blacks with portrayals of the stereotypical scared black in a series of films beginning in 1922. Numerous versions of *Uncle Tom's Cabin* came out in the early film days, mostly with whites in blackface playing Tom. Throughout the 1920's and 1930's, the black represented in motion pictures was that of the singing, dancing, comical, and subservient stereotyped figure. The only relief from this imagery came in the 1940's, when black roles slowly began to recognize the individual rather than the stereotype. The South reacted to this belated recognition with bans and censorship; Lena Horne was removed from the Southern version of *Ziegfeld Follies*, and another film was banned because in it a white star tipped his hat to a black.[1]

Songs played important roles in the portrayal of black stereotypes in motion pictures. Most of the songs used in films enjoyed further exploitation on radio. This dual exposure helped to promote and to fix the stereotypical black in the minds of Americans; many black entertainers were themselves associated with fixed images: Ethel Waters was the ideal "Mammy" figure; Lena Horne became the symbol of sexuality in the black female; Bill "Bojangles" Robinson was the happy, dancing darky; and so on ad infinitum. White performers in blackface cultivated the corresponding imagery, highlighted by song. Al Jolson, Eddie Cantor, Bing Crosby, Fred Astaire, Mickey Rooney, and Judy Garland are only a few of those who adopted blackface at one time or another in order to convey stereotypical black imagery.

In the East, another type of revolution was being effected in the American musical theater. Black influence spread from Harlem, center of the so-called "Harlem Renaissance," to the musical stage in a wave of enthusiasm for things black; Gilda Gray, in the 1922 edition of *Ziegfeld Follies*, sang "It's Getting Dark On Old Broadway"[2] in which the black invasion is described:

> Ev'ry cafe now has the dancing coon.
> Pretty choc'late babies
> Shake and shimmie ev'rywhere
> Real darktown entertainers hold the stage,
> You must black up to be the latest rage.
> Yes, the great white way is white no more,
> It's just like a street on the Swanee shore;
> It's getting very dark on old Broadway.

This development had its roots in pre-World War I days, during which time black entertainers had demonstrated their unique capabilities, but the movement was given further impetus by the advent of jazz. The exotic effect of exercising newly acquired social freedoms seemed to fascinate whites; in associating with black entertainers, they somehow felt that they were expressing the essence of the new liberalism. The black, on the other hand, was seriously attempting to find self-identity through literary and other arts; the impact of his contribution during this period must be weighed against those who maintain that his failure to divorce himself from Euro-American culture represents a failure of the movement.[3]

It is true that much of the music produced by blacks was indistinguishable from that of whites during this period, but this was always the case. Francis Johnson, a hundred years earlier, had produced music in precisely the same fashion as that of his white contemporaries. Songwriters of the 1920's and 1930's eagerly accepted the contributions of their black counterparts, not as musical aberrations, but as a new and exciting dimension to popular expression. The degrading coon song died a well-deserved death largely through the newer approach, a contribution worthy of attention and consideration in the question of the success of the Harlem effort.

The black composers, lyricists, musicians, and entertainers did manage to blunt the cutting insult of the coon song; still, they replaced it with imagery of the black that was essentially white. *Shuffle Along*, with lyrics and music by Noble Sissle and Eubie Blake, contained a number of songs that have no direct reference to color, but it also contained songs which offer little to dispel preconceived notions concerning blacks, such as "Old Black Joe and Uncle Tom," "Pickaninny Shoes," "Liza, Quit Vamping Me," and "If You've Never Been Vamped By A Brown Skin."[4] In this latter song, the imagery of the black female as a vamp—a supercharged sex symbol—was delineated in the manner that was to become the norm for the ideal "red hot mama":

> If you've never been vamped by a brown skin
> You've never been vamped at all;
> For the vamping-est vamp is a brown skin,
> And believe me now that ain't no stall.
> A high brown gal will make you break out of jail,
> A choc'late brown will make a tadpole smack a whale,
> A pretty seal skin brown, I mean one long and tall
> Would make the silent sphinx out in the desert bawl,
> If you've never been vamped by a brown skin,
> You've never been vamped at all!

Black composers also exploited the imagery of the happy, dancing darky, exemplified by James P. Johnson's "Charleston"[5] written in collaboration with Cecil Mack. There was, in each of the new dance crazes, something that hinted at excitement engendered by the slightly wicked nature of black dance:

> If you ain't got religion in your feet,
> You can do this prance and do it neat.

Black and white songwriters alike produced songs designed to emphasize the lack of moral restraint and the sensual pleasure to be gained from each new dance. "Tain't No Sin"[6] by Edgar Leslie and Walter Donaldson suggested that the new dances encouraged the rejection of normal behavior and held concupiscence as a viable alternative. Conservatives of the day were in complete agreement with this view, although their conclusions were entirely different from those of the songwriters:

> When the lazy syncopation,
> Of the music softly moans,

> 'Tain't no sin, to take off your skin.
> And dance around in your bones.

The slyly wicked, lascivious associations made with respect to the so-called black dances were made to order for the rebellion against outmoded morality. The relaxed manner of black dance was translated into loosened moral strictures through suggestive descriptions of bodily movements (shake, shiver, squirm, shimmy, etc.). These, in turn, suggested sexual activity. Expressions such as "hot" and "warm" further intensified sexual connotations of the dances. Often these terms were combined in the same song:

> When you do the Harlem River Quiver,
> All your little nerves begin to shiver,
> Ev'ry baby's willing to deliver
> Ev'rything she's got,
> Then you start to rock her helter skelter,
> She'll admit that she has never felt a
> More peculiar feeling, then you melt her
> Till she's good and hot!
>
> First you give it this and give it that,
> And start it off with a wow,
> Then you start to squirm like a river worm,
> You will make her, and how!
>
> Dance around until you shake her toes off,
> Keep it up until you shake her clothes off,
> Learn to do the Harlem River Quiver,
> Give it to her now.[7]

Both black and white conservatives saw all this as evidence that American youth was being corrupted by the new dance crazes and jazz. Black critics were concerned about the "worldly" aspects of jazz as compared to black sacred expression in song; the white critics attacked it mainly on the grounds that they found it difficult to attribute musical value to any form of black expression, particularly the loud and irreverent jazz. Even the word "jazz" was held to be unclean, as explained by Clay Smith:

The highly vulgar dances that accompany some of the modern jazz are sometimes far too suggestive of the ugly origin of the word. . . .[8]

Scott Godard, in his review of R.W.S. Mendl's *The Appeal of Jazz*, recognized the conservative's view of jazz as "subversive to law and order," noting that:

There are those who still consider its influence baneful, or imagine that it is made up solely of noises which are so disgusting as to be positively harmful to the ears, and even to the morals of the hearers.[9]

But it was not actually jazz that was causing the harm. Most of the music against which the critics railed was, in fact, commercial white attempts to exploit current crazes for black expression. The so-called "King of Jazz" was not a black artist, but Paul Whiteman. Even black expression sounded suspiciously white at times, as when Lucille Hegamin, "The Palmetto Songbird" (or the "Cameo Girl"), sang:

> Down in Louisana in that sunny clime,
> They play a class of music that is superfine,
> And it makes no difference if it's rain or shine,
> You can hear that jazzin' music playing all the time.[10]

Songwriters seemed to relish tweaking the sensibilities of staid moralists. Conservatives could hardly avoid being grossly offended by lyrics that attacked the very foundation of society, the family. One such song, "Jazz Baby,"[11] suggested that the entire family was under the unholy spell of jazz:

> My daddy was a trombone player,
> My mammy was a ragtime cabareter,
> They met one day at a tango tea,
> There was a syncopated wedding and then came me.

Such a casual attitude toward the sacred and basic unit of American society was bad enough when attributed to blacks, but "Jazz Baby" was white—from the illustrated sheet music cover to the composer and lyricist.

Surely the nation's moral guardians could see nothing but decadence and social ruin in "Sugar Foot Stomp"[12] in which "high steppin' mammas" shouted:

Oh Daddy—sweet daddy
Rock your mamma like a cradle—
Sweet papa
I must let my doggies romp
Do the dance with me
They call the sugar foot stomp.

Virtually all the dances are represented as having originated in the south or in Harlem. This was no doubt a holdover of the "happy, singing, dancing plantation darky." In point of fact, hardly any of the dances sprang from anywhere other than Tin Pan Alley. The eighth annual edition of *George White's Scandals* contained an example of one such dance, the famous "Black Bottom,"[13] imitated widely and on occasion, successfully, as in "Mississippi Mud."[14] This type of song throve on the euphoria created by the new music; it was never criticized for its outrageously distorted concept of the Southern black. Dissenters were concerned primarily by the assumption that such music would have a deleterious effect on white morality. The picture of unrestrained behavior was normally accepted as a portrayal of the black; but "Black Bottom" invited whites to indulge in a hedonistic display:

Oh, the black bottom of the Swanee River,
    Sometimes liked to shake and shiver,
And it makes the darkies feel like strutting around.
By watching they found a way to imitate it,
    I know they exaggerate it,
But I wish that you could see the dance that they found.
Ev'ry high-brown gal and her bonbon buddy
    Go down where the flats are muddy,
To do a step that soon will be renowned.
They call it Black Bottom
    A new twister;
It's sure got' em,
    And oh, Sister.
They clap their hands and do a raggedy trot,
    Hot!
Old fellows with lumbago,
    And high yellows,
Away they go:
    They jump right in and give it all that they've got!

> They say that when the river bottom coverd with ooze,
> Start in to squirm.
> Couples dance and that's the movement they use:
> Just like a worm!
> Black Bottom
>   A new rhytm [*sic*]
> When you spot 'em,
>   You go with 'em,
> And do that Black, Black Bottom all the day long!

White interest in the new dance crazes was not curbed in the slightest degree by critics, however. Professors warned Americans that they were "being turned back to an age of barbarism" by jazz;[15] musical giants fought out the pro and con of jazz in print; church leaders passed resolutions and even initiated lawsuits against jazz performances; Harvard University's coach, J.T. Knox, warned that "jazz and autos" were ruining American youth;[16] and Queen Mary requested that no jazz be played at one of her affairs.[17] None of these criticisms had sufficient power to dampen the enthusiasm of fanatics. Two wholesome white female entertainers, the Farber Sisters, for example, took the stage to flaunt the current spirit of social, sexual, and racial freedom by offering a pitch for the "Darktown Dancin' School":[18]

> Now that's the place to learn the new steps,
> Better come with me right now—
> Mister Dancin' Mose
> Dress'd in evenin' clothes
> Will be there to show you how;
> Say, when it comes to dancin' teachers,
> He's the greatest of his time,
> And doggone him,
> No one's got it on him
> In the Jazzbo dancin' line.

Actually, the argument for and against jazz and related dances was wholly misplaced, for virtually all of the music under discussion was popular song, exploitative of jazz, but certainly not jazz as conceived by its originators. It is not the purpose of this study to resolve the many questions pertaining to jazz, but there is little doubt that the endless dilution of jazz by white composers left few vestiges of the original contribution of blacks, as had been the case with ragtime earlier in the century. And, as had happened with the spiritual, blues, ragtime, and other musical expression of the black, white domination led even the black composers to debase their own art as an expedient to survival.

White composers were willing to acknowledge the black as the fountainhead of jazz, not as a gesture of generosity, however, but because they could produce no evidence that it was a white creation. Furthermore, the black was the social outcast who threatened to corrupt white America, so why attempt to arrogate jazz, which, according to many, threatened to do the same thing? Besides, jazz accomodated itself neatly to the conception of what black music should be. Thus white composers made a point of attributing jazz to the Southern black, stating that "Jazz Time Came From The South":[19]

> Jazz time—American jazz time—
> That raggedy jazz time—
> Came from the South.

George White's Scandals of 1926 was blessed with an enduring hit. "The Birth Of The Blues,"[20] a highly romanticized version of the origin of blues that is still accepted by some as authentic:

> Oh! They say some darkies long ago
>   Were searching for a different tune,
> One that they could croon
>   As only they can.
>   They only had the rhythm,
> So—they started swaying to and fro,
>   They didn't know just what to use,
> That is how the blues really began:
>
> They heard the breeze in the trees
>   Singing weird melodies
> And they made that the start of the blues.
> And from a jail came the wail
>   Of a downhearted frail,
> And they played that as part of the blues.
>
> From a whippoorwill
> Out on a hill

They took a new note,
Pushed it through a horn
'Til it was worn
Into a blue note!

And then they nursed it, rehearsed it,
    And gave out the news
That the Southland gave birth to the blues!

The distinction between jazz and blues is perhaps nowhere more obscured than in the popular song of the 1920's. Jazz, as a functional music related to dance, was associated with blues primarily because the practioners of both were, in the beginning, black. Handy called his "Saint Louis Blues" jazz, despite the fact that it is a finished composition.[21] But the blues that was the black secular expression was lost in the mad scramble to exploit the commercial possibilities of the new musical phenomenon. The cold blue despair that typifies the blues was distorted into superficial misery, or, perhaps more often, forgotten entirely in the haste to portray the excitement of "hot" jazz. This latter effect was the object of "Hot Lips":[22]

He's got hot lips
    When he plays jazz,
He draws out steps,
    Like no one has,
You're on your toes,
    And shake your shoes,
Boy, how he goes,
    When he plays Blues.

I watch the crowd
    Until he's through,
He can be proud,
    They're "cuckoo" too;
His music's rare,
    You must declare,
The boy is there
    With two hot lips.

Artificial blues proliferated to the point of becoming an inside joke among musicians; any tune became "blues" by simply adding that word to the end of the title. Handy's "Yellow Dog Rag" became blues in the popular mind after he changed the title to "Yellow Dog Blues";[23] Noble Sissle and Eubie Blake included three "blues" songs in their score of *Shuffle Along*: "Oriental Blues," "Low Down Blues," and "Gypsy Blues"; Clarence Williams wrote "Sugar Blues," a song destined to make Clyde McCoy famous through a rendition of a growling trumpet. Among these and thousands like them, hardly any so-called "blues" were actually the straightforward expression of the black. The personal and social problems that confronted blacks on a daily basis were ignored by these songs; worse, these songs took the surface manifestations of black grief and twisted them to fit prevailing stereotypes. "Sing! It's Good For Ya' "[24] offered the typical solution to black problems:

> Folks of all description,
>   Suffer from the Blues;
> You don't have to worry,
>   I've got some real good news.
> Here's a good prescription,
>   Makes you feel like new,
> Really very simple,
>   Here's all you have to do. Just—
>
> Sing! keep your Spirits high,
> Sing! pass ol' worry by,
> Sing! 'till the day you die,
> It's good for ya'.

This, of course, is the imagery of the happy plantation darky that formed a basic unit of the black stereotype in American song. Far from dying out as a result of contact between the races in the 1920's, the type flourished as a main feature of whites' conception of the black. Its direct descent from the carry-me-back can be traced in many songs but perhaps is best exemplified by "Alabam' Banjo Man":[25]

> That Alabam' Banjo man,
>   Syncopates like no one can,
> When he begins his joyful strumming,
>   (Sweet and pretty)
> All the pickaninnies sing
>   Harmony and ev'rything,

Just like the folks down home
(On the Swanee River)
"In the Gloaming"
Sweet refrain,
Takes me roaming back again.
Where the cotton blossoms grow,
To the land of Old Black Joe
And the music of the Alabam' Banjo man.

This imagery was connected to the past through songs lauding the "good old days" as well; the musical, *Rufus Le Maire's Affairs*, contains a song[26] which pleads:

Oh! won't you bring back, bring back those minstrel days
Out of the long ago—
Bring back those old faces in black—
Features we all loved so—

Although "Bring Back Those Minstrel Days" represented one of the links to earlier black imagery, there were ample songs showing the identical picture in a contemporary setting. "I'm A Swingin' Dingin' Daddy"[27] by Jerry Johnson and Irving Mills was written in the same stereotypical vein as were the earlier "Old Dan Tucker" types which showed the black equating virility with physical and sexual prowess as a prime value:

If I was swingin' now like I was swingin' then,
I could swing better than a hundred men,
I'm a swingin', dingin', daddy growing old.

If I still had feet and they still could kick,
I could keep better time than a drummer's sticks,
But I'm a swingin', dingin', daddy growing old.

I swung with a girl named Bernice,
A gal of society.
Well, I was her human furnace,
And she shovelled coal for me.

But I ain't no more like I used to was,
And I can't do things like I did because
I'm a swingin', dingin', daddy growing old.

It might be stated that the attitude of an entire era between world wars predicated the black as inherently musical, and little else. Certainly the black portrayed in song was based upon the assumption of a happy, singing, playing, and dancing black whose life-style fit the changing times. From the early "That's What Makes A Wild Cat Wild" to the World War II "Cymbal Sockin' Sam," the imagery was the same: musical hedonism. White children learned the stereotype at an early age through piano teaching materials such as "Banjo-Pickaninnies" by T. Robin MacLachlin (Figure 52).[28]

There was no shortage of traditionally formed carry-me-backs during this period; indeed, the sentimental longing for a mythical South was intensified in song, with many enduring hits being produced in both serious and comic moods. The connection between the female figure and Dixie imagery was also more pronounced, with the female, in many instances, becoming totally white. The associated "mammy" song became an established type and the entertainment business was inundated with vapid imitations of the Jolson imagery of "My Mammy." Older favorites, such as C.A. White's "I'se Gwine Back To Dixie," were dusted off and reprinted to serve the seemingly insatiable craving to see the South as an earthly paradise. The Chicago publisher, T.S. Denison, initiated a series of minstrel opening choruses and finales designed to exploit the nostalgia. Completely reactionary in spirit, these publications dredged up such outdated imagery as:

> There's a low green valley on the old Kentucky shore,
> Where I've whiled many happy hours away,
> A sitting and singing by the little cottage door,
> Where lived my darling Nellie Gray.[29]

The paradise on earth theme was either implied or openly stated, as in "Away Down South In Heaven":[30]

> Oh! the sun shines bright on the fields of white,
> And the birds make music all day—
> I mean away down South in Heaven, Heaven. . . .

Or, as stated by Kate Smith in the Paramount picture *Hello Everybody!*:

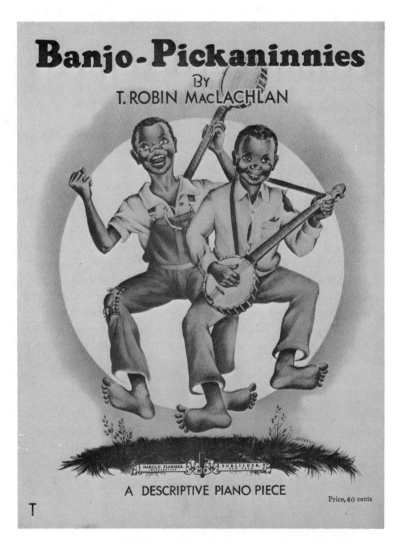

Figure 52

> Great big watermelons roll around and get in your way,
> In the Pickaninnies' Heaven.
> Luscious pork chop bushes growin' right outside your doorway,
> In the Pickaninnies' Heaven.
> They've even got a Swanee River
> Made of real lemonade
> And tho the good Lord took your mammy,
> She'll be waiting for you
> In the Pickaninnies' Heaven, Heaven.[31]

The outpouring of sentiment for the mythical South completely ignored reality. This South, to which so much warm friendliness and motherly love was attributed, was the same South that had lynched 2,522 blacks between 1885 and 1918. The murder of blacks at the hands of white mobs was sanctioned, in a sense, by the steadfast refusal of Southern lawmakers to allow any anti-lynch laws on the books. It was the South that clamored for the death of the so-called Scottsboro Boys in 1931 and undoubtedly would have succeeded, excepting for the intervention of the Communist-oriented International Labor Defense, which came to the side of the defense. It was, in short, a seething cauldron of racial hatred, this South that was pictured in song with such a tender brush.

But it was hardly a matter of questioning the truthfulness of the carry-me-back types that inspired the insipid, "Is It True What They Say About Dixie?"[32]

> Is it true what they say about Dixie?
> Does the sun really shine all the time?
> Do the sweet Magnolias blossom at ev'rybody's door?
> Do folks keep eating possum,
> Till they can't eat no more?

The question posed by this natural piece of Jolsoniana remained unanswered for nine years until Fred Clarkson composed the inevitable "Yes It's True What They Say About Dixie."[33]

Throughout this period, songs which portrayed the real South did not exist, perhaps because of the truism which holds that the entertainment business as a whole was scared stiff of the racial issue. Certainly the moguls of entertainment were reluctant to offend their

Southern markets where strong organizations such as the United
Daughters of the Confederacy proclaimed in song:

> Hail to the U.D.C.!
> Who lift on high
> The torch of memory,
> Lighting the sky
> That men may see afar
> The beacon bright
> Calling to all the South
> To banish night.

This song, "Hail To The U.D.C.,"[34] shows (in case an explanation
might be necessary) that the Civil War was by no means over in the
minds of Southern whites. The last line of the verse can easily be
interpreted "To oppress blacks," but the final verse bears directly
upon the point concerning the acceptability of songs dealing with the
Dixie myth:

> Sing we in Dixie land
> Songs that we love,
> Home where the heart's at home
> No more to rove.

Intimidated by unbending Southern attitudes, song publishers
poured out a veritable avalanche of "songs that we love," meaning, of
course, songs that did nothing to alter prevailing stereotypes of the
black. As late as 1952, these publishers were still issuing such music,
both in sheet music and in collections such as *Al Jolson's Old-Time
Minstrel Show*,[35] in which could be found not only a heavy sampling
of carry-me-backs, but instructions on how to produce a minstrel
show.

The past practice of singling out states, cities, rivers, and other
Southern localities began to lose its magic as a way of dealing with the
Dixie myth. Regardless of the Southern locality chosen for fatuous
praise, the carry-me-back was devoid of inventiveness; it seemed as
though a Procrustean conformity gripped composers' imaginations
the moment they faced any aspect of the Dixie myth. "On The Gin,
Gin, Ginny Shore"[36] could hardly avoid being mimicked by an
equally straightfaced "Bam, Bam, Bamy Shore."[37] And the choruses

of both "Swanee River Moon"[38] and "Carolina Moon"[39] are virtually interchangeable with the identical rhythm and melodic incipits. The success of the dance hit, "Charleston," assured that there would soon appear a "Charleston Charley"[40] or a "I'm Gonna Charleston Back To Charleston."[41] The imagery of " 'Way Down Yonder In New Orleans"[42] was unwavering in its adherence to the myth:

> 'Way down yonder in New Orleans,
> In the land of dreamy scenes,
> There's a garden of Eden,
> That's what I mean. . . .

The endless claptrap flowing from the pens of Tin Pan Alley's composers reached a climax of sorts in the middle 20's, when an inconsequential, though refreshingly waggish, "I Haven't Mentioned Mammy"[43] complained:

> Remember, remember, I haven't mentioned Swanee,
> But that is where my heart goes pitter pat,
> Remember, remember, I won't refer to cotton,
> Or fields of corn or anything like that,
> Remember now I'm blue as can be,

"I Haven't Mentioned Mammy" had no effect at all on the output of carry-me-backs, nor was it intended to. The year following its appearance, the Dixie myth gained support from many songs, among which "I Wish I Was In Dixie"[44] was repeating the familiar strain:

> Ev'ry cloud has a silver linin'
> And the sun is always shinin'
> That's the reason why
> I wish I was in Dixie.
> In the state that I was born in,
> Little song birds say "Good mornin' "
> That's the reason why
> I wish I was in Dixie.
> I'll say goodbye to trouble,
> Far away from harm;
> I'll just cuddle
> In my mammy's arms,
> There's a million kisses due her,

And I want to pay them to her,
That's the reason why
I wish I was in Dixieland.

The "mammy" figure was often replaced by the figure of the younger female in the carry-me-back, yet the mother image remained strong enough to form a distinct type of carry-me-back, the so-called "mammy song." Al Jolson was the undisputed king of the mammy song with his widely imitated "My Mammy,"[45] the lachrymose prototype of all such songs. Hardly anyone could outdo the fake sentimentality of Jolson on bended knee, in blackface, tearfully yammering:

Mammy, Mammy,
The sun shines East, the sun shines West,
But I've just learned where the sun shines best,
Mammy, Mammy,
My heart strings are tangled around Alabamy;
I'se a comin'—
Sorry that I made you wait,
I'se a comin'—
Hope and pray I'm not too late,
Mammy, Mammy,
I'd walk a million miles for one of your smiles,
My Mammy.

Other mammy songs attempted to reach the sickening sweetness of "My Mammy," but few succeeded. Harold A. Hummer's "Dear Old Georgia Mammy"[46] almost achieved the revolting level needed in order to compete with:

Dear old Georgia Mammy,
    Sing again to me.
Sing about the dear old days that used to be.
    I can well remember
When I sat upon your knee.
    Uncle Joe would play a tune on his banjo,
Little piccaninnies danced with hearts aglow.
    Dear old Georgia Mammy,
Won't you sing again to me.

Actually, it was another Jolson favorite, "I'd Love To Fall Asleep And Wake Up In My Mammy's Arms,"[47] which was the prime example of the musical Oedipus complex despite the fact that it was "My Mammy" that was most often copied. Granted that most songs of the period were corporate efforts involving producers and performers, one cannot help wondering about the psychological condition of those responsible for publicly proclaiming:

> I'd love to fall asleep and wake up in my mammy's arms,
> Just to feel her kissin' me,
> What a wonderful dream that would be!
> Mammy, mammy, with your lullabyes;
> Wake your baby;
> Open my eyes.
> 'Most ev'ry night thru fields of white, I wander way back home,
> And in those dreams my lonely heart keeps cryin';
> "Hold me mammy, fold me mammy, with your tender charms";
> I'd love to fall asleep and wake up in my mammy's arms.

The "mammy" of the song was clearly black; the younger female figure in the carry-me-back was not always distinguished by color. She was often pictured on cover illustrations of sheet music editions as being white, thus completing the transformation of the pre-minstrel "Coal Black Rose" through the "Yaller Rose Of Texas" into a white "Magnolia,"[48] "My Trixie From Dixieland,"[49] or a racially indistinct "Sweet Georgia Brown."[50] The cover illustration of "You've Got To See Mamma Ev'ry Night"[51] is that of a white woman, whereas the words imply a female of the older coon song type:

> You've got to see Mamma ev'ry night,
> Or you can't see Mamma at all,
> You've got to kiss Mamma, treat her right,
> Or she won't be home when you call. . . .

Conversely, the cover illustrations were sometimes the strongest clue leading to the racial identification of the female subject. "Red Hot Mamma"[52] has definite textual implications to the effect that the subject is black, but the silhouette of a black woman on the cover confirms the point.[53]

The imagery of both "You've Got To See Mamma Ev'ry Night" and "Red Hot Mamma" reinforced the stereotype of the young black female as a desirable, although often unmanageable, sex object. This, of course, was not new; but the rather casual lack of racial distinction between white and black female in songs of this period suggests that perhaps the white woman was being lowered from the lofty, untouchably pure position she had enjoyed in the past as a subject of song—it most certainly did not represent an improvement in attitudes concerning the black woman. The new morality of the era might account in part for such a phenomenon; women were beginning to throw off many of the restrictions that had prevented their meeting men on common ground, and men could be expected to react by reducing them to a more traditional level of subservience. Whatever the reasons, the fact remains that the "Red Hot Mama" image was applied to both white and black females during the 1920's and 1930's.

There were songs in which the crinolined Southern belle imagery was portrayed, albeit without significant success. Sam Coslow's "That's Southern Hospitality"[54] recreates the genteel quality of the Cavalier myth with his picture of a compliant, "dark-eyed southern miss" who, among her other attributes, is "not so bad at cookin' chicken dinners." It is not made clear whether the subject of this song is black or white; it is abundantly clear, however, that the protagonist would be categorized in today's society as a hard-shell male chauvinist indulging in his fantasy of what a woman should be.

Similarly, "When A Lady Meets A Gentleman Down South"[55] seems completely out of place among the "Red Hot Mamas" and "Flamin' Mamies" of the period. While it is possible that there were those who preferred to retain the image of a magnolia-scented South with all its pretensions of gentle charm, there were many more who perceived the phony picturesqueness of all the hackneyed phrases and words that had built this distorted view over the years. Cute "down-home" phrases such as, "If that's not sweet romance, then hush my mouth," confirmed that "When A Lady Meets A Gentleman Down South" was only another commerical song about the South. It never achieved popularity.

While "That's Southern Hospitality" and "When A Lady Meets A Gentleman Down South" fit the requirements for the Dixie myth very well, with its Southern "belle" up on her pedestal where she belonged, the songs of the two decades prior to World War II cast the young female more often than not in an earthier role.

Creamer and Layton were closer to the ideal with their "Strut,

Miss Lizzie"[56] in which "Miss Lizzie" reverts to being both black and sexy.

> Won't you strut, Miss Lizzie, get busy
> I want to see you walk—
> For the folks all state the way you syncopate
> Is the whole town talk.
> When you move so pretty, it's a pity,
> The other girls frown,
> But the men you meet like the way you shake your feet—
> Oh, you knock 'em dizzy,
> Strut, Miss Lizzie Brown.

Imagery of the fickle black female, such a formidable opponent to the black male in the coon song, softened somewhat during this period. The blues mainly concentrated on the sadness of separation, but the reaction seemed to favor two moods: the wronged party was either immobilized by grief or delighted to have done with the affair. The latter type is typified by a song that technically can be considered a holdover from the coon song, Andrew B. Sterling and Harry Von Tilzer's "I Ain't'en Got'en No Time To Have The Blues":[57]

> I ain't'en got'en no time to have the blue-oo-oo-oos,
>   No how.
> I'se goten another daddy now sweet Papa,
>   Oh, Papa, I'm in love.
> I ain't'en got'en no time for mournful new-oo-oo-oos. . . .

The rather fretful lamentation of the jilted lover has many examples, among which the great hit, "How Come You Do Me Like You Do?"[58] is a suitable specimen. Many people, not having heard the verse or not having seen the sheet music cover of "How Come You Do Me Like You Do?," never realized that its subjects were black, yet this song became one of the all-time favorites of the period.

The really tough women, "Hard Hearted Hannah"[59] or "Hard Boiled Rose,"[60] were cast as white, while the "Rose" of "Sweetest Little Rose In Tennessee"[61] and the "Hannah" of "Oh, Miss Hannah"[62] were not just black, they were truly lovable characters. "Sweet Georgia Brown," shown on the illustrated sheet music cover as white, and in the text as black, is pictured as quite engaging, with none of the brittle hardness of the imagery of white women of the period:

> She just got here yesterday,
>   Things are hot here now, they say,
> There's a big change in town—
>   Gals are jealous, there's no doubt,
> Still the fellows rave about
>   Sweet, sweet Georgia Brown,
> And ever since she came,
>   The colored folks all claim, Say
>
> No gal made has got a shade on Sweet Georgia Brown,
> Two left feet—but oh, so neat—has Sweet Georgia Brown,
> They all sigh and wanna die for Sweet Georgia Brown,

This cheerful imagery is consistent in many of the songs about the black female. "Lulu's Back In Town"[63] and "Ida! Sweet As Apple Cider,"[64] both hits of the thirties, demonstrate the fact that a fundamental change was taking place in the imagery of the black female in popular song—or was it that the American public was slowly inching its way to the realization that sexual attractiveness was not only possible, but desirable in the black woman? If this were indeed the case, it did not seriously affect white attitudes toward the real-life black woman; there were those in the country who deplored such songs as "Pretty Quadroon,"[65] especially when performed by white entertainers. The maudlin chorus struck some listeners as simply too sincere to be socially acceptable:

> Oh, my pretty Quadroon—
>   The flower that faded too soon;
> My heart's like the strings of my banjo—
>   All broke for my pretty Quadroon.

"Louisville Lou,"[66] comparable to the imagery of the white female, was less venomous; whereas songwriters could have viewed the liberated white female as something of a threat to their manhood, the black woman pictured in "Louisville Lou" was really sexy—more threatening to her female companions than to the male. The castration complex that permeates the white female imagery becomes in "Louisville Lou" little more than sheer awe at the subject's prowess in "vamping" males:

> Cullud gals, you'd better look out,
> > If you've got a man you're crazy about,
> 'Cause he may be the best of men,
> > But he's bound to weaken now and then
> Give him plenty lovin' each night;
> > Don't you ever leave him out of your sight,
> 'Cause if he meets this high brown doll,
> > Then you haven't got a chance at all.

Those composers who aspired to greater heights than crass commercialism tried to present a more sympathetic figure in their portrayal of the young black female subject. Most of these efforts were flawed in one respect or another; one of the lovelier songs in this manner, Lily Strickland's "Mah Lindy Lou,"[67] is burdened with a text cast in the thick pseudo-black dialect reminiscent of early minstrelsy. This unnecessary attempt at realism obscures a truly beautiful melody and the tender sentiment:

> Honey, did you heah dat mockin' bird sing las' night?
> O Lawd, he wuz singin' so sweet in de moonlight!
> In de ole magnolia tree,
> Bustin' his heart wid melody!
> I know, he wuz singin' ob you,
> Mah Lindy Lou, Lindy Lou!
> O Lawd, I'd lay right down an' die,
> Ef I could sing lak dat bird sings to you,
> Mah liddle Lindy Lou!

Songs of this type pictured a young black male, simple and sincere in his devotion, carrying his magnolia-scented message of love through song and "sweet talk," some of which contained unintentional connotations of a casual attitude toward sex that had been built up over the years in less serious songs. Apart from its title, John Prindle Scott's "Romeo In Georgia"[68] suggests that the hero of the song had less than honorable intentions toward his maid as he croons:

> Hurry up, Eliza,
> I's waitin' to surprise ye,
> Down here by the 'simmon tree....

Black capability for deep and lasting love was portrayed in "Chlo-e,"[69] a song which recalled the lost wives and lovers of earlier carry-me-backs. Listeners seemed to overlook the anomalies of the text, in which the lover goes roaming through the smoke and flame of a dismal swamp, and the musically fashioned cry, "Chlo-e!" is described as a sigh; audiences were too entranced with the imagery of a black lover vainly searching for his woman to pay much attention to details. Besides, these songs were commonly sung by white performers, not black.

The male black lover was pictured as something less than a paragon of fidelity in the commercial songs of the period. Indeed, the past imagery of the male dandy, the bully, and the irresistibly attractive lover remained the staple subjects.

Inspired by the example of Rudolph Valentino's popular success in the silent film *The Sheik*, Jack Yellen and Milton Ager cast their black "Romeo" as superior to the movie idol in matters of love in their "Lovin' Sam (The Sheik of Alabam')":[70]

> Listen, sisters and brothers,
>   I suppose you've heard of the Sheik;
> They say that he's the lovin' champ,
>   There ain't a woman he can't vamp,
> But let me tell you about a man I know:
>   He's the greatest of lovers
> Ever kissed a gal on the cheek.
>   There ain't a high brown gal in town
> Who wouldn't throw her daddy down
>   To be the bride of this cullud Romeo.

The description of this black Lochinvar is comparable to the imagery of the "vamp" female subject; with only slight textual changes the chorus of "Lovin' Sam" could be applicable to a woman. This phenomenon is perhaps the best example of the deficiencies of imagination that characterized such songs and made them sound so much alike. "Sam," then, is not very much different from his female counterpart, as described here:

> People call him Lovin' Sam,
>   He's the Sheik of Alabam',
> He's a mean love makin'—a heart breakin' man!
> And when the gals go strollin' by,
>   Boy! he rolls a wicked eye!

> Does he step?
> Does he strut?
> That's what he doesn't do nothin' else but!

The male vamp imagery persisted throughout the twenties with such songs as "Georgia Gigolo"[71] being modeled on the same order as "Lovin' Sam":

> I've seen Sheiks of the desert,
>   And "He" vamps on the screen,
> Dapper Dans upon Broadway,
>   Some betwixt and between;
> But there's a man I know, down south below,
>   The Mason Dixon line,
> A Romeo,
> Sweet Gigolo,
> The girls think he's divine. . . .

The "Dapper Dans upon Broadway" mentioned in "Georgia Gigolo" was a reference to Lew Brown and Albert Von Tilzer's "Dapper Dan,"[72] a song of the black male lover featured by Eddie Cantor "with terrific success" in the production *Midnight Rounders*. The only feature of this song which distinguishes it from others of the type is the chorus in which "Dan" presents himself in the first person, rather than the customary presentation in the third person:

> If I lose my gal in Tennessee,
>   That won't worry me,
> 'Cause I've got another honey lamb
>   Waitin' for me down in Alabam.
> And if I lose my gal in Alabam,
>   I won't feel blue
> 'Cause I got one in Georgia
>   That I can march right to.
> If I lose my gal in Georgia,
>   Bet that I won't pine,
> 'Cause I've got another mamma waiting,
>   Down in sunny Caroline.

The sexual connotations of such songs were always present and clearly understood, if not stated openly. In the thirties, however, song texts began to evidence trends toward a heavier innuendo that skirted the edges of obscenity in many instances. As stated previously, sex was not at any time considered an open subject in popular song, yet the decade before World War II found singers describing their lovers in such a way that only the most naive listener could fail to understand their meanings. No one, for instance, required an explanation of Ethel Waters' meaning as she sang Andy Razaf's "My Handy Man":[73]

> He shakes my ashes, greases my griddle;
> Churns my butter, strokes my fiddle;
> He threads my needle, creams my wheat;
> Heats my heater, chops my meat. . . .

The black as a desirable lover, with a remarkable performance level in satisfying a woman's passion, was naturally associated with song and dance, as was his female counterpart. "Charleston Charley,"[74] associated with the dance derived from the song "Charleston," of course, showed that the dance had brought out many of his latent talents for attracting women:

> I know a red-hot stepper,
>   Yes, he is full of pepper,
> The women follow him around, round, round, round;
> He used to be so lazy,
>   Now he is Charleston crazy,
> That dance has got him stepping 'round.
>
> They call him Charleston Charley, he's so jolly,
>   He sure does know his stuff,
> He never gets enough,
>   Women crave him 'cause he's rough. . . .

Another song of this type, "Charleston Baby Of Mine,"[75] tells of a similarly attractive character who "meets 'em and greets 'em and then he just let's 'em pine." The musical attraction of the black lover reflected widespread beliefs that his propensity for music and dance gave him an allure not possessed by ordinary males.

"Hi-de-ho Romeo"[76] by Benny Davis and J. Fred Coots went into Shakespearean allusions in order to find its "handle," or "gimmick." The "King of Hi-de-ho," Cab Calloway, featured this song in the third edition of the *Cotton Club Parade*, a revue exploiting the black theme in the late thirties. The black male's imagery was by now standardized to the point of making unnecessary any lengthy explication of the male characteristics of the subject; it was sufficient to give only a few key glimpses of the subject in order to establish his character:

> I'm just a HI-DE-HO ROMEO
> Lookin' for a Juliet.
> At this Barrymore bus'ness
> I may be new,
> But up in Harlem
> I'll teach Brother John a thing or two . . . .

This is confirmed by other songs of the late thirties, such as "Rag Picker,"[77] in which the subject is outlined in a relatively short text:

> Hear him singin' on his wagon,
> "Any rags or bottles today?"
> "How's your bones today, Miss Jones?
> Let me swing 'em all away"
> Junkey Joe has he got rhythm!
> All the gals are beggin' to strut
> Picks a rag, and does he shag!
> Nothin' else but . . . .

At least one song of the black lover eschewed the use of primarily black stereotypical imagery in order to outline character: "I'm Just Wild About Harry,"[78] which appeared in the first part of the twenties and became a lasting favorite, was a Sissle and Blake creation included in their *Shuffle Along*. Nothing in the musical content nor in the text indicates either a black subject or black origin; the only clue, beyond its inclusion in a black revue, is the cover illustration showing two black performers on stage. It is doubtful that many white performers realized that black associations existed in this piece, inasmuch as all the key words are missing.

Such was not the case with another Sissle and Blake song from the same show, their "Daddy, Won't You Please Come Home."[79] This was Gertrude Saunders's big hit in *Shuffle Along*, and all of the stereotypical imagery accruing to the fickle male was brought to bear in delineating the character of this particular "daddy":

> My daddy went away and quit me cold,
> And believe me when I say he ruined my soul.
> I surely miss his loving smile,

His hug and kisses that set me wild;
Today he called me on the 'phone,
    And when I heard his voice,
You should have heard me moan:

Oh, daddy—Da-Da-Da-Daddy,
Daddy, why don't you please come home? (etc.)

The picture of the woman grovelling at the feet of the faithless lover is that of the bully figure's woman of the coon song era, modernized but little changed in basic character. Songwriters were less explicit in describing the proclivity to physical combat displayed by this figure in songs of the past, perhaps owing to the very real and deadly serious exhibitions of black prowess during the racial disturbances of the period. In the twenties, when the songwriters wrote that their subject was a mean man, they expected the audience to believe it without lengthy corroboratory material typical of the coon song. Al Bernard's "Stavin' Change, The Meanest Man In New Orleans"[80] is one example:

I'm gonna tell you 'bout a bad man,
    Down in New Orleans,
Now you can rave about your Jessie James,
    But this man sure was mean,
He sure was rough, he used to strut his stuff,
    Up and down the Avenues,
He was a long, tall dressed up Brown,
    From his hat down to his shoes.

I'm gonna tell you now how Stave loved,
    Gal named Lindy Lee,
He always told the men around the town,
    That gal belongs to me,
She sure was bold, just like the story old,
    Trifled on him one sad day,
He shot poor Lindy through the heart,
    That's why folks down there all say:

Stavin' Change,
    The good Lord knows he was bad,
Stavin' Change,
    He made the sweet mammas glad—and sad. . . .

The bully figure was more often seen as the victim of the wrathful wronged woman; "Stavin' Change," the outraged lover who revenged himself by taking the life of his sweetheart, was overshadowed by female figures who threatened to equal or exceed that punishment for him. In "Aggravatin' Papa,"[81] an imperious female warns her lover:

> Aggravatin' papa,
>> Don't you try to two-time me,
> I said, 'don't two-time me!'
>> Aggravatin' papa,
>> Treat me kind or let me be,
> I mean, 'just let me be.'
> If you step out with a high brown baby,
>> I'll smack you down and I don't mean maybe.

Eddie Cantor sang "Birmingham Papa, Your Memphis Mamma's Comin' To Town,"[82] a song with virtually identical sentiments:

> Oh! Birmingham papa, your Memphis mamma's comin' to town,
>> You better watch your step,
> Birmingham papa, your Memphis mamma's got the low down,
>> Ain't nothin' else excep',
> Listen honey-lamb, when I reach Birmingham,
>> I'm gonna straighten you out.
> Babe, I'm tellin you,
> After I get thru,
>> You won't know what it's all about. . . .

The black bully occasionally became entangled with a type that could be considered worse than the vipers just described—the clinging vine. This female figure could not be dislodged by abuse, of which the bully had an ample supply. Lew Leslie's *Rhapsody In Black*, with an all-black cast, contained "You Can't Stop Me From Lovin' You,"[83] a preposterous song that is demeaning both to the male and female images as the truckling protagonist declaims:

> Oh! you great big brute—
>> How you mistreat me,
> Oh! you great big brute—
>> You can't defeat me;
> You can shower me with abuse,
>> You'll never shake me loose.
> Oh! you great big brute—
>> You can brow-beat me,
> But I'm tellin' you it's no use.

> Say I get in your hair,
> But baby, I don't care. . . .

By the end of the twenties, imagery of the desperately dependent or lonely black female had at least something more credible and recognizable in the treatment given by "Black and Blue."[84] The female in this song is lonely and knows why—she is black. Music and text complement each other in setting a sad mood:

> Out in the street, shufflin' feet,
> Couples passin' two by two,
> While here am I, left high and dry,
> Black, and 'cause I'm black I'm blue.
> Browns and yellers all have fellers;
> Gentlemen prefer them light,
> Wish I could fade, can't make the grade,
> Nothin' but dark days in sight.

Frankness concerning the black's real problem, the inability of whites to accept him for himself without being constantly reminded of his color, were indeed rare. Sincerity was not a common commodity in the songs produced between World War I and World War II. The very paucity of realism in popular song—especially with regard to black subjects—causes some degree of suspicion when sincerity is at last encountered. The weight of so much misrepresentation of the black in song may have been one of the reasons for the introductions Robert MacGimsey provided for many of his songs, as in "Old Slave,"[85] a serious song dedicated to a friend of his childhood, "old Uncle Olmstead." But even this precaution did not, as shall be seen later, prevent performers from making a mockery of honest efforts to present the black in a favorable light.

Songs showing the black as a viable figure were hardly the means to success in the entertainment business; it was far more profitable to follow current practice and deal with the stereotype. Pseudo-philosophy of the black became increasingly popular, as did those songs deriving from the pseudo-spiritual. Americans did not want to be reminded that pressing social and racial problems remained unsolved while they were in the midst of the greatest economic disaster—the Great Depression—the country had ever known.

Songs, such as "Shine,"[86] served a dual role of cheering up a despondent populace and reinforcing racial stereotypes. Those on the breadlines could cheer themselves with visions of a happy black singing:

> 'Cause I'm glad I'm living,
>> Take troubles smiling, never whine, whine, whine,
> 'Cause my color's shady
> And it's slightly diff'rent, maybe
>> That's why they call me "SHINE."

The misery of the Great Depression was heightened by Prohibition, which denied even the solace of the bottle to those who felt they needed its support. The black in song was not one to let the finer points of law prevent his having the drink that was so much a part of his stereotype; even before the Depression, Bert Williams had introduced two songs of this type, "The Moon Shines On The Moonshine"[87] and "I Makes Mine Myself."[88] The former song was one of the hits made by Williams in the *Ziegfeld Follies*, while the latter was introduced in *Broadway Brevities* at the Winter Garden. "The Moon Shines On The Moonshine" laments the advent of Prohibition and the closing of normal supply sources, the distilleries and bars. It informs the listeners that "in the mountain tops—far from the eyes of cops" there is still hope, provided the secret is kept.

Although "The Moon Shines On The Moonshine" was the song that was more closely associated with Williams's stage personality, "I Makes Mine Myself" is technically a better song. It describes the joy of the man who has plenty in the midst of want:

> Today I meets big Moses Jackson,
>> Limpin' down de street,
> Dat poor ole boy was laggin',
>> And a draggin' of his feet,
> I says to him: "Mah dear old friend,
>> How come yo' look so blue?"
> Says he: "I ain't absorbin'
>> What I'se been accustomed to,"
> "I see," says I, "They's put the goldfish
>> In your flowing bowl:
> Now me, I'se got most ev'rything
>> For any thirsty soul.
> Yessah, at my house
>> They's varieties fifty-seven,

> I opens up mah ice box door,
>   An' steps right into Heaven!
> 'Cause I makes mine myself (etc.).

The imagery of these songs reinforced the notion that the black was peculiarly addicted to drink and tended to obscure the very real fact that Prohibition, far from being a matter of sly racial humor, was indeed the legal windfall which allowed organized crime its golden opportunity to establish itself. Songs of black criminality were far more common than those about monolithic crime syndicates of the era.

Gambling was represented in such songs as "Seven Or Eleven; My Dixie Pair O' Dice,"[89] which managed to inject an outrageous pun on the "Paradise" of Dixie along with the stereotyped black gambler. The ideas in the title matched those of the text as well:

> At the railroad station
>   Almost ev'ry day
> Hangin' round the porters there
>   Tryin' hard to win his fare
> You'll see Rufus Johnson
>   Gamblin' his dough away
> Down on his knees with the dotted ivories
>   You can hear old Rufus say:
>
> Seven or Eleven means ev'rything to me,
>   Means I'm gonna see my Mammy,
>   Down in sunny Alabammy
> Seven or Eleven, that's what it's got to be

Other songs of the black criminal stereotype included "Waitin' For The Evenin' Mail (Sittin' On The Inside, Lookin' At The Outside)"[90] by Billy Baskette, in which the prisoner was in jail for "foolin' with the ev'nin' mail," or a more likely stereotype, the wifebeater brought before the court on the complaint "Oh Judge, He Treats Me Mean."[91] This latter song, of course, represents the bully brought to justice, although the text of the song does not inform the listener of the results of the trial but merely describes the complaint:

> Oh Judge! He treats me mean
>   (He wants to beat me—mistreats me)
> (etc.)

The decades between world wars saw an increased interest in black religion and philosophy, both of which found numerous outlets in serious and commercial songs. Folksongs were collected and arranged, as were the spirituals, in a belated effort to preserve a rapidly disappearing body of song. Folksong was disseminated primarily in collections, but the spiritual was brought before the public in collections, sheet music, and choral arrangements. Naturally, the commercial songwriters were busily exploiting the surface manifestations of black musical expression without being overly concerned that their product misrepresented their subject in most instances.

Composers and their publishers could see nothing incongruous in commercial exploitation of the secular or sacred folk expression of blacks; as in the early days of minstrelsy, the songs were offered to the public as authentic black song, regardless of origin. "I'm A Wand'rin!"[92] was advertised as an "old slave song," even though Samuel Richard Gaines took credit for both words and music without a backward glance at the logical impossibility of such an accomplishment.

The method normally followed in producing the pseudo-folk song was to employ known melodic peculiarities of black music, along with a characteristic rhythm, and to fit these to a text containing a thought that matched prevailing attitudes concerning the black. Syntax and spelling were both garbled to produce the wretched dialect expected of all blacks and, lo!—a black folk song was born. It could be labelled "old slave song," or anything else; the public could be persuaded to accept it.

This was the technique used in producing "Singin' A song (I'se Tired)."[93] wherein the protagonist is "woefully tired," "woefully fired," and "woefully mired;" yet he keeps "singin' a song" in order to cheer himself and to heal his pride—just as the "happy darkies do." Appropriately, this song was dedicated to Lawrence Tibbett, the Metropolitan Opera star who had created the role of Emperor Jones in Gruenberg's famous opera. It was the white singers, in short, who brought most of the white pseudo-folk songs to American audiences; black singers, such as Jules Bledsoe and Paul Robeson, were not overly enthusiastic about them, understandably enough.

The pseudo-folk song carried much the same message as commercially produced popular song. Indeed, there is hardly a valid reason for not considering the two types as two approaches to the

same end; J. Will Callahan and Oscar J. Fox saw their black hero as
being happy when the rain washes away everything he owns in their
"Rain And The River":[94]

> Let the river take my cabin,
>   And the rain soak the groun',
> I'll build another cabin
>   When the flood goes down. . . .

Anticipating the later craze for Calypso song, Frank Glick produced "Carryin' Coals,"[95] with a descriptive note on the singing that
accompanies the coaling of ships in Caribbean ports, and a text that
appears to derive more from the North American black than from the
Caribbean:

> I'm so weary and I'm so tired,
>   I often wish I was dead—
> From carryin' coals from morn till night. . . .

The commercial counterpart of "Carryin' Coals" could be found
in several songs, among which "Dusky Stevedore"[96] painted a
slightly different picture of the black dock worker:

> He's just a Stevedore,
>   Down on that Swanee shore,
> Workin' and singin' a song;
>   His dusky brow is wet,
> He doesn't mind the sweat,
>   A-scuffalin' all the day long;
> See his ragtime shuffalin' gait,
>   Happy, 'cause he's handlin' freight,
> The levee's heaven for,
>   The Dusky Stevedore. . . .

In the pseudo-folk idiom, the popular attitude was summed up by the
line in "Without A Song":[97]

> A darky's born, but he's no good no-how
>   Without a song.

Some commercial pseudo-folk song attempts resemble the
laments of early minstrelsy. Don Drew and Louis Breau produced

"Trubble,"[98] which differs from the carry-me-back only in that the protagonist never mentions a wish to be carried back to his loved ones in that earthly paradise, Dixie.

Among the sillier examples of the pseudo-folk song, few equal "Pickin' Cotton,"[99] featured in the ninth annual edition of *George White's Scandals*:

> Down where they have lazy weather
> When those darkies get together
> Cotton pickin' is a kind of a spree.
> There's a leader starts a rhythm
> As he picks they pick right with 'im
> They don't need a bossy Simon Legree.
> There's a beat, there's a measure
> For each cotton row,
> They make work seem a pleasure
> Dancing as they go.

William Arms Fisher was doubtlessly sincere in his appreciation of Dvořák's great symphony *From The New World*, but his enthusiasm was mired in the stereotyped image of the black as he attempted to capture the mood of the spiritual and to adapt the *Largo* with words and a new title, "Goin' Home":[100]

> Goin' home, goin' home,
> I'm a-goin' home;
> Quiet like, some still day,
> I'm jes' goin' home.

The equally genuine attempts by others to "arrange" the true spirituals were reminiscent of post-Civil War efforts along the same lines. Very few arranged spirituals captured the vast spectrum of emotion inherent in the originals. Both William Arms Fisher and Charles Fonteyn Manney arranged "Steal Way" with unsatisfying results in each instance. J. Rosamund Johnson's arrangement of the same spiritual comes as close to the original as is possible to capture on paper, but even here, the necessity for a lengthy introduction to the spiritual was deemed essential to correct interpretation.[101]

Some of the arranged spirituals appeared in stage productions such as Marc Connelly's *The Green Pastures*, for which Hall Johnson "selected and arranged" "City Called Heaven."[102] In it, evidence of commercialism leads to the suspicion that whatever beauty the original possessed was largely "selected and arranged" out of the piece.

Among the best of the arranged spirituals, William L. Dawson's *Tuskegee Choir Series* retained much of the original strength and glorious beauty of the genre. The simple explanation for this is that Dawson was following a tradition laid down years before by his group rather than trying to impress the uninitiated public; the essentially untrained quality of the spiritual is unsuited to refinements imposed by Western musical traditions. Dawson could succeed by the use of materials at hand whereas a Lawrence Tibbett could sing "arranged" black songs forever without once capturing the essence.

The immediate result of the renewed interest in black spirituals and folk expression was desecration at the hands of commercial songwriters. Treatment of the spiritual ranged from the standard practice of the coon song to the no less demeaning attempt to fuse current popular styles with that of the true spiritual. Regardless of which approach the songwriters used, their songs retained the imagery of the arm-swinging, catachrestical hypocrite preacher delivering his harangue against sin to a credulous flock.

"Oh Death Where Is Thy Sting"[103] shows that the coon song died a lingering death; it is a first-rate example of the tenacity of the popularly held belief that black religion is in reality a comic phenomenon.

> Now, Parson Brown, one Sunday morn,
>   Was giving good advice,
> He warn'd his congregation to
>   Refrain from sin and vice,
> He drew a fiery picture 'bout
>   The devil down below,
> And said folks, quit your sinnin'
>   Or to him you're bound to go.
> Why Hell is full of vampire women,
>   Whiskey, gin and dice,
> Make Satan get behind you
>   Now prepare for Paradise.
> Mose Johnson jump'd up from his chair,
>   Said, "Parson, is that true?
> That Hell is full of what you said,
>   Then let me say to you:

> If what you say is the positive truth,
>> O Death where is thy sting?
> I don't care now 'bout the pearly gates,
>> Or hear those angels sing;
> With booze and women down below,
>> Mister devil and I will put on a show,
> If what you say is the positive truth,
>> O Death where is thy sting."

The *Grand Street Follies* of 1925 featured a Dan Walker tune, "Glory! Glory! Glory!"[104] in which black religion is part of the story of the small town girl led astray in the big city:

> Now Liza Jane came to New York town,
>> From her home way down in Tennessee,
> There she walked the streets and she looked for work
>> As blue as she could be,
> And then one dark day, someone said,
>> "Liza Jane, you're awful pretty, where's your head?
> Go get yourself a job in a Broadway show."
>> So she joined the Ziegfeld Follies—where you know:
>
>> She has been Glory, Glory, Glory,
>> She has been Glorified!

Bogus morality and phony homiletics persisted into the thirties without letup. Enthusiasm for savoring the forbidden fruit of black social experience brought little understanding of the deeper meanings within the realms of black religion as expressed in song. The fake sermon of "Is That Religion?"[105] demonstrates how slight was the white grasp of black religion:

> Sisters, you strut the aisle,
>> All dress'd to kill with style,
> You wink your eye and smile,
>> IS THAT RELIGION?
> One thing I do despise,
>> You catch my deacon's eyes—
> That's where their weakness lies,
>> IS THAT RELIGION?
> You see your parson's vex'd,
>> You've got him so perplex'd,

His mind ain't on his text,
  IS THAT RELIGION?
There's some cheatin' gonna be did,
  And you all done took off the lid,
Tryin' to get your parson to skid,
  IS THAT RELIGION?

The second chorus turns the "parson's" wrath against the male members of the congregation:

Brothers, mind what I say—
  Each day you're mighty gay,
Instead of work, you play,
  IS THAT RELIGION?
Get into gamblin' scraps—
  Play poker and shoot craps,
Hide aces in your laps,
  IS THAT RELIGION?
You are always doin' those things,
  And on Sunday when the choir sings,
You just start in flappin' your wings,
  IS THAT RELIGION?

This frivolous attitude toward black religion was inevitably reflected in songs that became lasting favorites. Vincent Youmans used black religiosity repeatedly to produce some of his greatest hits: *Hit The Deck* (1927) contained "Hallelujah!" while his *Great Day* (1929) had for its title song the pseudo-sermon "Great Day." Both songs have become classics of the popular repertoire. Among Gershwin's several efforts in the same vein, "Clap Yo' Hands"[106] stands alongside the Youmans songs as a monument to excellence in melody writing and poor taste in texts. Written by his brother Ira, the text of "Clap Yo' Hands" contains the essence of the psuedo-sermon that dominated the Broadway stage, film, and radio for over two decades and proved convincingly that Tin Pan Alley was totally ignorant of black religion.

Gather around, you children,
And we will lose that evil spirit called the Voodoo.
Nothin' but trouble if he has found,
  If he has found you, children,
But you can chase the Hoodoo with the dance that you do.

> Let me lead the way;
> Jubilee today.
> He'll never hound you, stamp on the ground, you children!
> Come on!

One of Cole Porter's contributions to the lively pseudo-spiritual style was "Blow, Gabriel, Blow"[107] from *Anything Goes*. Here again, the talents of a first-rank composer were debased by an inflexible stereotype of black religion:

> Blow Gabriel, blow,
> Go on and blow Gabriel, blow!
> I've been a sinner, I've been a scamp,
> But now I'm willin' to trim my lamp
> So blow Gabriel, blow!

The fast tempo of these pseudo-spirituals was designed to lend authenticity to the genre; jittery, syncopated melodies were considered typical of black religious song, as evidenced in actual spirituals such as "Ain'-a That Good News." But composers and lyricists seemed incapable of shaking off the sheen of their technical perfection—a vital necessity on Broadway—in order to grovel in the same dirt from which the true spiritual sprang.

Many songwriters attempted to mask these inadequacies by adopting a slower tempo and a more serious stance in the lyrics. The fake solemnity of these efforts shows the appalling gap that existed between the songwriters and their subjects. In trying to show compassion for the black, songsmiths created gross horrors of misplaced sympathy that can only be considered as among the worst songs ever written on the subject of black religion. Lew Brown and Ray Henderson share honors for having produced one such song for *George White's Scandals* of 1931, "That's Why Darkies Were Born":[108]

> Someone had to pick the cotton,
> Someone had to plant the corn.
> Someone had to slave and be able to sing,
> That's Why Darkies Were Born.

> Someone had to laugh at trouble,
> Though he was tired and worn,
> Had to be content with any old thing,
> That's Why Darkies Were Born.

This song was enormously successful and the inspiration for countless imitations, not the least of which was "That's How Rhythm Was Born," a joint effort of George Whiting, Nat Schwartz, and J.C. Johnson. Perfection of this embarrassingly ludicrous pseudo-spiritual type was achieved when Ethel Waters appeared in the film *Cabin In The Sky* to sing the title song. She had also performed the song in the stage version of *Cabin In The Sky*, but the screen brought the song to millions more people than could have heard it on Broadway. The sight of a black singer performing "Cabin In The Sky"[109] touched many people, driving the inherent silliness of the song into the background and convincingly reinforcing the imagery of superficiality in black religion. How could anyone gainsay the warmly sympathetic figure of matriarchal prefiguration who promised her irreverent man:

> We will be oh so gay,
> Eat fried chicken ev'ry day
> As the angels go sailing by;
> That is why my heart is flying high, baby,
> 'Cause I know we'll have a Cabin in the Sky.

In all fairness, it should be pointed out that the second chorus of "Cabin In The Sky," sung by Eddie "Rochester" Anderson, rejects the promise of future joy and the denial of present pleasure, but this represented a strengthening of the black male stereotype rather than a commentary on the song itself.

Away from Broadway, the more serious songwriters added their contributions to the circumscribed imagery of black religion. David W. Guion's "Voodoo"[110] recalled the dichotomy of superstition and Christianity coexisting in black religion—the "proof" of superficiality that the coon song had used to great comic effect. Dramatic treatment for the concert hall rather than less pretentious media only intensified the demeaning image of the wide-eyed black as he sang:

> De air am full o' tings
> Wid wings, m-m-m
> De eyes ob snakes an' bats
> An' rats—m-m-m
> Am some po' sinner's soul turned col',
> Chained t' de Debble in de Debble's own hole,
> Longin' fo' t' git out an' shout.

> A voodoo gal knows how t' he'p 'em,
>   How t' he'p 'em break up dat spell,
> A voodoo gal knows how t' he'p 'em,
>   How t' he'p 'em git out ob hell.
> A voodoo gal knows how t' free 'em
>   From de ragin' fires Biblical,
> A voodoo gal knows how t' free 'em,
>   But dey got t' he'p a voodoo gal.

Lily Strickland's "Run On Home"[111] also dealt with black superstition. The imagery of the black's fear of death and graveyards is the theme of this song. Its chorus contains what might be considered the white threat—obviously far more real than that of the "graveyahd rabbit," who says:

> Run on home, nigger, run on home!
> Run on home, nigger, run on home!
> Run on home, nigger, run on home!
> You bedder keep a-runnin' on home!

Robert MacGimsey, mentioned earlier, was unquestionably sincere in his effort to bring authentic black expression to the public; his publishers claimed that he came "closer in his songs to the Negro's 'natural' mode of rendition than any other composer."[112] It is true that MacGimsey encumbered many of his songs with forewords, pronunciation guides, footnotes, and directions for performance, but it is equally true that he perpetrated and perpetuated great absurdities concerning black religion. MacGimsey assumed, for instance, that "twisting of the text" was characteristic of black preaching; he also created the impression that his songs were "collected" first-hand, a rather irresponsible claim that he never refuted.

Clothed in the comforting assurance of white respectability, many of MacGimsey's songs challenged the popularity of the commercially inspired Broadway products. Introduced and featured by Thomas L. Thomas, his "Shadrack" became a minor classic of popular music. This catachrestical sermon is more than merely a continuation of the pseudo-spiritual, it is evidence of the potential of an idea exploited by one familiar with the subject and, at the same time, aware of a public receptiveness. MacGimsey was acquainted with black music through his Southern childhood; his shrewd assessment of his material and his public could have resulted in a more significant, or even scholarly, contribution to knowledge of black expression—he chose, rather, the profitable low road.

"Shadrack" is written in a dialect so thick that an accompanying translation is needed to understand the words. For all the effort expended by MacGimsey, however, the text remains unconvincing:

> Thah was three chillun frum nuh lan' uv Isriel,
>   Shadrack, Meshack, Abednego,
> An nay took a trip into the lan' uv Babylon,
>   Shadrack, Meshack, Abednego.
> Nebucudnezza wus uh King uv Babylon,
>   Shadrack, Meshack, Abednego,
> He took a lot uh goal an' e made an idol,
>   Shad (noisily inhale, exhale) rack (noisily inhale, etc.)

MacGimsey continued to present himself as an expert in black music throughout the thirties. Notes accompanying the songs had a ring of authority about them, partly because MacGimsey arrogated unto himself an attitude, common among white Southerners, that he was privy to the innermost feelings of the Southern black. Wholehearted acceptance of his "authority" was a mark of the gullibility of Northern publishers and the public.

The explanatory notes to MacGimsey's "Land Uv Degradashun"[113] include his opinions concerning the general characteristics of the spiritual as well as a lengthy note concerning the song in hand. The general directions flatly warn: "When Negro spirituals are being sung with the real native inflections, the melody should not be played on the piano or any other accompanying instrument if the best effect is desired." This type of information, disregarding its rather unclear meaning, is well enough; but the directions for singing "Land Uv Degradashun" itself seem to presume too much when they tell the performer: "Bear in mind that Pharaoh and his army represent the Devil and all that is evil in the mind of the Negro. . . ." While commentary such as this might be needed for a correct interpretation of the song, there is yet another view possible: the paternalistic white Southerner finds it difficult to admit that there might be something about the black that he does not know.

MacGimsey became more adventuresome in his commentary in some of his later songs; "Daniel In The Lions' Den"[114] suggests that "the singer sit down, pat his feet in rhythm and sing the melody against the beat just as the old Negroes sang. Syncopations come easily this way, for that is how they were born in Negro music." MacGimsey's simplistic explication could have saved musicologists hours of study, had they but known!

Imagery of the black child during this period continued to flourish, although without significant change. Older themes were reworked, and occasionally new interpretations attempted, as in *Topsy and Eva*, adapted by Catherine C. Cushing from Harriet Beecher Stowe's *Uncle Tom's Cabin* and starring the Duncan Sisters. The imagery of this production centered around the subject of childhood, particularly the black-white relationship of Topsy and Eva, which was pictured as one of ineffable love. The child imagery that had grown from Stowe's novel, the unbelievably pure white child contrasted with the illiterate and mischievous black child, was too far removed from the "mammy" imagery of the times to be wholeheartedly accepted, however.

It was the lullaby of the "mammy" that dominated the imagery of the black child during this period and, incidentally, culminated in Gershwin's famous lullaby, "Summertime." Most lullaby treatments were harldly equal to "Summertime," excepting perhaps George H. Clutsam's "Ma Curly-Headed Babby," characterized by its composer, even at this late date, as a "Plantation Song." The typical lullaby, regardless of whether written by an expert or a mere formula writer, was still the cliché-ridden musical atrocity that seemed to have a permanent place as a Tin Pan Alley type.

In 1921, Haven Gillespie and Egbert Van Alstyne had produced "Honey, Dat's All,"[115] in which the black child is presented as:

> Jes' a little honey bee
> Buzzin' 'roun' yo' mammy's knee,
> Black and inky,
> Haid so kinky,
> Sweet as yo' can be,
> Angels brought yo' in da night,
> Done forgot to make yo' white.

By 1933, Hoagy Carmichael had corrected, at least in his title, the angels' oversight with his "Snowball":[116]

> Your two hands and feet are jes' as black as tar,
> But don' you cry, why say:

> The good Lord said He used an apple dumplin'
> To make your head,
> You know that's really sumpin'

Numerous songs were written on the food predilections attributed to the black child: "Cawn Bread"[117] by Thekla Hollingsworth and Jacques Wolfe is little more than a menu of so-called "soul food," while Wolfe's "adaptation" of "Shortnin' Bread"[118] has become one of the classics of the type.[119]

An example of the "scare lullaby," in which the black child is frightened to sleep, is furnished by "Li'l Black Nigger":[120]

> Li'l black nigger hide yo' head, um! um!
> Snuggle yo' self up in dat bed, um! um!
> Make out like yo' is pow'ful sick
> Else de witch gwine come right quick
> Carry yo' off on her ol' broom stick, um! um!

Playfulness of the black child was the theme of "Kinky Kids' Parade"[121] by Gus Kahn and Walter Donaldson:

> Hear the root-toot-toot-toot
> Of a secon-handed flute;
> That's Mammy Jinny's little picaninnies,
> My they're cute!
> Kinda drowsy from the heat,
> But their weary little feet,
> Gotta keep on steppin' lively
> When they hear that big drum beat.

"Pickin' On Your Baby"[122] was an attempt to evoke pity for the black child as a victim of racial discrimination. The lachrymose text of Paul V. Reynolds, set to the doleful melody of Billy James, converted a very real problem into the same limp-handed lamentation style that had so weakened the Abolitionists' efforts before the Civil War. It is not surprising that, having recognized an existing evil, the composer foiled his own exposition of it through the ubiquitous stereotyping of his characterization:

> "Mammy why?" said Pickaninny,
> Crying to his mammy Jinny

"Do the white boys pick on me—
Tell me why they never let me be—
And I must not play in their yard,
Ain't I just as nice as they are?
They won't let me in their games,
And they call me names—

　Are they pickin' on your baby,
　'Cause I'm a 'pickaninny rose'
　Mammy don't they know
　That they should not treat me so—
Don't they know that ev'ry dark cloud
Inside is silv'ry lined.
Mammy why are they pickin' on me all the time—
Won't you tell them all about me;
Ain't I the sweetest rose that grows
That's what you said and I suppose you know,
Now ain't that so?
Day by day in ev'ry way when they get together,
They go from bad to worse instead of getting better,
Are they pickin' on your baby,
'Cause I'm a pickaninny rose.

Mammy please just tell your Sammy,
Ain't I sweet as choc'late candy?
When I stay where I belong
Even then there's always something wrong—
You know why, but you won't tell me,
Don't you cry, for that won't help me;
They don't take me where they go
And I want to know—

　Are they pickin' on your baby (etc.).

Amid all the misrepresentations of the black in songs that flooded the twenties and thirties, it was inevitable that a few composers rebelled against prevailing imagery. The "mammy" song, the "hot-cha" image of the black female, the persistent picture of the black male as inferior, black religion as a joke—none of this had any bearing on the true black. Either through realization that prevailing stereo-types were false and outdated, or through a desire to capture and represent the genuine black, some producers of entertainment began searching for ways in which to accomplish a better image. It should be stated at the outset that, while the movement was generally a failure, it was at least a gesture in the right direction.

The first significant rumblings of discontent with black imagery came from the Broadway stage. Motion pictures and radio did not lose their timidity until after World War II. All-black revues and musicals had, of course, been a staple item in New York all during the twenties, but the imagery was virtually a fantasy of misconceptions. In 1927, however, Oscar Hammerstein II and Jerome Kern created a sensation with their handling of black characterization in their adaptation of Edna Ferber's *Show Boat*. Not only was the black presented with some degree of sympathy, but that taboo of all taboos, miscegenation, was shown to be admissable on stage without a concurrent collapse of American societal values.

In spite of their best intentions, Hammerstein and Kern were victims of the years of conditioning that had preceded them. Joe and the male chorus singing "Ol' Man River" paint a standard picture that contains the bulk of white preconceptions of the period. There were grumblings from the black community over the opening words, "Niggers all work . . .," which was later altered to read, "Colored folks work . . .," and there was a still later version, primarily for radio presentation, but these were complaints over details; the entire song, considered rather revolutionary at the time, does not achieve the new imagery that was being sought.

Other songs from *Show Boat*, "Bill," and "Can't Help Lovin' Dat Man," were even less of a departure from type. "Bill," of course, was an interpolation intended for an earlier show, while "Can't Help Lovin' Dat Man" is essentially the imagery of the "bully" song presented in the manner of a sentimental ballad.

The success of *Show Boat* suggested that perhaps the way to portray the black on the stage was to borrow from other literary forms. Louis Gruenberg made an opera of Eugene O'Neill's play *Emperor Jones*, Michael Todd produced a *Hot Mikado*, and Billy Rose presented Oscar Hammerstein II's *Carmen Jones*, to name only a few.

Although Gruenberg's *Emperor Jones* is both dramatic and musically exciting, the casting of the white baritone Lawrence Tibbett as the Emperor Jones weakened the opera, especially when compared to the stage version, which included the far more credible Paul Robeson in the title role. The most notable feature of the *Hot Mikado* was the casting of Bill "Bojangles" Robinson in the title role; in other respects it consisted of little more than an excuse to put black actors and singers on stage to parody Gilbert and Sullivan with topical lyrics such as:

> Whenever I find things are not copecedic,
> In this domain of mine,
> I'll double the taxes, and frame up an axis,
> Between me and Father Divine. . . .

Carmen Jones aimed toward loftier heights; Hammerstein explained that his choice of blacks as his principal figures in his adaptation was not an "eccentric theatrical stunt." He further explains his methods and aims for achieving an acceptable opera in English, concluding with the remark, "If... I have desecrated a masterpiece, I can only say... 'I am sorry. I didn't mean to.' "[123] Hammerstein's crime—if his adaptation of Bizet's masterpiece may be characterized in such manner—is small compared to the outrage committed against the dignity of blacks. It is one thing to concern oneself with the propriety of borrowing a classic for popularization; it is quite another to equate the desire to present opera in English with a willingness to ignore the demeaning effects of stereotypical imagery, as in the transformation of the "Habanera" into "Dat's Love," which portrays Carmen as a black man-killer, or in changing the "Flower Song" into a trivial "Dis Flower," in which Joe (José) exclaims: "She ain' de bes'."

This white conceptualization of black speech and thought patterns is the worst aspect of *Carmen Jones* and other attempts to adapt white works to black characterization. The originals could survive such treatment, but the imagery of the black lost far more than it gained.

By all means, the most impressive attempt to use literary works as a basis for serious treatment of the black in music was George Gershwin's *Porgy and Bess*. Du Bose Heyward's novel, *Porgy*, served as a literary, dramatic, and musical inspiration for years before it was transformed into opera. And opera it is, whether critics agree or not.

Gershwin had proven his ability to transcend the Broadway musical stage with several serious works prior to his last and greatest work, *Porgy and Bess*, the technical deficiencies of which are certainly not of an order that would deny it a place alongside other operas.

It is not necessary to review the entire history of *Porgy and Bess* in order to determine its place in the long evolution of the black theme in music; but one facet of *Porgy*'s development as a musical theme is rarely mentioned: it had been treated musically before Gershwin elevated it to opera.

Lew Leslie's *Blackbirds of 1928* contained a song, "Porgy,"[124] in which Bess sings her love for Porgy. This embryonic view of the main characters' relationship offered only a slight hint of later musical treatment of the theme, however, for none of the drama of the operatic version is present. It stands merely as another love song with a black character singing:

> I got a man now, I got Porgy,
> I understand now, I got Porgy,
> I'm thru wid by ways and his ways is my ways,
>   forevermore!

But Gershwin, affectionately though erroneously known as the "Beethoven of Jazz," drew upon his own repertoire of black imagery to recreate the characters in *Porgy*. A long line of songs utilizing stereotypical black subjects had been written by Gershwin before he created his masterpiece. "Swanee" had shown that Gershwin fully understood the "carry-me-back;" "Clap Yo' Hands" demonstrated his ability to distort black religion; "Liza" was a contribution to the black love song imagery, etc.

Not content to rely solely on this background, Gershwin undertook well-publicized visits to South Carolina to hear black singing at the source. It was not so well publicized that the primary purpose of these visits was to confer with Heyward on the progess and development of the opera. All in all, it can be stated that Gershwin was probably as well qualified to give *Porgy* its operatic treatment as any other white composer of the time. Hall Johnson put the matter fairly with his observation: "Nobody should have expected it to be a perfect Negro opera."[125]

In spite of the best of intentions, Gershwin perpetrated stereotypes in much the same way that well-meaning Harriet Beecher Stowe had done with her *Uncle Tom's Cabin* nearly a century earlier. The "happy darky," Porgy, cheerfully emulates Uncle Tom with his "I got plenty o' nuttin'."

The "no 'count darky" is faithfully reproduced by Sportin' Life, who undermines everyone's faith with his Biblical criticism in "It ain't necessarily so."

Hall Johnson considers "It Ain't Necessarily So" "so un-Negroid in thought and structure, that even (John W.) Bubbles cannot save it."[126]

Hardly any of the critics who reviewed *Porgy and Bess* bothered to comment on the fact that stereotypes constituted the major part of the characterizations. Commentary centered around the question of whether or nor a purely "American opera" had been achieved; only much later did Hall Johnson and others penetrate beyond this issue to point out that *Porgy and Bess* is a monument to the white conception of the black. Howard Taubman correctly assessed Gershwin's great work:

Thanks to his sincerity of emotion, Porgy and Bess endures despite its now outdated white man's view of the Negro as a simple lovable child of nature.[127]

Such was the imagery of the black in popular music as the United States entered World War II; troops were entertained at the beginning of the conflict with the latest boogie woogie and re-entered civilian life to the lively sounds of bebop. Black characterizations in song remained virtually unchanged, with the possible exception of a dearth of songs showing the black soldier as self-serving and cowardly.

The best efforts of Gruenberg, Kern, Gershwin, and others to unburden the black of his stereotypical image in music had to be counted a failure. Composers of the twenties and thirties were victims of the past as much as its inheritors; the climate for success in their endeavor called for a nonexistent social change. Fixed racial attitudes and the lack of intimate knowledge of their subjects made the sympathetic treatment of the black seem more a temporary aberration than the beginning of a movement. The black in song had been fixed by traditions too basic to break the mould.

Black entertainers and composers were trapped in the same net, desecrating their own images while at the same time showing an amazing capacity for influencing musical trends of the era. It was, after all, black music which set the mood between world wars, and no amount of copying, parodying, or outright stealing of black styles by whites could alter the essential character of the music.

Perhaps more significantly, racial barriers between white and black entertainers began to crumble as a result of the demand for blackness in popular music. The stage was being set for fulfillment of the observation of Langston Hughes and Milton Meltzer:

... in the profession itself it is generally agreed that there is less intolerance among performers than in any other field of American endeavor.[128]

Although still submerged under layers of stereotypical obfuscation, the black in song was slowly taking shape as an individual, but agonizing social changes remained to be achieved before the whole man could be seen.

Chapter Ten

Executive Order 8802 and After

Blacks in America at the outbreak of World War II remembered all too well the indignities they had suffered during previous wars. This time, however, they undertook to forestall a recurrence of past discriminatory practices by acting early in the war to demand that white patriotic rhetoric be translated into acts of justice; no longer were they willing to abide in silence the edicts of segregation in the armed forces and job discrimination on the home front.

Under the threat of a massive black protest march on Washington, President Roosevelt in 1941 issued Executive Order 8802, which stipulated that "there shall be no discrimination in the employment of workers in defense industries because of race, creed, color or national origin. . . ." This, of course, did not end the unfair treatment of blacks, but it did represent a substantial gain over Wilsonian policies of World War I.

Racial violence marked the entire war, yet blacks in uniform demonstrated the same valor they had shown in earlier wars. But it was not until World War II was over that President Truman ordered integration within the armed forces. The significant factor during the war was the conviction among blacks that they would never again settle for the second-class citizenship that had been their lot since Emancipation. However long and bloody the struggle, the opening shots in the fight for equality began in earnest and, more importantly, began to show signs of success during World War II.

In the main, white America went to war singing songs reminiscent of earlier wars: syrupy sentimental songs bemoaned the necessary separation from home and loved ones; a grimly determined patriotism promised ultimate victory; humorous songs attacked the enemy as well as the hardships of life in the armed forces. What was conspicuously absent was the body of song of previous wars in which the black was pictured as cowardly and lacking in true patriotism.

Blacks, for their part, produced their own distinct body of song separate from that of whites, just as they had in the past. These songs, the so-called "race songs," were made by blacks for blacks and were listed in the back pages of the record catalogs, whereas the songs that whites had long associated with the black were listed up front with the other white titles.[1]

Black influence remained strong in the white music, however. Blues and boogie-woogie flourished alongside the more relaxed style of swing. Black vocal groups, such as the Mills Brothers and the Golden Gate Quartette, sang songs with little relationship to race.

But it was not easy for America to alter its racial stereotypes simply on the strength of Presidential edict. Nor was there a sudden and universal change of heart. The United States had, for once, entered a war under quite unfavorable conditions; a new scapegoat, the enemy, pushed the black into the background as a target for attack in song for the moment. Minimized, but not forgotten, black imagery in song reverted to older "verities": "Dixie, Mother and You" types were dusted off and sung again rather than significantly producing new and original types. Black characterization retained all the demeaning qualities of the past treatments despite a reduced output of songs during the forties and fifties.

Minstrelsy, declared officially dead since the turn of the century, lived on as a favorite form of amateur entertainment. It had been kept alive after World War I through numerous publications of songs, skits, and directions for production of minstrel shows. None of these collections, or folios, as they were sometimes called, made the slightest acknowledgement of the demeaning nature of the genre until the early fifties. The attitude of the pre-war folio publishers is expressed in *The World's Best Complete Minstrel Folio:*[2]

We wish to impress upon you that the material contained in this book is suitable for the home, church, socials, theatre or any form of entertainment.

By 1953 the attitude had changed to the extent that Fred Hillebrand's *Burnt Cork & Melody, A New Minstrel Folio* cautioned users that:

All dialect has been omitted from the script of "Burnt Cork and Melody." It may be used at the director's and cast's discretion, but it is respectfully suggested that anything offensive or derogatory be carefully omitted.[3]

This change, in essence, is that which affected portrayal of the black in popular music from World War II through the fifties. Society was under pressure from a more militant black threat as the rhetoric that had served to keep him in a subservient position in the past began to sound unconvincing, even to large numbers of whites. Popular songwriters responded by reducing the flood of songs on black subjects and by slowly diminishing the ego-maiming quality of texts. It must be remembered, however, that it took two decades of bitter, and often confused, soul-searching by composers, lyricists, and publishers before there was even an acknowledgement that the overwhelming majority of songs on black subjects *had* desecrated the image of blacks over the centuries.

The black point of view was stated at the outset of World War II. Andy Razaf, Eubie Blake, and Charles L. Cooke collaborated to produce "We Are Americans Too,"[4] in which Americans were reminded once more of the blacks' role in various wars of the United States.

Typically, white songwriters skirted racial problems at home, while citing freedom as almost uniquely American. Incredibly naive, "There'll Never Be Another War!"[5] recalled the vain hopes of World War I in calling upon all Americans to sacrifice heavily in order to " . . . wipe those Japanazis right off the map, because we wanna make sure, THERE'LL NEVER BE ANOTHER WAR," after which " . . . all the downtrodden peoples will be free from fear once more, because we wanna make sure, THERE'LL NEVER BE ANOTHER WAR." The American black was not mentioned as belonging to the downtrodden group.

By the end of the war, however, there were those who could see injustices in the treatment afforded the American black. Privately printed and never popular, "There Will Be No Colored Line"[6] showed that some songwriters remembered the black at home and, no matter how slightly, the attitude toward him was being changed.

Professional songwriters attempted to retain the basic stereotypes even after society had begun to discard them. Male imagery, for example, was plagued by the established figures of the dandy, the happy, singing darky, the savage and other types. "Prince Charming"[7] by Al Dubin and LeRoy Holmes is representative of the dandy imagery of the forties:

> Slick, doesn't miss a trick,
> He knows what it is makes her ticker tick.

> Slick, doesn't work a lick,
> Grabs himself a pick,
> Kisses with a kick.

The happy, singing darky imagery permeated a great deal of the song literature. From Walt Disney's film, *Song of the South*, came "Zip-a-dee-doo-dah"[8] which reassured Americans that everything was "satisfactch'll."

Food stereotypes, pseudo-philosophy, and religion continued to dominate a large proportion of black imagery in song. Songs linking the black to popular concepts of primitive savagery were written as late as 1949, when "The Cannibal's Menu"[9] made the protagonist the main item on the bill of fare. "The Hottentot Song"[10] by Brown Bolte, Harry Mack, and Jane Douglass had explained earlier:

> A Hottentot is not so hot,
> A fuzzy head is all he's got. . . .

Most song references to black preferences in food related in some degree to Dixie imagery, somewhat in the manner of the carry-me-back. In the main, these songs eschewed the sentimentality of the carry-me-back for a bouncy, lively approach to imagery of the lip-smacking, wide-eyed black anticipating the wealth of food offered by Southern mammies. Andy Razaf's "That's What I Like About The South"[11] is little more than a full menu of what is termed today "soul food":

> Fried chicken, nice and sweet,
> Cornpone and possum meat,
> Mince pie that can't be beat;
> THAT'S WHAT I LIKE ABOUT THE SOUTH.
> Pigtails and black-eyed peas,
> Hog Maw and cottage cheese,
> You eat much as you please!
> THAT'S WHAT I LIKE ABOUT THE SOUTH.
>
> Biscuits? (grunt) umph!
> You ought to taste the ones Aunt Jenny makes!
> Flap-jacks? (grunt) umph!
> Don't stand a show with Jenny's good hoecakes!
>
> Hot bread and turnip greens,
> "Fat back" and lima beans,

> They know what livin' means,
> THAT'S WHAT I LIKE ABOUT THE SOUTH.

"By" Dunham and Terry Shand collaborated on "Possum Song,"[12] a description of a futile possum hunt, and Dinah Shore featured Bob Hilliard and Dave Mann's "Down In Nashville, Tennessee,"[13] a rather nonsensical invitation to:

> Chick-a-ling-bone, come with me
> Down to Nashville, Tennessee.
> You'll find your kind of real home cookin'
> Why keep lookin'?
> Come with me!

Food imagery, intermingled with the pleasures of music or Southern hospitality, went hand-in-glove with accepted stereotypes, although the black was seldom mentioned in the song directly. Thus, it was not necessary to specify to which race the "happy people" of "Struttin' With Some Barbeque"[14] belonged; within the context of the lyric, the meaning was clear:

> STRUTTIN' WITH SOME BARBEQUE,
> Swingin' with the band;
> Like the happy people do,
> Way down in Dixie land.

Don Raye, writer of the lyric of "Struttin' With Some Barbeque," had another hit with a similar song, "Down The Road A Piece,"[15] for which he also supplied the music. This song was published with a spoken dialogue reminiscent of early minstrelsy:

> Spoken dialogue:
> 1st: "Hey there boy, what cha doin' around these parts?"
> 2nd: "Aw, I was just lookin' for a little excitement, like some Dixie, or some Boogie."
> 1st: "Oooh! Sounds fine!"
> 2nd: "You like that kind of jazz?"
> 1st: "Man, any body that don't like that, just don't like fried chicken!"

The song then describes a place where good boogie and "chicken fried in bacon grease" can be enjoyed, ending with the two companions

glutted with fine music and food, running over a cow in their automobile when they leave. This was black imagery without the ritual
blackface.

Cole Porter's "Now You Has Jazz"[16] from the motion picture
High Society is also permeated with black imagery without once
mentioning the black. Similar in design to "The Birth Of The Blues,"
Porter's song lists ingredients presumed to be essential to the jazz
style including instrumentation and the reaction to jazz in foreign
countries. Hardly an accurate musicological description, to be sure,
but filled with enough black connotations to make it clear to the
"gentle folk of Newport" that jazz was black music.

Black male stereotypes included the coon song bully figure, as
exemplified by "Stone Cold Dead In The Market,"[17] made famous by
Ella Fitzgerald and Louis Jordan alike. Having black stars feature
this song assured that the connection with black imagery would be
strong without the necessity of being specific in the text, which
described a wife killing her husband who beat her after coming home
drunk.

Laziness was a pertinacious theme in a large number of songs,
among which "Lazy Hoe"[18] by Juanita Roos and Mischa Portnoff
and "Sun Tan Sam"[19] by Diane Lampert and John Gluck, Jr. were
typical. Here again, evocation of the "Sunny South" imagery and the
stereotype of the black as inherently lazy are enough to identify the
subject of the songs as the black male, whether child or adult.

"Lazy Hoe" adopts the pseudo-dialect and the affected black
"cornpone philosophy" to reinforce its imagery. This is a direct
descendant of "Do I Do I Don't Do Nothing" of 1825 through the
great hit of 1933, "Lazybones,"[20] by the songwriting team Johnny
Mercer and Hoagy Carmichael. Such songs relied heavily upon food
imagery and the great effort required to produce food or wealth with
which to buy food. "Lazybones," for example, was unwilling to either
work *or* play as long as the supply of watermelons and chicken gravy
lasted.

"Sun Tan Sam" is more direct in ascribing laziness as a black
characteristic. The protagonist is a black woman scolding her lazy
mate for "Snoozin' in de hot hot sun" while the work piles up.

One of the greatest hits following World War II dealt with the
black chicken thief theme, again, without specifically mentioning that
the culprit was black. But it was unnecessary to do so, since the well-
worn imagery of black propensity for chicken stealing made the title,

"There Ain't Nobody Here But Us Chickens,"[21] clear enough in intent.

> One night Farmer Brown was takin' the air
> After lockin' up the barn with the greatest of care,
> Then down in the hen house something stirred,
> When he shouted "Who's there?"
> This is what he heard.
> You can believe it or not.
>
> There ain't nobody here but us chickens,
> There ain't nobody here at all—
> So quiet yourself and stop that fuss
> There ain't nobody here but us.
> We chickens tryin' to sleep and you bust in
> And hobble, hobble, hobble, hobble with your chin.

Black infidelity was the theme of "Is You Is, Or Is You Ain't (Ma Baby)"[22] by Billy Austin and Louis Jordan. The syntax and the pseudo-black dialect used in the song stamp the subject as indelibly black, as in the beginning of the chorus:

> IS YOU IS, OR IS YOU AIN'T, ma baby,
> The way you're acting lately makes me doubt.
> You'se is still my baby, baby,
> Seems my flame in your heart's done gone out.

"Sixty Minute Man"[23] by William Ward and Rose Marks is the 1950's version of the bragging, virile black, although once more there is no direct mention of the subject's blackness. The lyric of "Sixty Minute Man" was a bit too suggestive for radio audiences of the day, and a second "radio version" was included in the sheet music. Both versions, while equally steeped in black imagery that hardly ennobles the male figure, seem tame by today's standards. It is interesting to note, however, that the terms "rock and roll," in the original version, carried strong sexual connotations and were deleted from the radio version, while the invitation to adultery in the last four lines was not. The original lyric reads:

> Look-a here, girls, I'm tellin' you now
> They call me Lovin' Dan.
> I rock 'em, roll 'em, all night long;

I'm a SIXTY MINUTE MAN.
If you don't believe I'm all I say,
Come up and take my hand.
When I let you go you'll cry "Oh, yes,
He's the SIXTY MINUTE MAN."

There'll be fifteen minutes of kissin'
Then you'll holler please don't stop.
There'll be fifteen minutes of teasin'
And fifteen minutes of squeezin'
And fifteen minutes of blowin' my top.

If your man ain't treatin' you right,
Come up and see your Dan.
I rock 'em, roll 'em, all night long;
I'm a SIXTY MINUTE MAN.

Augustinian confusion seemed to dominate the antiseptic radio version; the deletion of what was considered offensive had the effect of making much of the lyric more suggestive of concupiscence than the original, even though the changes were slight.

Look-a here, girls, I'm tellin' you now
They call me Lovin' Dan.
I'm a killer, a diller, all night long;
I'm a SIXTY MINUTE MAN.
If you don't believe I'm all I say,
Come up and take my hand.
When I let go you'll cry "Oh, yes,
He's the SIXTY MINUTE MAN.

There'll be fifteen mintues of schoolin'
Then you'll holler please don't stop.
There'll be fifteen minutes to kiss,
And fifteen minutes of bliss,
And fifteen minutes of . . . (instrumental)

(last four lines as in original version)

Black religion seemed as unfathomable and elusive to composers of this period as it had to those of the past. Some composers tried to treat the subject with respect but were thwarted by gross misunderstanding of the black religious impulse; others destroyed legitimate spirituals through heavy-handed arrangements, while still others chose to regard black religion as comedy.

The arbitrary association of black Christianity and voodoo persisted in song. "Voodoo Spirits"[24] with lyrics by Della Hayward and music by Frank La Forge is an attempt to make an art song of outdated and thoroughly demeaning imagery of the superstitious black. Worse, the pseudo-black dialect adopted for the lyric is a throwback to some of the most degrading examples of minstrelsy. Too long to quote fully, the final portion of "Voodoo Spirits" illustrates the ease with which not a few composers reverted to earlier types when confronted with themes that required understanding they did not possess:

> Mah heart's so troubled mah head's turned white.
> Ah's scared in de daytime an' terrified at night.
> In all de dark co'ners
> Ah hear de awf'lest rappin',
> Chills run up mah back;
> Ah knows sumpin's gwine-a happen,
> Bats flyin' in de air, queerest noises ever'where.
> Oh Lawdy, it's de debbil,
> He's a-poundin' on de wall,
> I hear de cats a-cryin' an' a-yowlin' in de hall,
> Lemme be, lemme be,
> Ah's gwine to de ribber, ain't comin' back no mo',
> Fo' dere's Voodoo sperrits flyin' roun'.

"Similau,"[25] on the other hand, had the advantage over "Voodoo Spirits" in that it *sounded* authentic; in the absence of knowledge concerning voodoo and its music the steady beat of the drum and somber melodic line was accepted as a genuine expression of pagan religion. Inasmuch as this type derived from Latin America and claimed African roots, it was rarely questioned; yet "Similau" and other songs of the type were disseminated primarily through night club circuits, movies, and radio, hardly the settings for serious presentation of serious musicological discoveries. The fact of the matter is that these songs were the product of commercial songsmiths who had discovered yet another stereotype that could be exploited. In its ignorance, the American public relied upon an instinct that had been consistently misled, until finally there was no way in which slick commercialism could be distinguished from honest musical representation.

Frank La Forge never did arrive at the point where he understood the needs of post-World War II audiences for a new, but only slightly

changed, black image in song. In his devotion to the ideal of black art
song, he continued to rely on material that was hopelessly outdated.
His "Camp Meetin' Song,"[26] for which he provided both words and
music, harks back to the pseudo-spiritual of the 1870's as he struggles
to cope with the complexities of black religion. La Forge's confusion
is evidenced by the inability to focus imagery on a fixed point; the
characterization is actually neither black nor white in the lyric that
begins:

> Oh, dance for me, ye pretty little maids,
> As I strum my old guitar.
> The moon shines bright wid a kind er yeller light:
> It is camp meetin' night.
> Oh, Lord! Oh, Lord!
> It is camp meetin' night.
>
> But I see de good folks walkin' all aroun',
> An' I is afraid.
> I hear all de brethern singin' far an' wide,
> Singin' all de hymns on de old countryside.
> Dere a-singin' an' shoutin' an' dancin' all aroun',
> De old folks an' de little folks,
> Jes' listen to de sound!
>
> De music so sweet dat it stirs de soul,
> I feel de shivers thrillin' me:
> Goin' up an' down.
> Dey's running an' singin' an' jumpin' here an' dere,
> Wid all de good old gospel toons jes' fillin' up de air.
> An' I was alone, a shiverin' wid fear.
>
> De Debbil was comin' after me.
> Oh, Lord! Oh, Lord!
> I got religion den.
>
> Dere de young an' de old was a-singin' all dere toons,
> Dere voices loudly singin'.
> An' dey said, "If you ain't got religion in your soul,
> You better not stick aroun'.

Less pretentious treatments of the pseudo-spiritual included the
numerous examples that seemed to be an indispensable part of any
motion picture with blacks in the cast. "Glory Day" by Lee Robin and
Ralph Rainger provided a touching moment in *Tales of Manhattan*,
yet the temptation to inject "chicken fry" and "jubilee" into the song

as part of the assumed black concept of heaven could not be resisted and thereby reduced the song to mere trivia.

"Deacon" songs lasted into the forties, with such songs as "Deacon Jones" by Johnny Lange, Hy Heath, and Richard Loring.[27] Here again, the black stereotypical preacher was seen in familiar terms; the text is further reinforced by the cover illustration of Deacon Jones in his dress suit with a chicken leg in his hand. The expression markings include the tempo marking: "Tempo, Meetin' House."

This type of forced cleverness was beginning to pall, however. Many performers and publishers found this material out of step with the times and a distinctly embarrassing liability. In groping for alternatives, they hit upon the notion—hardly a novel one—that a more serious approach to the true spiritual style would bring satisfactory results. Most of these attempts were failures simply because the composers were culturally worlds away from the subject.

Larry Hooper sang "Hallelujah Brother!"[28] in all sincerity, but the song suffered from most of the clichés of the pseudo-spiritual and sounded at best a slick commercial product.

Arrangements of authentic spiritual melodies continued to attract the public. As in the past, few of the spirituals were improved by such tampering with their inherent beauty. "He's Got The Whole World In His Hands," adapted by Geoff Love,[29] was simply and effectively done, but in performance, the trickery of raising the key of each successive chorus one-half step became a cliché in its own right.

Needless embellishment, if not downright trickery, was the hallmark of many of the spirituals arranged under the collective heading of "Fred Waring Arrangements." These choral arrangements were not actually done by Waring but were sanctioned by him through performance by his group or use of his name for commercial exploitation. A common device was the syllabic accompaniment, or the use of "oo", "ah", or humming, as in the arrangement of "Let My People Go" (Go Down Moses).[30] Even poorer taste was shown in the arrangement of "Dry Bones,"[31] in which various percussion sounds were assigned the task of illustrating the different parts of the skeleton described in the text.[32]

Creditable arrangements, such as those by William L. Dawson, were less familiar, perhaps owing to their eschewal of imagery derived from popular song. Although the melodic interval of the augmented fourth in Hamilton Forrest's arrangement of "Rock De Cradle, Mary"[33] is uncharacteristic, the piece is done with serious intent and without the grasping for effect that permeates most spiritual arrangements.

The Dixie myth was given its greatest benediction by Walt Disney's *Song Of The South* produced in the forties. Uncle Remus's stories presented in animation reinforced an already strong image of a folksy, peaceful black Southerner who, as we have seen, had little on his mind except the celebration of each day with "Zip-A-Dee-Doo-Dah" trivia. The title song of *Song of the South*[34] paints the "carry-me-back" in familiar tones, while "Uncle Remus Said,"[35] written for the film by Johnny Lange, Hy Heath, and Eliot Daniel, distorts the Remus tales with devices such as having the hare lose the race with the tortoise because he dropped into "Barney's Place" for a drink before reaching the finish line.

This type of utter silliness was the culmination of years of treating the black outlook on life as though it were a joke; it was, of course quite an old subject for popular songwriters. Little effort was required to produce such songs during the forties and fifties, especially since the songwriters considered this approach to the black subject less demeaning. Serious objections could be raised against prevailing imagery of the black male or female, for instance, but pseudo-black pseudo-philosophy put songwriters beyond the reach of criticism—or so they thought. This assumption that blacks were an inherently happy, indolent people with a folksy, cheerful philosophical attitude toward life remained a stock characterization in songs of the two decades until the civil rights movement of the sixties revealed it as a stupendous lie.

One example, Edgar A. Guest's "The Callers," was set to music by William Ortmann in 1941 with the subtitle "Who's Dat Knockin' At De Do'?"[36] The protagonist refuses entry to "Trouble," "Worry," and "Discontent," but happily admits "Mister Smile," "Sunshine," and "Joy" into his life. Given this insipid characterization of the black, it is not difficult to imagine the shock felt by whites two decades later as the civil rights movement destroyed the "happy darky" image.

The film version of *Cabin In The Sky*, another distortion of black philosophy, contained a topical song, "Things Ain't What They Used To Be,"[37] reminding blacks that they could walk with pride since they were part of the armed forces of World War II and that change for the better was taking place. This contradicted actual conditions of the soldiers who, for the most part, were segregated just as they had been in civilian life. While in a sense the sentiments expressed in "Things Ain't What They Used To Be" were prophetic of change, any improvements in black life would have to be gained through bitter struggle on the home front after the war.

Cabin In The Sky reverted to a more commonplace type of black pseudo-philosophy with "Life's Full Of Consequence,"[38] in which Lena Horne and Eddie "Rochester" Anderson sang of life's being "full o' honey and . . .wine," marred only by "Dat ole debbil Consequence." This was closer to the accepted stereotype of pseudo-spiritual homiletics that the public was accustomed to hearing. Black and beautiful Lena Horne was, in the white mind, the perfect embodiment of black sexuality—enormously appealing yet untouchable. Eddie "Rochester" Anderson was the reincarnation of the Mungo figure who included elements of genial indifference to responsibility and homespun logic that exasperated the "boss" or "massa" figure. Together, Horne and Anderson assured the success of a song such as "Life's Full of Consequence."

Many songs of pseudo-black philosophy offered nothing more than bootless cries against the slings and arrows of outrageous fortune. "That Lucky Old Sun"[39] by Haven Gillespie and Beasley Smith is typical of generally sympathetic, but totally impotent, commentary on black life:

> Oh Lawd! Oh Lawd!
> I'm tired and weary of pain;
> Please lawd! Please Lawd!
> Forgive me if I complain.
>
> Up in the mornin' out on the job,
>   Work like the devil for my pay,
> But that lucky old sun has nothin' to do
>   But roll around heaven all day.
> Fuss with my woman, toil for my kids,
>   Sweat 'til I'm wrinkled and gray,
> While that lucky old sun has nothin' to do
>   But roll around heaven all day.
> Lawd above, can't you know I'm pinin',
>   Tears all in my eyes;
> Send down that cloud with a silver linin',
>   Lift me to Paradise.
> Show me that river, take me across

And wash all my troubles away,
Like that lucky old sun, give me nothin' to do
But roll around heaven all day.

During and following World War II, the search for fresh
approaches in popular song reached significant proportions; the endless repetition of themes derived from the twenties and thirties had
made both the musical and textual material of American popular song
thoroughly predictable and boring. The scramble for novelty inevitably led to borrowings from Latin American and Caribbean musical
styles. Thus, musical techniques of the songsmiths were immeasur-
ably enhanced, while the imagery of song texts remained largely
unchanged.

Imagery in these texts was unmistakably black; Americans could
not shake themselves free from the notion that all people south of the
border were "colored," if not black. Thus, the imagery of "Happiness
(Hoppiness)"[40] contains the elements that might be expected were the
protagonist a North American black. The setting made the principal
difference: rather than sitting by "de ol' cabin do'," the protagonist
sits beneath a banana tree, singing a song of barnyard philosophy
which holds that "ev'rybody's searching for happiness."

The extensive search for regenerative material in the songwriting
business was less successful when African sources were tapped.
"Skokian,"[41] a South African song by August Msarurgwa, was
provided an American English text by Tom Glazer. This text is a
preposterous blend of foreign musical idiom and homegrown stereotyping. Faltering under the pressures of centuries of prejudice, Glazer
could hardly be expected to portray a real African, and the lyric for
"Skokian" shows that he certainly did not:

Ho Ho—Far away in Africa
Happy, happy Africa
They sing a-bing, a-bang, a-bingo
They have a ball and really go Skokian.
Ho Ho—Take a trip to Africa
Any ship to Africa
Come along and learn the lingo
Beside a jungle bungalow.

The hot drums are drummin'
The hot strings are strummin'

And warm lips are blissful
They're kiss-full of Skokian.

Geoffrey North was no more successful with African influences than Glazer. His attempt to provide suitable lyrics for "Kwela-Kwela,"[42] a love song, resulted in:

KWELA! (Chi-boom, boom, boom!)
KWELA! (Chi-boom, boom, boom!)
Won't you offer your love to me!
(Chi-boom, boom! Chi-boom, boom, boom!)

At the same time, older, indigenous styles, influenced by swing and jazz, degenerated into utter silliness in the portrayal of male-female relationships. Derived from the black imagery of the twenties and thirties, many songs of this type made no mention at all of color; the blackness of the prototype was thus lost to the younger generation, for whom these songs had been written. But the subject of "Bim Bam Baby"[43] by Sammy Mysels is a direct descendant of the "Red Hot Mama" of earlier times. Her lover, the "Bim Bam Baby," is himself descended from the aggressive lover of the past.

The combination of foreign and indigenous styles, with input from folk elements both black and white, produced in the 1950's what has loosely come to be known as rock. At first, professional musicians and songwriters looked upon rock and roll as a passing fad, but to teen-agers, to whom this new expression was directed, it was the embodi-ment of everything they stood for. In a remarkably short time, rock dominated the musical scene and drove older established musical traditions into the background.

Dances accompanying the various stages of rock developed into solo performances; no longer did couples embrace or even touch. Lyrics of the songs reflected this separation, which could be charac-terized as the alienation of youth from the so-called Establishment. It also reflected the social turmoil that was just around the corner for Americans.

The changing status of women was also reflected in rock. The female was rapidly losing her image of helplessness; the stereotype of the lily white princess, which began a long process of erosion in the twenties, finally died in the sixties. The female is dominant—albeit ridiculously pictured—in "She Say (Oom Dooby Doom)"[44] in which the male protagonist follows her every whim. By the end of the seventies, however, she would be the independent, self-reliant person of "I Am Woman"[45] and many other songs.

The male, on the other hand, was pictured in rock as impotent much of the time; he often reverted to self-pity in attempting to rationalize his shortcomings. "The Great Pretender"[46] by Buck Ram is typical:

> Oh, yes, I'm the great pretender,
> Pretendin' I'm doin' well;
> My need is such, I pretend too much,
> I'm lonely, but no one can tell.

The male was hopelessly torn between love and hatred for an imposing female figure. With such beginnings as "Caldonia,"[47]

> CALDONIA! CALDONIA!
> What makes your big head so hard?
> But I love you, love you just the same.

through the irreverent "I Want To Be Evil,"[48]

> I want to be evil, I want to spit tacks,
> I want to be evil, and cheat at jacks,
> I want to be wicked, I want to tell lies,
> I want to be mean, and throw mud pies. . . .

and "The Cajun Queen,"[49]

> She kinda breezed into town from New Orleans,
> Said, "Boys, I'm Big John's CAJUN QUEEN.
> I didn't come here to argue or waste anybody's time,
> I just come to get my man from your dirty old mine,
> 'Cause he moves me!"

to "Venus,"[50]

> Her weapons were her crystal eyes
>   making ev'ry man mad.
> Black as dark night she was,
>   got what no one else had.

the black female imagery was overwhelming in its aggressiveness by the time it reached the rock era. Male reaction to such imagery in song was often feeble retreat to earlier stereotypes. "Watermelon Man"[51] by Gloria Lynne and Herbie Hancock associated the plump watermelon with suggestions of sexual prowess in the male subject:

> Oh, Watermelon man, Ah! Watermelon man,
> 'Cause he's got the best watermelon
> He's a real good watermelon man.
> Ev'rybody dig watermelon man.
>
> Oh! Watermelon man, Ah! Watermelon man,
> They are just as round as they can be;
> Make you almost want to eat the seeds.
> Ev'rybody dig watermelon man.

Woman's fickleness was thrown back at her accusingly in "Step Down, Brother, Next Case!"[52]

> You told me you loved me, baby,
> You told me you'd be true;
> But tell me how come baby,
> I saw you with somebody new?
> STEP DOWN, BROTHER, NEXT CASE! Yeah,
> STEP DOWN, BROTHER, NEXT CASE!

In times past, such give-and-take imagery had sufficed to satisfy commonly held attitudes toward blacks, but the 1960's found these responses sadly lacking and, indeed, even damaging. Black self-respect, one of the major objectives of the civil rights movement, required an imagery in song that was a more accurate reflection of the true black; it is fitting that this need was answered not by commercial songwriters, but by black composers, joined later by a newer, more aggressively concerned group of whites. Starting with "Keep The Faith, Baby,"[53] sung by Brook Benton, blacks made it clear that for them, at least, the old black image was dead; they at last announced that those blacks in the entertainment business would henceforward try to shake the image of the inferior black, happy to accept whatever fate decreed by white America. From this time on, he would:

> Stand up tall,
> Face it all. . . .

Perhaps the best song of this type was James Brown's "Say It Loud—I'm Black and I'm Proud."[54] The message and tone of the song is unmistakeable:

> Say It Loud: I'm Black and I'm Proud:
> Say It Loud: I'm Black and I'm Proud:
> Some people say we got a lot of malice,
> Some say it's a lot of nerve,
> But I say we won't quit moving
> Until we get what we deserve.

The mood of this song fit the events of the day far better than any commercial product had so far. It was instantly recognized that this was a type that appealed to current audiences. It was not the older "Establishment" that had to be appeased any longer; the young constituted the listening audience, sang the songs, and bought the recordings. Older Americans, with all their prejudices, were simply bypassed in the new music; even the established publishers lost ground through their inability to grasp the mood of the times and alter their prejudices accordingly. The publishing industry began to move from New York to such unlikely spots as Nashville and Los Angeles.

"A Natural Man" by Sandy Brown and Bobby Hebb came from the Hollywood publisher, Beresofsky-Hebb (1971), and proclaimed the self respect of black manhood; from Nashville songs such as "Buffalo Soldier"[55] came as a shock to those who had seen the South as unbending and even rabid in its racism; yet from a former stronghold of the Confederacy now came:

> When are they gonna call, call you a man?
> Yeh, tell me
> When are they gonna call, call you a man?
> I wanna know
> When, oh, will they call, call you a black man,
> A white man, call you a yellow man, for goodness sake,
> Nothin' but a fellow man.

A clearer perspective on the change in attitudes can be gained through comparison of the handling of a specific subject: Bill "Bojangles" Robinson, the fabulous entertainer of pre-war stage and motion pictures, was himself often the subject of song. He had demon-

strated his talents, in the main, in ways that satisfied the white
expectations of what the black entertainer should be—much as had
Bert Williams. In the thirties, whites expressed their approval of
Robinson's capitulation to stereotype by singing:

> Oh! Bojangles of Harlem, you dance with such hot stuff!
> Young folks love you in Harlem, they say you've got stuff!
> Tough guys rumba out of poolrooms,
> And kids start "Truckin' " out of schoolrooms.
> Oh! Bojangles of Harlem!
> The whole town's at your heels![56]

By contrast, in the sixties, "Bojangles" was seen as a tragic figure,
exploited and cast aside, in the wistfully beautiful "Mr. Bojangles":[57]

> I knew a man Bojangles and he danced for you,
> In worn out shoes.
> With silver hair, a ragged shirt and baggy pants,
> The old soft shoe.
> He jumped so high, jumped so high,
> Then he lightly touched down.
>
> I met him in a cell in New Orleans
> I was down and out.
> He looked at me to be the eyes of age
> As he spoke right out.
> He talked of life, talked of life,
> He laughed, slapped his leg a step . . .
>
> He said his name, Bojangles,
> Then he danced a lick across the cell.
> He grabbed his pants a better stance
> Oh he jumped up high.
> He clicked his heels.
> He let go a laugh, let go a laugh. . . .

This imagery was light years away from that of "Jim Crow" of
minstrelsy; it represents a totally fresh approach to the black in song.
This change in attitudes could be found on the stage as well.

From the blackface inanities of Al Jolson, Eddie Cantor, and the
like, the decades following World War II witnessed a change in the
presentation of black characterizations; performers such as Richard
"Lord" Buckley, a white nightclub entertainer, began searching in

earnest for honest ways in which to deal with the black subject. Buckley could—and did—perform black characterizations in all-black clubs; however, he never wore blackface and never belittled his subject.

The new attitudes created inexplicable confusion in the ranks of older songwriters, performers and, in no small measure, in their audiences. Taught through centuries of conditioning to regard black as ugly, evil, or comic, America was unprepared for such songs as "Black is Beautiful":[58]

> Black is so beautiful it makes you cry.

In the past, audiences had rejected such imagery, as in "She's Black, But That's No Matter" or "To A Brown Girl Dead,"[59] the lovely poem of Countee Cullen set to music by Magaret Bonds. But given the new social situation, "black" became a term that demanded attention and respect.

It was not as though the older generation of popular song producers and their audiences were moral imbeciles in their confused efforts to understand what amounted to a cultural revolution taking place around them; there simply had been nothing in the known history of American popular song which would indicate that the sixties would spawn an entirely new conceptualization of the black image in song. This new breed was having no part of the "Establishment" rhetoric of freedom and equality when, in fact, there were millions of Americans who were anything but free or equal.

Even beyond the question of hypocrisy in the old rhetoric, the younger generation seemed to be groping for a solution to the question Emerson posed in his *Nature*: Why should we not also enjoy an original relation to the universe? Thus, the issue became universalized into a concern with the brotherhood of man. As this concept expanded in the songs of the sixties, there arose the additional concept that man was destroying himself on his planet through his life-style of greed, corruption, pollution, and so on. This was heady stuff for popular song, but the younger generation seemed ready for a fight.

The new breed of songwriters saw a beloved America torn away from its most cherished ideals by the older generation—the "Establishment." They attacked bureaucratic resistance to change and became the mouthpiece for contemporary demands for freedom and equality without equivocation. Curtis Mayfield, in his "This Is My Country,"[60] came right to the point:

> Some people think we don't have the right to say
>   "It's my Country."
> Before they give in, they'd rather fuss and fight than say
>   "It's my Country."
> I paid three hundred years or more,
> Of slave driving sweat and whelps on my back,
>   This is my country.

Mayfield's song was not an exception; Roger Cook and Roger Mayfield proposed a worldwide solution in their "Melting Pot":[61]

> Take a pinch of white man
> Wrap it up in black man
> Add a touch of blue blood
> And a little bitty bit of Red Indian boy—Mm—
> Well, you've got a recipe for a get along scene
> Oh what a beautiful dream
> If it could only come true you know, you know,
> What we need is a great big melting pot
> Big enough to take the world and all it's got
> Keep it stirring for a hundred years or more
> Turn out coffee coloured people by the score.

This open invitation to participate in that most dread horror envisaged by racists, miscegenation, was the subject of several songs. Richard Adler's *Kwamina* (1961), a musical concerning the love between an African black and a white woman, anticipated the mood of the times, but only ran for thirty-two performances. "Nothing More To Look Forward To,"[62] from *Kwamina*, laments the ill-fated romance:

> Nothing more to look forward to.
> Why were you so swee-eet?
> Nothing more to be living for,
> No longer can we meet, ca-an we meet.

Never again to lie so close
I can see myself in your eyes.
Never again to kiss good-bye
As the sun is starting to rise.

"Society's Child"[63] by Janis Ian is somewhat more to the point
and, incidentally, icily objective in its assessment of contemporary
society.

Come to my door, baby,
Face is clean and shining black as night,
My mother went to answer you know—
That you looked so fine.
Now I could understand your tears and your shame,
When she wouldn't let you inside,
When she turned and said,
"But honey, he's not our kind."
She says I can't see you any more, baby,
Can't see you any more.

Walk me down to school, baby,
Ev'rybody's acting deaf and dumb,
Until they turn and say,
"Why don't you stick to your own kind."
My teachers all laugh, the smirking stares,
Cutting deep down in our affairs.
Preachers of equality, think they believe it;
Then why won't they just let us be?
They say I can't see you any more, baby,
Can't see you any more.

One of these days I'm gonna stop my list'ning,
Gonna raise my head up high,
One of these days I'm gonna raise up my glistening wings and fly.
But that day will have to wait for a while
Baby, I'm only Society's Child.
When we're older things may change,
But for now this is the way they must remain.
I say I can't see you any more, baby,
Can't see you any more.
No.
I don't want to see you any more, baby.

In real-life situations, racially mixed marriages were becoming
commonplace. Many songwriters and performers began to practice

what the lyrics preached, often with gratifying results. The songwriter Norman Curtis and his black wife, Patricia Taylor Curtis, collaborated on several productions which reflected the racial situation in the United States during the time they were written. *Walk Down Mah Street!*, an off-Broadway musical revue, was given 135 performances at Players Theatre in New York, while their *Unfinished Business!*, another revue, ran seventy-eight performances at New York City's Theatre East.[64]

Unfinished Business! concerns white involvement with the civil rights movement in 1964, as seen in "But I Do,"[65] sung by a young white girl and a young white boy on the picket line:

> HE: When the sun is burning hot on my shoulders
> I could cool off in that all-white swimming pool
> I don't have to take this sign
> And take my place in line
> But I do. But I do.
>
> SHE: My neighbor thinks our school is next to perfect
> It's a place, she says, where only whites should be
> I don't want to intervene
> I don't want to start a scene
> But I do. But I do.
>
> Then she talks about those slum schools in ghettoes
> About their bringing Negroes to our school
> I don't want to lose respect
> For her age or intellect
> But I do. But I do.
>
> I'm always in one scrap or another
> When friends of mine blow the racists' horn
> I get so mad if I don't speak I'll smother
> At times I wish that I had not been born.
>
> When we pledge the flag in school every morning
> And the words liberty and justice fill the room
> I sometimes want to cry
> 'Cause we've made those words a lie
> And I do. And I do.

Songs of this type reflect the agony of youth concerned with much larger issues than are expected of those of that age; rather than singing of sweethearts and affairs of young love, these young hotspurs were plumbing the depths of racism, injustice, misplaced patriotism, and every other perceived social ill. The vaunted traditional values that had been collectively known as "the American way" had proven false in application, and youth felt that it held the answers for a return to the verities of the founding fathers.

While there were successes accruing to the youth movement of the sixties, the net result was failure in the attempt to alter society. Among the reasons for this failure were: the failure to accurately gauge the intensity of prejudices held by society; the failure to offer attractive, or even reasonable, alternatives to the system; and the failure to realize the self-defeating effect of violence. Burnings, bombings, and other activist measures, regardless of how justified the alienated youth might have felt in adopting them, repelled most Americans, who saw only the destruction of society, not the repressive governmental violence to which the activists were trying to draw attention.

Inevitably, there was a reaction in song to the new liberalism. Few in number, and rarely mentioning the American black, songs such as "Okie From Muskogee"[66] and "Welfare Cadillac"[67] embodied much of middle-class America's reactionary mood. According to a Reuters release, Merle Haggard, who collaborated with Roy Edward Burris on "Welfare Cadillac" and performed it, "tapped, perhaps for the first time in popular music, a vast reservoir of resentment among Americans against the long-haired young and their 'underground society.' "[68]

But the ugliest reaction against the ideals represented by the youth movement was "Battle Hymn Of Lt. Calley,"[69] a song which extolled a convicted murderer of women and children in the Vietnamese war. This sick, shameful song reflected the paranoia afflicting and dividing the country. It was not only an inaccurate, dishonorable attempt to excuse atrocities committed in the name of duty and a warped sense of patriotism, it attacked those trying to stop the senseless killing. As a measure of the moral bankruptcy of the country during this period, it may be fairly stated that in many respects the radical youth won their point easily.

The question of what such songs have to do with black imagery returns at this point, not answerable by simply stating that many of the same people used similar methods in demonstrating for civil rights and other causes. So many factors were involved in the developing events of the sixties that explanations tend to become oversimplifications that satisfy no one.

In style and substance, the protest of the sixties merged to become a broader reality in which racism was seen as an integral part of universal evil. Man could no longer be indifferent to his fellow man.

Thus, the black theme in song of this period lurks in virtually every musical commentary on contemporary society. From the early "If I Had A Hammer"[70] and the so-called Freedom Songs through songs such as "Give A Damn,"[71] the black image is present in the appeal for racial justice and an end to racial hostility—whether mentioned specifically or not.

Hal David and Burt Bacharach, in their "What The World Needs Now Is Love,"[72] speak to the same humanitarian ideals without mentioning race as they did in their "All Kinds Of People,"[73] in which race is the main concern:

> Light kind of people should feel compassion
> For dark kind of people,
> Should feel compassion and care for one another. . . .

Black imagery in this new music produced some truly startling results. Oscar Brown's recording of his "Bid 'Em In"[74] is a chilling re-enactment of the auctioning of a young black girl on the slavery block. Older themes, such as the Dixie myth and the "Mammy" figure, became confused ramblings.

Phil Trimm's "Mammy Blue"[75] mumbles over and over again the title phrase. Faltering and unsure of its imagery, this song demonstrates above all that it is totally out of place in the company of all the songs of protest.

Bobby Russell's "South,"[76] a song which attempts to keep alive the Dixie myth, characterizes the region as "the land of the free," repeating the phrase no less than five times, as though repetition would convince everyone that the repugnant lie was really true, and that all the cross-burnings, killing, and beating of civil rights workers, the searing hatred of integration and Federal power enforcing it—that all this was just bad press against the magnolia-scented South.

The older imagery simply failed to match the mood and style of modern music. It was as though an older ideology based upon what society needed to believe for its own peace of mind had come into conflict at last with reality—and reality had won.

The imagery of the plantation darky was only slightly more credible; "Black Hands White Cotton,"[77] a song of the Southern Alabama black field hand, ends with:

Lord, can't you hear me talkin' to ya?
A new day is dawnin',
A black night it turns mornin',
Black hands a-demanding some respect and understanding.
White man; black brother, hand in hand
    with one another, singin'
Glory, Glory Hallelujah!

The sentiment expressed in "Black Hands White Cotton" is
visionary on at least two counts: the Southern white had never indicated his willingness to join blacks (nor, for that matter, had overwhelming numbers of Northern whites), and in Mississippi, in the
summer of 1966, the black leaders had dismissed the theme of "black
and white together," making it clear that "black power" meant
exclusion of the liberal white from the struggle for black justice in
America.

Hurt, but undaunted by this black rebuff, white songwriters continued to attack the larger ills of contemporary society. One can
sense that the edge had been blunted in some of their songs, however.
John Lennon's "Power To The People"[78] is an almost predictable
response, as though repeating a rote lesson, in its halfhearted appeal
for revolt. By way of contrast, the black composer Eugene Record, in
a song on the identical theme, maintains the vitality of black protest;
his "Give More Power To The People"[79] comes directly to the
heart of the matter:

There's some people up there hoggin' ev'rything;
Tellin' lies, givin' alibis 'bout the people's money and things.
If they're gonna throw it away, might as well give some to me,
Yeah.
They've seen and heard of, but never had misery.

There are some people who are starving to death,
Never knew, but only heard of, and they never had happiness.
If you don't have enough to eat, how can you think of love?
You don't have time to care—so it's crime you're guilty of.

For God's sake, give more power to the people.

This jeremiad parallels the mood of the times closely, cutting
through the well-meaning but unconvincing laments on the black
condition by white composers.

While the new breed of black composer was shaking off the tremendous burden imposed by centuries of stereotyping and prejudice, many of the white spokesmen for civil rights reverted to the somewhat vague, limp-handed protest style of the pre–Civil War Abolitionists, producing ineffectual songs such as John Lennon's "Imagine."[80] In this song, the listener is asked to comtemplate living in a world without national boundaries or religion, the rationale being that without political or religious encumbrances upon humankind, there would be no reason for war or killing. Assuming that Lennon was seriously proposing a solution to contemporary woes of mankind, "Imagine" had to be one of the most visionary songs of the sixties; most protest songs were directed at changing rather than abolishing politics and religion.

The writers, both black and white, were at their best, however, when eulogizing the martyrs and heroes of their movement. "Abraham, Martin and John"[81] by Dick Holler is a quietly beautiful tribute to Lincoln, John F. and Robert Kennedy, and Martin Luther King. Reverend King, in many respects a more credible symbol of black aspirations than Lincoln or either of the Kennedys, was memorialized in individual works, among which "Didn't The Angels Sing"[82] and "Elegy For Martin Luther King" (for piano solo) are worthy of mention.

The tragic killing of four students at Kent State University in May, 1970 during a protest against the Cambodian invasion elicited the scathing "Ohio,"[83] a denunciation of the entire situation:

> Tin soldiers and Nixon's coming
> we're finally on our own
> this summer I hear the drumming
> four dead in Ohio.

The equally tragic and senseless killing of black students at Jackson State College in Mississippi around the same time has not, as far as can be ascertained, brought forth comment in song.

But the song which bludgeons the listener with its intense outrage against the endless brutality visited upon the black in America is Bob Dylan's memorial to George Jackson. Jackson, who became a revolutionary dialectician and leader of his militant fellow inmates at the state prison in Soledad, California, aroused violent and often conflicting emotions among those who felt that he was a prime example of the black in conflict with "The System." He, along with John Clutchette and Fleeta Drumgo, the so-called "Soledad Brothers," were charged with murdering John Mills, a guard at Soledad. Seven months later, in August, 1970 George Jackson's younger brother, Jonathan, attempted to effect the release of the Soledad Brothers through the kidnapping of a judge and others at the Marin County courthouse; the proposal to trade the hostages for the freedom of the prisoners ended in a bloody standoff in which both Jonathan and the judge were among the dead.

About a year later, George Jackson was killed by guards at San Quentin, who claimed that he had tried to escape—in full daylight view of his captors.

Jackson was greatly feared for his outspoken criticism and revolutionary attitude toward contemporary society and so was doomed to be consumed by that society. Dylan's song tells Jackson's story in the manner of an old ballad:

> I woke up this mornin':
> There were tears in my bed.
> They killed a man I really loved,
> Shot him through the head.
>
> > Lord, Lord, they cut George Jackson down;
> > Lord, Lord, they laid him in the ground.
>
> Sent him off to prison
> For a seventy dollar robb'ry;
> Closed the door behind him
> And they threw away the key.
>
> He wouldn't take shit from no one,
> He wouldn't bow down or kneel.
> Authorities they hated him
> Because he was just too real.
>
> The prison guards, they cursed him
> As they watched him from above,
> But they were frightened of his power;
> They were scared of his love.
>
> Sometimes I think this whole world
> Is one big prison yard,
> Some of us are prisoners—
> The rest of us are guards.[84]

This is the ultimate irony in the history of black imagery in song. The black is at last met face-to-face as a reality that demands consideration, yet the figure chosen represents one of the most feared and despised men in America. We finally meet a real black in song only to find that our preconceptions have misled us—he is not the happy, dancing, and stupid nonentity that we have been led to expect, but a tortured soul who somehow managed to maintain self-respect despite society's rejections. Small wonder that George Jackson became a symbol of the universally oppressed, at least in the eyes of many liberals.

Apart from the symbolism attached to George Jackson as a contemporary idol of black militancy, the use of the Jackson theme in music serves as a measure of the effectiveness of black imagery in song over the years. In Jackson, the cumulative effect of years of racism in song stands as a monumental infamy; we can hardly expect the reaction to three hundred years of misrepresentation of the black in song to be less than a scathing rebuke.

Appendix I

Charles Mathews and
American Minstrelsy

Tracing the antecedents of American minstrelsy inevitably leads to
the trail of the great English actor, mimic, and comedian, Charles
Mathews, whose two important tours of the United States (1822–
1823 and 1834–1835) had such a profound effect on the development
of low comedy on our native stage. Francis Hodge, in his *Yankee
Theatre* (Austin, 1964), characterizes Mathews as the paterfamilias
of the Yankee theatre and the progenitor of all native American dialect
comedy.[1] Hans Nathan concurs in Hodge's assessment of Mathews's
talent for mimicry of national types he developed through his travels;[2]
Scottish, Irish, Welsh, English, German, Dutch, and many other
types were Mathews's stock in trade and, combined with the famed
Mathews wit, the sketches he made from these types formed impressive insights into the comic nature of national characteristics.

Both Hodge and Nathan tread on rather dangerous ground, however, when they uncritically accept the Mathews types as "realistically conceived," particularly with regard to his conception of the
American black, which he developed from his first tour. Three centuries of white American misunderstanding of the black have rendered
the distinguishing of the "real" black nearly impossible. It remains
very much an open question whether Mathews, Hodge, Nathan, or
any white is—or was—qualified to speak with authority on the "real"
black. The white view of what the black was expected to be is
probably a more accurate description of the Mathews black.

Mathews claimed that his portrayals of American types, including
blacks, were based on fact. This practice may account for the
numerous instances in which pre-minstrel composers and performers
attributed their material to a black source without bothering to
substantiate in any way their claims. Later researchers tended to

accept these claims without demanding proof. This, in turn, obscured the true origin of the materials of minstrelsy and gave rise to a totally erroneous conclusion that the songs, dances, speech patterns, and dialect were an accurate reflection of the Southern plantation slave. A re-examination of Mathews's role in the formative period of minstrelsy may shed new light on the matter of authenticity and, at the same time, help dispel some of the misconception that has fed the stereotype of the American black.

A highly complex Charles Mathews is revealed in his *Memoirs of Charles Mathews, Comedian* (London, 1839), a sort of diary consisting mainly of letters to his wife and others. It would be difficult to imagine a personality less likely to find empathy with the egalitarianism and adolescent self-assertiveness of Americans than Mathews. Possessed of phenomenal self-esteem, the imperious Mathews was largely unprepared for the Americans, who, by his standards, were generally uncivilized. He put Americans into three categories: the "upper orders," or those whose behavior he could tolerate because it differed only slightly from the English; the "middle orders"—shopkeepers, landlords, and those we think of today as the great middle class; and the "lower orders," or those he found to be "inexcusably boorish."[3]

In his first letters to his wife, Mathews mentioned that he wished to be fair in his assessment of the American people and to avoid snap judgments in the manner of the Frenchman, Pillet, who had written a highly biased book on English manners after only a short stay there. Yet it took Mathews only six days to form his opinions of the Americans, opinions that were to remain essentially unchanged throughout the rest of his life.[4]

Mathews found that the "lower orders" must "necessarily prevent a European from being comfortable, if he has not made up his mind very resolutely to look on, laugh, and thoroughly despise." Innkeepers, landlords, waiters, coachmen, and all others meant to serve were "unendurable" and "educated to be insolent." Mathews found it inconceivable that these lower orders could with impunity fail to "bow, tip their hats, etc."[5] The servility of blacks was more to his liking: "I have not met with a white waiter, and (barring the *musk*) I am glad of it."[6]

Mathews arrived in New York harbor in September of 1822 but did not land there owing to an outbreak of yellow fever in the city. His first landing was made at Baltimore, from whence he made his way back up the coast through Philadelphia, performing before enthusiastic crowds. His arrival in New York coincided with cleanup operations following the epidemic. Far from being sympathetic or even superficially understanding in the face of the recent calamity, Mathews complained bitterly of the noise and the "want of cheerfulness and civility" of the "lower orders," which he found calculated to "produce a smile of thorough contempt rather than anger."[7] In this same letter, he elaborates the theme:

> It consists of a studied sullenness, the determination never to be civil . . . to a fellow creature, and not to bow, or say thank ye, to a person they know to be their superior. . . .

As for the barbaric behavior of Mathews's "lower orders," he was prompted to write: "If this be the effect of a Republican government, give me a monarch even if he be a despot."[8] The "upper orders," said Mathews, either liked it or were compelled to submit to it. He asked a prominent judge how he could endure such "familiarity" from the working classes and was given the prudent answer, "All such men have votes."

Mathews was enormously successful among the Americans he found so despicable. Eight nights' performances brought him $12,962, which he admitted was "superior to anything I ever did out of London."[9]

He confined his social life to the "upper orders" and began to avoid shopkeepers and other members of the "lower orders" as much as possible. He wrote to his wife in January of 1823, "The society here (the upper ranks—I have literally had no intercourse with any other) is quite delightful."

If his decision to confine his social activity to this so-called upper order is to be taken at face value, as he says it must, the validity of his observations and later representations of the American character should be questioned. Given the revulsion he felt toward the "lower orders," it cannot be said that he understood any part of the nation's drama so boisterously unfolding about him. There is no proof that Mathews's conception of Americans was a clear, unbiased appraisal. The hypercritical and highly sophisticated Mathews was incapable of accepting this rough new country. Instead of attempting to fathom the depths of this new situation, Mathews's own ego prevented his seeing anything other than mere externals. To credit his impressions of Americans as "realistic" is, under these circumstances, a tenuous conclusion.

Reality was less of a problem for Mathews than it has been for his later critics, however. He was merely searching for material suitable for inclusion in his act. His disappointment in not finding it is evident throughout his correspondence and reflects his inability to fathom the American spirit. In a letter to his wife, dated January 7, 1823, he wrote:

I have heard a black preacher, who was rather amusing. The pranks that are played in the "nigger meetings," as they are called, are beyond belief— yelling, screeching, and groaning, resembling a fox-chase much more than a place of worship.

The white man saw only the surface, as might be expected. Mathews's view of the black religious experience as "rather amusing" became an enduring stereotype in blackface minstrelsy and the pseudo-spiritual of Reconstruction America.

The "upper orders" did not provide Mathews with much comic material. He found them "more grave and humorless than the English—almost melancholy, in fact." But a young firebrand preacher, the Reverend Paschal Strong, delivered a sermon attacking Mathews, telling his flock that all their troubles, including the recent epidemic of yellow fever, were traceable to their fondness for Mr. Mathews's performances in America. The patent stupidity of this attack was a comic windfall to Mathews, who could not resist replying to Strong, thanking him for his free gift of comic material and promising to attend the following Sunday's service, if it should be on the same subject, "in order to study his style and action."[10] He signed his reply " . . . your obliged, angelic, yellow-fever-producing friend."

By February, 1823, Mathews was writing home that the search for comic material was his chief motive for staying in the United States, but he complained, "It will require all your ingenuity, all your fancy (and more than ever *I* possessed), to find real materials in this country for humorous entertainment." He lamented the "universal sameness of manner and character, so uniform a style of walking and looking, of dressing and thinking" which made parody so difficult.[11] In the same letter, Mathews found the American black, the "real unadulterated natives," equally without humor:

They never joke themselves, and they cannot see it in others. They would stare at *you* as a white wonder; and be perfectly amazed that any man . . . could possibly have collected so many jokes. . . .

This letter also reveals part of the Mathews's method for acquiring material:

. . . I feel perfect conviction that I am never amusing without I assume the manner of another, I know not how to suggest matter for comic effects out of mere observations.

These are telling points in attempting to understand Mathews's quandary. He had to know his subject thoroughly before comedy could be molded from it, yet he found the common American so personally repulsive that he could not bring himself to endure the close proximity necessary to perfect his imagery. As evidence of his confusion Mathews stated, " . . . though I have used the term *lower*, I hardly know who they are, where they are, or how they exist." He continues: "If I enter into a conversation with a coachman, he is Irish; if a fellow brings me a note, he is Scotch. If I call a porter, he is a Negro. I can't come at the American without I go to the porter-houses, and that I cannot condescend to do."

Mathews could not see the trees for the forest; all those Irish, Scotish, and even all those blacks, were the real Americans for whom he was vainly searching.

The black as a subject for comedy was about the only hope left to Mathews. He noted (*not* with the amazement claimed by Nathan) that "A very fat negro, with whom I met, driving a stage-coach . . . and urging his horses by different tunes on a fiddle, while he ingeniously fastened the reins round his neck" would "give an opportunity for the only costume which differs from that of our own country." He also comments upon the commonplace sight of black women dressed as Quakers, not noted, however, with excitement, but almost in desperation.

He says, "With respect to songs, I really fear that I shall hardly be able to suggest subjects. The only striking subject for a pattersong is the inordinate love of title; a remarkable instance of the weakness and inconsistency of these *simple* republicans." This love of titles, he goes on to explain, included all ranks of persons, who "are more ridiculously ostentatious of the petty titles that are recognized than any people under the sun. On every road, even at the meanest pothouse, it is common to call out, 'Major, bring me a glass of toddy!' 'Captain Obis, the segars and change for a dollar!' 'Why are we so long changing horses, colonel?' This was addressed to our coachman—a fact!"

But it was the landlord, not the black, who offered the strongest possibility of caricature. Great heights of scorn were reached in Mathews's disdain for this character, of whom he said, "I won't spare him an inch. He is . . . the most insolent rascal I ever encountered; he is the double distilled of those qualities I described as apertaining to the middle orders. Here I can *personate* to advantage. It will be my main stay, my sheet anchor." And so it was in the subsequent parodies of American life that Mathews developed.

This exceptionally long letter to his friend James Smith concludes with a partial account of Mathews's version of the American black's humorous possiblities:

I shall be rich in black fun. I have studied their broken English carefully. It is pronounced the real thing, even by the Yankees. It is a pity that I dare not touch upon a preacher. I know its danger, but perhaps the absurdity might give a *colour* to it—a black Methodist! I have a specimen from life, which is relished highly in private. A *leetle* bit you shall have. By the by, they call the *nigger* meetings "Black Brimstone Churches."

My wordy bredren, it a no use to come to de meetum-house to ear de most hellygunt orashions if a no put a de *cent* into de plate; de spiritable man cannot get a on widout de temporalities; twelve 'postles must hab de candle to burn. You dress a self up in de fine blue a cot, and bandalore breechum, and tink a looklike a gemman, but no more like a gemman dan put a finger in a de fire, and take him out again, widout you put a de money in a de plate, He lend a to de poor, lend to de Law (Lord), if you like a de secoority drop a de cents in to de box. My sister in a de gallery too dress em up wid de poke a de bonnet, and de furbelow-tippet, and look in de glass and say, 'Pretty Miss Phyllis, how bell I look!' but no pretty in de eye of de Law (Lord) widout a drop a cent in de plate. My friend and bredren, in my endeavor to save you, I come across de bay in de stim a boat. I never was more shock dan when I see de race a horse a rubbin down. No fear o' de Law afore dere eye on de Sabbat a day, ben I was tinking of de great enjawment my friend at a Baltimore was to have dis night, dey rub a down de horse for de use of de debbil. Twixt you and I, no see what de white folk make so much fun of us, for when dey act so foolish demselve, dey tink dey know ebery ting, and dat we poor brack people know noting at all amose (almost). Den shew dem how much more dollars you can put in de plate dan de white meetum-houses. But, am sorry to say, some of you put three cent in a plate, and take out a quarter a dollar. What de say ven you go to hebben? Dey ask you what you do wid de twenty-two cent you take out of de plate when you put in de tree cent? What you go do den?

Mathews also included what he considered to be authentic black songs:

I have several specimens of these black gentry that I can bring into play, and particularly scraps of songs, and malaprops, such as Mahometan below Caesar (Thermometer below zero) &c.

Song

Oh! love is like de pepper-corn;
　　It make me act so cute.
It make de bosom feel so warm,
　　And eye shine like new boot!
I meet Miss Phillis tudder day
　　In berry pensive mood;
She almost cry her eyes away
　　From Pomp's ingratitude.

O lubby brushing maid, said I,
　　What makee look so sad?
Ah! Scip, de brooteous virgin cry,
　　I feel most debblish bad!
For Pomp he stole my heart away,
　　Me taught him berry good;
But he no lub me now he say!
　　Chah! what ingratitude!

Disregarding the obvious flaws in Mathews's conception of the American black, it strains the imagination to consider this an authentic view. By his own testimony, Mathews was unable to pierce the surface of any American characteristic, much less the reality of the black, who was at the very end of the social scale as constructed by Mathews. It is not likely that the sermon was actually heard by him in one of the "Brimstone Churches," although Nathan maintains that it was.[12] One who could not condescend to frequent the porterhouses would hardly extend himself even further down the social scale to mix with blacks. Not only had the fastidious Mathews complained repeatedly of the "musk" of the blacks, his wife makes known in Volume IV of the *Memoirs* his great fear of crowds. His memoirs, so detailed in other respects, does not, in fact, mention a single instance of a visit to a black church, although there are suggestions of an awareness of them. Awareness does not necessarily mean knowledge or understanding, however.

Mathews states that the sermon was taken from life but does not elaborate on the point. Authentication for him rested upon the assertion that it was the "real thing," verified "even by the Yankees." Closer examination of the sermon reveals certain elements that are difficult to accept as typically Negroid: the repetitious "a" after certain words (it a, if a, stim a boat, etc.) has come to be accepted as the English form of Italian, not black dialect; discrepancies in certain words—both in usage and spelling—strain for comic effect (hellygunt orashions; no more like a gemman dan put a finger in a de fire, and take him out again; etc.); final "er" and "or" sounds, commonly dropped in attempts to capture black speech, are uncertainly handled by Mathews ("more" for "mo," "finger" for "fingah," etc.). The list could continue, but it is clear that Mathews's conception of the American black was not that of contemporary songwriters, particularly in his rendition of the dialect. Very little imagination is needed to visualize a poor Italian immigrant saying "stim a boat," or "lend a to de poor," or a German saying "ven you go." One can even imagine an Indian scout using the form, "meetum-house." All in all, Mathews's version of black dialect fell far short of realism.

Mathews himself acknowledged the impropriety of using religion as a platform for comedy, but neither he nor the other white comic songwriters who followed him imagined that the danger lay in the insult to the black; it was uncertainty over the reaction of white audiences that gave him pause. In this instance Mathews had good reason to be wary, for he knew that the emissaries of God took a dim view of the acting profession generally, and he, not being a particularly religious man, did not enjoy a perfect relationship with them.

But the racially-oriented religious slander exists in Mathews's sermon, whether recognized or not. Mathews's difficulty in finding suitable material for his act could hardly account for such a gross and tasteless travesty. Perhaps he felt safer in venting his scorn for

Americans in general by attacking the most vulnerable and helpless segment of the population; he more probably operated under the assumption that the black was incapable of intelligent worship of the white divinity. In any event, if we credit Nathan's contention that Mathews's rude sermon was "the very first stump speech,"[13] then it is Mathews who must bear the blame for having established the stereotypical black preacher and the catachrestical sermon that ridiculed any attempt by blacks to adopt Christianity.

Mathews developed two entertainments from the material collected in the United States. His *Trip to America* was presented in London on March 25, 1824, and his *Jonathan in England* opened in September of the same year. London audiences found both pieces amusing, but Americans were enraged. When he returned to the United States ten years later in 1834, he was met by placards "of the most abominable nature, inviting hostility towards Mr. Mathews. . . ."[14] One of the placards read:

NOTICE

We understand Charles Mathews is to play on Monday evening, the 13th instant. The scoundrel ought to be pelted from an American stage, after his writing that book which he did about six years ago, called 'Mathews Caricature on America.' This insult upon Americans ought to be met with the contempt it deserves. After using the most vile language against the "too easily duped Yankees," as he calls us, he thinks thus to repay us for our kindness towards him. But we hope they will show him that we are not so easily duped this time as we were then, and drive the ungrateful slanderer from our stage forever.

Mathews was deeply shocked by this rebuke, even fearing for his life on a few occasions at the beginning of his second American tour. He went out of his way to soothe the outraged Yankees and soon was able to write home to his son, "I have only time to say that all's well!"

But all was not well. America was greatly changed from his first visit. Old friends had forgotten him; others had died. Mathews himself had grown older and less resilient; the effect of coping with the inhospitable reception in New York took a heavy toll upon his health and spirits. He considered an early return to England and his wife, writing to her son, said, "He is not *ill*, observe—but he is *not well*." A month later Mathews wrote his son, "This *will not do*. I must *come* back—I am blighted. I cannot work."

Mathews and his wife departed for England on February 18, 1835, after having written to a friend, "This visit has destroyed all the pleasing recollections of the country . . . I congratulate you on the return of the Tories. I wish you could send all the Whigs here. I should like no better punishment than their being compelled to visit America in search of liberty."

Mathews never saw London again. His health was so poor upon arrival in England that he was confined to Plymouth, where he died that spring, on the morning of his 59th birthday.

There is little to gain by belaboring Mathews's confused conceptualization of the American black. He was so thoroughly bemused by Americans in general, as contrasted with other types he so successfully exploited, that he never knew how to approach the subject. Indeed, it is a serious mistake to credit his observations of the American people as anything other than those of a pertinacious Englishman on a par with Mrs. Trollope or Captain Basil Hall.

Appendix II

Method

This study of the imagery of the black in American popular music is based upon several premises that have currency among those concerned with the sociology of music today. Foremost among these is the assertion, best enunciated by Willi Apel in the *Harvard Dictionary of Music* (2d ed., Cambridge, 1969), that:

Musical types and forms . . . are greatly influenced by social forces, generated by and flourishing in response to particular social conditions and functional demands.

Another premise holds that there is a recognizable distinction between popular music and other musical manifestations such as folk music and serious music. Henry Edward Krehbiel makes the distinction between folk music and popular music in his *Afro-American Folksongs* (New York, 1914):

Folksong is not popular song in the sense in which the word is most frequently used, but the song of the folk; not only the song admired by the people but, in a strict sense, the song created by the people.

Both folk music and serious music, moreover, were—at least until the current decade—created for rather special audiences, limited to rather restricted geographical areas. Folk music pertains to the people who produced it; serious music, for all its universality, remains the special province of an educated elite. Popular music, on the other hand, aims at reaching the widest audience possible, regardless of social class or geographical location. Its prime goal is commercial success.

The continual search for success tends to make popular music more reflective of broad public attitudes than other musical types. The public demands support, not criticism, of its self-image in song. This is why producers of popular song are reluctant to advance songs that do not strike a chord in sympathy with public ideals of the moment.

Thus, in the complex web of cultural dynamics in America, popular music plays an important, although often unnoticed, role. It serves as an authentication of popular attitudes or, on occasion, as argument against them. It provides a forum upon which ideas can be publicly tested. Wide dissemination of popular music tends to unify public sentiment and to strengthen the immediate conceptions of the society from which it springs. The study of large quantities of the popular music of given moments of history confirms the thesis that popular music is a reflection of current attitudes, providing insights that are unavailable through other sources. Therefore, the study of America's popular music on the subject of black imagery goes beyond the pronouncements of scholars, statesmen, and others who wrote, spoke and even fought over the "black problem" throughout our history. Through examination of song texts, a better picture of public attitudes toward the black emerges. Additionally, sheet music artifacts can provide signs of attitudes held by those responsible for their production. These producers (authors, composers, publishers, and performers) revealed, often inadvertently, their low esteem for blacks through generally lower standards for the production of sheet music on black subjects. Musical and printing standards were generally lower than those obtaining for other types of sheet music; cover illustrations were often more degrading to the image of the black than were either the texts or musical settings of the songs; performers frequently delighted in having themselves outrageously caricatured in blackface to provide these cover illustrations.

The prime source for songs making up the sample for this study was the Sheet Music Collection of the Free Library of Philadelphia, with some 200,000 titles in sheet music, songster, and broadside forms. Known holdings of other large collections of popular music such as those in the Library of Congress, New York Public Library, and the British Museum were also used, as were several private collections of significant proportions, most notably the Kean Archives in Philadelphia.

Catalogs, advertisements, bibliographies, and special lists functioned to suggest other titles and as an aid in location of texts.

Valuable data was obtained from these sources, especially in those instances in which annotations were provided.

Some titles were included for their prominence in the history of American music. These songs, such as Emmett's "Dixie," or several of Foster's songs, could not be omitted from any study of the black image in music if for no other reason than to investigate the many testimonials to the effect that such songs enhance black imagery.

An estimated 4,000 titles made up the large sample of songs in which the black subject is either manifest or implied. A primary analysis of the texts of these songs provided a basis upon which to separate the examples according to various categories of black imagery: black male; black female; black child; religion; philosophy; politics; nostalgia for plantation life; and mixed and variant types.

These types were divided into historical periods roughly corresponding to the important stages of the history of the black in America. Added consideration was given to those social forces directly affecting musical forms and types. For example, both the anti-slavery movement and Reconstruction caused powerful reactions in song. Historical division was rendered easy upon discovering a strong relationship between such social forces and the several types and forms.

Within the categories historically arranged, a smaller sample of representative titles was chosen for the actual study. Popularity indicators (number of editions, variants, imitations, printings, etc.) became a factor in selecting this sample, but no attempt was made to "load" the sample by confining it to only popular favorites. It is obvious, however, that any study of popular music should include some examples that have achieved so-called "hit" status, since these, in many cases, are the very songs which reflect popular attitudes that are the object of this study.

Consideration of such functional demands of popular music suggested still another factor: the purposes for which many of the songs were produced. Research on the songs and their producers was compared with known facts of history in an attempt to determine when, how, and most importantly, why a particular type was produced. Here, it must be stated, the greatest margin of error among scholars became apparent: myths surrounding some important songs had been uncritically accepted and passed along to others who repeated the myths as fact not only in music histories, but in social histories as well.

It became necessary to re-examine these myths in the light of available evidence and common sense logic in order to determine their effect upon black imagery in the songs. The song texts themselves were analysed for clues which would either verify or disprove these myths. It soon became clear that discarding the invalid beliefs—the myths—concerning our popular song was to be a most difficult, thankless part of the study.

The smaller sample, some 750 titles, was selected as it related to sociological, geographic, psychological, economic, religious, political, and of course, racial factors during the periods covered in this study. Most of the various postures maintained by whites toward blacks are well chronicled throughout America's history; it was one of the purposes of this study to identify these postures within the song lyrics for comparison.

Theories of prejudice have been a major factor in this study, as have various theories of laughter and humor. Taken together, prejudice and humor have a definite impact upon the popular music of any given moment in history. It was the further purpose of this study to consider all these factors and to present them as objectively as possible, knowing full well that any such attempt is inevitably tinctured by the perceptions of contemporary society.

Analysis of the smaller sample was also devoted to specifics of popular attitudes: the use of preconceived dialects; textual patterns that recur in various songs of a given period; repeated misconceptions concerning blacks; illustrative exaggerations; all these and any other manifestations of racial attitudes were considered evidence concerning the black imagery in song.

In the final analysis, of course, the judgment was a personal choice. Every attempt was made to assure objectivity in selecting, analyzing, and presenting the conclusions of this study, yet it must be admitted that here, as in virtually any music criticism, the personal predilections of the researcher are manifest.

Notes

CHAPTER ONE

1. Charles Read Baskerville, *The Elizabethan Jig and Related Song Drama* (New York, 1965), pp. 314–315, 3, 113.

2. *Ibid.*, pp. 315, n. 2.

3. Lorenzo J. Greene, *The Negro in Colonial New England, 1620–1776* (Port Washington, New York, 1942), p. 16.

4. *Ibid.*, pp. 23–24.

5. *Ibid.*, p. 61. See also Cotton Mather, *The Negro Christianized* (Boston, 1706), p. 2.

6. Oscar G. Sonneck, *Miscellaneous Studies in the History of Music* (New York, 1921), p. 16.

7. Phyllis Hartnoll, "Negro in the American Theatre," in *The Oxford Companion to the Theatre*, 2d ed. (London, 1957).

8. Thomas Southerne, *Oroonoko: A Tragedy as it is Acted at the Theatre-Royal* (London, 1696), Act II, Scene iii, p. 243.

9. Both songs taken from *Plays Written by Thomas Southerne, Esq.* (London, 1774), II: 302–303.

10. Oscar G. Sonneck, *Francis Hopkinson and James Lyon* (Washington, D.C., 1905), pp. 125ff.

11. Herbert J. Muller, *Freedom in the Ancient World* (New York, 1961), pp. 195, 236, 247, 248, 261, 286.

12. Sonneck, *Miscellaneous Studies*, pp. 23–45.

13. Edmond McAdoo Gagey, *Ballad Opera* (New York, 1965), p. 215.

14. Sonneck, *loc. cit.*

15. *Pennsylvania Gazette*, Wednesday, April 16, 1767, as quoted in Sonneck, *loc. cit.*

16. Hans Nathan, *Dan Emmett and the Rise of Early Negro Minstrelsy* (Norman, Oklahoma, 1962) p. 20, cites the 1768 date, whereas Hartnoll, *op. cit.*, p. 565, gives the date as 1769.

17. George O. Seilhamer, *History of the American Theatre* (Philadelphia, 1888), I: 249–250.

18. Seilhamer, *loc. cit.*

19. Nathan, *op. cit.*, p. 30.

20. H.G. Sear, "Charles Dibdin, 1745–1814," in *Music and Letters*, XXVI (1945):61.

21. Sheet Music Collection of the Free Library of Philadelphia. The overwhelming majority of the examples are taken from this collection. Only those examples taken from other sources will henceforth be acknowledged.

22. Oscar G. Sonneck, *A Bibliography of Early Secular American Music*, rev. and enl. by William Treat Upton (Washington, D.C., 1945), p. 335.

23. *Ibid.*, p. 106.

24. The version cited is entitled "The Desponding Negro, A Favorite Song. Price 20 Cents. Philadelphia, Printed for Carr & Co. At their Music Store, No. 136 High Street. . . ." The 1793 date is given in Sonneck, *Bibliography*, p. 106.

25. *Songs of Innocence* (1789).

26. T.S. Grimshawe, ed., *The Works of William Cowper* (New York, 1868). The depth of Cowper's indignation toward slavery is further illustrated by the following extract from his *Charity*:

> Canst thou, and honour'd with a Christian name,
> Buy what is woman-born, and feel no shame?
> Trade in the blood of innocence, and plead
> Expedience as a warrant for the deed?

27. Sonneck, *Bibliography*, pp. 517, 202. See also Oscar G. Sonneck, *Early Concert Life in America* (Leipzig, 1907), pp. 218, 243.

28. Nathan, *op. cit.*, p. 6.

29. Nathan, *loc. cit.*

30. Nathan, *loc. cit.* Nathan cites the short title, "The Negro Boy," quoting "I sold a *blooming.* . . . " rather than "*guiltless*" Negro boy. Additionally, Edward Miller is named as the composer. The Moulds version is the better known setting of the song, although Nathan inaccurately maintains that it can only be found in *The Musical Repertory* (Boston, 1796).

31. Sonneck, *Bibliography*, p. 505.

32. Nathan, *op. cit.*, p. 13.

33. Published in *Proceedings of the Association for Promoting the Discovery of the Interior Parts of Africa* (London). A more complete account was published in London in 1799.

34. Nathan, *op. cit.*, pp. 6–7.

35. Benjamin Carr, "A Negro Song," from *The Musical Journal* (Baltimore, *ca.* 1801), II, No. 43:39.

36. Probably Charles Stokes (1784–1839). *Cf.* Richard J. Wolfe, *Secular Music in America, 1801–1825)* (New York, 1964), II:883.

37. *Danish and Norwegian Melodies*, selected by A. Anderson Feldborg; harmonized and arranged . . . by C. Stokes; the poetry translated by William Sidney Walker (London, 1815), pp. 47–49.

38. Francis Hodge, *Yankee Theatre; The Image of America on the Stage, 1825–1850* (Austin, Texas, 1964), p. 61.

39. Nathan, *op. cit.*, p. 46. Most folksong collectors do not attribute folk origins to "Possum Up a Gum Tree," preferring to cite merely the circumstances under which the song was found, listing variants, and so on. Botkin, in *American Play-party Song* (New York, 1937), does venture the guess that the song is "based on songs of folk and minstrel origin" (*cf.* p. 295).

40. See John A. Lomax and Alan Lomax, *American Ballads and Folk Songs* (New York, 1934), p. 238; Vance Randolph, *Ozark Folksongs* (Columbia, Missouri, 1948), Vol. II, p. 280; Newman I. White, *American Negro Folksongs* (Cambridge, Massachusetts, 1928), pp. 237–238.

41. See Appendix I.

42. Joanne Grant, editor, *Black Protest; History, Documents and Analyses, 1619 to the Present* (Greenwich, Connecticut, 1968), pp. 18–19.

43. Possibly Thomas Linley (1732–1795), or his son, Thomas Linley, Jr. (1756–1778), both of whom were prolific composers for the English stage.

44. Nathan, *op. cit.*, p. 10.

CHAPTER TWO

1. Nathan, *op. cit.,* p. 34; pp. 34–35 footnote.

2. Harry Dichter and Elliot Shapiro, *Early American Sheet Music; Its Lure and Its Lore* (New York, 1941), p. 51. See also Nathan, *op. cit.*, pp. 35–36. The version taken for this study is found in *The Negro Forget-Me-Not Songster* published by Turner and Fisher (Philadelphia, *ca.* 1850), pp. 211–212.

3. Title actually reads: "Back Side of Albany."

4. Nathan, *op. cit.*, p. 35.

5. *The Nightingale; or, Musical Companion, Being a Collection of Entertaining Songs* (New York, 1814), pp. 67–68.

6. See Richard J. Wolfe, *Secular Music in America, 1801–1825*, 3 vols. (New York, 1964), 2:635 (item 6484).

7. S. Foster Damon, *Brown University, Harris Collection of American Poetry and Plays, Series of Old American Songs*, No. 9.

8. Frederick Douglass, *Narrative of the Life of Frederick Douglass, An American Slave*, reprint edition (New York, 1968), p. 32. Douglass speaks also of the actual music of the slave, attributing to such music his "first glimmering conception of the dehumanizing character of slavery." *Supra.*

9. Solomon Northrup, *Twelve Years a Slave* (Auburn, Buffalo, 1854), Chapter XII.

10. Repeated lines omitted.

11. Damon, *op. cit.*, No. 13. The words were probably written by White Snyder, although John Clemens has also been cited as the author. See Robert A. Gerson, *Music in Philadelphia* (Philadelphia, 1940), p. 86.

12. Damon, *loc. cit.*

13. "Coal Black Rose" was also popular abroad, as shown by an early pirated edition which appeared in London, called "Life in Philadelphia; or, Coal Black Rose." This edition lifted the music, text and illustrations from the American versions.

14. See Joshua Coffin, *Slave Insurrections* (New York, 1860; reprinted by Negro History Press, 1969?), pp. 7–8.

15. Benjamin Quarles, *The Negro in the Making of America* (New York, 1964), p. 71.

16. There are three editions of "Sambo's Address" in the Sheet Music Collection of the Free Library of Philadelphia. The example cited is entitled "Sambo's 'Dress To He' Bred'ren, As sung with the most enormous applause, At Mr. Davis' Musical Parties, On Friday Evenings, Broadway House, by Mr. Brower (*not* Frank Brower), the Celebrated Comic Singer ... Arranged ... by James B. Taylor" (New York, 1833).

17. Joseph Botkin, "Sambo, The National Jester in Popular Culture," in Gary B. Nash and Richard Weiss, ed., *The Great Fear; Race in the Mind of America* (New York, 1970), p. 169.

18. Nathan, *op. cit.*, pp. 166; 171–172.

19. Nathan, *op. cit.*, p. 52.

20. Damon, *op. cit.*, No. 15.

21. *Cf.* Nathan, *op. cit.*, pp. 52ff.

22. Sir Edward Michael Packenham, the British general in charge of the expedition against New Orleans during the War of 1812. He was killed in battle on January 8, 1815.

23. The practice of referring in song to other currently popular songs offers valuable clues concerning the relative popularity of the songs mentioned.

24. This is probably a reference to Robert Young Hayne (1791–1839), United States Senator from 1823 to 1832, and a leading opponent of the protective tariff. The famous debate between Hayne and Daniel Webster in 1830 began as an argument over the sale of public lands, but the dispute widened to include the whole issue of state's rights versus federal powers. Hayne championed the cause of nullification, which held that a state could nullify federal laws within its own boundaries—a direct ancestor of the secessionist theory which led to the Civil War.

25. For an interesting discussion of factors involved in perpetuating slavery in the 1830's, see Stanley M. Elkin, *Slavery*, 2d ed. (Chicago, 1968), pp. 27–36.

26. Probably a reference to Tristam Burges (1770–1853), Congressman from Rhode Island from 1825 to 1835. Burges's logic and sarcasm won him wide fame as a debater.

27. Also known as "There Was an Old Soldier Who Had a Wooden Leg."

28. Carl Wittke, *Tambo and Bones* (Durham, North Carolina, 1930), p. 17.

29. Nathan, *op. cit.*, p. 166.

30. Damon, *op. cit.*, No. 20.

31. Gilbert Chase, *America's Music* (New York, 1965), pp. 278–279.

32. Original title: "Old Tare River." This version is taken from the *Negro Forget-Me-Not Songster* (Philadelphia, *ca.* 1850), pp. 176–177.

33. Probably a slanting reference to Charles Dickens, whose works were widely pirated in the United States. In an attempt to curb his losses from this practice, Dickens visited America in 1842. His *American Notes* (1842) and *Martin Chuzzlewit* (1843) contained forthright, often unfavorable comments on American customs and institutions such as slavery. Considerable ill will between Dickens and the American public was generated by his observations, although much of what he recorded was accurate.

34. Nathan, *op. cit.*, pp. 52–55.

35. This edition, published by John Cole and Son (Baltimore), is the earliest found. *Cf.* Dichter and Shapiro, *op. cit.*, p. 51, and Sigmund Spaeth, *A History of Popular Music in America* (New York, 1948), p. 72.

36. Dichter and Shapiro, *op. cit.*, p. 52.

37. Robert A. Gerson, *Music in Philadelphia* (Philadelphia, 1940), pp. 84–85. When Johnson's band visited Providence, Rhode Island, the home of the abolitionist movement, they were not allowed to play because of their color, for example.

38. Damon, *op. cit.*, No. 14.

39. Chase, *op. cit.*, p. 289. See also John Tasker Howard, *Stephen Foster, America's Troubadour* (New York, 1939), p. 83.

40. Damon, *op. cit.*, No. 24. See also Edward L. Rice, *Monarchs of Minstrelsy, From "Daddy" Rice to Date* (New York, 1911), p. 24.

41. See Chase, *op. cit.*, pp. 262–263. While Chase characterizes the theory of Sweeney's having invented the five-string banjo as "rather mythical," the basis on which this judgment is made is somewhat tenuous, inasmuch as the illustration of Sweeney's "Whar Did You Cum From" is cited as proof that the instrument had only four strings. Examination of this illustration reveals scant support for either theory of the number of strings due to the lack of definition of the print; if the number of tuning machines on the instruments depicted on the cover is taken as an indication of the number of strings, the issue is even further clouded, for there are machines for *six* strings!

42. There are several title variants, such as "Johnny Booker," etc. Harold Courlander, *Negro Folk Music, U.S.A.* (New York, 1963), pp. 187–188, cites an "Old John Booker" which is totally unlike the version cited here in either textual content or meter.

43. Damon, *op. cit.*, No. 28. Damon cites a source for this song: *The Book of a Thousand Songs* (New York, n.d.), which contains lines destined for fame through "another college song. . . ."

> Oh, dar was a bull dog on a bank,
> An' a bull frog in a pool,
> An' de bull dog called de frog
> A damn cold water fool.

These lines appear in, and were probably taken from another song: "Whar Did You Cum From; or, Oh, Mr. Coon, " since they are in precisely this form within the song. *Cf. The Negro Forget-Me-Not Songster*, pp. 74–75.

44. Wittke, *op. cit.*, p. 33.

45. George C.D. Odell, *Annals of the New York Stage* (New York, 1928), IV:232.

46. John Tasker Howard, *Our American Music*, 3d ed., rev. (New York, 1946), p. 179.

47. Nathan, *op. cit.*, p. 169.

CHAPTER THREE

1. Odell, *op. cit.*, IV: *passim.*

2. Odell, *op. cit.*, IV: 603.

3. Nathan, *op. cit.*, p. 144. Christy's contention that blackface minstrelsy originated with his troupe can be discounted on the technical grounds that neither his methods nor his materials were clearly stated. See Nathan, *ibid.*

4. See Beatrice Landeck, *Echoes of Africa in Folk Songs of the America's,* 2d ed., rev. (New York, 1969), pp. 170–177. Landeck's assertion that "Both black and white troupes travelled the country over, adapting Afro-American vocal and instru-

mental music for the white public" remains unverified and thus untenable as a generality, particularly with regard to the early period of minstrelsy.

5. George Washington Cable, "The Dance in the Place Congo, " *The Century Magazine*, XXXI (February, 1886): 517–532, as reprinted in Bernard Katz, ed., *The Social Implications of Early Negro Music in the United States* (New York, 1969), p. 40.

6. *Ibid.*, p. 3. Katz's inability to distinguish between black music and that of whites is evident in his Introduction (pp. 1–7) exemplified by his assertion that Stephen Foster was "the Joel Chandler Harris of Negro music." The fact that both Foster and Harris capitalized on the stereotypical image of the black and that Foster kept his music strictly within the established white formulas has a significance that seems to have escaped Katz and other scholars.

7. Robert E. Spiller, *et al.*, eds., *Literary History of the United States* (New York, 1953), p. 40.

8. Vernon Louis Parrington, *Main Currents in American Thought*, 3 vols. in 1 (New York, 1958), II: 6–7.

9. Parrington, *loc. cit.*

10. From a bound volume of broadsides inscribed "Catalogue of Songs. Arranged by S.(?)H. Ettla, Aug 30th, 1855." To distinguish this from a similar compilation by Ettla, the present source is hereinafter cited as *Ettla No. 1*. The other compilation, although dated "Aug 24th, 1855," is designated in the present study as *Ettla No. 2*.

11. Philadelphia, c1846.

12. pp. 199–200.

13. From *The Lover's Forget-Me-Not, and Songs of Beauty . . . With All the Late Negro Melodies* (Philadelphia, 1847), pp. 91–92.

14. *The Negro Forget-Me-Not Songster* (Philadelphia, ca. 1855), pp. 116–117. A similarly short-lived song, "De Nigga Gineral" in *The Lover's Forget-Me-Not Songster* (p. 13), relates to a slave uprising seen as a specific plot. The date of the song suggests that it may have been inspired by the Nat Turner insurrection of 1831, but the reference to "Uncle Gabel" in the text points to the Gabriel conspiracy of 1800, which caused national concern for years after its occurrence. Omitting needless repetitions, the song is as follows:

> Oh, don't you know your uncle Gabel?
> O, he was a Nigger General.
> He was the chief of the insurgents,
> Dey raised demselves down in Northampton,
> O, de whites dey caught him and dey fought him.
> Dey drove him to de gallows wid four gray horses,
> O Johnson Ben he drove de waggon,
> And dey hang him and dey swung him,
> So dat was de last ob uncle Gabel.

15. *The Negro Forget-Me-Not Songster*, p. 195.

16. *Op. cit.*, p. 229.

17. *Christy's Panorama Songster* (New York, n.d.), p. 113. There are several variants of this song. Nathan, *op. cit.* (p. 292), cites a "Come Back Steben " by D.D. Emmett which is probably not identical with those under consideration in the present study.

18. Boston, c1843. Published by Chas. H. Keith, 67 & 69 Court St.

19. Also parodied as "The Fine Old Southern Gentleman." See Sigmund Spaeth, *A History of Popular Music in America* (New York, 1948), p. 94.

20. Pp. 62–63; 144–145.

21. Chase, *op. cit.*, p. 167.

22. Published by Lee and Walker (Philadelphia, 1847).

23. Wittke, *op. cit.*, p. 56.

24. *Ettla No. 2*, p. 117. A second edition was published in sheet music form by Lee and Walker (Philadelphia, 1853).

25. *Negro Forgt-Me-Not Songster*, pp. 110–111.

26. Published by Henry McGaffrey (Baltimore, 1853).

27. As quoted in Eric L. McKitrick, *Slavery Defended; The Views of the Old South* (Englewood Cliffs, New Jersey, 1963), p. 40.

28. *Ibid.*,p. 47.

29. *Ibid.*,p. 56.

30. Fitzhugh, for example, held that communism was "precisely the system of domestic slavery with us"; that the North was controlled by millionaires—"men of cold hearts and weak minds"; and that free workers under capitalism were "little better than trespassers on this earth given by God to all mankind." *Ibid.*, pp. 44, 46, 47. William Grayson produced a long heroic poem, *The Hireling and the Slave* (Charleston, 1856), in which he extolled the advantages enjoyed by slaves as compared with the bitter life of the free worker:

> Vainly the starving white, at every door,
> Craves help or pity for the hireling poor;
> But that the distant black may softlier fare,
> Eat, sleep, and play, exempt from toil and care.

Ibid. , p. 61.

31. *Negro Forget-Me-Not Songster*, pp. 25–27.

32. *Ettla No. 1*, p. 169.

33. *Ettla No. 2*, p. 197.

34. Published by Firth, Pond & Co. (New York).

35. *Ettla No. 1*, p. 172.

36. *Ettla No. 1*, p. 95.

37. *Ettla No. 2*, p. 177. Three sheet music editions, two published by William Hall & Son (New York, 1847), one by George Willig, Jr. (Baltimore, 1848), all agree with the broadside version.

38. *Ettla No. 2*, p. 180.

39. An earlier "Mary Blane," from which these samples derive, was published by C.G. Christman (New York, 1846), with William Whitlock credited as composer. The melody of this song is essentially the same as the later versions; the text, however, is that of the love song and is more properly discussed under that heading. (*q.v.*).

40. *Ettla No. 1*. p. 274.

41. Published by Henry Prentiss (Boston, 1844).

42. *Ettla No. 2*. p. 9.

43. Published by A. Fiot (Philadelphia, 1844).

44. Published by W.C. Peters (Cincinnati, 1847).

45. Published by James E. Boswell (Baltimore, 1855).

46. Dr. Cartwright of New Orleans, "1. Diseases and Peculiarities of the Negro Race," *DeBow's Review*,II (September, 1851): 331–334, as quoted in William L. Katz, *Eyewitness: The Negro in American History* (New York, 1967), pp. 131–132.

47. Published by A. Fiot (Philadelphia, 1846).

48. *Negro Forget-Me-Not Songster*, p. 20.

49. Published by Wm. A. Pond (New York, 1858).

50. Published by F.D. Benteen (Baltimore, 1849).

51. *Ettla No. 1*, p. 293.

52. Published by Firth, Pond & Co. (New York, 1850).

53. Published by Firth, Pond & Co. (New York, 1853). The version cited is from *The Negro Forget-Me-Not Songster*, pp. 17–18.

54. *A Treatise on Sociology, Theoretical and Practical*, as quoted in McKitrick, *Slavery Defended*, p. 53.

55. *Negro Forget-Me-Not Songster*, p. 34.

56. *Christy's Panorama Songster*, pp. 84–85; also in *Negro Forget-Me-Not Songster*, pp. 209–210.

57. Arthur Tappan (1786–1865), was one of the most ardent abolitionists. He served as the first president of the American Anti-Slavery Society and later organized the American and Foreign Anti-Slavery Society. His aid to fugitive slaves and his formidable opposition to the institution of slavery lead to his being held up to ridicule in numerous minstrel songs, as the present instance illustrates.

58. *Ettla No. 2*, p. 8.

59. *Negro Forget-Me-Not Songster*, p. 236.

60. *Ettla No. 1*, p. 233.

61. *Negro Forget-Me-Not Songster*, p. 206.

62. J. Thomas Scharf and Thompson Westcott, *History of Philadelphia, 1609–1884* (Philadelphia, 1884), pp. 637, 641–642, 663.

63. Published by J. Torr (Philadelphia, n.d.).

64. *Ettla No. 1*, p. 108.

65. *Negro Forget-Me-Not Songster*, pp. 226–227.

66. Published by E.H. Wade (Boston, 1849).

67. *Ettla No. 1*, p. 178.

68. Mounted patrols, called MP's, were maintained in all slaveholding states for the obvious purposes of forestalling revolt and apprehension of runaway slaves.

69. Published by Firth & Hall (New York, 1843). The edition cited in this study was arranged by J.T. Norton and published by A. Fiot (Philadelphia, 1844).

70. *Lady's Musical Library Extra: Music of the Ethiopian Serenaders, Nine Songs and a Set of Cotillions* (Philadelphia, 1845).

71. Published by Jaques & Brother (New York, 1847).

72. *Negro Forget-Me-Not Songster*, p. 208.

73. *Ibid.*, p. 199.

74. Probably a reference to the great Leonid shower, which appeared over America on November 13, 1833, and led many to believe that the end of the world had come.

75. T.D. Rice, for example, in one of the many parodies of his "Jim Crow" entitled, "Trip to A Nigga Meeting," perverts the religious impulse of the black with wildly inaccurate explications of Biblical stories thusly:

He says dat Cane was de fuss man,
Julycome Cesar was de toder,
Dey put Adam on de treden mill,
Kase he kill him brodder.
And den dat Mr. Sampson,
Was de man who build de ark,
Mr. Jones was de fisherman,
Who swallowed down de shark.

Negro Forget-Me-Not Songster, pp. 224–225.

76. Published by Firth, Pond & Co. (New York, 1854); see also Edward D. Andrews, *The Gift to be Simple; Songs, Dances and Rituals of the American Shakers* (New York, 1940), p. 159.

77. Compare, for example, the curious Shaker song, "Black Bill's Wonderment," *ibid.*, p. 121.

78. Published by Oliver Ditson (Boston, 1853). An earlier edition, entitled "Jordan Am A Hard Road To Trabel," does not credit a composer nor an author, although it is dedicated to a "W.K. Northall, Esq., by T.F. Briggs." This edition, published by Horace Waters (New York, 1852), does not invalidate Emmett's claim of authorship however.

79. Parodies and variations were so numerous, in fact, that publishers were often compelled to distinguish them by numbering them: "Jordan . . . No. 1," "Jordan . . . No. 2," and so on. Some publishers borrowed and shortened the title to "Jordan" (*Ettla No. 1*, p. 97), or altered it: "The Other Side of Jordan;" or "Jordan Ain't A Hard Road To Travel." Despite the manifold variations, most of the songs retained the chorus of the original with few alterations.

80. *Ettla No. 1*, p. 97.

81. *Ibid.*, p. 101.

82. *Ibid.*, p. 102.

83. *Loc. cit.*

84. *Ettla No. 1*,p. 98. Probably a reference to the United States citizens who accompanied Narciso López on his expedition in August 1851 aimed at freeing Cuba from Spanish rule. Lacking popular support, the effort failed, with López and most of his followers being captured and shot.

85. This verse is in reference to Lajos Kossuth (1802–1894), Hungarian patriot and statesman, who visited the United States after his release from a Turkish prison in 1851.

86. Franklin Pierce (1804–1869), 14th President of the United States, was inaugurated in 1853. Pro-slavery and expansionary in his views, he tacitly supported the scheme to annex Cuba to the United States as a slave state—by force, if necessary—and acted to extend slavery into the Louisiana Territory, thereby nullifying the Missouri Compromise of 1820. Pierce's actions added to growing tensions over the slavery issue although he is reputed to have been sincere in his efforts to conciliate Northern and Southern points of view.

87. *Negro Forget-Me-Not Songster*, p. 115.

88. *Ettla No. 2*, p. 139.

89. *Negro Forget-Me-Not Songster*, p. 211.

90. *Ibid.*, pp. 223–224.
91. *Ibid.*, p. 24.
92. *Ibid.*, p. 29.
93. *Ibid.*, pp. 206–207.
94. *The Lover's Forget-Me-Not Songster*, p. 103.
95. *Negro Forget-Me-Not Songster*, pp. 182-183.
96. *Ibid.*, p. 221.
97. *Ibid.*, pp. 214–215.
98. *Ibid.*, p. 61.
99. *Ibid.*, p. 86.

CHAPTER FOUR

1. Alice Dana Adams, *The Neglected Period of Anti-Slavery in America, 1808–1831* (Gloucester, 1964), p. 252.
2. Jairus Lincoln, *Anti-Slavery Melodies: For Friends of Freedom. Prepared for the Hingham Anti-Slavery Society* (Hingham, 1843), pp. 8–9, 30–31, 41, 64–65, 70–71. It is an interesting coincidence that the preface of this work is dated February 22, 1843, only sixteen days after the first confirmed minstrel show performance,
3. George W. Clark, *The Harp of Freedom* (New York, 1856). In this collection, "Lucy Neal" became "We're Free" (p. 321), "Lucy Long" became "The Poor Voter's Song" (p. 297), to name only a few examples of borrowings from minstrelsy's repertoire.
4. Clark, *op. cit.*, pp. 97–98.
5. Clark, *loc. cit.*
6. Clark, *op. cit.*, pp. 46–48. Words are by L.F. Blanchard and music by George W. Clark.
7. *Ibid.*, pp. 51–52.
8. Lincoln, *op. cit.*, p. 5.
9. Clark, *op. cit.*, pp. 312–313.
10. Performed in 1816 at Covent Garden. See also Nathan, *op. cit.*, p. 14.
11. Full title: "The Chase—Set Every Inch of Canvas." Composed by Henry Russell for his new entertainment "Negro Life," words by Angus B. Reach, Esq. (n.p., n.d.).
12. Published by Fiot, Meignen & Co. (Philadelphia, *ca.* 1838).
13. *Ettla No. 1*, p. 164.
14. *Minstrel Songs, Old and New* (Boston, 1882), pp. 190–191.
15. Published by Oliver Ditson (Boston, 1844). Used through courtesy of William Petrecca, Academy of Musical Americana, Philadelphia. Repetitions omitted.
16. Published by Henry Prentiss (Boston, 1844). Used through courtesy of William Petrecca, Academy of Musical Americana, Philadelphia.
17. Published by Jesse Hutchinson, Jr. (Boston, 1844).
18. Odell, *Annals*, IV: 684–685.

19. With his by now expected lack of accuracy, Ewen states that "Get Off The Track" was written by Jesse Hutchinson (Sr.?) and that the tune was "an old slave melody." See Ewen, *Popular American Songs* (New York, 1966), p. 119.

20. Published by S. Brainard & Co. (Cleveland, 1854).

21. Dan Rice, *Dan Rice's Original Comic and Sentimental Poetic Effusions* (Philadelphia, 1860), p. 71.

22. Edward Wagenknecht, *Harriet Beecher Stowe: The Known and the Unknown* (New York, 1965), p. 6; Catherine Gilbertson, *Harriet Beecher Stowe* (New York, 1937), pp. 143–144.

23. Philip Van Doren Stern, *The Annotated Uncle Tom's Cabin* (New York, 1964), pp. 8–9. On the perpetuation of black stereotypes, Stern says:

> During the last few decades, more and more people, white as well as black, became increasingly aware of the fact that stereotypes of Negro behavior were hurting his efforts to escape from the inferior role that had been placed upon him. As a result, Negroes themselves began to resent the Uncle Tom image.

24. *Ibid.*, p. 27.

25. *Ibid.*, pp. 26–27.

26. Frank J. Metcalf, *American Writers and Compilers of Sacred Music* (New York, 1925), pp. 281–285.

27. Published by Oliver Ditson (Boston, 1852). Both words and music are by Woodbury.

28. Published by E.H. Wade (Boston, 1858).

29. F.O. Jones, ed., *A Handbook of American Music and Musicians* (New York, 1886).

30. Jones, *loc. cit.*

31. Joseph T. Shipley, *Guide to Great Plays* (Washington, D.C., 1956), pp. 11–13.

32. Published by Oliver Ditson (Boston, n.d.). Oliver Ditson published at the address shown on this edition (115 Washington St.) between 1844 and 1857. See Dichter and Shapiro, *op. cit.*, p. 185.

33. Published by H. Waters (New York, 1854).

34. Published by Oliver Ditson (Boston, 1852). Words are by Miss M.A. Collier, music by E.J. Loder.

35. Published by Oliver Ditson (Boston, 1852).

36. Rice, *op. cit.*, p. 29.

37. Published by Henry McCaffrey (Baltimore, 1853). See also Stern, *op. cit.*, pp. 32–33.

38. Richard B. Harwell, *Confederate Music* (Chapel Hill, 1950), pp. 26–40.

39. *Foster Hall Reproductions. Songs, Compositions and Arrangements by Stephen Collins Foster, 1826–1864* (Indianapolis, 1933). Only the first, third, and eighth verses are cited.

40. *Ibid.*

41. Clark, *op. cit.*, pp. 316–317.

42. *Dixey's Songster* (Philadelphia, 1860), pp. 16–17. Written by H. Angelo, and sung by Dixey. Music published by Coulston, 147 N. Eighth St.

43. *Ibid.*, p. 73.

44. Rice, *op. cit.*, pp. 30–32.
45. *Ibid.*, p. 24.

CHAPTER FIVE

1. Emmett originally entitled his masterpiece "Dixie's Land," which was changed to "I Wish I Was In Dixie's Land" by the publisher, Firth, Pond (New York, 1860). Although many title variants exist, the tune is commonly known simply as "Dixie."

2. Nathan, *op. cit.*, Chapter 16. This is perhaps the most reasoned of the numerous studies of "Dixie." Nathan weighs the various myths concerning the song against available evidence, with the perhaps unfortunate result that much of the romantic fabrication is stripped away. More fanciful accounts can be found in Ernest K. Emurian, *Stories of Civil War Songs* (Natick, 1960), pp. 11–18; Ewen, *op. cit.*, pp. 86–88; Spaeth, *op. cit.*, pp. 137–142 *et passim*. See also Charles B. Galbreath, "Song Writers of Ohio," in *Ohio State Archeological and Historical Society Publications*, XIII: 504–550. Galbreath recounts much of Emmett's own version—recorded in the composer's later life—of how he came to write "Dixie," after he had already given several different and often contradictory accounts of the story.

3. In 1969, the student council of the University of Virginia asked the student band to stop playing "Dixie," which the band refused to do. Despite protests, the same situation was found to exist at Georgia Tech, Tulane, Mississippi, and other universities, *Newsweek*, October 13, 1969, p. 28. Additionally, Whitney Young Jr. called the singing of "Dixie" an insult to all blacks, *The Sunday Bulletin* (Philadelphia), February 8, 1970. At the celebration of the 110th anniversary of the First Battle of Manassas, the 75th U.S. Army Band refused to accompany the chorus in a rendition of "Dixie," and after it was remarked that the song should have been played anyway, a black member of the band was heard to say, "We won the war, Baby," (AP) *The Evening Bulletin* (Philadelphia), July 19, 1971.

4. A measure of the popularity of "Dixie" is found in the many arrangements, transcriptions, and translations that have appeared, such as a choral edition designed for American-German male chorus published by Oliver Ditson (Boston, 1892). It boggles the mind to imagine the "happy plantation slave" proclaim the opening lines: "O wär ich doch, wo wir Baumvoll' pfluckten. . . ."

5. Richard B. Harwell, *Confederate Music* (Chapel Hill, 1950), pp. 87; 93; 89–90.

6. Wittke, *op. cit.*, p. 235.

7. "Words concocted by Ye Tragic; Music gotten up by Ye Comic." Published by Blackmar & Bro. (Augusta, 1864).

8. Benjamin Butler, *Butler's Book* (Boston, 1892), pp. 256–257. See also William A. Katz, *Eyewitness: The Negro in American History* (New York, 1967), p. 210.

9. Published by Horace Waters (New York, 1861), reprinted in *Clark's School Visitor* (Philadelphia, ca. 1862), p. 48.

10. Words by "Moses," arranged by Thomas Baker. Published by Horace Waters (New York, 1861).

11. Arranged by C.S. Brainard. Published by S. Brainard (Cleveland, 1862).

12. Words by Lucy Lovell; music by Mrs. Parkhurst. Published by Horace Waters (New York, 1864).

13. Published by Oliver Ditson (Boston, *ca.* 1861). The words for "Uncle Sam's Hotel" were given another setting by J.R. Adams, who retitled the piece "The Contraband's Hotel." This version was published by J.L. Peters (New York, 1862), and also in the South. See Harwell, *op. cit.*, p. 109.

14. Published by Oliver Ditson (Boston, 1861). See Willard A. and Porter W. Heaps, *The Singing Sixties* (Norman, 1960), p. 287.

15. Published by Root & Cady (Chicago, 1962). Other "skedaddle" songs included George Danskin's "Skedaddle," and another "New Skedaddle," with words by Eugene T. Johnston and music by John Durnal. See also Heaps and Heaps, *op. cit.*, pp. 78, 89.

16. Based on the title page of "The New Skedaddle," which lists Scott as the composer of "Kingdom Coming," perhaps Work's best-known Civil War hit.

17. Published by Root & Cady (Chicago, 1862). The edition cited bears an 1863 copyright date, but is in all respects identical to the earlier edition.

18. Published by Root & Cady (Chicago, 1862).

19. Published by Root & Cady (Chicago, 1861).

20. Published by Root & Cady (Chicago, 1864).

21. George Frederick Root, "Congregational Singing Among Negroes," in *The New York Musical Review and Choral Advocate* (New York), VI: 7, March 29, 1855, p. 107. Root indicates a strong preference for the congregational singing over the choir singing heard during this visit to a Richmond, Virginia Negro church. He was deeply affected by the spontaneous singing of that congregation, and noted that there was "no mincing the matter here; no humming the melody two octaves below the pitch for fear of being conspicuous; but strong, mellow tones, full of pathos, singing 'as unto God, and not unto men.' " Root could not escape his own white musical conceptions, however, as he notes: "The tune was not altogether appropriate, and they filled it with odd turns and embellishments, and did not keep remarkably well together. . . . "

22. Published by Root & Cady (Chicago, 1862).

23. "A Parody on the Phantom Chorus in La Sonnambula, as arranged and sung by the Christy's Minstrels" (New York, 1848).

24. Published by Firth, Pond (New York, 1849).

25. Published by Louis Tripp (Louisville, 1864).

26. Published as a broadside by H. De Marsan (New York, *ca.* 1863). Sung to the tune, "Wait For The Wagon."

27. Words by George Cooper. Published by Firth, Son & Co. (New York, 1863).

28. Also known by the title "Raw Recruits."

29. Spaeth, *op. cit.*, p. 129; Irwin Silber, *Songs of the Civil War* (New York, 1960), pp. 91ff., 99–103. The two versions included in this study: "Abraham's Daughter or, Raw Recruits," published by Firth, Son & Co. (New York, 1862) and by Septimus Winner (Philadelphia, 1861); and "Abraham's Daughter," arranged by F.H.H. Oldfield, published by M. Gray (San Francisco, *ca.* 1863).

30. Published by Root & Cady (Chicago, 1863).

31. Advertisement on the last page of "Babylon Is Fallen." (1863 edition).

32. Words and music composed by Dan D. Emmett. Wm. A. Pond & Co. (New York, 1864).

33. Published by Horace Waters (New York, 1864).

34. Published by Wm. Hall & Son (New York, 1864).

35. Silber, *op. cit.*, p. 309.

36. *Buckley's Melodist; A Repertoire of Choice Songs and Ballads, With Choruses, As Sung at the Concerts of Buckley's Serenaders*. Published by Henry Tolman & Co. (Boston, 1864), p. 109.

37. Published by Root & Cady (Chicago, 1864).

38. Published by Wm. Hall & Son (New York, 1864).

39. Words by Charles C. Sawyer; music by John M. Loretz. Published by Sawyer and Thompson (Brooklyn, 1863).

40. *Carncross & Dixey's Minstrel Melodies, a Collection of Popular Songs . . . as Sung by Them . . .* (Philadelphia, 1864), pp. 60–61.

41. As quoted in Peter M. Bergman and Mort N. Bergman, *The Chronological History of the Negro in America* (New York, 1969), p. 228.

42. Full title: "Young Eph's Lamentation; or, Whar Will I Go If De War Breaks De Country Up." Written by J.B. Murphy, and published by Jacob Endres (St. Louis, 1862).

43. *Carncross & Dixey's Minstrel Melodies*, p. 37.

44. Published by Oliver Ditson (Boston, 1863).

45. Music by H.T. Merrill. Published by Root & Cady (Chicago, 1862).

46. Music by W.O. Perkins. Published by Oliver Ditson (Boston, 1862).

47. Published by H.M. Higgins (Chicago, 1862).

48. January 1, 1863.

49. Published by Root & Cady (Chicago, 1863).

50. From Edith Fowke and Joe Glazer, *Songs of Work and Freedom* (New York, 1961), p. 173.

51. John Tasker Howard, *Stephen Foster, America's Troubadour* (New York, 1939), pp. 82, 382.

52. Facsimile published by *Musical Americana* (Philadelphia, 1956) of the edition published by Blodgett & Bradford (Buffalo, 1860). See also Dichter and Shapiro, *op. cit.*, p. 109.

53. See Forrest G. Wood, *Black Scare: The Racist Response to Emancipation and Reconstruction* (Berkeley and Los Angeles, 1968), pp. 53ff.

54. Published by J. Marsh (Philadelphia, 1864). Foster could hardly have known who the candidates for this election were, for he died on January 13, 1864, and the candidates were not chosen until the following summer.

55. Published by W.W. Whitney (Toledo, 1865).

56. Published by Oliver Ditson (Boston, 1861).

57. Published by Russell & Pattee (Boston, 1862). "Sally Come Up! or, A Nigger's Holiday," as Mackney's version was called, had a considerably altered melody and extended text.

58. Published by Wm. A. Pond (New York, 1864). "Nancy Fat" was set to music by T. McNally and arranged by C. (Charles W.?) Glover. (Charles W. Glover died in 1863).

59. *Buckley's Melodist*, pp. 84–86.

60. *Ibid.*, pp. 91–92.

61. *Ibid.*, pp. 102–103.

62. *Ibid.*, pp. 92–93.

63. Marshall McLuhan, with Wilfred Watson, *From Cliché to Archetype* (New York, 1970), p. 133.

64. Published by Root & Cady (Chicago, 1865).

65. Published as a broadside by D.A. Warden (Philadelphia, 1862).

66. Arranged by J.E. Smith and published by J.W. Davies & Sons (Richmond, 1864).

67. "A Chaunt to the Wild Western Melody, 'Joe Bowers,' " by R I (or I R?) n.d., n.p.. See also Dichter and Shapiro, *op. cit.*, p. 123.

CHAPTER SIX

1. Leaders of the American Anti-Slavery Society felt that the achievement of emancipation rendered the further existence of their organization unnecessary. Douglass, Phillips, Purvis, and others felt that the black was not truly free until civil and political rights were secured by federal law, however, and led the effort to maintain the Society until such goals had been reached. See Herbert Aptheker, ed., *A Documentary History of the Negro People in the United States*, 2 vols. (New York, 1951). II: 547–550. Sumner also recognized the necessity of federal guarantees of equality for freedmen, as stated in his Senate speech of February 5, 1866. See W.E. Burghardt DuBois, *Black Reconstruction* (New York, 1935), pp. 192–197.

2. Milton R. Konvitz, *A Century of Civil Rights* (New York, 1961), p. 17.

3. *Ibid.*, p. 46.

4. Wood, *op. cit.*, p. 15.

5. "As sung with immense eclat by the inimitable Billy Emerson. Dedicated to Gen. Ben Butler." (!) Words by T.E. Garrett, Esq., music by Alfred von Rochow. Published by Balmer & Weber (St. Louis, 1868).

6. Words by H.F. Greene, music by W.F. Walker. Published by S. Brainard's Sons (Cleveland, 1866).

7. *The Singer's Journal* (New York, 1869), p. 117.

8. *Op. cit.*, pp. 62ff.

9. *The Singer's Journal*, p. 115.

10. "Oh! My!" (by) Howard. From the cover of "We'll Show Them When We Come To Vote" by Frank Howard. Published by W.W. Whitney (Toledo, 1869).

11. L. Fayette Sykes, comp., *Garfield and Arthur Campaign Song Book* (New York, 1880), No. 17.

12. *Ibid.*, No. 18.
13. *Ibid.*, No. 13.
14. *Ibid.*, No. 5. "Sung to the tune: Battle Hymn of the Republic."
15. Words by George M. Vickers, music by John Ford. Published by Lee & Walker (Philadelphia, 1880).
16. For an excellent account of the black in the post-Reconstruction era see Rayford W. Logan, *The Betrayal of the Negro* (New York, 1965).
17. Adapted and arranged by "B. R. H." Published by Root & Cady (Chicago, 1866).
18. These and many other toys built on black subjects may be seen in the Perelman Antique Toy Museum, Philadelphia.
19. Words by Frank Green. Published by Lee & Walker (Philadelphia, 1869).
20. Attributed to "Julius Crow." Published by C. Sheard (London, n.d.).
21. Published by S.W. Blair (Boston, 1891).
22. Published by J.M. Russell (n.p., 1881).
23. Published by P.I. Magoun (Bath, Maine, 1884).
24. Published by T.B. Harms (New York, 1887).
25. Published by W.A. Evans & Bro. (n.p., 1885).
26. Reprinted in *The Singer's Journal*, p. 42.
27. The version quoted is the Oliver Ditson reprint (Boston, 1920).
28. Published by White, Smith (Boston, 1878).
29. Published by White, Smith (Boston, 1876).
30. Published by S. Brainard's Sons (Cleveland, 1866).
31. Published by S. Brainard's Sons (Cleveland, 1866).
32. In *Songs of the Times*. W.F. Shaw (n.p., 1883).
33. In *Minstrel Songs Old and New*. Oliver Ditson (Boston, 1882), pp. 81–83.
34. Words by Ed(ward) Harrigan, music by Dave (David) Braham. Published by Wm. A. Pond (New York, 1876).
35. Words by Frank Dumont, music by James K. Stuart, *ca.* 1873. In *Minstrel Songs Old and New*, pp. 46–48.
36. Wood, *op. cit.*, p. 143.
37. In *The Singer's Journal*, No. 2, p. 11.
38. Published by William J.A. Lieder (New York, 1881).
39. Copyright 1887, by Geo. W. Richardson.
40. Words and music by Harry Bennett; arranged by F.W. Zaulig. Published by William A. Pond (New York, 1876).
41. Published by Saul Ser-Trew (New York, 1867).
42. In *The Singer's Journal*, No. 7, p. 53.
43. Arranged by F. Louis. Published by P.R. McCargo (Boston, 1880).
44. In *The Singer's Journal*, No. 10, p. 75.
45. *Ibid.*, No. 3, p. 21.
46. Words and melody by Henry Hart, arranged by James E. Stewart. Copyright 1873, by J.L. Peters. In *Minstrel Songs Old and New*, pp. 58–60.
47. See Spaeth, *op. cit.*, p. 174; Ewen, *op. cit.* While it is of course possible that black troops actually sang "Shew Fly, Don't Bother Me" during the Civil War, Spaeth and Ewen both neglect to indicate their source for this information. In addition to the

1869 copyright date, the last part of the first verse points more directly to a later white origin for the song:

> I feel, I feel, I feel,
> That's what my mother said,
> The angels pouring 'lasses down,
> Upon this nigger's head.

48. Published by J.L. Peters (n.p., 1872). In *Minstrel Songs Old and New*, pp. 61–63.

49. Published by Compton & Doan (St. Louis, 1868).

50. From the Broadside Collection, Free Library of Philadelphia. The original "Full Moon Union" is by Edward Harrigan and David Braham, published by Wm. A. Pond (New York, 1880).

51. Published by White, Smith (Boston, 1879).

52. Written and composed by Donly. Published by E.H. Harding (New York, 1879).

53. Published by E.H. Harding (New York, 1880).

54. Arranged by Louis Bodecker. Published by National Music (Chicago, 1882).

55. Spaeth, *op. cit.*, pp. 179–191.

56. Harrigan was born in New York on October 26, 1845; Hart was born in Worcester, Massachusetts, on July 25, 1855; Braham was born in 1838.

57. Words by Edward Harrigan, music by Dave (David) Braham. Published by Wm. A. Pond (New York, 1875).

58. Words by Edward Harrigan, music by David Braham. Published by Wm. A. Pond (New York, 1879).

59. Words by Edward Harrigan, music by Dave (David)Braham. Published by Wm. A. Pond (New York, 1879).

60. Words by Ed (Edward) Harrigan, music by Dave (David) Braham. Published by Wm. A. Pond (New York, 1881).

61. Published by S. Brainard's Sons (Cleveland and Chicago, 1883). Also in *Songs of Dixie*, S. Brainard's Sons (New York, 1890), p. 128.

62. Published by S. Brainard's Sons (Cleveland and Chicago, 1884).

63. Published by Balmer & Weber (n.p., 1887). Also reprinted in (Henry J.) *Wehman's Collection of 127 Songs* (New York, 1891), p. 9.

64. Published by C.D. Blake (Boston, 1884).

65. Words and music by Harry Talbert. Copyright by W.A. Evans (n.p., 1883).

66. Words by Frank Dumont, music by James E. Stewart. Published by J.L. Peters (New York, 1873).

67. Words by Bobby Newcomb, music by Eddy Fox, arranged by Frank Cardella. Published by R.J. Compton (St. Louis, 1867).

68. Arranged by T. Brigham Bishop. Published by J.J. Dobmeyer (Cincinnati, 1868).

69. Published by C.M. Tremaine (New York, 1868).

70. Words and music by H.J. Whymark. Published by Oliver Ditson (Boston, 1865).

71. By Dondere. Published by W.W. Whitney (Toledo, *ca.* 1869), from an advertisement on the cover of "We'll Show You When We Come To Vote."

72. Words and music by Monroe H. Rosenfeld. Copyright by W.A. Evans & Bro. (n.p., 1885).

CHAPTER SEVEN

1. Gustavus D. Pike, *The Jubilee Singers and Their Campaign for Twenty Thousand Dollars* (Boston, 1873), pp. 163–164; also, Gustavus D. Pike, *The Singing Campaign for Ten Thousand Pounds* (New York, 1875), pp. 205–206; J.B.T. Marsh and F.J. Loudin, *The Story of the Jubilee Singers* (Cleveland, 1892), pp. 155–156.

2. See William Frances Allen, *et al.*, *Slave Songs of the United States* (New York, 1867), p. i ff.

3. Copyright 1885, by W.F. Shaw (n.p.).

4. Words written and adapted by "A.L.," published by Lee & Walker (Philadelphia, 1880). The cover illustration was done by Connelly Company, Boston.

5. Words and music by D.S. McCosh. Published by Chicago Music (Chicago, 1880), and Wm. A. Pond & Co. (New York, 1880).

6. Words by Harry B. Smith, music by George Schleiffarth. Published by Bowen and Schleiffarth (Chicago, 1886).

7. Published by White, Smith & Co. (Boston, 1879).

8. Published by White, Smith & Co. (Boston, 1879).

9. Words by James Hosey. Copyright 1881, by W.F. Shaw (n.p.), reprinted in *Songs of the Times* (1883). Repeated phrases have been omitted.

10. Published by W.C. Woodward (Memphis, 1879).

11. Published by George D. Newhall (Cincinnati, 1878).

12. Thus, the allegation that "Keep In De Middle Ob De Road" is generally considered a true black spiritual demonstrates not only the gullibility of the scholar, but a measure of insensitivity to the message of the text as considered within its historical context. See Spaeth, *op. cit.*, p. 159.

13. Published by The John Church Co. (Cincinnati, 1885). Only the third verse is quoted.

14. Published by The John Church Co. (Cincinnati, 1885).

15. Robert Green Ingersoll (1833–1899), noted lawyer, author, and lecturer, whose freethinking attacks on what he termed the "superstitions of religion" earned him the epithet of "the great agnostic."

16. Lily Langtry (1852–1929), famous English actress, whose company made the first of many successful American tours in 1882. The reference in this song alludes to her exploitation of a stage career to maintain her well-known propensity for the high life.

17. Benjamin Franklin Butler (1818–1893) had a stormy career as a politician and as a brigadeer general during the Civil War. His radical politics and his support of blacks made him the butt of much criticism.

18. Spaeth, *op. cit.*, pp. 230–233.

19. Spaeth, *loc. cit.* Rosenfeld used the pseudonym, F. Heiser, in this instance. Published by T.B. Harms (New York, 1884), and Willis Woodward (New York, 1884).

20. Published by George D. Newhall (Cincinnati, 1878).

21. One of the lines of the four-part setting of this chorus reads: "Dar's no use in try'ng to *get* away," an obvious misprint which nonetheless reveals the psychological message of the song.

22. Published by George D. Newhall (Cincinnati, 1883).

23. Copyright 1886, by W.F. Shaw (n.p.).

24. Published by New York Variety Co. (New York, 1885).

25. Published by Oliver Ditson (Boston, 1875).

26. Cf. Spaeth, *op. cit.*, pp. 197–198.

27. Published by John F. Perry (Boston, 1877).

28. Published by White, Smith and Co. (Boston, 1880).

29. Arranged by F. Louis. Published by John F. Perry (Boston, 1880).

30. Copyright 1880, by Thompson & Odell (Boston).

31. Published by P.R. McCargo & Co. (Boston, 1880).

32. Published by W.A. Evans (Boston, 1882).

33. Published by National Music Co. (Chicago, 1883).

34. Published by W.A. Evans (Boston, 1882).

35. Published by W.A. Evans and Brother (Boston, 1883).

36. Published by Balmer & Weber (St. Louis, 1883).

37. Published by J.C. Groene (Cincinnati, 1886).

38. Published by T.B. Harms (New York, 1885).

39. Published by Hitchcock's Music Store (New York, 1884).

40. Published by M. Witmark & Sons (New York, 1888).

41. Words by Theodore D.C. Miller, music by William W. Bentley. Published by Mrs. Pauline Lieder (New York, 1880).

42. Published by W.F. Shaw (Philadelphia, 1882).

CHAPTER EIGHT

1. Frederick Douglass, "Lynch Law In The South," in *North American Review*. CLV (1892): 117–124.

2. "Got Your Habits On." Words and Music by John Queen. Published by Feist and Frankenthaler (New York, 1899).

3. From "Impressions Of The Philippines," (author unknown), in Wilhelm H. Orf, comp., *The Great American Soldier and Other Selections* (Manila, 1913), pp. 112–114.

4. "On The South Sea Isle." Words and Music by Harry Von Tilzer. Published by Harry Von Tilzer (New York, 1916). The Spanish-speaking dependents were seen as black from the early days of the American occupation. James G. Dewey's love song,

"My Filipino Baby," published by Wright and Kochman (San Francisco, 1899), was characterized as "a coon simplicity," with a verse that begins:
'Way down in Manila lives a lady
A choc'late-colored dazzler, she's a dream. . . .
The female protagonist sang "I Want A Filipino Man," by Irving Jones (F.A. Mills, New York, 1899), in which the Spanish-speaking male is described as:
A real coon born in a foreign land,
One with that straight black silky hair. . . .

5. Isaac Goldberg, *Tin Pan Alley* (New York, 1930), p. 139.
6. Andre Hodier, *Jazz: Its Evolution and Essence* (New York, 1956), p. 40; Barry Ulanov, *Handbook of Jazz* (New York, 1955), p. 5.
7. Gunther Schuller, *Early Jazz: Its Roots and Musical Development* (New York, 1968), pp. 32–33.
8. *Op. cit.*, pp. 150–151.
9. *Op. cit.*, p. 155.
10. From a sheet music advertisement, *ca.* 1900.
11. Published by Theodore Presser (Philadelphia, 1898).
12. Published by F.A. Mills (New York, 1895).
13. Published by F.A. Mills (New York, 1898).
14. Published by F.A. Mills (New York, 1899).
15. Published by F.A. Mills (New York, 1897).
16. Words by Andrew B. Sterling, music by Harry Von Tilzer. Published by Feist and Frankenthaler (New York, 1898).
17. Published by Will Rossiter (Chicago, 1899).
18. Words by Harry Zaun, music by Halsey K. Mohr. Published by Henry Krey Music (Boston, 1906).
19. Words by Al Simmonds, music by Garnett Lee. Published by Evans Hill (New York, 1906).
20. Words by Raymond A. Browne, music by Henry Clay Smith. Published by Sol Bloom (New York, 1905).
21. Published by M. Witmark and Sons (New York, 1901).
22. Words by Ed. Gardenier, music by Jack L. Ottenheimer. Published by Sol Bloom (New York, 1903).
23. Words and music by Leon Berg. Published by Shapiro, Bernstein (New York, 1903).
24. Published by Sol Bloom (New York, 1904).
25. Words by Will D. Cobb, music by Gus Edwards. Published by Howley, Haviland (New York, 1899).
26. Published by George Willig (Baltimore, 1898).
27. Book by John J. McNally, lyrics by William Jerome, music by Jean Schwartz. Published by Shapiro (New York, 1909).
28. Published by Jerome H. Remick & Co. (New York, 1905)
29. Published by Howley, Haviland and Dresser (New York, 1901).
30. Words and music by Thomas S. Allen. Published by George M. Krey (Boston, 1902).

31. Words by Arthur Longbrake, music by George Fairman. Published by Joseph Morris (Philadelphia, 1906).

32. Words and music by Lee Johnson. Published by Zeno Mauvais (San Francisco, 1896).

33. Words and music by Alex Rogers. Published by Attucks (New York, 1904).

34. By (Ed) Rose and (Ted) Snyder. Published by F.A. Mills (New York, 1905).

35. Words and music by Lew Sully. Published by Howley, Haviland (New York, 1897).

36. Published by M. Witmark and Sons (New York, 1896).

37. Ewen, *op. cit.*, p. 10; Goldberg, *op. cit.*, p. 156. Rather surprisingly, Ewen fails to interpret even the story situation correctly, holding that the female is being jilted by the male!

38. Isidore Witmark and Isaac Goldberg, *From Ragtime to Swingtime*. (New York, 1939), pp. 94, 148–149, 170.

39. "I'se Got Another Nigger On Ma Staff." Words by Andrew B. Sterling, music by Harry Von Tilzer. Published by Feist and Frankenthaler (New York, 1897).

40. Words and music by Hughie Cannon. Published by Howley, Haviland and Dresser (New York, 1902).

41. Words by Frank Fogerty, music by Woodward and Jerome. Published by Howley, Haviland and Dresser (New York, 1902).

42. Words by Billy Johnson, music by Seymour Furth. Published by Howley, Haviland and Dresser (New York, 1902).

43. Words by Bob Cole and J.W. Johnson, music by Rosamund Johnson. Published by Joseph W. Stern (New York, 1901).

44. Words by Edward Furber, music by Bert W. Williams. Published by Joseph W. Stern (New York, 1898).

45. Words and music by Edward A. Paulton. Published by M. Witmark and Sons (New York, 1906).

46. "I'm The Toughest, Toughest Coon." Words by Carl Stowe, music by L. Mauran Bloodgood. Published by Walter Jacobs (Boston, 1904).

47. Published by White-Smith (Boston, 1896).

48. Words and music by Mark Beam. Published by May Irwin (New York, 1904), and sung by her in *Mrs. Black Is Back*.

49. Published by Joseph W. Stern (New York, 1901).

50. Words by Felix F. Feist, music by Joseph S. Nathan. Published by Leo Feist (New York, 1906).

51. Published by Oliver Ditson (Boston, 1893).

52. Words and music by Charles Shackford. Published by E.T. Paull (New York, 1897).

53. Both published by Lyceum (New York, 1903).

54. Words and music by Dan Lewis. Published by National Music (Chicago, 1882).

55. Words and music by Harry Freeman. Published by Lyon and Healy (Chicago, 1897).

56. Published by M. Witmark and Sons (New York, 1894).

57. Katz, *op. cit.*, p. 389.

58. Words by Brandon Walsh, music by Ernest Breuer. Published by Will Rossiter (Chicago, 1914).

59. For an excellent, although brief, account of the black in American wars, see *Ebony*, August, 1968.

60. Words by Jimmie Marten, music by Mitch LeBlanc. Published by Thomas Goggan (Houston, 1917). Courtesy of Kean Archives.

61. Words by Bernie Grossman, music by Billy Winkle. Published by Joe Morris (New York, 1918).

62. Words and music by Harry Carroll. Published by Shapiro, Bernstein (New York, 1918).

63. Words by Alfred Bryan, music by Ernest Breuer. Published by Richmond (New York, 1918).

64. Published by Clark-Levy (San Francisco, 1917).

65. Words and music by Smith and Bowman. Published by Walter Jacobs (Boston, 1903).

66. Words and music by Joe Arizona. Published by Joseph Morris (Philadelphia, 1904).

67. Words by Marshall Walker, music by Will E. Skidmore. Published by Joseph W. Stern (New York, 1918).

68. Words by Renton Tunnah, music by Will E. Skidmore. Published by Will E. Skidmore (New York, 1916).

69. Words and music by Will E. Skidmore and Marshall Walker. Published by Skidmore Music (New York, 1919).

70. Published by Joseph W. Stern (New York, 1904).

71. Words and music by Lee Johnson. Published by Zeno Mauvais (San Francisco, 1896).

72. Published by Hurtig and Seamon (New York, 1890).

73. Published by Joseph W. Stern (New York, 1906), and featured in Cole and Johnson's *The Shoo-fly Regiment*.

74. Words by Ed. Rose, music by Nat Osborne. Published by Howley, Haviland (New York, 1902).

75. Words and music by Arthur Longbrake. Published by Jos. Morris (Philadelphia, 1908).

76. Published by Jerome H. Remick (New York, 1906).

77. Published by S. Brainard's Sons (Chicago, 1895).

78. Published by T.B. Harms (New York, 1894).

79. Words by Arline Wyatt, music by Tom McRae. Published by Jos. W. Stern (New York, 1912).

80. Words by William Osborne, music by Nellie Sylvester. Published by Carleton Cavanagh (New York, 1897).

81. Words by Gene Jefferson, music by Leo Friedman. Published by Sol Bloom (Chicago, 1900).

82. Published by Jerome H. Remick (New York, 1907).

83. Published by Waterson, Berlin and Snyder (New York, 1918).

84. The former: words by Andrew B. Sterling, music by Harry Von Tilzer. Published by Harry Von Tilzer (New York, 1903). The latter song has words by

Charles McCarron and Charles S. Alberte, music by Albert Von Tilzer. Published by Broadway Music (New York, 1906).

85. Published by Jerome H. Remick (New York, 1917).

86. Words by Irving Caesar. Published by T.B. Harms (New York, 1919).

87. Both songs published by Waterson, Berlin and Snyder (New York, 1912). Snyder collaborated with Berlin on "I Want To Be In Dixie," but the extent of his contribution is not known.

88. Published by Al Piantadosi (New York, 1917).

89. Published by Vandersloot (Williamsport, 1907).

90. Published by Edward B. Marks (New York, 1901).

91. Published by George W. Meyer (New York, 1913).

92. Published by Leo Feist (New York, 1919).

93. Words by James Royce (under the pseudonym, J.R. Shannon), music by Frederick Knight Logan. Published by Forster (Chicago, 1905). "Missouri Waltz" has had high-level political associations as well: it was not only the "theme song" of former President Truman, but was included in a tasteless display by President Nixon at a Washington Gridiron Club banquet, wherein he and Vice President Agnew engaged in a lampoon of their so-called Southern strategy. See *Time*, March 30, 1970, p. 42.

94. Published by Waterson, Berlin and Snyder (New York, 1914). Caption title reads: "When It's Night Time in Dixie Land."

95. Words by Al Trahern, music by Lee Orean Smith. Published by Vandersloot (New York, 1902).

96. Words by Jack Yellen, music by George L. Cobb. Published by Jerome H. Remick (New York, 1915).

97. Words by Tell Taylor, music by Earl K. Smith. Published by Tell Taylor (Chicago, 1917).

98. Published by M. Witmark and Sons (New York, 1913).

99. Words by Charles E. Baer, music by Johann C. Schmid. Published by Jos. M. Morris (Philadelphia, 1905).

100. Words and music by Max S. Witt. Published by Shapiro (New York, 1912).

101. Words by Jean Lenox, music by Harry O. Sutton. Published by Jos. W. Stern & Co. (New York, 1905).

102. Published by Howley, Haviland and Dresser (New York, 1903).

103. Words by Alfred Bryan, music by Harry Tierney. Published by Jerome H. Remick (New York, 1916).

104. Published by Jerome H. Remick (New York, 1916).

105. Published by Harry Von Tilzer (New York, 1919).

106. From a collective cover title page on "Nobody Belongs To Me." Published by M. Witmark and Sons (New York, 1908).

107. Words by Jack Caddigan, music by James A. Brennan. Published by Daly (Boston, 1918).

108. Words and music by John Redmond and Lee David. Published by Mills (New York, 1937).

109. Words by Jack Yellen, music by George L. Cobb. Published by M. Witmark and Sons (New York, 1915).

110. Published by Wm. B. Gray (New York, 1899).

111. Published by M. Witmark and Sons (New York, 1912).

112. Words by M.F., music by George H. Clutsam. Published by Chappell (New York, 1900).

113. Words by William Moore, music by Will Marion Cook. Published by G. Schirmer (New York, 1907).

114. Words by Wm. H. Gardner. Published by M. Witmark and Sons (New York, 1914).

115. Published by M. Witmark and Sons (New York, 1906).

116. Published by F.A. Mills (New York, 1897).

117. Published by Shapiro, Bernstein and Von Tilzer (New York, 1901).

118. Words by Alfred Bryan, music by George W. Meyers. Published by F.B. Haviland (New York, 1908).

119. Words by Clarence S. Brewster, music by A. Baldwin Sloane. Published by M. Witmark and Sons (New York, 1898).

120. Words by John Gilroy, music by Harry Linton. Published by Sol Bloom (New York, 1902).

121. Words by J. Adrian, music by Carl Bruno. Published by The Walrus Co. (Pittsburg, 1903).

122. Words by Henry S. Creamer, music by Silvio Hein. Published by Marie Cahill (New York, 1909).

123. Words by William Murray, music by Ernest Hogan. Published by Sol Bloom (New York, 1902).

124. Words by Thomas J. Keating, music by Lyn Udall. Published by M. Witmark and Sons (New York, 1901).

125. Words by Will A. Heelan, music by Harry Von Tilzer. Published by Wm. C. Dunn (New York, 1899).

126. Published by Howley, Haviland and Dresser (New York, 1902).

127. Published by M. Witmark and Sons (New York, 1903).

128. Words by Edward Madden, music by Theodore Morse. Published by F.B. Haviland (New York, 1904).

129. Words and music by Adelaide Sullivan. Published by Zeno Mauvais (San Francisco, 1899).

130. Words by Ed. H. Jacobs, music by Fr(ank) L. Neddermeyer. Published by F.L. Neddermeyer (Columbus, 1896).

131. Words by Joe Hayden, music by Theodore A. Metz. Published by Willis Woodward (New York, 1896).

132. Words by Will J. Harris, music by Harry I. Robinson. Published by Will Rossiter (Chicago, 1909).

133. Words by Benjamin Hapgood Burt, music by Silvio Hein. Published by Jos. W. Stern (New York, 1906).

134. Words and music by Max Hoffman. Published by Shapiro, Bernstein & Co. (New York, 1902).

135. Published by Howley, Haviland and Dresser (New York, 1902).

136. Words by W.S. Gilbert, music by George Schleiffarth. Published by S. Brainard's Sons (New York, 1889).

137. Published by Jos. W. Stern (New York, 1902).

138. Dichter and Shapiro, *op. cit.*, p. 101.

139. Words by Jack Drislane, music by Theodore Morse. Published by F. B. Haviland (New York, 1907).
140. Words by Edward Madden, music by Theodore Morse. Published by F.B. Haviland (New York, 1908).
141. Words by Jack Drislane, music by Henry Frantzen. Published by F.B. Haviland. (New York, 1909).
142. Words by Dave Oppenheimer, music by Joe Cooper. Published by Shapiro (New York, 1911).
143. Published by T.B. Harms (New York, 1898).
144. Published by York Music (New York, 1910).
145. Words by Edgar Leslie and E. Ray Goetz, music by George W. Meyer. Published by Waterson, Berlin and Snyder (New York, 1917).
146. Words and music by Thomas S. Allen. Published by Walter Jacobs (Boston, 1904).
147. Published by Sherman, Clay (San Francisco, 1916).
148. Words by C.S. Montanye, music by Frank H. Grey. Published by M. Witmark and Sons (New York, 1919).
149. Words by Richard Henry Buck. Published by White-Smith (Boston, 1896).
150. Words by A.C., music by T. Channing Moore. Published by N. Weinstein (New York, 1904).
151. Published by Edwin H. Morris (New York, 1897).
152. Published by Albright Music (Chicago, 1899).
153. Published by Theodore Presser (Philadelphia, 1904).
154. Published by M. Witmark and Sons (New York, 1911).
155. Published by M. Witmark and Sons (New York, 1906).
156. Words by Raymond Egan, music by Richard Whiting. Published by Jerome H. Remick (New York, 1916).
157. Words by Ring W. Lardner, music by G. Harris White. Published by Harold Rossiter (Chicago, 1916).
158. Words by William H. Gardner, music by Adam Geibel. Published by Shapiro, Remick (New York, 1904).
159. Allport, *op. cit.*, pp. 170–171. Conflict between the mother-child imagery and the black stereotyped figure caused some songwriters to resort to fantasy for solutions, as in Charles Shackford's "Only A Little Yaller Coon," in which the color of the black child magically changes to "yaller":

> Dah's a mighty heap of truble brewin' down in Tennessee
> And its all about a little yaller coon.
> Now this little pickaninny was as black as he could be,
> On de mornin' he was born de fust of June,
> Now de cause ob dis commotion was de fact dat ober night,
> Exactly on de fullnes ob de moon,
> Dat dis little pickaninny changed his skin from black to white
> In de morn dey found a little yaller coon.

160. Words by Karl Kennett, music by Lyn Udall. Published by M. Witmark and Sons (New York, 1899).

161. Words by Charles R. Fisher, music by Joe Santly. Published by M. Witmark and Sons (New York, 1903).

162. Published by M. Witmark and Sons (New York, 1902).

163. "Honey, You'se Ma Lady Love; A Coonlet Courtship." Words and music by Nat. D. Mann. Published by M. Witmark and Sons (New York, 1897).

164. Published by Carrie Jacobs-Bond and Son (Hollywood, 1903).

165. Words by E.P. Moran, music by J. Fred Helf. Published by Helf and Hager (New York, 1908).

166. Words and music by Bob Cole and Billy Johnson. Published by Howley, Haviland and Co. (New York, 1899).

167. Published by Saxx Music (Boston, 1899).

168. Tom Fletcher, *The Tom Fletcher Story; One Hundred Years of the Negro in Show Business* (New York, 1954), p. xx.

CHAPTER NINE

1. Langston Hughes and Milton Meltzer, *Black Magic: A Pictorial History of the Negro in American Entertainment* (Englewood Cliffs, 1967), p. 313.

2. Words and music by Louis A. Hirsch, Gene Buck, and Dave Stamper. Published by Harms (New York, 1922).

3. George E. Kent, "Taking Off the Minstrel Mask," in the *New York Times Book Review*. LXXVII: 2, pp. 4–20.

4. Published by M. Witmark and Sons (New York, 1921).

5. Words and music by Cecil Mack (pseudonym of Richard C. McPherson) and Jimmy (James P.) Johnson. Published by Harms (New York, 1923).

6. Published by Donaldson, Douglass and Gumble (New York, 1929).

7. "Harlem River Quiver." Words by Dorothy Fields, music by Jimmy McHugh. Published by Jack Mills (New York, 1928).

8. Quoted in Henry O. Osgood, *So This Is Jazz* (Boston, 1925), pp. 16–17.

9. In *Music and Letters* (1927), VIII: iv, pp. 483–484.

10. "The Jazz Me Blues," by Tom Delaney. Published by Palmetto Music (New York, 1921).

11. Words by Blanche Merrill, music by M.K. Jerome. Published by Waterson, Berlin and Snyder (New York, 1919).

12. Words by Walter Melrose, music by Joe Oliver. Published by Melrose (New York, 1926).

13. Words by B.G. De Sylva and Lew Brown, music by Ray Henderson. Published by Harms (New York, 1926).

14. By James Cavanaugh and Harry Harris. Published by Shapiro, Bernstein (New York, 1927).

15. *New York Times*, January 27, 1925, 12:8.

16. *New York Times*, October 11, 1924, 16:1.

17. *New York Times*, July 28, 1922, 3:2.

18. Words by Jack Yellen, music by Albert Gumble. Published by Jerome H. Remick (New York, 1920). Introduced by the Farber Sisters in *Sinbad*.

19. Words by Grant Clarke and Roy Turk, music by George W. Meyer and Arthur Johnson. Published by Irving Berlin (New York, 1924). Featured in A.H. Woods' musical *Dixie to Broadway*.

20. Words by B.G. De Sylva and Lew Brown, music by Ray Henderson. Published by Harms (New York, 1926).

21. W.C. Handy, *Father of the Blues, An Autobiography* (New York, 1955), p. 123.

22. Words and music by Henry Busse, Henry Lange, and Lou Davis. Published by Leo Feist (New York, 1922).

23. Handy, *op. cit.*, p. 305.

24. Words by Hughie Prince, music by Harold Mooney. Published by Luz Brothers (New York, 1932).

25. Words and music by Art Conrad and Frank Gillen. Published by Edw. B. Marks (New York, 1924).

26. "Bring Back Those Minstrel Days." Words by Ballard MacDonald, music by Martin Broones. Published by Shapiro, Bernstein (New York, 1926).

27. Published by Mills (New York, 1937).

28. Published by Harold Flammer (New York, 1928).

29. "Denison's Minstrel Opening Chorus," by Jeff Branen, arranged by Harry L. Alford. (Chicago, 1922).

30. Words by Bud Green, music by Harry Warren. Published by Shapiro, Bernstein (New York, 1927).

31. "Pickaninnies' Heaven." Words by Sam Coslow, music by Arthur Johnston. Published by Famous Music (New York, 1932).

32. Words and music by Irving Caesar, Sammy Lerner, and Gerald Marks. Published by Irving Caesar (New York, 1936).

33. Published by Nordyke (Hollywood, California, 1945).

34. Words by Virginia Carter Castleman, music by Anita Schrade. Published by Anita Schrade (n.p., 1931).

35. Published by Warock Music (New York, 1952).

36. Words by Edgar Leslie, music by Walter Donaldson. Published by Shapiro, Bernstein (New York, 1921).

37. Words by Mort Dixon, music by Ray Henderson. Published by Jerome H. Remick (New York, 1925).

38. Words and music by H. Pitman Clarke. Published by Leo Feist (New York, 1921).

39. Words by Bennie Davis, music by Joseph Burke. Published by Joe Morris (New York, 1928).

40. By Gene Austin, Emmet O'Hara, and Irving Mills. Published by Jack Mills (New York, 1924).

41. By Roy Turk and Lou Handman. Published by Jerome H. Remick (New York, 1925).

42. By Creamer and Layton. Published by Shapiro, Bernstein (New York, 1922).
43. Words by Ray Sherwood, music by Marion Schott. Published by F.B. Haviland (New York, 1926).
44. Words by William Tracey, music by Dan Dougherty. Published by Shapiro, Bernstein (New York, 1927).
45. Words by Sam Lewis and Joe Young, music by Walter Donaldson. Published by Irving Berlin (New York, 1921).
46. Published by Denton & Haskins (New York, 1924).
47. Words by Sam M. Lewis and Joe Young, music by Fred E. Ahlert. Published by Waterson, Berlin and Snyder (New York, 1920).
48. By B.G. DeSylva, Lew Brown and Ray Henderson. Published by DeSylva, Brown and Henderson (New York, 1927).
49. Words by Jeff Branen, music by Henry S. Sawyer. Published by T.S. Denison (Chicago, 1925).
50. Words and music by Ben Bernie, Maceo Pinkard, and Kenneth Casey. Published by Remick (New York, 1925).
51. By Billy Rose and Con Conrad. Published by Leo Feist (New York, 1923).
52. By Gilbert Wells, Bud Cooper, and Fred Rose. Published by Rainbow Music (New York, 1924), assigned to Irving Berlin (New York, 1924).
53. The technical device of depicting the black by means of the silhouette on illustrated sheet music covers was popular during the 1920's and 1930's, perhaps as a reflection of the movement away from the thoroughly demeaning covers of the coon song.
54. Published by Popular Melodies (New York, 1937).
55. Words and music by Dave Oppenheim, Michael Cleary, and Jaques Krakeur II. Published by Popular Melodies (New York, 1936).
56. Published by Jack Mills (New York, 1921). Introduced by Van and Schenck in the *Ziegfeld Follies of 1921.*
57. Published by Harry Von Tilzer (New York, 1919).
58. Words and music by Gene Austin and Roy Bergere. Published by Stark and Cowan (New York, 1924).
59. By Jack Yellen, Bob Bigelow, and Charles Bates. Published by Ager, Yellen and Bornstein (New York, 1924).
60. By Al Dubin, Jimmie McHugh, Irving Mills, and Irwin Dash. Published by Jack Mills (New York, 1924).
61. By Cal DeVoll. Published by Ted Browne (Chicago, 1924).
62. Words by Thekla Hollingsworth, music by Jessie L. Deppen. Published by Harms (New York, 1924).
63. Words by Al Dubin, music by Harry Warren. Published by M. Witmark and Sons (New York,1935).
64. Words by Eddie Leonard, music by Eddie Munson. Published by Edward B. Marks (New York, 1930).
65. Words and music by Fred Howard and Nat Vincent. Published by Vincent-Howard-Preeman (Los Angeles, 1930); copyright assigned to M.M. Cole (Chicago, 1935).
66. Words by Jack Yellen, music by Milton Ager. Published by Advanced Music (New York, 1923).

67. Published by G. Schirmer (New York, 1920).

68. Published by R.L. Huntzinger (New York, 1919).

69. Words by Gus Kahn, music by Neil Moret. Published by Villa Moret (San Francisco, 1927).

70. Published by Ager, Yellen and Bornstein (New York, 1922).

71. Words and music by Spencer Williams and Howard Johnson. Published by Triangle Music (New York, 1929).

72. Published by Broadway Music (New York, 1921).

73. Published by Triangle Music (New York, 1928).

74. By Gene Austin, Emmet O'Hara, and Irving Mills. Published by Jack Mills (New York, 1924).

75. Words by Bernie Grossman, music by Danny Dougherty. Published by Stark and Cowan (New York, 1925).

76. Published by Mills Music (New York, 1937).

77. Words by Raymond Leveen and George Hayes, music by Frankie Carle. Published by Jewel Music (New York, 1939).

78. Published by M. Witmark and Sons (New York, 1921).

79. Published by M. Witmark and Sons (New York, 1921).

80. Published by Joe Morris (New York, 1923).

81. By Roy Turk, J. Russell Robinson, and Addy Britt. Published by Waterson, Berlin and Snyder (New York, 1922).

82. By Al Bernard. Published by Henry Waterson (New York, 1924).

83. Words by Mann Holiner, music by Alberta Nichols. Published by Shapiro, Bernstein (New York, 1931).

84. Words by Andy Razaf, music by Thomas Waller and Harry Brooks. Published by Mills (New York, 1929).

85. Published by Carl Fischer (New York, 1939).

86. Words by Cecil Mack and Lew Brown, music by Ford Dabney. Published by Shapiro, Bernstein (New York, 1924).

87. Words by Francis DeWitt, music by Robert Hood Bowers. Published by Shapiro, Bernstein (New York, 1920).

88. Words by Francis De Witt, music by Robert Hood Bowers. Published by Shapiro, Bernstein (New York, 1921).

89. Words by Lew Brown, music by Walter Donaldson. Published by Shapiro, Bernstein (New York, 1923).

90. Published by Waterson, Berlin and Snyder (New York, 1923).

91. Words and music by James F. Hanley. Published by Shapiro, Bernstein (New York, 1920).

92. Published by White-Smith (Boston, 1922).

93. Words by George Murray Brown, music by Keith Crosby Brown. Published by Harold Flammer (New York, 1935).

94. Published by C.C. Birchard (Boston, 1936).

95. Published by Maxwell Weaner (New York, 1939).

96. Words by Andy Razaf, music by J.C. Johnson. Published by Triangle Music (New York, 1928).

97. Words by William Rose and Edward Eliscu, music by Vincent Youmans. Published by Miller Music (New York, 1929).

98. Published by Shapiro, Bernstein (New York, 1925).

99. Words and music by B.G. De Sylva, Lew Brown, and Ray Henderson. Published by De Sylva, Brown and Henderson (New York, 1928).

100. Words and adaptation by William Arms Fisher, music by Anton Dvořák. Published by Oliver Ditson (Boston, 1922).

101. See James Weldon Johnson and J. Rosamund Johnson, *The Book of American Negro Spirituals* (New York, 1925), pp. 11–15, 114–117.

102. Published by Robbins (New York, 1930).

103. Words and music by Clarence A. Stout. Published by Handy Bros. Music (New York, 1920).

104. Published by Edward B. Marks (New York, 1925).

105. By Maceo Pinkard and Mitchell Parrish. Published by Mills Music (New York, 1930).

106. Published by Harms (New York, 1926).

107. Published by Harms (New York, 1934).

108. Published by De Sylva, Brown and Henderson (New York, 1931).

109. Words by John Latouche, music by Vernon Duke. Published by Leo Feist (New York, 1940).

110. Words by Marie Lussi. Published by G. Schirmer (New York, 1929).

111. Published by G. Schirmer (New York, 1920).

112. "A Note On Robert MacGimsey," in "Shadrack." Words and music by Robert MacGimsey. Published by Carl Fischer (New York, 1931).

113. Published by Carl Fischer (New York, 1934).

114. Published by Carl Fischer (New York, 1939).

115. Published by Van Alstyne and Curtis (New York, 1921).

116. Published by Southern (New York, 1933).

117. Published by G. Schirmer (New York, 1939).

118. Words edited by Clement Wood. Published by Harold Flammer (New York, 1928).

119. Ewen, in his *American Popular Songs*, attributes "Shortnin' Bread" to Wolfe, mentioning that several black composers claimed to have written it. Another adaptation was made by David W. Guion and published by Robbins Music (New York, 1941).

120. Words by Betty Reynolds, music by Edward Morris. Published by Edward Morris (New York, 1924).

121. Published by Leo Feist (New York, 1925).

122. Published by Clarence Williams (New York, 1924).

123. Oscar Hammerstein II, *Carmen Jones* (New York, 1945), p. xiii ff.

124. Words by Dorothy Fields, music by Jimmie McHugh. Published by Mills Music (New York, 1928).

125. "Porgy and Bess—A Folk Opera?" in Lindsay Patterson, comp. and ed., *Anthology of the American Negro in the Theatre* (New York, 1967), p. 187ff.

126. *Ibid.*, p. 192.

127. Howard Taubman, *The Making of the American Theatre*, rev. ed. (New York, 1967), p. 219.

128. Taubman, *op. cit.*, p. 282.

CHAPTER TEN

1. "The Music America Loves Best," record catalog of Radio Corporation of America (Camden, 1943). Stephen Foster, James Bland, Dan Emmett, George Gershwin, and other composers using black subject matter and imitative styles of blacks are listed in the front of the catalog, under "Classic Works and Established Favorites." Composers and performers of black music, such as Doc Clayton, Golden Gate Quartet and Memphis Slim, are at the rear of the catalog, under "Race Entertainment."

2. By Al Bernard. Published by Amsco Music (New York, 1933).

3. Published by Edward B. Marks (New York, 1953).

4. Published by Handy Brothers Music (New York, 1941). After World War II, Charles L. Cooke collaborated with W.C. Handy in producing a tribute to President Truman, "The Big Stick Blues March" (1951), which praised his stand on civil rights with:

> All men up!
> Not some men down,
> Said Harry T's.
> Civil Rights Bill.

5. Words and music by Nelson Cogane, Ira Schuster, and Joseph Meyer. Published by Paull-Pioneer Music (New York, 1942).

6. Words by Mrs. Julianna Hill, music by Joseph A. Sarcini. Published by Samaritan Sacred Song Publishers (St. Louis, 1946). The back cover of the sheet music edition of another song, "There's A New Flag On Iwo Jima" (Leeds Music, New York, 1945), by Harold Adamson and Jimmy McHugh, contains Chaplain Roland B. Gittlesohn's "Sermon on the Dedication of [the] 5th Marine Division Cemetery on Iwo Jima," in which all the ideals for which the nation was fighting were enumerated. Speaking of the dead, Gittlesohn said: "Among those men there is no discrimination. No prejudice. No hatred." Of the living, he promised "the birth of a new freedom for the sons of men everywhere." Lofty ideals often become the subject matter for popular song, but seldom have racial problems been so specifically mentioned as in these two instances.

7. Published by Edwin H. Morris (New York, 1943).

8. Words by Ray Gilbert, music by Allie Wrubel. Published by Santly-Joy (New York, 1946).

9. Words and music by Tade Dolan, Tom Erwin, Frances Dolen, and Chris Bowden. Published by General Music (New York, 1949).

10. Published by Bob Miller (New York, 1945).

11. Published by Southern Music (New York, 1944).

12. Published by Harry Warren (New York, 1947).

13. Published by Harms (New York, 1951).

14. Words by Don Raye, music by Louis Armstrong. Published by Leeds Music (New York, 1950).

15. Published by Leeds Music (New York, 1941; 1952; 1955).

16. Published by Buxton-Hill (New York, 1956).

17. Words and music by Wilmoth Houdini. Published by Miller Music (New York, 1946).

18. Published by Omega Music Edition (New York, 1946).

19. Published by Redd Evans (New York, 1956).

20. Published by Southern Music (New York, 1933). An interesting sequel, "Lazy Bones Gotta Job Now," sung by Joe Morrison in the motion picture *It's A Great Life*, failed to achieve success. Leo Robin and Lewis E. Gensler, writers of the song, made some technical errors in their black imagery by having "Lazy Bones" working at a government job and by having his motivation for getting the job his desire to earn enough money to get married. Apart from any other faults, these violations of prevailing stereotypes were sufficient to insure failure for the song.

21. Published by Sun Music (New York, 1947).

22. Published by Leeds Music (New York, 1943, 1944).

23. Published by Armo Music (Cincinnati, 1951).

24. Published by Carl Fischer (New York, 1946).

25. Words by Harry Coleman, music by Arden Clar. Published by Campbell Music (New York, 1948).

26. Published by Carl Fischer (New York, 1952).

27. Published by Pyramid Music (New York, 1943).

28. Words and music by Jan Matus and George R. Brown. Published by Southwest (Hollywood, California, 1953).

29. Published by Chappell (New York, 1957).

30. Arranged by Tom Scott. Published by Shawnee Press (East Stroudburg, Pennsylvania, 1943).

31. Arranged by Livingston Gearhart. Published by Words and Music (New York, 1946).

32. The "head bone," for example, was to be illustrated by a "bong" sound, made by a deep-toned temple block; the "neck bone," by the "Z-z-z-zip" of a rachet; and so on. The obvious intent is to exploit aural comic imagery of the black as had been developed over years of minstrel and vaudeville slapstick experience.

33. From the Marion Kerby original collection of Negro Exaltations. Published by Mills Music (New York, 1952).

34. Words by Sam Coslow, music by Arthur Johnston. Published by Santly-Joy (New York, 1946).

35. Published by Santly-Joy (New York, 1946).

36. Published by Braun Music (Chicago).

37. Words by Ted Parsons, music by Mercer Ellington. Published by Tempo Music (New York, 1943).

38. Words by E.Y. Harburg, music by Harold Arlen. Published by Leo Feist (New York, 1943).

39. Published by Robbins Music (New York, 1949).

40. Words by Herb Magidson, music by Ben Oakland. Published by George Simon (New York, 1957).

41. Published by Shapiro, Bernstein (New York, 1952 and 1954).

42. Music by Nico Carstens, Charles Segal, Viv Styger, and Anton De Waal. Published by Trutone (Africa, 1954); Peer International (New York, 1955).

43. Published by Case Music (New York, 1952).

44. By Barry Mann and Mike Anthony. Published by Stratton Music (New York, 1959).

45. Words and music by Helen Reddy and Ray Burton. Published by Buggerlugs Music, c/o Artie Mogull (Los Angeles, 1971, 1972).

46. Published by Panther Music (New York, 1955).

47. Words and music by Fleecie Moore. Published by Warock Music (New York, 1945).

48. Words and music by Raymond Taylor and Lester Judson. Published by Duchess Music (New York, 1952).

49. By Wayne P. Walker. Published by Cedarwood (Nashville, 1961).

50. Words and music by R. van Leeuwen. Published by Dayglow Music N.V. (Hilversum, Holland, 1969).

51. Published by Hancock Music (New York, 1962; 1963; 1965).

52. Words by Jack Lee, music by Frank Owens. Published by Edwin H. Morris (New York, 1967).

53. Words and music by Luchi De Jesus, Mayme Watts, and Lila Lerner. Published by Anne-Rachel Music (New York, 1967).

54. Published by Dynatone (Cincinnati, 1968).

55. Words and music by David Barnes, Myra Smith, and Margaret Lewis. Published by Shelby Singleton Music and Hip Hill Music (1969).

56. "Bojangles of Harlem," words by Dorothy Fields, music by Jerome Kern. Published by Chappell (New York, 1936). Featured in the RKO Radio motion picture *Swing Time.*

57. Words and music by Jerry Jeff Walker. Published by Cotillon Music and Daniel Music (New York, 1968).

58. Words by Charles Wood, music by John Cacavas. Published by Chappell (New York, 1968).

59. Published by R.D. Row (Boston, 1956).

60. Published by Camad Music (Chicago, 1968).

61. Published by Cookaway Music (London, 1969).

62. Words and music by Richard Adler. Published by Sahara Music (n.p., 1961).

63. Published by Dialogue Music (n.p., 1966).

64. Letter to the author from Norman Curtis, dated April 1, 1971.

65. Words by Patricia Taylor Curtis, music by Norman Curtis. Copyright by the authors, 1964.

66. Words and music by Merle Haggard and Roy Edward Burris. Published by Blue Book Music (Bakersfield, California, 1969).

67. Words and music by Guy Drake. Published by Birmingham Music (1969), assigned to Bull Fighter Music (Nashville, 1970).

68. In *The Philadelphia Inquirer.* April 22, 1970.

69. By Julian Wilson and James M. Smith. Published by Shelby Singleton Music and Quickit Publishing Co. (Nashville, 1971).

70. Words and music by Lee Hays and Pete Seeger. Published by Ludlow Music (New York, 1962).

71. Words and music by Stuart Scharf. Published by Takya Music (New York, 1968). Theme song for the New York Urban Coalition Campaign.

72. Published by Blue Seas Music and Jac Music (New York, 1965).

73. Published by Blue Seas Music (New York, 1971).
74. ~~Published by Kicks Music (n.p., 1960)~~; recorded on Columbia (CL 1577).
75. Music by Hubert Giraud. Published by Maxim Music (New York, 1971).
76. Published by Pix-Russ (Nashville, 1970).
77. Words and music by Kenneth Bell, Coy Reeves, and David Bell. Published by Wren Music (New York, 1969, 1970).
78. Published by Northern Songs, Ltd. (London, 1971); Maclen Music (New York).
79. Full title: "For God's Sake, Give More Power To The People." Published by Julio-Brian Music (New York, 1971).
80. Published by Northern Songs Ltd. (London, 1971).
81. Published by Roznique Music (New York, 1968).
82. Words by Noble Sissle, music by Eubie Blake. Published by Leo Feist (New York, 1968).
83. Words and music by Neil Young. Published by Cotillon Music and Broken Arrow Music (New York, 1970).
84. Published by Ram's Horn Music (n.p., 1971).

APPENDIX I

1. *Vide* pp. 60–77.
2. *Op. cit.*, pp. 44–49.
3. *Memoirs*, III: 309.
4. *Ibid.*, p. 307.
5. *Loc. cit.*
6. *Op. cit.*, p. 315. Italics are Mathews's.
7. *Op. cit.*, p. 322.
8. *Op. cit.*, p. 307.
9. *Op. cit.*, p. 332.
10. *Op. cit.*, pp. 343–345.
11. *Op. cit.*, p. 381.
12. Nathan, *op. cit.*, p. 45.
13. *Loc. cit.*
14. Mathews, *op. cit.*, IV: 294–297.

Bibliography

Adams, Alice Dana. *The Neglected Period of Anti-Slavery in America, 1808–1831.* Gloucester, Massachusetts: Radcliffe College Monographs, 1964. Originally published by P. Smith, 1908.

Allport, Gordon U. *The Nature of Prejudice.* Abridged. Garden City, New York: Doubleday, 1958. Originally published by Addison-Wesley Publishing Co. in 1954.

Andrews, Edward D. *The Gift to be Simple: Songs, Dances and Rituals of the American Shakers.* New York: J.J. Augustin, Inc., 1940.

Aptheker, Herbert, editor. *A Documentary History of the Negro People in the United States.* 2 vols. New York: Citadel Press, 1966.

Baskerville, Charles Read. *The Elizabethan Jig and Related Song Drama.* New York: Dover, 1965.

Bennett, Lerone, Jr. *Before the Mayflower: A History of the Negro in America, 1619–1964.* Revised edition. Baltimore: Penguin Books, 1969.

Bergler, Edmund. *Laughter and the Sense of Humor.* New York: Intercontinental Book Corp., 1956.

Bergman, Peter M., and Bergman, Mort N. *The Chronological History of the Negro in America.* New York: Harper & Row, 1969.

Bergson, Henri. *Essai sur la Signification du Comique.* 173ᵉ ed. Paris: Presses Universitaires de France, 1962.

Brandel, Rose. *The Music of Central Africa; An Ethnomusicological Study: The Former Belgian Congo, Ruanda-Urundi, Uganda, Tanganyika.* The Hague: Martinus Nijhoff, 1961.

Brawley, Benjamin. *A Social History of the American Negro.* New York: Macmillan, 1970.

Broucek, Jack Wolf. "Eighteenth Century Music in Savannah, Georgia." Ph.D. dissertation, Florida State University, 1963.

Butcher, Margaret Just. *The Negro in American Culture.* New York: Alfred A. Knopf, 1969.

Butler, Benjamin. *Butler's Book.* Boston: Thayer, 1892.

Captain Canot; or, Twenty Years of an African Slaver. Written out and edited from the Captain's Journals, Memoranda, and Conversations by Brantz Mayer. New York: D. Appleton & Company, Inc., 1854.

Carter, Albert E. "The Louisiana Negro and His Music." Master's thesis, Northwestern University, 1947.

Charles, Norman. "Social Values in American Popular Songs (1890–1950)." Ph.D. dissertation, University of Pennsylvania, 1958.

Charters, Ann. *Nobody: The Story of Bert Williams.* New York: Macmillan, 1970.

Chase, Gilbert. *America's Music.* 2nd revised edition. New York: McGraw-Hill, 1965.

Coffin, Joshua. *Slave Insurrections.* New York: American Anti-Slavery Society 1860. Reprinted by Negro History Press, 1969.

Colvig, Richard. *Black Music: A Checklist of Books.* Oakland, California: Oakland Public Library, 1969.

Courlander, Harold. *Negro Folk Music, U.S.A.* New York: Columbia University Press, 1963.

Curtis, Natalie. *Songs and Tales from the Dark Continent.* New York: G. Schirmer, Inc., 1920.

Davidson, Frank Costellow. *The Rise, Decline and Influence of the American Minstrel Show.* Ph.D. dissertation, New York University, 1952.

Dichter, Harry, and Shapiro, Elliot. *Early American Sheet Music: Its Lure and Its Lore.* New York: Bowker, 1941.

Douglass, Frederick. *Narrative of the Life of Frederick Douglass, An American Slave.* Reprint edition. New York: Belknap Press, 1968.

DuBois, W.E. Burghardt. *Black Reconstruction 1860–1880.* New York: Russell & Russell, 1935.

————. *The Souls of Black Folk, Essays and Sketches.* Greenwich, Connecticut: Fawcett, 1961.

Dunson, Josh. *Freedom in the Air: Song Movements of the Sixties.* New York: International Publishers, 1965.

Elkins, Stanley M. *Slavery: A Problem in American Institutional and Intellectual Life.* 2nd edition. Chicago: University of Chicago Press, 1968.

Emurian, Ernest K. *Stories of Civil War Songs.* Natick, Massachusetts: W.A. Wilde, 1960.

Ewen, David. *American Popular Songs: From the Revolutionary War to the Present.* New York: Random House, 1966.

Fishel, Leslie H., Jr., and Quarles, Benjamin. *The Negro American; A Documentary History.* Glenview, Illinois: Scott, Foresman & Co., 1967.

Fisher, Miles Mark. *Negro Slave Songs in the United States.* New York: Citadel Press, 1953.

Fletcher, Tom. *The Tom Fletcher Story: One Hundred Years of the Negro in Show Business.* New York: Burdge, 1954.

Freud, Sigmund. *Jokes and their Relation to the Unconscious.* Newly translated from the German and edited by James Strachey. New York: W.W. Norton, 1960.

Gagey, Edmond McAdoo. *Ballad Opera.* New York: B. Blom, 1965.

Gelbertson, Catherine. *Harriet Beecher Stowe.* New York: Appleton-Century, 1937.

Gerson, Robert A. *Music in Philadelphia.* Philadelphia: Theodore Presser, 1940.

Goldberg, Isaac. *Tin Pan Alley*. New York: F. Ungar, 1930.

Gossett, Thomas F. *Race: The History of an Idea in America*. Dallas: Southern Methodist University Press, 1963.

Grant, Joanne, editor. *Black Protest: History, Documents and Analyses, 1619 to the Present*. Greenwhich, Connecticut: Fawcett World Library, 1968.

Greene, Lorenzo J. *The Negro in Colonial New England, 1620–1776*. Port Washington, New York: Atheneum, 1942.

Grimshawe, T.S., editor. *The Works of William Cowper*. New York, 1868.

Handy, W.C. *Father of the Blues, An Autobiography*. New York: Macmillan, 1955.

———, ed. *Unsung Americans Sung*. New York: Handy Brothers, 1944.

Hartnoll, Phyllis. "Negro in the American Theatre." In *The Oxford Companion to the Theatre*. 2nd edition. London: Oxford University Press, 1957.

Harwell, Richard B. *Confederate Music*. Chapel Hill, North Carolina: University of North Carolina Press, 1950.

Heaps, Porter W. *The Singing Sixties*. Norman, Oklahoma: University of Oklahoma Press, 1960.

Herskovitz, Melville J. *The Myth of the Negro Past*. Boston: Beacon Press, 1941.

Herzberg, Max J., and Mones, Leon. *Humor of America*. New York: Appleton-Century-Crofts, 1945.

Hodge, Francis. *Yankee Theatre: The Image of America on the Stage, 1825–1850*. Austin, Texas: University of Texas Press, 1964.

Hodier, Andre. *Jazz: Its Evolution and Essence*. New York: Grove Press, 1956.

Howard, John Tasker. *Our American Music*. 3rd edition, revised. New York: Thomas Y. Crowell, 1946.

————. *Stephen Foster, America's Troubadour.* New York: Tudor Publishing Co., 1939.

Hughes, Langston, and Meltzer, Milton. *Black Magic: A Pictorial History of the Negro in American Entertainment.* Englewood Cliffs, New Jersey: Prentice-Hall, 1967.

Jenkins, William Sumner. *Pro-slavery Thought in the Old South.* Gloucester, Massachusetts: Peter Smith, 1960.

Johnson, James Weldon. *Along This Way: The Autobiography of James Weldon Johnson.* New York: Viking Press, 1954.

————, and Johnson, J. Rosamund. *The Book of American Negro Spirituals.* New York: Viking Press, 1925.

Jones, F.O., editor. *A Handbook of American Music and Musicians.* New York: Jones, 1886.

Kahn, E.J., Jr. *The Merry Partners: The Age and Stage of Harrigan and Hart.* New York: Random House, 1955.

Kardiner, Abram, and Ovesey, Lionel. *The Mark of Oppression: Explorations in the Personality of the American Negro.* Cleveland: World, 1951.

Katz, Bernard, editor. *The Social Implications of Early Negro Music in the United States.* New York: Arno Press, 1969.

Katz, William A. *Eyewitness: The Negro in American History.* New York: Pitman Publishing Co., 1967.

Kemble, Frances Anne. *Journal of a Residence on a Georgia Plantation in 1838–1839.* Edited by John A. Scott. New York: Alfred A. Knopf, 1961.

Krehbiel, Henry Edward. *Afro-American Folksongs: A Study in Racial and National Music.* New York: G. Schirmer, 1914.

Kwabena Nketia, J.H. *African Music in Ghana.* Evanston, Illinois: Northwestern University Press, 1963.

LaBrew, Arthur. *Studies in Nineteenth Century Afro-American Music.* Detroit: LaBrew, n.d.

Landeck, Beatrice. *Echoes of Africa in Folk Songs of the America's.* 2nd edition, revised. New York: David McKay, 1969.

Lester, Julius. *Look Out, Whitey! Black Power's Gon' Get Your Mama!* New York: Dial Press, Inc., 1968.

Litwack, Leon F. *North of Slavery: The Negro in the Free States, 1790–1860.* Chicago: University of Chicago Press, 1961.

Locke, Alain. *The Negro and His Music.* Port Washington, New York: Kennikat Press, 1936.

Logan, Rayford W. *The Betrayal of the Negro from Rutherford B. Hayes to Woodrow Wilson.* New enlarged edition. New York: Collier Books, 1965.

Lomax, John A., and Lomax, Alan. *American Ballads and Folk Songs.* New York: Macmillan, 1934.

McKitrick, Eric L. *Slavery Defended: The Views of the Old South.* Englewood Cliffs, New Jersey: Prentice-Hall, 1963.

McLuhan, Marshall, with Watson, Wilfred. *From Cliché to Archetype.* New York: Viking, 1970.

Marcuse, Maxwell F. *Tin Pan Alley in Gaslight.* Watkins Glen, New York: Century House, 1959.

Marsh, J.B.T., and Loudin, F.J. *The Story of the Jubilee Singers.* Cleveland: Cleveland Printing & Publishing Co., 1892.

Mates, Julian. *The American Stage Before 1800.* New Brunswick, New Jersey: Rutgers University Press, 1962.

Mathews, Charles. *Memoirs of Charles Mathews, Comedian.* London, 1839).

Merriam, Alan P. *The Anthropology of Music.* Evanston, Illinois: Northwestern University Press, 1964.

Metcalf, Frank J. *American Writers and Compilers of Sacred Music.* New York: Abingdon Press, 1925.

Meyer, Hazel. *The Gold in Tin Pan Alley.* New York: J.B. Lippincott, 1958.

Muller, Herbert J. *Freedom in the Ancient World*. New York: Bantam Books, Inc., 1961.

Mullin, Gerald W. *Flight and Rebellion: Slave Resistance in 18th Century Virginia*. New York: Oxford University Press, 1972.

Myrdal, Gunnar, with the assistance of Richard Sterner and Arnold Rose. *An American Dilemma: The Negro Problem and Modern Democracy*. 2 vols. New York: Harper & Row, 1962.

Nash, Gary B., and Weiss, Richard, editors. *The Great Fear: Race in the Mind of America*. New York: Holt, Rinehart & Winston, 1970.

Nathan, Hans. *Dan Emmett and the Rise of Early Negro Minstrelsy*. Norman, Oklahoma: University of Oklahoma Press, 1962.

Nicoll, Allardyce. *A History of English Drama, 1660–1900*. 6 vols. London: Cambridge University Press, 1960.

Northrup, Solomon. *Twelve Years a Slave*. Edited by Sue Eakin and Joseph Logsdon. Baton Rouge: Louisiana State University Press, 1968.

Odell, George C.D. *Annals of the New York Stage*. New York: Columbia University Press, 1928.

Odum, Howard W., and Johnson, Guy B. *The Negro and His Songs: A Study of Typical Negro Songs in the South*. Hatboro, Pennsylvania: Folklore Associates, 1964.

Oliver, Paul. *The Story of the Blues*. Philadelphia: Chilton, 1969.

Olmstead, Frederick Law. *The Cotton Kingdom; A Traveller's Observations on Cotton and Slavery in the American United States*. Edited by Arthur M. Schlesinger. New York: Alfred A. Knopf, 1953.

Osgood, Henry O. *So This Is Jazz*. Boston: Little, Brown & Co., 1925.

Parkman, Daily, and Spaeth, Sigmund. *"Gentlemen, Be Seated!" A Parade of the Old-Time Minstrels*. New York: Doubleday, Doran & Co., 1928.

Parrington, Vernon Louis. *Main Currents in American Thought.* 3 vols. in one. New York: Harcourt, Brace & World, 1958.

Parrish, Lydia. *Slave Songs from the Georgia Sea Islands.* New York: Creative Age Press, Inc., 1942.

Patterson, Lindsay, compiler and editor. *Anthology of the American Negro in the Theatre.* New York: Publishers Co., 1967.

Pike, Gustavus D. *The Jubilee Singers and Their Campaign for Twenty Thousand Dollars.* Boston: Lee and Shepard, 1873.

————. *The Singing Campaign for Ten Thousand Pounds; or, The Jubilee Singers in Great Britain.* Revised edition. New York: American Missionary Association, 1875.

Quarles, Benjamin. *The Negro in the Making of America.* New York: Collier Books, 1964.

Quinn, Arthur Hobson. *A History of the American Drama from the Beginning to the Civil War.* 2nd edition. New York: Appleton-Century-Crofts, 1943.

Rice, Edward L. *Monarchs of Minstrelsy, From "Daddy" Rice to Date.* New York: Kenney Publishing Co., 1911.

Scharf, J. Thomas, and Westcott, Thompson. *History of Philadelphia, 1609–1884.* Philadelphia: Everts, 1884.

Scheer, Robert, editor. *Eldridge Cleaver: Post-Prison Writings and Speeches.* New York: Random House, 1967.

Schuller, Gunther. *Early Jazz: It's Roots and Musical Development.* New York: Oxford University Press, 1968.

Schwartz, Barry N., and Disch, Robert. *White Racism: Its History, Pathology and Practice.* New York: Dell Publishing Co., 1970.

Seilhamer, George O. *History of the American Theatre.* Philadelphia: Globe, 1888.

Shipley, Joseph T. *Guide to Great Plays.* Washington, D.C.: Public Affairs Press, 1956.

Siebert, Wilbur H. *The Underground Railroad from Slavery to Freedom.* New York: Arno Press and *The New York Times,* 1968.

Silber, Irwin. *Songs America Voted By.* Harrisburg: Stackpole Books, 1971.

———. *Songs of the Civil War.* New York: Columbia University Press, 1960.

Sonneck, Oscar G.T. *A Bibliography of Early Secular American Music.* Revised and enlarged by William Treat Upton. Washington, D.C.: Library of Congress, 1945.

———. *Early Concert Life in America.* Leipzig: Breitkopf & Hartel, 1907.

———. *Francis Hopkinson and James Lyon.* Washington, D.C.: H.L. McQueen, 1905.

———. *Miscellaneous Studies in the History of Music.* New York: Macmillan, 1921.

Southern, Eileen. *The Music of Black Americans: A History.* New York: W.W. Norton, 1971.

———. *Readings in Black American Music.* New York: W.W. Norton, 1971.

Southerne, Thomas. *Oroonoko: A Tragedy as it is Acted at the Theatre-Royal.* London: 1696.

Spaeth, Sigmund. *A History of Popular Music in America.* New York: Random House, 1948.

Spiller, Robert E., *et. al.*, editors. *Literary History of the United States.* New York: Macmillan, 1953.

Stampp, Kenneth M. *The Peculiar Institution: Slavery in the Ante-Bellum South.* New York: Vintage Books, 1956.

Stearns, Marshall, and Stearns, Jean. *Jazz Dance: The Story of American Vernacular Dance.* New York: Macmillan, 1968.

Sterling, Dorothy. *Tear Down the Walls! A History of the Black Revolution in the United States.* New York: New American Library, 1968.

Stern, Philip Van Doren. *The Annotated Uncle Tom's Cabin.* New York: Paul S. Erikson, 1964.

Taubman, Howard. *The Making of the American Theatre*. Revised edition. New York: Coward-McCann, 1967.

Thomas, John L., editor. *Slavery Attacked: The Abolitionist Crusade*. Englewood Cliffs, New Jersey: Prentice-Hall, 1965.

Thompson, Edgar T., and Hughes, Everett C., editors. *Race: Individual and Collective Behavior*. Glencoe, Illinois: The Free Press, 1958.

Toll, Robert C. *Blacking Up: The Minstrel Show in Nineteenth-Century America*. New York: Oxford University Press, 1974.

Trotter, James M. *Music and Some Highly Musical People*. Boston: Lee & Shepard, 1883.

Ulanov, Barry. *Handbook of Jazz*. New York: Viking, 1955.

United States Commission on Civil Rights. *Freedom to the Free; Century of Emancipation, 1863–1963. A report to the President by the United States Commission on Civil Rights*. Washington, D.C.: U.S. Government Printing Office, 1963.

Wagenknecht, Edward. *Harriet Beecher Stowe: The Known and the Unknown*. New York: Oxford University Press, 1965.

Washington, Booker T. *Up From Slavery: An Autobiography*. New York: Bantam Books, 1956.

Weyl, Nathaniel. *The Negro in American Civilization*. Washington, D.C.: Public Affairs Press, 1960.

White, Newman I. *American Negro Folksongs*. Cambridge, Massachusetts: Harvard University Press, 1928.

The White Problem in America. The editors of *Ebony*. New York: Lancer Books, 1965.

Whitman, Wanda Willson. *Songs That Changed the World*. New York: Crown Publishers, 1969.

Whitmark, Isadore, and Goldberg, Isaac. *From Ragtime to Swingtime*. New York: L. Furman, 1939.

Whittke, Carl. *Tambo and Bones*. Durham, North Carolina: Duke University Press, 1930.

Wish, Harvey, editor. *Slavery in the South*. New York: Noonday Press, 1964.

Wolfe, Richard J. *Secular Music in America, 1801–1825*. Three vols. New York: The New York Public Library, 1968.

Wood, Forrest G. *Black Scare: The Racist Response to Emancipation and Reconstruction*. Berkeley and Los Angeles: University of California Press, 1968.

Woodson, Carter G., and Wesley, Charles H. *The Negro in Our History*. 11th edition. Washington, D.C.: Associated Publishers, 1966.

Wynns, Charles E., editor. *The Negro in the South Since 1865*. University, Alabama: University of Alabama Press, 1965.

SONGSTERS AND COLLECTIONS

Al Jolson's Old-Time Minstrel Show. New York: Warock, 1952.

Allen, William Frances, *et. al.*, editor. *Slave Songs of the United States*. New York: A Simpson & Co., 1867.

Brown, William Wells, compiler. *The Anti-Slavery Harp: A Collection of Songs for Anti-Slavery Meetings. Compiled by William W. Brown, a Fugitive Slave*. Boston: Bela Marsh, 1848.

Buckley's Melodist; A Repertoire of Choice Songs and Ballads, With Choruses, as Sung at the Concerts of Buckley's Serenaders. Boston: Henry Tolman & Co., 1864.

Burleigh, H.T. *Plantation Melodies Old and New*. Words by R.E. Phillips, *et. al.*, music composed, or transcribed and adapted by H.T. Burleigh. New York: G. Schirmer, 1901.

Carawan, Guy, and Carawan, Candy. *We Shall Overcome: Songs of the Southern Freedom Movement*. New York: Oak, 1963.

Carncross and Dixey's Minstrel Melodies: A Collection of Popular Songs . . . as Sung by Them. Philadelphia: Simpson & Co. 1864.

Carr, Benjamin. *The Musical Journal*. Baltimore: *ca.* 1801.

Chaff, Gumbo (pseud.). *The Ethiopian Glee Book; A Collection of Popular Negro Melodies, Arranged for Quartet Clubs. By Gumbo Chaff, A.M.A. First Banjo Player to the King of Congo.* Boston: Elias Howe, 1848.

Christy's Panorama Songster. Containing the Songs as Sung by the Christy, Campbell, Pierce's Minstrels, and Sable Brothers. New York: Wm. H. Murphy.

Clark, George W. *The Harp of Freedom.* New York: Miller, Orton & Mulligan, 1856.

Coleridge-Taylor, Samuel. *Twenty-Four Negro Melodies. Op. 59.* Boston: Oliver Ditson, 1905.

Damon, S. Foster, editor. *Series of Old American Songs.* Providence: Brown University Library, 1936.

Danish and Norwegian Melodies, Selected by A. Anderson Feldborg; Harmonized and Arranged . . . by C. Stokes; The Poetry Translated by William Sidney Walker. London: 1815.

Dixey's Songster. Philadelphia: A. Winch, 1860.

Ettla, S.H. *Sam's Songster: Being a Choice Collection of the Most Fashionable Songs of the Present Day.* First edition. Harrisburg: Ettla, 1855.

[Foster, Stephen Collins.] *Songs, Compositions and Arrangements by Stephen Collins Foster, 1826–1864.* Indianapolis: Foster Hall Reproductions, 1933.

Fowke, Edith, and Glazer, Joe. *Songs of Work and Freedom.* Garden City, New York: Doubleday, 1961.

Haviland's Hundred Hits. Song Album. New York: F.B. Haviland, 1908.

Johnson, James Weldon, and Johnson, J. Rosamund. *The Books of American Negro Spirituals.* New York: Viking, 1940.

Jubilee and Plantation Songs. New York: Oliver Ditson, 1887.

Lady's Musical Library Extra: Music of the Ethiopian Serenaders, Nine Songs and a Set of Cotillions. Philadelphia: Turner & Fisher, 1845.

Lincoln, Jairus. *Anti-Slavery Melodies: For Friends of Freedom. Prepared for the Hingham Anti-Slavery Society.* Hingham, Massachusetts: Elijah B. Gill, 1843.

Love and Sentimental Songster. New York: Dick & Fitzgerald, 1862.

The Lover's Forget-Me-Not, and Songs of Beauty . . . With All the Late Negro Melodies. Philadelphia: John B. Perry, 1847.

Mills Favorite Old Timers. No. 2. New York: Mills, 1935.

The Minstrel; A Collection of Celebrated Songs, Set to Music. Baltimore: F. Lucas, 1812.

Minstrel Songs, Old and New. Boston: Oliver Ditson, 1882.

Moore, Frank, editor. *Songs and Ballads of the American Revolution.* Port Washington, New York: Kennikat Press, 1964.

The Negro Forget-Me-Not Songster. Philadelphia: Turner & Fisher, 1855.

The Nightingale; or, Musical Companion, Being a Collection of Entertaining Songs. New York: Smith & Forman, 1814.

Orf, Wilhelm H., compiler. *The Great American Soldier and Other Selections.* Manila: 1913.

Rice, Dan. *Dan Rice's Original Comic and Sentimental Poetic Effusions.* Philadelphia: 1860.

Ryan's Mamoth Collection. 1050 Reels and Jigs, Hornpipes, Clogs, Walk-Arounds, Essences, Strathspeys, Highland Flings and Contra Dances, With Figures, and How To Play Them . . . Boston: Elias Howe, 1883.

Siegmeister, Elie. *Songs of Early America, 1620–1830.* New York: Edward B. Marks, 1944.

Songs of Dixie. New York: S. Brainard's Sons, 1890.

Songs of the Sunny South. New York: Leo Feist, n.d.

Songs of the Times: 100 Popular Favorites. Boston: W.F. Shaw, 1883.

Sykes, L. Fayette, compiler. *Garfield and Arthur Campaign Song Book.* New York: Coleman House, 1880.

The United States Songster. A Choice Selection of About One-Hundred and Seventy of the Most Popular Songs: Including Nearly All the Songs Contained in the American Songster. Cincinnati: U.P. James, 1836.

Vance, Randolph. *Ozark Folksongs* Columbia, Missouri: 1948.

Wehman's Collection of 127 Songs. New York: Henry J. Wehman, 1891.

Index of Names

Index of Songs